Mastering Algorithms with C

Kyle Loudon

O'REILLY®

Beijing · Cambridge · Farnham · Köln · Paris · Sebastopol · Taipei · Tokyo

Mastering Algorithms with C
by Kyle Loudon

Copyright © 1999 O'Reilly & Associates, Inc. All rights reserved.
Printed in the United States of America.

Published by O'Reilly & Associates, Inc., 101 Morris Street, Sebastopol, CA 95472.

Editor: Andy Oram

Production Editor: Jeffrey Liggett

Printing History:

August 1999:   First Edition.

This book is printed on acid-free paper with 85% recycled content, 15% post-consumer waste.
O'Reilly & Associates is committed to using paper with the highest recycled content available
consistent with high quality.

ISBN: 1-56592-453-3

Table of Contents

Preface

When I first thought about writing this book, I immediately thought of O'Reilly & Associates to publish it. They were the first publisher I contacted, and the one I most wanted to work with because of their tradition of books covering "just the facts." This approach is not what one normally thinks of in connection with books on data structures and algorithms. When one studies data structures and algorithms, normally there is a fair amount of time spent on proving their correctness rigorously. Consequently, many books on this subject have an academic feel about them, and real details such as implementation and application are left to be resolved elsewhere. This book covers how and why certain data structures and algorithms work, real applications that use them (including many examples), and their implementation. Mathematical rigor appears only to the extent necessary in explanations.

Naturally, I was very happy that O'Reilly & Associates saw value in a book that covered this aspect of the subject. This preface contains some of the reasons I think you will find this book valuable as well. It also covers certain aspects of the code in the book, defines a few conventions, and gratefully acknowledges the people who played a part in the book's creation.

Organization

This book is divided into three parts. The first part consists of introductory material that is useful when working in the rest of the book. The second part presents a number of data structures considered fundamental in the field of computer science. The third part presents an assortment of algorithms for solving common problems. Each of these parts is described in more detail in the following sections, including a summary of the chapters each part contains.

Part I

Part I, *Preliminaries*, contains Chapters 1 through 4. Chapter 1, *Introduction*, introduces the concepts of data structures and algorithms and presents reasons for using them. It also presents a few topics in software engineering, which are applied throughout the rest of the book. Chapter 2, *Pointer Manipulation*, discusses a number of topics on pointers. Pointers appear a great deal in this book, so this chapter serves as a refresher on the subject. Chapter 3, *Recursion*, covers recursion, a popular technique used with many data structures and algorithms. Chapter 4, *Analysis of Algorithms*, presents the analysis of algorithms. The techniques in this chapter are used to analyze algorithms throughout the book.

Part II

Part II, *Data Structures*, contains Chapters 5 through 11. Chapter 5, *Linked Lists*, presents various forms of linked lists, including singly-linked lists, doubly-linked lists, and circular lists. Chapter 6, *Stacks and Queues*, presents stacks and queues, data structures for sorting and returning data on a last-in, first-out and first-in, last-out order respectively. Chapter 7, *Sets*, presents sets and the fundamental mathematics describing sets. Chapter 8, *Hash Tables*, presents chained and open-addressed hash tables, including material on how to select a good hash function and how to resolve collisions. Chapter 9, *Trees*, presents binary and AVL trees. Chapter 9 also discusses various methods of tree traversal. Chapter 10, *Heaps and Priority Queues*, presents heaps and priority queues, data structures that help to quickly determine the largest or smallest element in a set of data. Chapter 11, *Graphs*, presents graphs and two fundamental algorithms from which many graph algorithms are derived: breadth-first and depth-first search.

Part III

Part III, *Algorithms*, contains Chapters 12 through 17. Chapter 12, *Sorting and Searching*, covers various algorithms for sorting, including insertion sort, quicksort, merge sort, counting sort, and radix sort. Chapter 12 also presents binary search. Chapter 13, *Numerical Methods*, covers numerical methods, including algorithms for polynomial interpolation, least-squares estimation, and the solution of equations using Newton's method. Chapter 14, *Data Compression*, presents algorithms for data compression, including Huffman coding and LZ77. Chapter 15, *Data Encryption*, discusses algorithms for DES and RSA encryption. Chapter 16, *Graph Algorithms*, covers graph algorithms, including Prim's algorithm for minimum spanning trees, Dijkstra's algorithm for shortest paths, and an algorithm for solving the traveling-salesman problem. Chapter 17, *Geometric Algorithms*, presents geometric algorithms, including methods for testing whether line segments intersect, computing convex hulls, and computing arc lengths on spherical surfaces.

Key Features

There are a number of special features that I believe together make this book a unique approach to covering the subject of data structures and algorithms:

Consistent format for every chapter

Every chapter (excluding those in the first part of the book) follows a consistent format. This format allows most of the book to be read as a textbook or a reference, whichever is needed at the moment.

Clearly identified topics and applications

Each chapter (except Chapter 1) begins with a brief introduction, followed by a list of clearly identified topics and their relevance to real applications.

Analyses of every operation, algorithm, and example

An analysis is provided for every operation of abstract datatypes, every algorithm in the algorithms chapters, and every example throughout the book. Each analysis uses the techniques presented in Chapter 4.

Real examples, not just trivial exercises

All examples are from real applications, not just trivial exercises. Examples like these are exciting and teach more than just the topic being demonstrated.

Real implementations using real code

All implementations are written in C, not pseudocode. The benefit of this is that when implementing many data structures and algorithms, there are considerable details pseudocode does not address.

Questions and answers for further thought

At the end of each chapter (except Chapter 1), there is a series of questions along with their answers. These emphasize important ideas from the chapter and touch on additional topics.

Lists of related topics for further exploration

At the end of each chapter (except Chapter 1), there is a list of related topics for further exploration. Each topic is presented with a brief description.

Numerous cross references and call-outs

Cross references and call-outs mark topics mentioned in one place that are introduced elsewhere. Thus, it is easy to locate additional information.

Insightful organization and application of topics

Many of the data structures or algorithms in one chapter use data structures and algorithms presented elsewhere in the book. Thus, they serve as examples of how to use other data structures and algorithms themselves. All dependencies are carefully marked with a cross reference or call-out.

Coverage of fundamental topics, plus more

This book covers the fundamental data structures and algorithms of computer science. It also covers several topics not normally addressed in books on the subject. These include numerical methods, data compression (in more detail), data encryption, and geometric algorithms.

About the Code

All implementations in this book are in C. C was chosen because it is still the most general-purpose language in use today. It is also one of the best languages in which to explore the details of data structures and algorithms while still working at a fairly high level. It may be helpful to note a few things about the code in this book.

All code focuses on pedagogy first

There is also a focus on efficiency, but the primary purpose of all code is to teach the topic it addresses in a clear manner.

All code has been fully tested on four platforms

The platforms used for testing were HP-UX 10.20, SunOs 5.6, Linux 5.1, and DOS/Windows NT/95/98. See the readme file on the accompanying disk for additional information.

Headers document all public interfaces

Every implementation includes a header that documents the public interface. Most headers are shown in this book. However, headers that contain only prototypes are not. (For instance, Example 12-1 includes *sort.h*, but this header is not shown because it contains only prototypes to various sorting functions.)

Static functions are used for private functions

Static functions have file scope, so this fact is used to keep private functions private. Functions specific to a data structure or algorithm's implementation are thus kept out of its public interface.

Naming conventions are applied throughout the code

Defined constants appear entirely in uppercase. Datatypes and global variables begin with an uppercase character. Local variables begin with a lowercase character. Operations of abstract datatypes begin with the name of the type in lowercase, followed by an underscore, then the name of the operation in lowercase.

All code contains numerous comments

All comments are designed to let developers follow the logic of the code without reading much of the code itself. This is useful when trying to make connections between the code and explanations in the text.

Structures have typedefs as well as names themselves

The name of the structure is always the name in the typedef followed by an underscore. Naming the structure itself is necessary for self-referential structures like the one used for linked list elements (see Chapter 5). This approach is applied everywhere for consistency.

All void functions contain explicit returns

Although not required, this helps quickly identify where a void function returns rather than having to match up braces.

Conventions

Most of the conventions used in this book should be recognizable to those who work with computers to any extent. However, a few require some explanation.

Bold italic

Nonintrinsic mathematical functions and mathematical variables appear in this font.

`Constant width italic`

Variables from programs, names of datatypes (such as structure names), and defined constants appear in this font.

Italic

Commands (as they would be typed in at a terminal), names of files and paths, operations of abstract datatypes, and other functions from programs appear in this font.

$\lg x$

This notation is used to represent the base-2 logarithm of x, $\log_2 x$. This is the notation used commonly in computer science when discussing algorithms; therefore, it is used in this book.

Comments and Questions

Please address comments and questions concerning this book to the publisher:

O'Reilly & Associates
101 Morris Street
Sebastopol, CA 95472
800-998-9938 (in the U.S. or Canada)
707-829-0515 (international or local)
707-829-0104 (FAX)

You can also send us messages electronically. To be put on our mailing list or to request a catalog, send email to:

info@oreilly.com

To ask technical questions or comment on the book, send email to:

bookquestions@oreilly.com

Acknowledgments

The experience of writing a book is not without its ups and downs. On the one hand, there is excitement, but there is also exhaustion. It is only with the support of others that one can truly delight in its pleasures and overcome its perils. There are many people I would like to thank.

First, I thank Andy Oram, my editor at O'Reilly & Associates, whose assistance has been exceptional in every way. I thank Andy especially for his continual patience and support. In addition, I would like to thank Tim O'Reilly and Andy together for their interest in this project when it first began. Other individuals I gratefully acknowledge at O'Reilly & Associates are Rob Romano for drafting the technical illustrations, and Lenny Muellner and Mike Sierra, members of the tools group, who were always quick to reply to my questions. I thank Jeffrey Liggett for his swift and detailed work during the production process. In addition, I would like to thank the many others I did not correspond with directly at O'Reilly & Associates but who played no less a part in the production of this book. Thank you, everyone.

Several individuals gave me a great deal of feedback in the form of reviews. I owe a special debt of gratitude to Bill Greene of Intel Corporation for his enthusiasm and voluntary support in reviewing numerous chapters throughout the writing process. I also would like to thank Alan Solis of Com21 for reviewing several chapters. I thank Alan, in addition, for the considerable knowledge he has imparted to me over the years at our weekly lunches. I thank Stephen Friedl for his meticulous review of the completed manuscript. I thank Shaun Flisakowski for the review she provided at the manuscript's completion as well. In addition, I gratefully acknowledge those who looked over chapters with me from time to time and with whom I discussed material for the book on an ongoing basis.

Many individuals gave me support in countless other ways. First, I would like to thank Jeff Moore, my colleague and friend at Jeppesen, whose integrity and pursuit of knowledge constantly inspire me. During our frequent conversations, Jeff was kind enough to indulge me often by discussing topics in the book. Thank you, Jeff. I would also like to thank Ken Sunseri, my manager at Jeppesen, for creating an environment at work in which a project like this was possible. Furthermore, I warmly thank all of my friends and family for their love and support throughout my writing. In particular, I thank Marc Loudon for answering so many of my questions. I thank Marc and Judy Loudon together for their constant encouragement. I thank Shala Hruska for her patience, understanding, and support at the project's end, which seemed to last so long.

Finally, I would like to thank Robert Foerster, my teacher, for the experiences we shared on a 16K TRS-80 in 1981. I still recall those times fondly. They made a wonderful difference in my life. For giving me my start with computers, I dedicate this book to you with affection.

I

Preliminaries

This part of the book contains four chapters of introductory material. Chapter 1, *Introduction*, introduces the concepts of data structures and algorithms and presents reasons for using them. It also presents a few topics in software engineering that are applied throughout the rest of the book. Chapter 2, *Pointer Manipulation*, presents a number of topics on pointers. Pointers appear a great deal in this book, so this chapter serves as a refresher on the subject. Chapter 3, *Recursion*, presents recursion, a popular technique used with many data structures and algorithms. Chapter 4, *Analysis of Algorithms*, describes how to analyze algorithms. The techniques in this chapter are used to analyze algorithms throughout the book.

1

Introduction

When I was 12, my brother and I studied piano. Each week we would make a trip to our teacher's house; while one of us had our lesson, the other would wait in her parlor. Fortunately, she always had a few games arranged on a coffee table to help us pass the time while waiting. One game I remember consisted of a series of pegs on a small piece of wood. Little did I know it, but the game would prove to be an early introduction to data structures and algorithms.

The game was played as follows. All of the pegs were white, except for one, which was blue. To begin, one of the white pegs was removed to create an empty hole. Then, by jumping pegs and removing them much like in checkers, the game continued until a single peg was left, or the remaining pegs were scattered about the board in such a way that no more jumps could be made. The object of the game was to jump pegs so that the blue peg would end up as the last peg and in the center. According to the game's legend, this qualified the player as a "genius." Additional levels of intellect were prescribed for other outcomes. As for me, I felt satisfied just getting through a game without our teacher's kitten, Clara, pouncing unexpectedly from around the sofa to sink her claws into my right shoe. I suppose being satisfied with this outcome indicated that I simply possessed "common sense."

I remember playing the game thinking that certainly a deterministic approach could be found to get the blue peg to end up in the center every time. What I was looking for was an *algorithm*. Algorithms are well-defined procedures for solving problems. It was not until a number of years later that I actually implemented an algorithm for solving the peg problem. I decided to solve it in LISP during an artificial intelligence class in college. To solve the problem, I represented information about the game in various *data structures*. Data structures are conceptual organizations of information. They go hand in hand with algorithms because many algorithms rely on them for efficiency.

Often, people deal with information in fairly loose forms, such as pegs on a board, notes in a notebook, or drawings in a portfolio. However, to process information with a computer, the information needs to be more formally organized. In addition, it is helpful to have a precise plan for exactly what to do with it. Data structures and algorithms help us with this. Simply stated, they help us develop programs that are, in a word, elegant. As developers of software, it is important to remember that we must be more than just proficient with programming languages and development tools; developing elegant software is a matter of craftsmanship. A good understanding of data structures and algorithms is an important part of becoming such a craftsman.

An Introduction to Data Structures

Data comes in all shapes and sizes, but often it can be organized in the same way. For example, consider a list of things to do, a list of ingredients in a recipe, or a reading list for a class. Although each contains a different type of data, they all contain data organized in a similar way: a list. A list is one simple example of a data structure. Of course, there are many other common ways to organize data as well. In computing, some of the most common organizations are *linked lists, stacks, queues, sets, hash tables, trees, heaps, priority queues*, and *graphs*, all of which are discussed in this book. Three reasons for using data structures are efficiency, abstraction, and reusability.

Efficiency

> Data structures organize data in ways that make algorithms more efficient. For example, consider some of the ways we can organize data for searching it. One simplistic approach is to place the data in an array and search the data by traversing element by element until the desired element is found. However, this method is inefficient because in many cases we end up traversing every element. By using another type of data structure, such as a *hash table* (see Chapter 8, *Hash Tables*) or a *binary tree* (see Chapter 9, *Trees*) we can search the data considerably faster.

Abstraction

> Data structures provide a more understandable way to look at data; thus, they offer a level of abstraction in solving problems. For example, by storing data in a stack (see Chapter 6, *Stacks and Queues*), we can focus on things that we do with stacks, such as pushing and popping elements, rather than the details of how to implement each operation. In other words, data structures let us talk about programs in a less programmatic way.

Reusability

> Data structures are reusable because they tend to be modular and context-free. They are modular because each has a prescribed interface through which

access to data stored in the data structure is restricted. That is, we access the data using only those operations the interface defines. Data structures are context-free because they can be used with any type of data and in a variety of situations or contexts. In C, we make a data structure store data of any type by using void pointers to the data rather than by maintaining private copies of the data in the data structure itself.

When one thinks of data structures, one normally thinks of certain actions, or *operations*, one would like to perform with them as well. For example, with a list, we might naturally like to insert, remove, traverse, and count elements. A data structure together with basic operations like these is called an *abstract datatype*. The operations of an abstract datatype constitute its *public interface*. The public interface of an abstract datatype defines exactly what we are allowed to do with it. Establishing and adhering to an abstract datatype's interface is essential because this lets us better manage a program's data, which inevitably makes a program more understandable and maintainable.

An Introduction to Algorithms

Algorithms are well-defined procedures for solving problems. In computing, algorithms are essential because they serve as the systematic procedures that computers require. A good algorithm is like using the right tool in a workshop. It does the job with the right amount of effort. Using the wrong algorithm or one that is not clearly defined is like cutting a piece of paper with a table saw, or trying to cut a piece of plywood with a pair of scissors: although the job may get done, you have to wonder how effective you were in completing it. As with data structures, three reasons for using formal algorithms are efficiency, abstraction, and reusability.

Efficiency

Because certain types of problems occur often in computing, researchers have found efficient ways of solving them over time. For example, imagine trying to sort a number of entries in an index for a book. Since sorting is a common task that is performed often, it is not surprising that there are many efficient algorithms for doing this. We explore some of these in Chapter 12, *Sorting and Searching*.

Abstraction

Algorithms provide a level of abstraction in solving problems because many seemingly complicated problems can be distilled into simpler ones for which well-known algorithms exist. Once we see a more complicated problem in a simpler light, we can think of the simpler problem as just an abstraction of the more complicated one. For example, imagine trying to find the shortest way to route a packet between two gateways in an internet. Once we realize that this problem is just a variation of the more general *single-pair shortest-paths problem* (see Chapter 16, *Graph Algorithms*), we can approach it in terms of this generalization.

Reusability

Algorithms are often reusable in many different situations. Since many well-known algorithms solve problems that are generalizations of more complicated ones, and since many complicated problems can be distilled into simpler ones, an efficient means of solving certain simpler problems potentially lets us solve many others.

General Approaches in Algorithm Design

In a broad sense, many algorithms approach problems in the same way. Thus, it is often convenient to classify them based on the approach they employ. One reason to classify algorithms in this way is that often we can gain some insight about an algorithm if we understand its general approach. This can also give us ideas about how to look at similar problems for which we do not know algorithms. Of course, some algorithms defy classification, whereas others are based on a combination of approaches. This section presents some common approaches.

Randomized algorithms

Randomized algorithms rely on the statistical properties of random numbers. One example of a randomized algorithm is *quicksort* (see Chapter 12).

Quicksort works as follows. Imagine sorting a pile of canceled checks by hand. We begin with an unsorted pile that we partition in two. In one pile we place all checks numbered less than or equal to what we think may be the median value, and in the other pile we place the checks numbered greater than this. Once we have the two piles, we divide each of them in the same manner and repeat the process until we end up with one check in every pile. At this point the checks are sorted.

In order to achieve good performance, quicksort relies on the fact that each time we partition the checks, we end up with two partitions that are nearly equal in size. To accomplish this, ideally we need to look up the median value of the check numbers before partitioning the checks. However, since determining the median requires scanning all of the checks, we do not do this. Instead, we randomly select a check around which to partition. Quicksort performs well on average because the normal distribution of random numbers leads to relatively balanced partitioning overall.

Divide-and-conquer algorithms

Divide-and-conquer algorithms revolve around three steps: *divide, conquer,* and *combine.* In the divide step, we divide the data into smaller, more manageable pieces. In the conquer step, we process each division by performing some operation on it. In the combine step, we recombine the processed divisions. One example of a divide-and-conquer algorithm is *merge sort* (see Chapter 12).

Merge sort works as follows. As before, imagine sorting a pile of canceled checks by hand. We begin with an unsorted pile that we divide in half. Next, we divide each of the resulting two piles in half and continue this process until we end up with one check in every pile. Once all piles contain a single check, we merge the piles two by two so that each new pile is a sorted combination of the two that were merged. Merging continues until we end up with one big pile again, at which point the checks are sorted.

In terms of the three steps common to all divide-and-conquer algorithms, merge sort can be described as follows. First, in the divide step, divide the data in half. Next, in the conquer step, sort the two divisions by recursively applying merge sort to them. Last, in the combine step, merge the two divisions into a single sorted set.

Dynamic-programming solutions

Dynamic-programming solutions are similar to divide-and-conquer methods in that both solve problems by breaking larger problems into subproblems whose results are later recombined. However, the approaches differ in how subproblems are related. In divide-and-conquer algorithms, each subproblem is independent of the others. Therefore, we solve each subproblem using recursion (see Chapter 3, *Recursion*) and combine its result with the results of other subproblems. In dynamic-programming solutions, subproblems are not independent of one another. In other words, subproblems may share subproblems. In problems like this, a dynamic-programming solution is better than a divide-and-conquer approach because the latter approach will do more work than necessary, as shared subproblems are solved more than once. Although it is an important technique used by many algorithms, none of the algorithms in this book use dynamic programming.

Greedy algorithms

Greedy algorithms make decisions that look best at the moment. In other words, they make decisions that are locally optimal in the hope that they will lead to globally optimal solutions. Unfortunately, decisions that look best at the moment are not always the best in the long run. Therefore, greedy algorithms do not always produce optimal results; however, in some cases they do. One example of a greedy algorithm is *Huffman coding*, which is an algorithm for data compression (see Chapter 14, *Data Compression*).

The most significant part of Huffman coding is building a *Huffman tree*. To build a Huffman tree, we proceed from its leaf nodes upward. We begin by placing each symbol to compress and the number of times it occurs in the data (its frequency) in the root node of its own binary tree (see Chapter 9). Next, we merge the two trees whose root nodes have the smallest frequencies and store the sum of the frequencies in the new tree's root. We then repeat this process until we end up with a single tree, which is the final Huffman tree. The root node of this tree contains the total number of symbols in the data, and its leaf nodes contain the original symbols and their frequencies. Huffman coding is greedy because it continually seeks out the two trees that appear to be the best to merge at any given time.

Approximation algorithms

Approximation algorithms are algorithms that do not compute optimal solutions; instead, they compute solutions that are "good enough." Often we use approximation algorithms to solve problems that are computationally expensive but are too significant to give up on altogether. The *traveling-salesman problem* (see Chapter 16) is one example of a problem usually solved using an approximation algorithm.

Imagine a salesman who needs to visit a number of cities as part of the route he works. The goal in the traveling-salesman problem is to find the shortest route possible by which the salesman can visit every city exactly once before returning to the point at which he starts. Since an optimal solution to the traveling-salesman problem is possible but computationally expensive, we use a *heuristic* to come up with an approximate solution. A heuristic is a less than optimal strategy that we are willing to accept when an optimal strategy is not feasible.

The traveling-salesman problem can be represented graphically by depicting the cities the salesman must visit as points on a grid. We then look for the shortest tour of the points by applying the following heuristic. Begin with a tour consisting of only the point at which the salesman starts. Color this point black. All other points are white until added to the tour, at which time they are colored black as well. Next, for each point v not already in the tour, compute the distance between the last point u added to the tour and v. Using this, select the point closest to u, color it black, and add it to the tour. Repeat this process until all points have been colored black. Lastly, add the starting point to the tour again, thus making the tour complete.

A Bit About Software Engineering

As mentioned at the start of this chapter, a good understanding of data structures and algorithms is an important part of developing well-crafted software. Equally important is a dedication to applying sound practices in software engineering in our implementations. Software engineering is a broad subject, but a great deal can be gleaned from a few concepts, which are presented here and applied throughout the examples in this book.

Modularity

One way to achieve modularity in software design is to focus on the development of *black boxes*. In software, a black box is a module whose internals are not intended to be seen by users of the module. Users interact with the module only through a prescribed interface made *public* by its creator. That is, the creator publicizes only what users need to know to use the module and hides the details about everything else. Consequently, users are not concerned with the details of how the module is implemented and are prevented (at least in policy, depending on the language) from working with the module's internals. These ideas are fundamental to *data hiding* and *encapsulation*, principles of good software engineering enforced particularly well by object-oriented languages. Although languages that are not object-oriented do not enforce these ideas to the same degree, we can still apply them. One example in this book is the design of abstract datatypes. Fundamentally, each datatype is a structure. Exactly what one can do with the structure is dictated by the operations defined for the datatype and publicized in its header.

Readability

We can make programs more readable in a number of ways. Writing meaningful comments, using aptly named identifiers, and creating code that is self-documenting are a few examples. Opinions on how to write good comments vary considerably, but a good fundamental philosophy is to document a program so that other developers can follow its logic simply by reading its comments. On the other hand, sections of self-documenting code require few, if any, comments because the code reads nearly the same as what might be stated in the comments themselves. One example of self-documenting code in this book is the use of header files as a means of defining and documenting public interfaces to the data structures and algorithms presented.

Simplicity

Unfortunately, as a society we tend to regard "complex" and "intelligent" as words that go together. In actuality, intelligent solutions are often the simplest ones. Furthermore, it is the simplest solutions that are often the hardest to find. Most of the algorithms in this book are good examples of the power of simplicity. Although many of the algorithms were developed and proven correct by individuals doing extensive research, they appear in their final form as clear and concise solutions to problems distilled down to their essence.

Consistency

One of the best things we can do in software development is to establish coding conventions and stick to them. Of course, conventions must also be easy to recognize. After all, a convention is really no convention at all if someone else is not able to determine what the convention is. Conventions can exist on many levels. For example, they may be cosmetic, or they may be more related to how to approach certain types of problems conceptually. Whatever the case, the wonderful thing about a good convention is that once we see it in one place, most likely we will recognize it and understand its application when we see it again. Thus, consistency fosters readability and simplicity as well. Two examples of cosmetic conventions in this book are the way comments are written and the way operations associated with data structures are named. Two examples of conceptual conventions are the way data is managed in data structures and the way static functions are used for private functions, that is, functions that are not part of public interfaces.

How to Use This Book

This book was designed to be read either as a textbook or a reference, whichever is needed at the moment. It is organized into three parts. The first part consists of introductory material and includes chapters on pointer manipulation, recursion, and the analysis of algorithms. These subjects are useful when working in the rest of the book. The second part presents fundamental data structures, including linked lists, stacks, queues, sets, hash tables, trees, heaps, priority queues, and graphs. The third part presents common algorithms for solving problems in sorting, searching, numerical analysis, data compression, data encryption, graph theory, and computational geometry.

Each of the chapters in the second and third parts of the book has a consistent format to foster the book's ease of use as a reference and its readability in general. Each chapter begins with a brief introduction followed by a list of specific topics and a list of real applications. The presentation of each data structure or algorithm begins with a description, followed by an interface, followed by an implementation and analysis. For many data structures and algorithms, examples are presented as well. Each chapter ends with a series of questions and answers, and a list of related topics for further exploration.

The presentation of each data structure or algorithm starts broadly and works toward an implementation in real code. Thus, readers can easily work up to the level of detail desired. The descriptions cover how the data structures or algorithms work in general. The interfaces serve as quick references for how to use the data structures or algorithms in a program. The implementations and analyses provide more detail about exactly how the interfaces are implemented and how each implementation performs. The questions and answers, as well as the related topics, help those reading the book as a textbook gain more insight about each chapter. The material at the start of each chapter helps clearly identify topics within the chapters and their use in real applications.

2

Pointer Manipulation

In C, for any type *T*, we can form a corresponding type for variables that contain addresses in memory where objects of type *T* reside. One way to look at variables like this is that they actually "point to" the objects. Thus, these variables are called *pointers*. Pointers are very important in C, but in many ways, they are a blessing and a curse. On the one hand, they are a powerful means of building data structures and precisely manipulating memory. On the other hand, they are easy to misuse, and their misuse often leads to unpredictably buggy software; thus, they come with a great deal of responsibility. Considering this, it is no surprise that pointers embody what some people love about C and what other people hate. Whatever the case, to use C effectively, we must have a thorough understanding of them. This chapter presents several topics on pointers and introduces several of the techniques using pointers that are employed throughout this book.

This chapter covers:

Pointer fundamentals

Including one of the best techniques for understanding pointers: drawing diagrams. Another fundamental aspect of pointer usage is learning how to avoid dangling pointers.

Storage allocation

The process of reserving space in memory. Understanding pointers as they relate to storage allocation is especially important because pointers are a virtual carte blanche when it comes to accessing memory.

Aggregates and pointer arithmetic

In C, aggregates are structures and arrays. Pointer arithmetic defines the rules by which calculations with pointers are performed. Pointers to structures are important in building data structures. Arrays and pointers in C use pointer arithmetic in the same way.

Pointers as parameters to functions

The means by which C simulates call-by-reference parameter passing. In C, it is also common to use pointers as an efficient means of passing arrays and large structures.

Pointers to pointers

Pointers that point to other pointers instead of pointing to data. Pointers to pointers are particularly common as parameters to functions.

Generic pointers and casts

Mechanisms that bypass and override C's type system. Generic pointers let us point to data without being concerned with its type for the moment. Casts allow us to override the type of a variable temporarily.

Function pointers

Pointers that point to executable code, or blocks of information needed to invoke executable code, instead of pointing to data. They are used to store and manage functions as if they were pieces of data.

Pointer Fundamentals

Recall that a pointer is simply a variable that stores the address where a piece of data resides in memory rather than storing the data itself. That is, pointers contain memory addresses. Even for experienced developers, at times this level of indirection can be a bit difficult to visualize, particularly when dealing with more complicated pointer constructs, such as pointers to other pointers. Thus, one of the best things we can do to understand and communicate information about pointers is to draw diagrams (see Figure 2-1). Rather than listing actual addresses in diagrams, pointers are usually drawn as arrows linking one location to another. When a pointer points to nothing at all—that is, when it is set to NULL—it is illustrated as a line terminated with a double bar (see Figure 2-1, step 4).

As with other types of variables, we should not assume that a pointer points anywhere useful until we explicitly set it. It is also important to remember that nothing prevents a pointer in C from pointing to an invalid address. Pointers that point to invalid addresses are sometimes called *dangling pointers*. Some examples of programming errors that can lead to dangling pointers include casting arbitrary integers to pointers, adjusting pointers beyond the bounds of arrays, and deallocating storage that one or more pointers still reference.

Storage Allocation

When we declare a pointer in C, a certain amount of space is allocated for it, just as for other types of variables. Pointers generally occupy one machine word, but

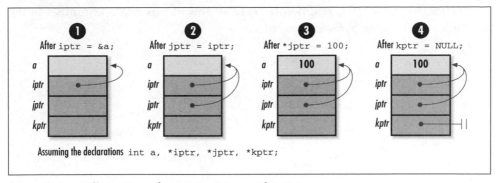

Figure 2-1. An illustration of some operations with pointers

their size can vary. Therefore, for portability, we should never assume that a pointer has a specific size. Pointers often vary in size as a result of compiler settings and type specifiers allowed by certain C implementations. It is also important to remember that when we declare a pointer, space is allocated only for the pointer itself; no space is allocated for the data the pointer references. Storage for the data is allocated in one of two ways: by declaring a variable for it or by allocating storage dynamically at runtime (using *malloc* or *realloc*, for example).

When we declare a variable, its type tells the compiler how much storage to set aside for it as the program runs. Storage for the variable is allocated automatically, but it may not be persistent throughout the life of the program. This is especially important to remember when dealing with pointers to *automatic variables*. Automatic variables are those for which storage is allocated and deallocated automatically when entering and leaving a block or function. For example, since *iptr* is set to the address of the automatic variable *a* in the following function *f*, *iptr* becomes a dangling pointer when *f* returns. This situation occurs because once *f* returns, *a* is no longer valid on the program stack (see Chapter 3, *Recursion*).

```
int f(int **iptr) {

int a = 10;
*iptr = &a;

return 0;

}
```

In C, when we dynamically allocate storage, we get a pointer to some storage on the heap (see Chapter 3). Since it is then our responsibility to manage this storage ourselves, the storage remains valid until we explicitly deallocate it. For example, the storage allocated by *malloc* in the following code remains valid until we call *free* at some later time. Thus, it remains valid even after *f* returns (see Figure 2-2), unlike the storage allocated automatically for *a* previously. The parameter *iptr* is a pointer to the object we wish to modify (another pointer) so that when *f* returns, *iptr* contains the address returned by *malloc*. This idea is explored further in the section on pointers as parameters to functions.

```
#include <stdlib.h>

int g(int **iptr) {

if ((*iptr = (int *)malloc(sizeof(int))) == NULL)
   return -1;

return 0;

}
```

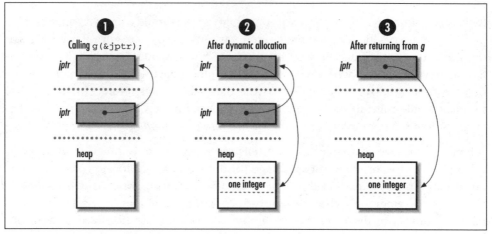

Figure 2-2. Pointer operations in returning storage dynamically allocated in a function

Pointers and storage allocation are arguably the areas of C that provide the most fodder for the language's sometimes bad reputation. The misuse of dynamically allocated storage, in particular, is a notorious source of *memory leaks*. Memory leaks are blocks of storage that are allocated but never freed by a program, even when no longer in use. They are particularly detrimental when found in sections of code that are executed repeatedly. Fortunately, we can greatly reduce memory leaks by employing consistent approaches to how we manage storage.

One example of a consistent approach to storage management is the one used for data structures presented in this book. The philosophy followed in every case is that it is the responsibility of the user to manage the storage associated with the actual data that the data structure organizes; the data structure itself allocates storage only for internal structures used to keep the data organized. Consequently, only pointers are maintained to the data inserted into the data structure, rather than private copies of the data. One important implication of this is that a data structure's implementation does not depend on the type and size of the data it stores. Also, multiple data structures are able to operate on a single copy of data, which can be useful when organizing large amounts of data.

In addition, this book provides operations for initializing and destroying data structures. Initialization may involve many steps, one of which may be the allocation of memory. Destroying a data structure generally involves removing all of its data and freeing the memory allocated in the data structure. Destroying a data structure also usually involves freeing all memory associated with the data itself. This is the one exception to having the user manage storage for the data. Since managing this storage is an application-specific operation, each data structure uses a function provided by the user when the data structure is initialized.

Aggregates and Pointer Arithmetic

One of the most common uses of pointers in C is referencing *aggregate data*. Aggregate data is data composed of multiple elements grouped together because they are somehow related. C supports two classes of aggregate data: *structures* and *arrays*. (Unions, although similar to structures, are considered formally to be in a class by themselves.)

Structures

Structures are sequences of usually heterogeneous elements grouped so that they can be treated together as a single coherent datatype. Pointers to structures are an important part of building data structures. Whereas structures allow us to group data into convenient bundles, pointers let us link these bundles to one another in memory. By linking structures together, we can organize them in meaningful ways to help solve real problems.

As an example, consider chaining a number of elements together in memory to form a *linked list* (see Chapter 5, *Linked Lists*). To do this, we might use a structure like *ListElmt* in the following code. Using a *ListElmt* structure for each element in the list, to link a sequence of list elements together, we set the *next* member of each element to point to the element that comes after it. We set the *next* member of the last element to NULL to mark the end of the list. We set the *data* member of each element to point to the data the element contains. Once we have a list containing elements linked in this way, we can traverse the list by following one *next* pointer after another.

```
typedef struct ListElmt_ {

void          *data;
struct ListElmt_   *next;

} ListElmt;
```

The `ListElmt` structure illustrates another important aspect about pointers with structures: structures are not permitted to contain instances of themselves, but they may contain *pointers to* instances of themselves. This is an important idea in building data structures because many data structures are built from components that are self-referential. In a linked list, for example, each `ListElmt` structure points to another `ListElmt` structure. Some data structures are even built from structures containing multiple pointers to structures of the same type. In a binary tree (see Chapter 9, *Trees*), for example, each node has pointers to two other binary tree nodes.

Arrays

Arrays are sequences of homogeneous elements arranged consecutively in memory. In C, arrays are closely related to pointers. In fact, when an array identifier occurs in an expression, C converts the array transparently into an unmodifiable pointer that points to the array's first element. Considering this, the two following functions are equivalent.

Array Reference	Pointer Reference
`int f() {`	`int g() {`

`int a[10], *iptr;`
`iptr = a;`
`iptr[0] = 5;`
	`int a[10], *iptr;`
	`iptr = a;`
	`*iptr = 5;`

`return 0;`	`return 0;`
`}`	`}`

To understand the relationship between arrays and pointers in C, recall that to access the *i*th element in an array *a*, we use the expression:

```
a[i]
```

The reason that this expression accesses the *i*th element of *a* is that C treats *a* in this expression the same as a pointer that points to the first element of *a*. The expression as a whole is equivalent to:

```
*(a + i)
```

which is evaluated using the rules of *pointer arithmetic*. Simply stated, when we add an integer *i* to a pointer, the result is the address, plus *i* times the number of bytes in the datatype the pointer references; it is not simply the address stored in the pointer plus *i* bytes. An analogous operation is performed when we subtract an integer from a pointer. This explains why arrays are zero-indexed in C; that is, the first element in an array is at position 0.

For example, if an array or pointer contains the address 0x10000000, at which a sequence of five 4-byte integers is stored, *a[3]* accesses the integer at address 0x1000000c. This address is obtained by adding $(3)(4) = 12_{10} = c_{16}$ to the address 0x10000000 (see Figure 2-3a). On the other hand, for an array or pointer referencing twenty characters (a string), *a[3]* accesses the character at address 0x10000003. This address is obtained by adding $(3)(1) = 3_{10} = 3_{16}$ to the address 0x10000000 (see Figure 2-3b). Of course, an array or pointer referencing one piece of data looks no different from an array or pointer referencing many pieces. Therefore, it is important to keep track of the amount of storage that a pointer or array references and to not access addresses beyond this.

The conversion of a multidimensional array to a pointer is analogous to converting a one-dimensional array. However, we also must remember that in C, multidimensional arrays are stored in row-major order. This means that subscripts to the right vary more rapidly than those to the left. To access the element at row *i* and column *j* in a two-dimensional array, we use the expression:

```
a[i][j]
```

C treats *a* in this expression as a pointer that points to the element at row 0, column 0 in *a*. The expression as a whole is equivalent to:

```
*(*(a + i) + j)
```

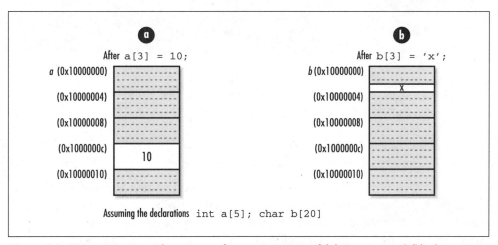

Figure 2-3. Using pointer arithmetic to reference an array of (a) integers and (b) characters

Pointers as Parameters to Functions

Pointers are an essential part of calling functions in C. Most importantly, they are used to support a type of parameter passing called *call-by-reference*. In call-by-reference parameter passing, when a function changes a parameter passed to it, the change persists after the function returns. Contrast this with *call-by-value* parameter passing, in which changes to parameters persist only within the function itself. Pointers are also an efficient means of passing large amounts of data in and out of functions, whether we plan to modify the data or not. This method is efficient because only a pointer is passed instead of a complete copy of the data. This technique is used in many of the examples in this book.

Call-by-Reference Parameter Passing

Formally, C supports only call-by-value parameter passing. In call-by-value parameter passing, private copies of a function's calling parameters are made for the function to use as it executes. However, we can simulate call-by-reference parameter passing by passing pointers to parameters instead of passing the parameters themselves. Using this approach, a function gets a private copy of a pointer to each parameter in the caller's environment.

To understand how this works, first consider *swap1*, which illustrates an incorrect implementation of a function to swap two integers using call-by-value parameter passing without pointers. Figure 2-4 illustrates why this does not work. The function *swap2* corrects the problem by using pointers to simulate call-by-reference parameter passing. Figure 2-5 illustrates how using pointers makes swapping proceed correctly.

Incorrect Swap	Correct Swap
`void swap1(int x, int y) {`	`void swap2(int *x, int *y) {`
`int tmp;` `tmp = x; x = y; y = tmp;`	`int tmp;` `tmp = *x; *x = *y; *y = tmp;`
`return;`	`return;`
`}`	`}`

One of the nice things about C and call-by-reference parameter passing is that the language gives us complete control over exactly how parameter passing is performed. One disadvantage, however, is that this control can be cumbersome since we often end up having to dereference call-by-reference parameters numerous times in functions.

Another use of pointers in function calls occurs when we pass arrays to functions. Recalling that C treats all array names transparently as unmodifiable pointers, passing an array of objects of type *T* in a function is equivalent to passing a pointer to an object of type *T*. Thus, we can use the two approaches interchangeably. For example, function *f1* and function *f2* are equivalent.

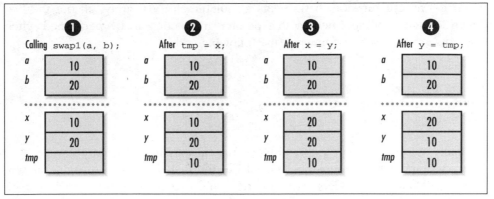

Figure 2-4. An illustration of swap1, which uses call-by-value parameter passing and fails to swap two integers in the caller's environment

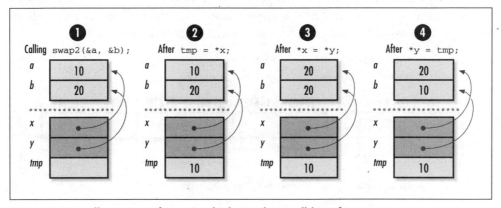

Figure 2-5. An illustration of swap2, which simulates call-by-reference parameter passing and successfully swaps two integers in the caller's environment

Array Reference	Pointer Reference
`int f1(int a[]) {`	`int f2(int *a) {`
`a[0] = 5;`	`*a = 5;`
`return 0;`	`return 0;`
`}`	`}`

Usually the approach chosen depends on a convention or on wanting to convey something about how the parameter is used in the function. When using an array parameter, bounds information is often omitted since it is not required by the compiler. However, including bounds information can be a useful way to document a limit the function imposes on a parameter internally. Bounds information plays a more critical role with array parameters that are multidimensional.

When defining a function that accepts a multidimensional array, all but the first dimension must be specified so that pointer arithmetic can be performed when elements are accessed, as shown in the following code:

```
int g(int a[][2]) {

a[2][0] = 5;

return 0;

}
```

To understand why we must include all but the first dimension, imagine a two-dimensional array of integers with three rows and two columns. In C, elements are stored in row-major order at increasing addresses in memory. This means that the two integers in the first row are stored first, followed by the two integers in the second row, followed by the two integers of the third row. Therefore, to access an element in any row but the first, we must know exactly how many elements to skip in each row to get to elements in successive rows (see Figure 2-6).

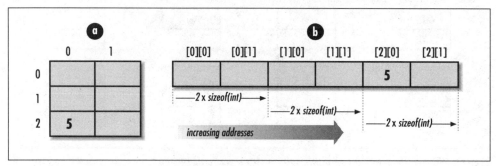

Figure 2-6. Writing 5 to row 2, column 0, in a 2 × 3 array of integers (a) conceptually and (b) as viewed in memory

Pointers to Pointers as Parameters

One situation in which pointers are used as parameters to functions a great deal in this book is when a function must modify a pointer passed into it. To do this, the function is passed a *pointer to the pointer* to be modified. Consider the operation *list_rem_next*, which Chapter 5 defines for removing an element from a linked list. Upon return, **data** points to the data removed from the list:

```
int list_rem_next(List *list, ListElmt *element, void **data);
```

Since the operation must modify the pointer **data** to make it point to the data removed, we must pass the address of the pointer **data** in order to simulate call-by-reference parameter passing (see Figure 2-7). Thus, the operation takes a pointer to a pointer as its third parameter. This is typical of how data is removed from most of the data structures presented in this book.

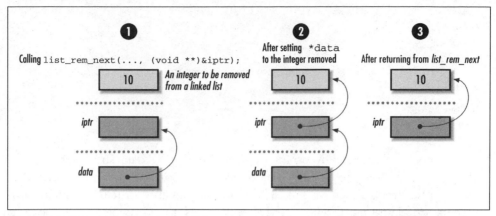

Figure 2-7. Using a function to modify a pointer to point to an integer removed from a linked list

Generic Pointers and Casts

Recall that pointer variables in C have types just like other variables. The main reason for this is so that when we dereference a pointer, the compiler knows the type of data being pointed to and can access the data accordingly. However, sometimes we are not concerned about the type of data a pointer references. In these cases we use *generic pointers*, which bypass C's type system.

Generic Pointers

Normally C allows assignments only between pointers of the same type. For example, given a character pointer *sptr* (a string) and an integer pointer *iptr*, we are not permitted to assign *sptr* to *iptr* or *iptr* to *sptr*. However, generic pointers can be set to pointers of any type, and vice versa. Thus, given a generic pointer *gptr*, we are permitted to assign *sptr* to *gptr* or *gptr* to *sptr*. To make a pointer generic in C, we declare it as a void pointer.

There are many situations in which void pointers are useful. For example, consider the standard C library function *memcpy*, which copies a block of data from one location in memory to another. Because *memcpy* may be used to copy data of any type, it makes sense that its pointer parameters are void pointers. Void pointers can be used to make other types of functions more generic as well. For example, we might have implemented the *swap2* function presented earlier so that it swapped data of any type, as shown in the following code:

```
#include <stdlib.h>
#include <string.h>

int swap2(void *x, void *y, int size) {
```

```
void *tmp;

if ((tmp = malloc(size)) == NULL)
   return -1;

memcpy(tmp, x, size); memcpy(x, y, size); memcpy(y, tmp, size);
free(tmp);

return 0;

}
```

Void pointers are particularly useful when implementing data structures because they allow us to store and retrieve data of any type. Consider again the *ListElmt* structure presented earlier for linked lists. Recall that this structure contains two members, *data* and *next*. Since *data* is declared as a void pointer, it can point to data of any type. Thus, we can use *ListElmt* structures to build any type of list.

In Chapter 5, one of the operations defined for linked lists is *list_ins_next*, which accepts a void pointer to the data to be inserted:

```
int list_ins_next(List *list, ListElmt *element, void *data);
```

To insert an integer referenced by *iptr* into a list of integers, *list*, after an element referenced by *element*, we use the following call. C permits us to pass the integer pointer *iptr* for the parameter *data* because *data* is a void pointer.

```
retval = list_ins_next(&list, element, iptr);
```

Of course, when removing data from the list, it is important to use the correct type of pointer to retrieve the data removed. Doing so ensures that the data will be interpreted correctly if we try to do something with it. As discussed earlier, the operation for removing an element from a linked list is *list_rem_next* (see Chapter 5), which takes a pointer to a void pointer as its third parameter:

```
int list_rem_next(List *list, ListElmt *element, void **data);
```

To remove an integer from *list* after an element referenced by *element*, we use the following call. Upon return, *iptr* points to the data removed. We pass the address of the pointer *iptr* since the operation modifies the pointer itself to make it point to the data removed.

```
retval = list_ins_next(&list, element, (void **)&iptr);
```

This call also includes a *cast* to make *iptr* temporarily appear as a pointer to a void pointer, since this is what *list_rem_next* requires. As we will see in the next section, casting is a mechanism in C that lets us temporarily treat a variable of one type as a variable of another type. A cast is necessary here because, although a void pointer is compatible with any other type of pointer in C, a pointer to a void pointer is not.

Casts

To cast a variable *t* of some type *T* to another type *S*, we precede *t* with *S* in parentheses. For example, to assign an integer pointer *iptr* to a floating-point pointer *fptr*, we cast *iptr* to a floating-point pointer and then carry out the assignment, as shown:

```
fptr = (float *)iptr;
```

(Although casting an integer pointer to a floating-point pointer is a dangerous practice in general, it is presented here as an illustration.) After the assignment, *iptr* and *fptr* both contain the same address. However, the interpretation of the data at this address depends on which pointer we use to access it.

Casts are especially important with generic pointers because generic pointers cannot be dereferenced without casting them to some other type. This is because generic pointers give the compiler no information about what is being pointed to; thus, it is not clear how many bytes should be accessed, nor how the bytes should be interpreted. Casts are also a nice form of self-documentation when generic pointers are assigned to pointers of other types. Although the cast is not necessary in this case, it does improve a program's readability.

When casting pointers, one issue we need to be particularly sensitive to is the way data is aligned in memory. Specifically, we need to be aware that applying casts to pointers can undermine the alignment a computer expects. Often computers have alignment requirements so that certain hardware optimizations can make accessing memory more efficient. For example, a system may insist that all integers be aligned on word boundaries. Thus, given a void pointer that is not word aligned, if we cast the void pointer to an integer pointer and dereference it, we can expect an exception to occur at runtime.

Function Pointers

Function pointers are pointers that, instead of pointing to data, point to executable code or to blocks of information needed to invoke executable code. They are used to store and manage functions as if they were pieces of data. Function pointers have a type that is described in terms of a return value and parameters that the function accepts. Declarations for function pointers look much like declarations for functions, except that an asterisk (*) appears before the function name, and the asterisk and name are surrounded by parentheses for reasons of associativity. For example, in the following code, *match* is declared as a pointer to a function that accepts two void pointers and returns an integer:

```
int (*match)(void *key1, void *key2);
```

This declaration means that we can set *match* to point to any function that accepts two void pointers and returns an integer. For example, suppose *match_int* is a function that accepts two void pointers to integers and returns 1 if the integers match, or 0 otherwise. Assuming the previous declaration, we could set *match* to point to this function by executing the following statement:

```
match = match_int;
```

To execute a function referenced by a function pointer, we simply use the function pointer wherever we would normally use the function itself. For example, to invoke the function referenced by *match* earlier, we execute the following statement, assuming *x*, *y*, and *retval* have been declared as integers:

```
retval = match(&x, &y);
```

One important use of function pointers in this book is to encapsulate functions into data structures. For example, in the implementation of chained hash tables (see Chapter 8, *Hash Tables*), the data structure has a *match* member similar to the function pointer just described. This pointer is used to invoke a function whenever we need to determine whether an element we are searching for matches an element in the table. We assign a function to this pointer when the table is initialized. The function we assign has the same prototype as *match* but internally compares two elements of the appropriate type, depending on the type of data in the table for which the table has been defined. Using a pointer to store a function as part of a data structure is nice because it is yet another way to keep an implementation generic.

Questions and Answers

Q: *One of the difficulties with pointers is that often when we misuse them, our errors are not caught by the compiler at compile time; they occur at runtime. Which of the following result in compile-time errors? Which of the following result in runtime errors? Why?*

a) ```
    char *sptr = "abc",*tptr;
    *tptr = sptr;
    ```

b)  ```
    char *sptr = "abc",*tptr;
    tptr = sptr;
    ```

c) ```
    char *sptr = "abc",*tptr;
    *tptr = *sptr;
    ```

d)  ```
    int *iptr = (int *)10;
    *iptr = 11;
    ```

e) ```
    int *iptr = 10;
    *iptr = 11;
    ```

f)  ```
    int *iptr = (int *)10;
    iptr = NULL;
    ```

A: a) A compile-time error occurs because when we dereference *tptr*, we get a character, whereas *sptr* is a pointer to a character. Thus, the code is trying to assign a character pointer to a character, which is a type conflict. b) No error occurs because both *tptr* and *sptr* are character pointers. c) A runtime error is likely to occur because no storage has been allocated for *tptr*. When we dereference *tptr*, we cannot be sure where it points. d) A runtime error is likely to occur because assigning an integer pointer a fixed address is dangerous. When dereferencing *iptr*, we try to write 11 at address 10, which is probably invalid. e) A compile-time error or warning occurs because the code is trying to initialize an integer pointer to an integer, which is a type conflict. f) No error occurs because although the code first performs the dangerous step of initializing *iptr* to a fixed address, it is then immediately reset to NULL, which is valid.

Q: *Recall that calculations with pointers are performed using pointer arithmetic. If p contains the address 0x10000000, what address does the following expression access? How many bytes are accessed at this address?*

```
*(p + 5)
```

A: The answer to this question depends on the type of *p*. Recall that when we add an integer *i* to a pointer *p*, the result is not the address stored in *p* plus *i* bytes, but the address in *p*, plus *i* times the number of bytes in the datatype *p* references. Since the question does not state *p*'s type, it is not possible to determine the address accessed as a result of the expression. The type of *p* is also required to determine how many bytes *p* accesses. Therefore, it is also impossible to determine the number of bytes accessed.

Q: *The operation* list_rem_next *removes an element from a linked list (see Chapter 5). If* iptr *is an integer pointer we would like set to an integer removed from a list, how might we call* list_rem_next *as an alternative to the approach presented in the chapter? A prototype for the function is shown here, where* list *is the list,* element *references the element preceding the one to remove, and upon return,* data *references the data removed.*

```
int list_rem_next(List *list, ListElmt *element, void **data);
```

A: An alternative way to call *list_rem_next* is shown here. In this approach, *iptr* is cast to a void pointer instead of a pointer to a void pointer. This method is acceptable because void pointers are compatible with all others. However, our original approach is clearer because it is consistent with the prototype of *list_rem_next*.

```
retval = list_rem_next(&list, element, (void *)&iptr);
```

Related Topics

C++

An object-oriented language that enforces many practices of good software engineering. As one example, it supports constructors and destructors for datatypes. These mechanisms provide a compact way of managing memory within instances of the type, thus avoiding many of the problems associated with memory leaks and pointers in C.

Heap-based allocation

The type of memory allocation provided by the C functions *malloc* and *realloc*. Heap-based allocation is often called *dynamic storage allocation*. This allows a program to request more memory as it needs it rather than allocating a fixed amount at compile time.

3

Recursion

Recursion is a powerful principle that allows something to be defined in terms of smaller instances of itself. Perhaps there is no better way to appreciate the significance of recursion than to look at the mysterious ways nature uses it. Think of the fragile leaf of a fern, in which each individual sprig from the leaf's stem is just a smaller copy of the overall leaf; or the repeating patterns in a reflection, in which two shiny objects reflect each other. Examples like these convince us that even though nature is a great force, in many ways it has a paradoxical simplicity that is truly elegant. The same can be said for recursive algorithms; in many ways, recursive algorithms are simple and elegant, yet they can be extremely powerful.

In computing, recursion is supported via recursive functions. A recursive function is a function that calls itself. Each successive call works on a more refined set of inputs, bringing us closer and closer to the solution of a problem. Most developers are comfortable with the idea of dividing a larger problem into several smaller ones and writing separate functions to solve them. However, many developers are less comfortable with the idea of solving a larger problem with a single function that calls itself. Admittedly, looking at a problem in this way can take some getting used to. This chapter explores how recursion works and shows how to define some problems in a recursive manner. Some examples of recursive approaches in this book are found in tree traversals (see Chapter 9, *Trees*), breadth-first and depth-first searches with graphs (see Chapter 11, *Graphs*), and sorting (see Chapter 12, *Sorting and Searching*).

This chapter covers:

Basic recursion

> A powerful principle that allows a problem to be defined in terms of smaller and smaller instances of itself. In computing, we solve problems defined recursively by using recursive functions, which are functions that call themselves.

Tail recursion

A form of recursion for which compilers are able to generate optimized code. Most modern compilers recognize tail recursion. Therefore, we should make use of it whenever we can.

Basic Recursion

To begin, let's consider a simple problem that normally we might not think of in a recursive way. Suppose we would like to compute the factorial of a number n. The factorial of n, written $n!$, is the product of all numbers from n down to 1. For example, $4! = (4)(3)(2)(1)$. One way to calculate this is to loop through each number and multiply it with the product of all preceding numbers. This is an *iterative* approach, which can be defined more formally as:

$$n! = (n)(n-1)(n-2) \ldots (1)$$

Another way to look at this problem is to define $n!$ as the product of smaller factorials. To do this, we define $n!$ as n times the factorial of $n - 1$. Of course, solving $(n - 1)!$ is the same problem as $n!$, only a little smaller. If we then think of $(n - 1)!$ as $n - 1$ times $(n - 2)!$, $(n - 2)!$ as $n - 2$ times $(n - 3)!$, and so forth until $n = 1$, we end up computing $n!$. This is a *recursive* approach, which can be defined more formally as:

$$F(n) = \begin{cases} 1 & \text{if } n = 0,\ n = 1 \\ nF(n-1) & \text{if } n > 1 \end{cases}$$

Figure 3-1 illustrates computing 4! using the recursive approach just described. It also delineates the two basic phases of a recursive process: *winding* and *unwinding*. In the winding phase, each recursive call perpetuates the recursion by making an additional recursive call itself. The winding phase terminates when one of the calls reaches a *terminating condition*. A terminating condition defines the state at which a recursive function should return instead of making another recursive call. For example, in computing the factorial of n, the terminating conditions are $n = 1$ and $n = 0$, for which the function simply returns 1. Every recursive function must have at least one terminating condition; otherwise, the winding phase never terminates. Once the winding phase is complete, the process enters the unwinding phase, in which previous instances of the function are revisited in reverse order. This phase continues until the original call returns, at which point the recursive process is complete.

Example 3-1 presents a C function, *fact*, that accepts a number n and computes its factorial recursively. The function works as follows. If n is less than 0, the function returns 0, indicating an error. If n is 0 or 1, the function returns 1 because 0!

$$F(4) = 4 \times F(3) \qquad \text{winding phase}$$
$$F(3) = 3 \times F(2) \qquad .$$
$$F(2) = 2 \times F(1) \qquad .$$
$$F(1) = 1 \qquad \text{terminating condition}$$

$$F(2) = (2)(1) \qquad \text{unwinding phase}$$
$$F(3) = (3)(2) \qquad .$$
$$F(4) = (4)(6) \qquad .$$
$$24 \qquad \text{recursion complete}$$

Figure 3-1. Computing 4! recursively

and 1! are both defined as 1. These are the terminating conditions. Otherwise, the function returns the result of n times the factorial of $n - 1$. The factorial of $n - 1$ is computed recursively by calling *fact* again, and so forth. Notice the similarities between this implementation and the recursive definition shown earlier.

Example 3-1. Implementation of a Function for Computing Factorials Recursively

```
/*****************************************************************************
 *                                                                           *
 * ------------------------------- fact.c --------------------------------- *
 *                                                                           *
 *****************************************************************************/

#include "fact.h"

/*****************************************************************************
 *                                                                           *
 * -------------------------------- fact --------------------------------- *
 *                                                                           *
 *****************************************************************************/

int fact(int n) {

/*****************************************************************************
 *                                                                           *
 *  Compute a factorial recursively.                                         *
 *                                                                           *
 *****************************************************************************/

if (n < 0)
   return 0;
else if (n == 0)
   return 1;
else if (n == 1)
   return 1;
else
   return n * fact(n - 1);

}
```

To understand how recursion really works, it helps to look at the way functions are executed in C. For this, we need to understand a little about the organization of a C program in memory. Fundamentally, a C program consists of four areas as it executes: a code area, a static data area, a heap, and a stack (see Figure 3-2a). The code area contains the machine instructions that are executed as the program runs. The static data area contains data that persists throughout the life of the program, such as global variables and static local variables. The heap contains dynamically allocated storage, such as memory allocated by *malloc*. The stack contains information about function calls. By convention, the heap grows upward from one end of a program's memory, while the stack grows downward from the other (but this may vary in practice). Note that the term *heap* as it is used in this context has nothing to do with the heap data structure presented in Chapter 10, *Heaps and Priority Queues*.

When a function is called in a C program, a block of storage is allocated on the stack to keep track of information associated with the call. Each call is referred to as an *activation*. The block of storage placed on the stack is called an *activation record* or, alternatively, a *stack frame*. An activation record consists of five regions: incoming parameters, space for a return value, temporary storage used in evaluating expressions, saved state information for when the activation terminates, and outgoing parameters (see Figure 3-2b). Incoming parameters are the parameters passed into the activation. Outgoing parameters are the parameters passed to functions called within the activation. The outgoing parameters of one activation record become the incoming parameters of the next one placed on the stack. The activation record for a function call remains on the stack until the call terminates.

Returning to Example 3-1, consider what happens on the stack as one computes 4!. The initial call to *fact* results in one activation record being placed on the stack with an incoming parameter of $n = 4$ (see Figure 3-3, step 1). Since this activation does not meet any of the terminating conditions of the function, *fact* is recursively called with n set to 3. This places another activation of *fact* on the stack, but with an incoming parameter of $n = 3$ (see Figure 3-3, step 2). Here, $n = 3$ is also an outgoing parameter of the first activation since the first activation invoked the second. The process continues this way until n is 1, at which point a terminating condition is encountered and *fact* returns 1 (see Figure 3-3, step 4).

Once the $n = 1$ activation terminates, the recursive expression in the $n = 2$ activation is evaluated as $(2)(1) = 2$. Thus, the $n = 2$ activation terminates with a return value of 2 (see Figure 3-3, step 5). Consequently, the recursive expression in the $n = 3$ activation is evaluated as $(3)(2) = 6$, and the $n = 3$ activation returns 6 (see Figure 3-3, step 6). Finally, the recursive expression in the $n = 4$ activation is evaluated as $(4)(6) = 24$, and the $n = 4$ activation terminates with a return value of 24 (see Figure 3-3, step 7). At this point, the function has returned from the original call, and the recursive process is complete.

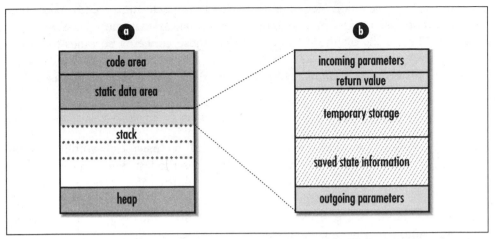

Figure 3-2. The organization in memory of (a) a C program and (b) an activation record

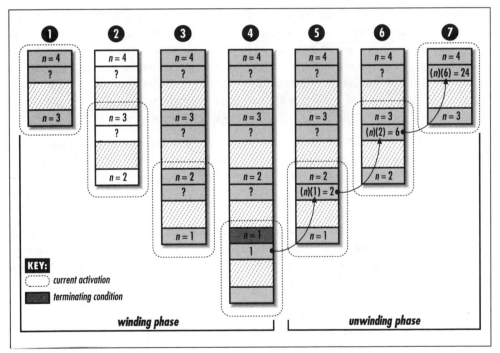

Figure 3-3. The stack of a C program while computing 4! recursively

The stack is a great solution to storing information about function calls because its last-in, first-out behavior (see Chapter 6, *Stacks and Queues*) is well suited to the order in which functions are called and terminated. However, stack usage does have a few drawbacks. Maintaining information about every function call until it returns takes a considerable amount of space, especially in programs with many recursive calls. In addition, generating and destroying activation records takes time because there is a significant amount of information that must be saved and restored. Thus, if the overhead associated with these concerns becomes too great, we may need to consider an iterative approach. Fortunately, we can use a special type of recursion, called *tail recursion*, to avoid these concerns in some cases.

Tail Recursion

A recursive function is said to be *tail recursive* if all recursive calls within it are tail recursive. A recursive call is tail recursive when it is the last statement that will be executed within the body of a function and its return value is not a part of an expression. Tail-recursive functions are characterized as having nothing to do during the unwinding phase. This characteristic is important because most modern compilers automatically generate code to take advantage of it.

When a compiler detects a call that is tail recursive, it overwrites the current activation record instead of pushing a new one onto the stack. The compiler can do this because the recursive call is the last statement to be executed in the current activation; thus, there is nothing left to do in the activation when the call returns. Consequently, there is no reason to keep the current activation around. By replacing the current activation record instead of stacking another one on top of it, stack usage is greatly reduced, which leads to better performance in practice. Thus, we should make recursive functions tail recursive whenever we can.

To understand how tail recursion works, let's revisit computing a factorial recursively. First, it is helpful to understand the reason the previous definition was not tail recursive. Recall that the original definition computed $n!$ by multiplying n times $(n - 1)!$ in each activation, repeating this for $n = n - 1$ until $n = 1$. This definition was not tail recursive because the return value of each activation depended on multiplying n times the return value of subsequent activations. Therefore, the activation record for each call had to remain on the stack until the return values of subsequent calls were determined. Now consider a tail-recursive definition for computing $n!$, which can be defined formally as:

$$F(n, a) = \begin{cases} a & \text{if } n = 0, n = 1 \\ F(n-1, na) & \text{if } n > 1 \end{cases}$$

This definition is similar to the one presented earlier, except that it uses a second parameter, a (initially set to 1), which maintains the value of the factorial computed thus far in the recursive process. This prevents us from having to multiply the return value of each activation by n. Instead, in each recursive call, we let $a = na$ and $n = n - 1$. We continue this until $n = 1$, which is the terminating condition, at which point we simply return a. Figure 3-4 illustrates the process of computing 4! using this approach. Notice how there is no work that needs to be performed during the unwinding phase, a signature of all tail-recursive functions.

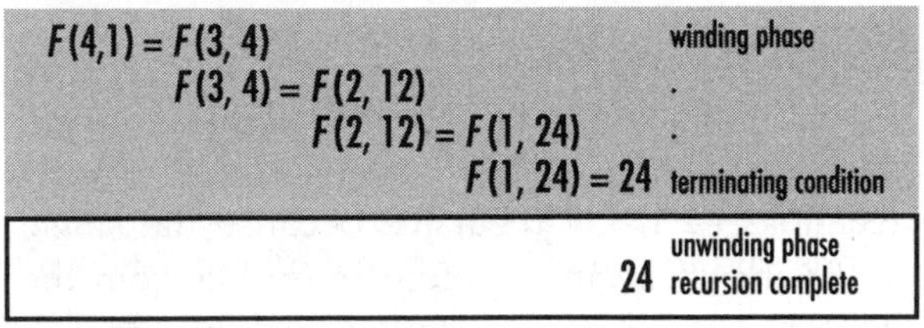

$$F(4,1) = F(3, 4) \qquad \text{winding phase}$$
$$F(3, 4) = F(2, 12)$$
$$F(2, 12) = F(1, 24)$$
$$F(1, 24) = 24 \quad \text{terminating condition}$$

unwinding phase
24 recursion complete

Figure 3-4. Computing 4! in a tail-recursive manner

Example 3-2 presents a C function, *facttail*, that accepts a number *n* and computes its factorial in a tail-recursive manner. This function also accepts the additional parameter *a*, which is initially set to 1. The function *facttail* is similar to *fact*, except that it uses *a* to maintain the value of the factorial computed thus far in the recursion. Notice the similarities between this implementation and the tail-recursive definition.

Example 3-2. Implementation of a Function for Computing Factorials in a Tail-Recursive Manner

```
/*****************************************************************************
 *                                                                          *
 *  --------------------------- facttail.c ---------------------------       *
 *                                                                          *
 *****************************************************************************/

#include "facttail.h"

/*****************************************************************************
 *                                                                          *
 *  ---------------------------- facttail ----------------------------       *
 *                                                                          *
 *****************************************************************************/

int facttail(int n, int a) {

/*****************************************************************************
 *                                                                          *
 *  Compute a factorial in a tail-recursive manner.                         *
 *                                                                          *
 *****************************************************************************/

if (n < 0)
   return 0;
else if (n == 0)
   return 1;
```

Example 3-2. Implementation of a Function for Computing Factorials
in a Tail-Recursive Manner (continued)

```
else if (n == 1)
   return a;
else
   return facttail(n - 1, n * a);

}
```

The function in Example 3-2 is tail recursive because the single recursive call to *facttail* is the last statement executed before returning from the call. It just happens that this is the last statement of *facttail* as well, but this does not have to be the case. In other words, there could have been other statements after the recursive call, provided they were executed only when the recursive call was not. Figure 3-5 illustrates the limited activity on the stack while computing 4! using this tail-recursive function. Contrast this with the activity on the stack in Figure 3-3.

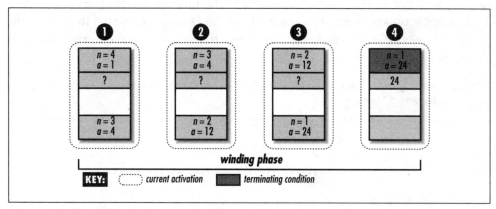

Figure 3-5. The stack of a C program while computing 4! in a tail-recursive manner

Questions and Answers

Q: *The following recursive definition has an error. What is it, and how can we fix it? For a positive integer* n, *the definition, in its proper form, is common in formally computing the running time of divide-and-conquer algorithms, such as merge sort (see Chapter 12). Merge sort divides a set of data in half, then divides the halves in half, and continues this way until each division contains a single element. Then, during the unwinding phase, the divisions are merged to produce a final sorted set.*

$$T(n) = \begin{cases} 1 & \text{if } n = 0 \\ 2\,T(n/2) + n & \text{if } n > 0 \end{cases}$$

A: The problem with this definition is that it never reaches the terminating condition, $n = 0$, for any initial value of n greater than 0. To fix the problem, it needs an obtainable terminating condition. The condition $n = 1$ works well, which means we should also change the second condition in the function. A recursive definition with an acceptable terminating condition is presented here:

$$T(n) = \begin{cases} 1 & \text{if } n = 1 \\ 2T(n/2) + n & \text{if } n > 1 \end{cases}$$

This happens to be the correct definition for the running time of merge sort. Such a function is called a *recurrence*. In more formal analysis, recurrences are used frequently to describe the running times of recursive algorithms.

Q: *Describe a recursive approach for computing the prime factors of a number. Determine whether the approach is tail recursive, and describe why or why not.*

A: Recursion is a natural way to find the prime factors of a number because factoring is really just the same problem over and over again, only a little smaller, as we determine each factor. A recursive approach to this problem can be defined as shown:

$$F(n, P) = \begin{cases} P \cup n & \text{if } n \text{ is prime} \\ F(n/i, P \cup i); i \text{ is smallest prime factor of } n & \text{if } n \text{ is not prime} \end{cases}$$

This definition says that to determine the prime factors of a number n recursively, determine its smallest prime factor i, record this in a set of factors P, and repeat the process for $n = n/i$. Continue this way until n is found to be prime itself, which is the terminating condition. This definition is tail recursive because there is nothing that needs to be done during the unwinding phase, as Figure 3-6 confirms.

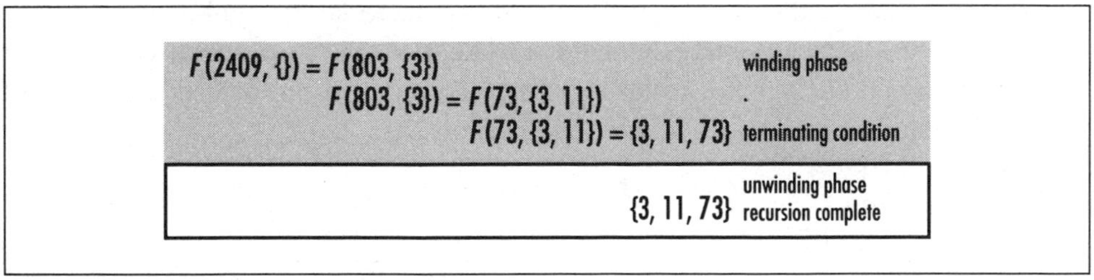

Figure 3-6. Computing the prime factors of 2409 in a tail-recursive manner

Q: *Considering how the stack is used in executing recursive functions, what happens when the winding phase of a recursive process never terminates, perhaps as a result of a malformed terminating condition, as in the first question?*

A: If the terminating condition of a recursive function is never reached, eventually the stack grows past an acceptable size and the program aborts from a *stack overflow.* A special pointer, called the *frame pointer,* keeps track of the top of the stack as a program executes. It is also used to determine when the stack has grown too large. An interrupt is raised to signal the error.

Q: *Recursive functions frequently offer simple yet concise ways to describe useful computations. Describe the computation that the following recursive definition describes:*

$$H(n) = \begin{cases} 1 & \text{if } n = 1 \\ H(n-1) + (1/n) & \text{if } n > 1 \end{cases}$$

A: This recursive definition calculates a series like the following one, called the *harmonic series.* For positive integers n, the function calculates the nth harmonic number. (The calculation proceeds in reverse order from what is shown, but the following form is more recognizable.)

$$H(n) = 1 + \frac{1}{2} + \frac{1}{3} + \frac{1}{4} + \frac{1}{5} + \ldots + \frac{1}{n}$$

Q: *Is the function in the previous question tail recursive? If so, describe why. If not, describe why not and present a tail-recursive version.*

A: The function defined in the previous question is not tail recursive because the return value of the recursive call is used in an expression. This expression becomes the return value of the current call. Therefore, each activation must remain on the stack until it gets the return value of subsequent activations. To make this function tail recursive, we can use an approach like the one presented earlier in the chapter for computing a factorial in a tail-recursive manner. We use an additional parameter a to keep a tally of the total value of the series computed thus far in the recursion. Formally, a tail-recursive version of the function in the previous question is as follows:

$$H(n, a) = \begin{cases} a + 1 & \text{if } n = 1 \\ H(n-1, a + 1/n) & \text{if } n > 1 \end{cases}$$

Related Topics

Compiler design

The basics behind the code translators that ultimately dictate how efficiently programs will run, at least at the instruction level. Whereas generally in algorithm design we focus on complexity as a measure of performance (see Chapter 4, *Analysis of Algorithms*), understanding the issues compilers deal with in translating code can help us tune performance in practice. Understanding tail recursion is a good example.

Tail recursion elimination

A process in which the final tail-recursive call in a function is replaced with an iterative control structure. This does not change the outcome of the function, but helps avoid the overhead of an extra function call. Tail recursion elimination is a fundamental principle studied in compiler design.

Recursion trees

Illustrations that help us visualize calling sequences with recursive functions. Recursion trees vary in their formality. Figures 3-1 and 3-4 for recursively computing a factorial and Figure 3-6 for determining the prime factors of a number are recursion trees. Recursion trees are most often used with functions containing two or more recursive calls within each activation.

4

Analysis of Algorithms

Whether we are designing an algorithm or applying one that is widely accepted, it is important to understand how the algorithm will perform. There are a number of ways we can look at an algorithm's performance, but usually the aspect of most interest is how fast the algorithm will run. In some cases, if an algorithm uses significant storage, we may be interested in its space requirement as well. Whatever the case, determining how an algorithm performs requires a formal and deterministic method.

There are many reasons to understand the performance of an algorithm. For example, we often have a choice of several algorithms when solving problems. Understanding how each performs helps us differentiate between them. Understanding the burden an algorithm places on an application also helps us plan how to use the algorithm more effectively. For instance, *garbage collection algorithms*, algorithms that collect dynamically allocated storage to return to the heap (see Chapter 3, *Recursion*), require considerable time to run. Knowing this, we can be careful to run them only at opportune moments, just as LISP and Java do, for example.

This chapter covers:

Worst-case analysis
> The metric by which most algorithms are compared. Other cases we might consider are the average case and best case. However, worst-case analysis usually offers several advantages.

O-notation
> The most common notation used to formally express an algorithm's performance. *O*-notation is used to express the upper bound of a function within a constant factor.

Computational complexity

The growth rate of the resources (usually time) an algorithm requires with respect to the size of the data it processes. *O*-notation is a formal expression of an algorithm's complexity.

Worst-Case Analysis

Most algorithms do not perform the same in all cases; normally an algorithm's performance varies with the data passed to it. Typically, three cases are recognized: the *best case*, *worst case*, and *average case*. For any algorithm, understanding what constitutes each of these cases is an important part of analysis because performance can vary significantly between them. Consider even a simple algorithm such as *linear search*. Linear search is a natural but inefficient search technique in which we look for an element simply by traversing a set from one end to the other. In the best case, the element we are looking for is the first element we inspect, so we end up traversing only a single element. In the worst case, however, the desired element is the last one we inspect, in which case we end up traversing all of the elements. On average, we can expect to find the element somewhere in the middle.

Reasons for Worst-Case Analysis

A basic understanding of how an algorithm performs in all cases is important, but usually we are most interested in how an algorithm performs in the *worst case*. There are four reasons why algorithms are generally analyzed by their worst case:

*   Many algorithms perform to their worst case a large part of the time. For example, the worst case in searching occurs when we do not find what we are looking for at all. Imagine how frequently this takes place in some database applications.

*   The best case is not very informative because many algorithms perform exactly the same in the best case. For example, nearly all searching algorithms can locate an element in one inspection at best, so analyzing this case does not tell us much.

*   Determining average-case performance is not always easy. Often it is difficult to determine exactly what the "average case" even is. Since we can seldom guarantee precisely how an algorithm will be exercised, usually we cannot obtain an average-case measurement that is likely to be accurate.

*   The worst case gives us an upper bound on performance. Analyzing an algorithm's worst case guarantees that it will *never* perform worse than what we determine. Therefore, we know that the other cases must perform at least as well.

Although worst-case analysis is the metric for many algorithms, it is worth noting that there are exceptions. Sometimes special circumstances let us base performance on the average case. For example, randomized algorithms such as quicksort (see Chapter 12, *Sorting and Searching*) use principles of probability to virtually guarantee average-case performance.

O-Notation

O-notation is the most common notation used to express an algorithm's performance in a formal manner. Formally, *O*-notation expresses the upper bound of a function within a constant factor. Specifically, if $g(n)$ is an upper bound of $f(n)$, then for some constant c it is possible to find a value of n, call it n_0, for which any value of $n \geq n_0$ will result in $f(n) \leq cg(n)$.

Normally we express an algorithm's performance as a function of the size of the data it processes. That is, for some data of size n, we describe its performance with some function $f(n)$. However, while in many cases we can determine f exactly, usually it is not necessary to be this precise. Primarily we are interested only in the *growth rate* of f, which describes how quickly the algorithm's performance will degrade as the size of the data it processes becomes arbitrarily large. An algorithm's growth rate, or *order of growth*, is significant because ultimately it describes how *efficient* the algorithm is for arbitrary inputs. *O*-notation reflects an algorithm's order of growth.

Simple Rules for O-Notation

When we look at some function $f(n)$ in terms of its growth rate, a few things become apparent. First, we can ignore constant terms because as the value of n becomes larger and larger, eventually constant terms will become insignificant. For example, if $T(n) = n + 50$ describes the running time of an algorithm, and n, the size of the data it processes, is only 1024, the constant term in this expression already constitutes less than 5% of the running time. Second, we can ignore constant multipliers of terms because they too will become insignificant as the value of n increases. For example, if $T_1(n) = n^2$ and $T_2(n) = 10n$ describe the running times of two algorithms for solving the same problem, n only has to be greater than 10 for T_1 to become greater than T_2. Finally, we need only consider the highest-order term because, again, as n increases, higher-order terms quickly outweigh the lower-order ones. For example, if $T(n) = n^2 + n$ describes the running time of an algorithm, and n is 1024, the lesser-order term of this expression constitutes less than 0.1% of the running time. These ideas are formalized in the following simple rules for expressing functions in *O*-notation.

- Constant terms are expressed as $O(1)$. When analyzing the running time of an algorithm, apply this rule when you have a task that you know will execute in a certain amount of time regardless of the size of the data it processes. Formally stated, for some constant c:

  $O(c) = O(1)$

- Multiplicative constants are omitted. When analyzing the running time of an algorithm, apply this rule when you have a number of tasks that all execute in the same amount of time. For example, if three tasks each run in time $T(n) = n$, the result is $O(3n)$, which simplifies to $O(n)$. Formally stated, for some constant c:

  $O(cT) = cO(T) = O(T)$

- Addition is performed by taking the maximum. When analyzing the running time of an algorithm, apply this rule when one task is executed after another. For example, if $T_1(n) = n$ and $T_2(n) = n^2$ describe two tasks executed sequentially, the result is $O(n) + O(n^2)$, which simplifies to $O(n^2)$. Formally stated:

  $O(T_1) + O(T_2) = O(T_1 + T_2) = \max(O(T_1), O(T_2))$

- Multiplication is not changed but often is rewritten more compactly. When analyzing the running time of an algorithm, apply this rule when one task causes another to be executed some number of times for each iteration of itself. For example, in a nested loop whose outer iterations are described by T_1 and whose inner iterations by T_2, if $T_1(n) = n$ and $T_2(n) = n$, the result is $O(n)O(n)$, or $O(n^2)$. Formally stated:

  $O(T_1)O(T_2) = O(T_1 T_2)$

O-Notation Example and Why It Works

The next section discusses how these rules help us in predicting an algorithm's performance. For now, let's look at a specific example demonstrating why they work so well in describing a function's growth rate. Suppose we have an algorithm whose running time is described by the function $T(n) = 3n^2 + 10n + 10$. Using the rules of O-notation, this function can be simplified to:

$$O(T(n)) = O(3n^2 + 10n + 10) = O(3n^2) = O(n^2)$$

This indicates that the term containing n^2 will be the one that accounts for most of the running time as n grows arbitrarily large. We can verify this quantitatively by computing the percentage of the overall running time that each term accounts for as n increases. For example, when $n = 10$, we have the following:

Running time for $3n^2$: $3(10)^2/(3(10)^2 + 10(10) + 10) = 73.2\%$

Running time for $10n$: $10(10)/(3(10)^2 + 10(10) + 10) = 24.4\%$

Running time for 10: $10/(3(10)^2 + 10(10) + 10) = 2.4\%$

Already we see that the n^2 term accounts for the majority of the overall running time. Now consider when $n = 100$:

Running time for $3n^2$: $3(100)^2/(3(100)^2 + 10(100) + 10) = 96.7\%$ (Higher)

Running time for $10n$: $10(100)/(3(100)^2 + 10(100) + 10) = 3.2\%$ (Lower)

Running time for 10: $10/(3(100)^2 + 10(100) + 10) < 0.1\%$ (Lower)

Here we see that this term accounts for *almost all* of the running time, while the significance of the other terms diminishes further. Imagine how much of the running time this term would account for if n were 10^6!

Computational Complexity

When speaking of the performance of an algorithm, usually the aspect of interest is its *complexity*, which is the growth rate of the resources (usually time) it requires with respect to the size of the data it processes. *O*-notation describes an algorithm's complexity. Using *O*-notation, we can frequently describe the worst-case complexity of an algorithm simply by inspecting its overall structure. Other times, it is helpful to employ techniques involving recurrences and summation formulas (see the related topics at the end of the chapter), and statistics.

To understand complexity, let's look at one way to surmise the resources an algorithm will require. It should seem reasonable that if we look at an algorithm as a series of k statements, each with some cost (usually time) to execute, c_i, we can determine the algorithm's total cost by summing the costs of all statements from c_1 to c_k in whatever order each is executed. Normally statements are executed in a more complicated manner than simply in sequence, so this has to be taken into account when totaling the costs. For example, if some subset of the statements is executed in a loop, the costs of the subset must be multiplied by the number of iterations. Consider an algorithm consisting of $k = 6$ statements. If statements 3, 4, and 5 are executed in a loop from 1 to n and the other statements are executed sequentially, the overall cost of the algorithm is:

$$T(n) = c_1 + c_2 + n(c_3 + c_4 + c_5) + c_6$$

Using the rules of *O*-notation, this algorithm's complexity is $O(n)$ because the constants are not significant. Analyzing an algorithm in terms of these constant costs is very thorough. However, recalling what we have seen about growth rates, remember that we do not need to be so precise. When inspecting the overall structure of an algorithm, only two steps need to be performed: we must determine which parts of the algorithm depend on data whose size is not constant, and then derive functions that describe the performance of each part. All other parts of the algorithm execute with a constant cost and can be ignored in figuring its overall complexity.

Assuming $T(n)$ in the previous example represents an algorithm's running time, it is important to realize that $O(n)$, its complexity, says little about the *actual* time the algorithm will take to run. In other words, just because an algorithm has a low growth rate does not necessarily mean it will execute in a small amount of time. In fact, complexities have no real units of measurement at all. They describe only how the resource being measured will be affected by a *change* in data size. For example, saying that $T(n)$ is $O(n)$ conveys only that the algorithm's running time varies proportionally to n, and that n is an upper bound for $T(n)$ within a constant factor. Formally, we say that $T(n) \leq cn$, where c is a constant factor that accounts for various costs not associated with the data, such as the type of computer on which the algorithm is running, the compiler used to generate the machine code, and constants in the algorithm itself.

Many complexities occur frequently in computing, so it is worthwhile to become familiar with them. Table 4-1 lists some typical situations in which common complexities occur. Table 4-2 lists these common complexities along with some calculations illustrating their growth rates. Figure 4-1 presents the data of Table 4-2 in a graphical form.

Table 4-1. Some Situations Wherein Common Complexities Occur

Complexity	Example
$O(1)$	Fetching the first element from a set of data
$O(\lg n)$	Splitting a set of data in half, then splitting the halves in half, etc.
$O(n)$	Traversing a set of data
$O(n \lg n)$	Splitting a set of data in half repeatedly and traversing each half
$O(n^2)$	Traversing a set of data once for each member of another set of equal size
$O(2^n)$	Generating all possible subsets of a set of data
$O(n!)$	Generating all possible permutations of a set of data

Table 4-2. The Growth Rates of the Complexities in Table 4-1

	$n = 1$	$n = 16$	$n = 256$	$n = 4K$	$n = 64K$	$n = 1M$
$O(1)$	1.000E+00	1.000E+00	1.000E+00	1.000E+00	1.000E+00	1.000E+00
$O(\lg n)$	0.000E+00	4.000E+00	8.000E+00	1.200E+01	1.600E+01	2.000E+01
$O(n)$	1.000E+00	1.600E+01	2.560E+02	4.096E+03	6.554E+04	1.049E+06
$O(n \lg n)$	0.000E+00	6.400E+01	2.048E+03	4.915E+04	1.049E+06	2.097E+07

Table 4-2. The Growth Rates of the Complexities in Table 4-1 (continued)

	$n = 1$	$n = 16$	$n = 256$	$n = 4K$	$n = 64K$	$n = 1M$
$O(n^2)$	1.000E+00	2.560E+02	6.554E+04	1.678E+07	4.295E+09	1.100E+12
$O(2^n)$	2.000E+00	6.554E+04	1.158E+77	—	—	—
$O(n!)$	1.000E+00	2.092E+13	—	—	—	—

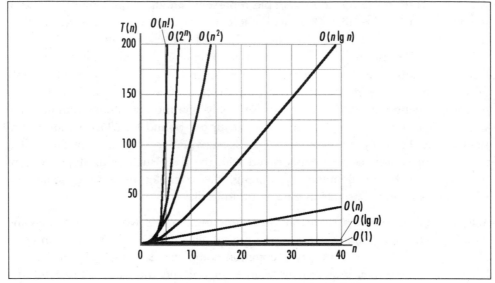

Figure 4-1. A graphical depiction of the growth rates in Tables 4-1 and 4-2

Just as the complexity of an algorithm says little about its actual running time, it is important to understand that no measure of complexity is necessarily efficient or inefficient. Although complexity is an indication of the efficiency of an algorithm, whether a particular complexity is considered efficient or inefficient depends on the problem. Generally, an efficient algorithm is one in which we know we are doing the best we can do given certain criteria. Typically, an algorithm is said to be efficient if there are no algorithms with lower complexities to solve the same problem and the algorithm does not contain excessive constants. Some problems are intractable, so there are no "efficient" solutions without settling for an approximation. This is true of a special class of problems called *NP-complete problems* (see the related topics at the end of the chapter).

Although an algorithm's complexity is an important starting point for determining how well it will perform, often there are other things to consider in practice. For example, when two algorithms are of the same complexity, it may be worthwhile to consider their less significant terms and factors. If the data on which the algorithms' performances depend is small enough, even an algorithm of greater complexity with small constants may perform better in practice than one that has a lower order of complexity and larger constants. Other factors worth considering are how complicated an algorithm will be to develop and maintain, and how we can make the actual implementation of an algorithm more efficient. An efficient implementation does not always affect an algorithm's complexity, but it can reduce constant factors, which makes the algorithm run faster in practice.

Analysis Example: Insertion Sort

This section presents an analysis of the worst-case running time of insertion sort, a simple sorting algorithm that works by inserting elements into a sorted set by scanning the set to determine where each new element belongs. A complete description of insertion sort appears in Chapter 12. The code for the sort is shown in Example 4-1.

We begin by identifying which lines of code are affected by the size of the data to be sorted. These are the statements that constitute the nested loop, whose outer part iterates from 1 to *size* – 1 and whose inner part iterates from $j - 1$ to wherever the correct position for the element being inserted is found. All other lines run in a constant amount of time, independent of the number of elements to be sorted. Typically, the generic variable n is used to refer to the parameter on which an algorithm's performance depends. With this in mind, the outer loop has a running time of $T(n) = n - 1$, times some constant amount of time. Examining the inner loop and considering the worst case, we assume that we will have to go all the way to the other end of the array before inserting each element into the sorted set. Therefore, the inner loop iterates once for the first element, twice for the second, and so forth until the outer loop terminates. Effectively, this becomes a summation from 1 to $n - 1$, which results in a running time of $T(n) = (n(n + 1)/2) - n$, times some constant amount of time. (This equation is from the well-known formula for summing a series from 1 to n.) Consequently:

$$O(T(n)) = O\left(\frac{n^2}{2} + \frac{n}{2} - n\right) = O\left(\frac{n^2}{2}\right) = O(n^2)$$

Example 4-1. Implementation of Insertion Sort from Chapter 12

```
/*****************************************************************************
*                                                                           *
*  ------------------------------- issort.c -------------------------------  *
*                                                                           *
*****************************************************************************/

#include <stdlib.h>
#include <string.h>

#include "sort.h"
```

Example 4-1. Implementation of Insertion Sort from Chapter 12 (continued)

```c
/*****************************************************************************
*                                                                          *
*  ------------------------------- issort --------------------------------  *
*                                                                          *
*****************************************************************************/

int issort(void *data, int size, int esize, int (*compare)(const void *key1,
   const void *key2)) {

char              *a = data;

void              *key;

int               i,
                  j;

/*****************************************************************************
*                                                                          *
*  Allocate storage for the key element.                                   *
*                                                                          *
*****************************************************************************/

if ((key = (char *)malloc(esize)) == NULL)
   return -1;

/*****************************************************************************
*                                                                          *
*  Repeatedly insert a key element among the sorted elements.              *
*                                                                          *
*****************************************************************************/

for (j = 1; j < size; j++) {

   memcpy(key, &a[j * esize], esize);
   i = j - 1;

   /*************************************************************************
   *                                                                      *
   *  Determine the position at which to insert the key element.          *
   *                                                                      *
   *************************************************************************/

   while (i >= 0 && compare(&a[i * esize], key) > 0) {

      memcpy(&a[(i + 1) * esize], &a[i * esize], esize);
      i--;

   }

   memcpy(&a[(i + 1) * esize], key, esize);

}
```

Example 4-1. Implementation of Insertion Sort from Chapter 12 (continued)

```
/*****************************************************************************
*                                                                           *
*   Free the storage allocated for sorting.                                 *
*                                                                           *
*****************************************************************************/

free(key);

return 0;

}
```

Questions and Answers

Q: *From lowest to highest, what is the correct order of the complexities $O(n^2)$, $O(3^n)$, $O(2^n)$, $O(n^2 \lg n)$, $O(1)$, $O(n \lg n)$, $O(n^3)$, $O(n!)$, $O(\lg n)$, $O(n)$?*

A: From lowest to highest, the correct order of these complexities is $O(1)$, $O(\lg n)$, $O(n)$, $O(n \lg n)$, $O(n^2)$, $O(n^2 \lg n)$, $O(n^3)$, $O(2^n)$, $O(3^n)$, $O(n!)$.

Q: *What are the complexities of $T_1(n) = 3n \lg n + \lg n$; $T_2(n) = 2^n + n^3 + 25$; and $T_3(n, k) = k + n$, where $k \le n$? From lowest to highest, what is the correct order of the resulting complexities?*

A: Using the rules of O-notation, the complexities of T_1, T_2, and T_3 respectively are $O(n \lg n)$, $O(2^n)$, and $O(n)$. From lowest to highest, the correct order of these complexities is $O(n)$, $O(n \lg n)$, and $O(2^n)$.

Q: *Suppose we have written a procedure to add m square matrices of size $n \times n$. If adding two square matrices requires $O(n^2)$ running time, what is the complexity of this procedure in terms of m and n?*

A: To add m matrices of size $n \times n$, we must perform $m - 1$ additions, each requiring time $O(n^2)$. Therefore, the overall running time of this procedure is:

$$O(m-1)O(n^2) = O(m)O(n^2) = O(mn^2)$$

Q: *Suppose we have two algorithms to solve the same problem. One runs in time $T_1(n) = 400n$, whereas the other runs in time $T_2(n) = n^2$. What are the complexities of these two algorithms? For what values of n might we consider using the algorithm with the higher complexity?*

A: The complexity of T_1 is $O(n)$, and the complexity of T_2 is $O(n^2)$. However, the algorithm described by T_1 involves such a large constant coefficient for n that when $n < 400$, the algorithm described by T_2 would be preferable. This is a good example of why we sometimes consider other factors besides the complexity of an algorithm alone.

Q: How do we account for calls such as memcpy *and* malloc *in analyzing real code? Although these calls often depend on the size of the data processed by an algorithm, they are really more of an implementation detail than part of an algorithm itself.*

A: Usually calls such as *memcpy* and *malloc* are regarded as executing in a constant amount of time. Generally, they can be expected to execute very efficiently at the machine level regardless of how much data they are copying or allocating. Of course, their exact efficiency may depend on the computer on which they execute as well as other factors (particularly in the case of *malloc*, which depends on the state of the system at the moment it is called).

Related Topics

Recurrences

Functions frequently used in the formal analysis of recursive algorithms. Recurrences are represented as recursive functions. A recursive function is a function that calls itself (see Chapter 3). Each successive call works on a more refined set of inputs, bringing us closer and closer to a solution. They are useful in describing the performance of recursive algorithms because they allow us to describe an algorithm's performance in terms of invoking the algorithm on a more and more refined set of inputs.

Summation formulas

Mathematical formulas useful in simplifying summations that describe the running times of algorithms. Summations occur frequently as the result of analyzing iterative control structures.

Θ-notation, Ω-notation, o-notation, and w-notation

Additional notations used to represent information about an algorithm's performance. Whereas *O*-notation expresses the upper bound of a function within a constant factor, Θ-notation expresses a bound from above and below. Ω-notation expresses strictly a lower bound within a constant factor. *o*-notation and *w*-notation are analogous to *O*-notation and Ω-notation but are more precise. *O*-notation often is used informally where other notations would be more specific.

NP-complete problems

A class of problems for which no polynomial-time algorithms are known, but for which no proof exists refuting the possibility either. Thus, NP-completeness has long been one of the most perplexing vexations in computer science. A polynomial-time algorithm is one whose complexity is less than or equal to $O(n^k)$, where k is some constant. Many useful and deceptively difficult problems fall into this class, such as the *traveling-salesman problem* (see Chapter 16, *Graph Algorithms*).

II

Data Structures

This part of the book contains seven chapters on data structures. Chapter 5, *Linked Lists*, presents various forms of linked lists, including singly-linked lists, doubly-linked lists, and circular lists. Chapter 6, *Stacks and Queues*, presents stacks and queues, data structures for sorting and returning data on a last-in, first-out and first-in, last-out order respectively. Chapter 7, *Sets*, presents sets and the fundamental mathematics describing sets. Chapter 8, *Hash Tables*, presents chained and open-addressed hash tables, including material on how to select a good hash function and how to resolve collisions. Chapter 9, *Trees*, presents binary and AVL trees. It also discusses various methods of tree traversal. Chapter 10, *Heaps and Priority Queues*, presents heaps and priority queues, data structures that help to quickly determine the largest or smallest element in a set of data. Chapter 11, *Graphs*, presents graphs and two fundamental algorithms from which many graph algorithms are derived: breadth-first and depth-first searches.

5

Linked Lists

Linked lists are some of the most fundamental data structures. Linked lists consist of a number of elements grouped, or *linked*, together in a specific order. They are useful in maintaining collections of data, similar to the way that arrays are often used. However, linked lists offer important advantages over arrays in many cases. Specifically, linked lists are considerably more efficient in performing insertions and deletions. Linked lists also make use of dynamically allocated storage, which is storage allocated at runtime. Since in many applications the size of the data is not known at compile time, this can be a nice attribute as well.

This chapter covers:

Singly-linked lists
> The simplest linked lists, in which elements are linked by a single pointer. This structure allows the list to be traversed from its first element to its last.

Doubly-linked lists
> Linked lists in which elements are linked by two pointers instead of one. This structure allows the list to be traversed both forward and backward.

Circular lists
> Linked lists in which the last element is linked to the first instead of being set to NULL. This structure allows the list to be traversed in a circular fashion.

Some applications of linked lists are:

Mailing lists
> Lists such as the ones found in email applications. Since it is difficult to predict how long a mailing list may be, a mailer might build a linked list of addresses before sending a message.

Scrolled lists

Components found in graphical user interfaces. Often data associated with items in scrolled lists is not displayed. One approach to managing this "hidden" data is to maintain a linked list wherein each element stores the data for one item in the scrolled list.

Polynomials

An important part of mathematics not inherently supported as a datatype by most languages. If we let each element of a linked list store one term, linked lists are useful in representing polynomials (such as $3x^2 + 2x + 1$).

Memory management (illustrated in this chapter)

An important role of operating systems. An operating system must decide how to allocate and reclaim storage for processes running on the system. A linked list can be used to keep track of portions of memory that are available for allocation.

LISP

An important programming language in artificial intelligence. LISP, an acronym for LISt Processor, makes extensive use of linked lists in performing symbolic processing.

Linked allocation of files

A type of file allocation that eliminates external fragmentation on a disk but is good only for sequential access. Each block of a file contains a pointer to the file's next block.

Other data structures

Some data structures whose implementations depend on linked lists are stacks, queues, sets, hash tables, and graphs, all of which are presented in this book.

Description of Linked Lists

Singly-linked list*s* , usually simply called *linked lists*, are composed of individual elements, each linked by a single pointer. Each element consists of two parts: a data member and a pointer, called the *next* pointer. Using this two-member structure, a linked list is formed by setting the *next* pointer of each element to point to the element that follows it (see Figure 5-1). The *next* pointer of the last element is set to NULL, a convenient sentinel marking the end of the list. The element at the start of the list is its *head*; the element at the end of the list is its *tail*.

To access an element in a linked list, we start at the head of the list and use the *next* pointers of successive elements to move from element to element until the desired element is reached. With singly-linked lists, the list can be traversed in only one direction—from head to tail—because each element contains no link to its predecessor. Therefore, if we start at the head and move to some element, and then wish to access an element preceding it, we must start over at the head (although sometimes we can anticipate the need to know an element and save a pointer to it). Often this weakness is not a concern. When it is, we use a doubly-linked list or circular list.

Conceptually, one thinks of a linked list as a series of contiguous elements. However, because these elements are allocated dynamically (using *malloc* in C), it is important to remember that, in actuality, they are usually scattered about in memory (see Figure 5-2). The pointers from element to element therefore are the only means by which we can ensure that all elements remain accessible. With this in mind, we will see later that special care is required when it comes to maintaining the links. If we mistakenly drop one link, it becomes impossible to access any of the elements from that point on in the list. Thus, the expression "You are only as strong as your weakest link" is particularly fitting for linked lists.

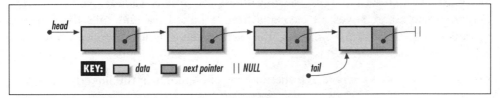

Figure 5-1. Elements linked together to form a linked list

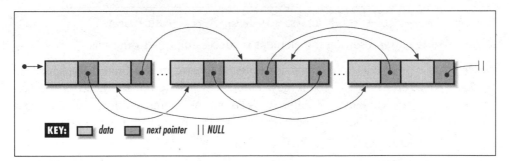

Figure 5-2. Elements of a linked list linked but scattered about an address space

Interface for Linked Lists

list_init

```
void list_init(List *list, void (*destroy)(void *data));
```

Return Value   None.

Description   Initializes the linked list specified by *list*. This operation must be called for a linked list before the list can be used with any other operation. The *destroy* argument provides a way to free dynamically allocated data when *list_destroy* is called. For example, if the list contains data dynamically allocated using *malloc*, `destroy` should be set to *free* to free the data as the linked list is destroyed. For structured data containing several dynamically allocated members, `destroy` should be set to a user-defined function that calls *free* for each dynamically allocated member as well as for the structure itself. For a linked list containing data that should not be freed, `destroy` should be set to NULL.

Complexity $O(1)$

list_destroy

```
void list_destroy(List *list);
```

Return Value   None.

Description   Destroys the linked list specified by `list`. No other operations are permitted after calling *list_destroy* unless *list_init* is called again. The *list_destroy* operation removes all elements from a linked list and calls the function passed as `destroy` to *list_init* once for each element as it is removed, provided `destroy` was not set to NULL.

Complexity $O(n)$, where n is the number of elements in the linked list.

list_ins_next

```
int list_ins_next(List *list, ListElmt *element, const void *data);
```

Return Value   0 if inserting the element is successful, or –1 otherwise.

Description   Inserts an element just after `element` in the linked list specified by `list`. If `element` is NULL, the new element is inserted at the head of the list. The new element contains a pointer to `data`, so the memory referenced by `data` should remain valid as long as the element remains in the list. It is the responsibility of the caller to manage the storage associated with `data`.

Complexity $O(1)$

list_rem_next

```
int list_rem_next(List *list, ListElmt *element, void **data);
```

Return Value   0 if removing the element is successful, or –1 otherwise.

Description   Removes the element just after `element` from the linked list specified by `list`. If `element` is NULL, the element at the head of the list is removed. Upon return, `data` points to the data stored in the element that was removed. It is the responsibility of the caller to manage the storage associated with the data.

Complexity $O(1)$

list_size

```
int list_size(const List *list);
```

Return Value   Number of elements in the list.

Description   Macro that evaluates to the number of elements in the linked list specified by *list*.

Complexity $O(1)$

list_head

```
ListElmt *list_head(const List *list);
```

Return Value   Element at the head of the list.

Description   Macro that evaluates to the element at the head of the linked list specified by *list*.

Complexity $O(1)$

list_tail

```
ListElmt *list_tail(const List *list);
```

Return Value   Element at the tail of the list.

Description   Macro that evaluates to the element at the tail of the linked list specified by *list*.

Complexity $O(1)$

list_is_head

```
int list_is_head(const ListElmt *element);
```

Return Value   1 if the element is at the head of the list, or 0 otherwise.

Description   Macro that determines whether the element specified as *element* is at the head of a linked list.

Complexity $O(1)$

list_is_tail

```
int list_is_tail(const ListElmt *element);
```

Return Value   1 if the element is at the tail of the list, or 0 otherwise.

Description   Macro that determines whether the element specified as `element`
is at the tail of a linked list.

Complexity $O(1)$

list_data

```
void *list_data(const ListElmt *element);
```

Return Value   Data stored in the element.

Description   Macro that evaluates to the data stored in the element of a linked
list specified by `element`.

Complexity $O(1)$

list_next

```
ListElmt *list_next(const ListElmt *element);
```

Return Value   Element following the specified element.

Description   Macro that evaluates to the element of a linked list following the
element specified by `element`.

Complexity $O(1)$

Implementation and Analysis of Linked Lists

Recall that each element of a linked list consists of two parts: a data member and a
pointer to the next element in the list. The structure `ListElmt` represents an individual element of a linked list (see Example 5-1). As you would expect, this structure has two members that correspond to those just mentioned. The structure `List`
is the linked list data structure (see Example 5-1). This structure consists of five
members: `size` is the number of elements in the list, `match` is a member not used
by linked lists but by datatypes that will be derived later from linked lists,
`destroy` is the encapsulated destroy function passed to *list_init*, `head` is a pointer
to the first of the linked elements, and `tail` is a pointer to the tail element.

Example 5-1. Header for the Linked List Abstract Datatype

```
/*****************************************************************************
*                                                                           *
*  ------------------------------- list.h -------------------------------   *
*                                                                           *
*****************************************************************************/
```

Example 5-1. Header for the Linked List Abstract Datatype (continued)

```c
#ifndef LIST_H
#define LIST_H

#include <stdlib.h>

/*****************************************************************************
*                                                                          *
*  Define a structure for linked list elements.                            *
*                                                                          *
*****************************************************************************/

typedef struct ListElmt_ {

void             *data;
struct ListElmt_  *next;

} ListElmt;

/*****************************************************************************
*                                                                          *
*  Define a structure for linked lists.                                    *
*                                                                          *
*****************************************************************************/

typedef struct List_ {

int              size;

int              (*match)(const void *key1, const void *key2);
void             (*destroy)(void *data);

ListElmt         *head;
ListElmt         *tail;

} List;

/*****************************************************************************
*                                                                          *
*  --------------------------- Public Interface ---------------------------  *
*                                                                          *
*****************************************************************************/

void list_init(List *list, void (*destroy)(void *data));

void list_destroy(List *list);

int list_ins_next(List *list, ListElmt *element, const void *data);

int list_rem_next(List *list, ListElmt *element, void **data);

#define list_size(list) ((list)->size)
```

Example 5-1. Header for the Linked List Abstract Datatype (continued)

```
#define list_head(list) ((list)->head)

#define list_tail(list) ((list)->tail)

#define list_is_head(list, element) ((element) == (list)->head ? 1 : 0)

#define list_is_tail(element) ((element)->next == NULL ? 1 : 0)

#define list_data(element) ((element)->data)

#define list_next(element) ((element)->next)

#endif
```

list_init

The *list_init* operation initializes a linked list so that it can be used in other operations (see Example 5-2). Initializing a linked list is a simple operation in which the `size` member of the list is set to 0, the `destroy` member to `destroy`, and the `head` and `tail` pointers to NULL.

The runtime complexity of *list_init* is $O(1)$ because all of the steps in initializing a linked list run in a constant amount of time.

list_destroy

The *list_destroy* operation destroys a linked list (see Example 5-2). Primarily this means removing all elements from the list. The function passed as `destroy` to *list_init* is called once for each element as it is removed, provided `destroy` was not set to NULL.

The runtime complexity of *list_destroy* is $O(n)$, where n is the number of elements in the list. This is because the $O(1)$ operation *list_rem_next* must be called once for each element.

list_ins_next

The *list_ins_next* operation inserts an element into a linked list just after a specified element (see Example 5-2). The call sets the new element to point to the data passed by the caller. The actual process of inserting the new element into the list is a simple one, but it does require some care. There are two cases to consider: insertion at the head of the list and insertion elsewhere.

Generally, to insert an element into a linked list, we set the `next` pointer of the new element to point to the element it is going to precede, and we set the `next` pointer of the element that will precede the new element to point to the new element (see Figure 5-3). However, when inserting at the head of a list, there is no element that will precede the new element. Thus, in this case, we set the *next* pointer of the new element to the current head of the list, then reset the head of the list to point to the new element. Recall from the interface design in the previous section that passing NULL for *element* indicates that the new element should be inserted at the head. In addition to these tasks, whenever we insert an element at the tail of the list, we must update the *tail* member of the list data structure to point to the new tail. Last, we update the size of the list by incrementing its *size* member.

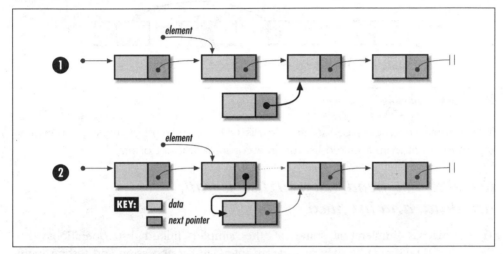

Figure 5-3. Inserting an element into a linked list

The runtime complexity of *list_ins_next* is O(1) because all of the steps in inserting an element into a linked list run in a constant amount of time.

list_rem_next

The *list_rem_next* operation removes from a linked list the element just after a specified element (see Example 5-2). The reasons for removing the element just after, as opposed to the element itself, are discussed in the questions and answers at the end of the chapter. As with inserting an element, this call requires consideration of two cases: removing an element from the head of the list and removing one elsewhere.

The actual process of removing the element from the list is a simple one, but it too requires some care (see Figure 5-4). Generally, to remove an element from a linked list, we set the *next* pointer of the element preceding the one being removed to point to the element after the element being removed. However, when removing an element from the head of a list, there is no element that precedes the element being removed. Thus, in this case, we set the head of the list to point to the element after the one being removed. As with insertion, NULL serves nicely as a sentinel passed in *element* to indicate that the element at the head of the list should be removed. In addition to these tasks, whenever we remove the element at the tail of the list, we must update the *tail* member of the list data structure to point to the new tail, or to NULL if removing the element has caused the list to become empty. Last, we update the size of the list by decreasing the *size* member by 1. Upon return, *data* points to the data from the element removed.

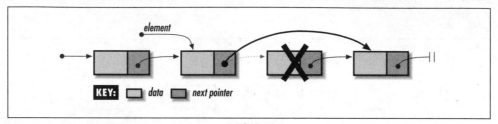

Figure 5-4. Removing an element from a linked list

The runtime complexity of *list_rem_next* is *O*(1) because all of the steps in removing an element from a linked list run in a constant amount of time.

list_size, list_head, list_tail, list_is_tail, list_data, and list_next

These macros implement some of the simpler linked list operations (see Example 5-1). Generally, they provide an interface for accessing and testing members of the *List* and *ListElmt* structures.

The runtime complexity of these operations is *O*(1) because accessing and testing members of a structure are simple tasks that run in a constant amount of time.

Example 5-2. Implementation of the Linked List Abstract Datatype

```
/*****************************************************************************
*                                                                           *
*  ------------------------------- list.c -------------------------------   *
*                                                                           *
*****************************************************************************/

#include <stdlib.h>
#include <string.h>

#include "list.h"

/*****************************************************************************
*                                                                           *
*  ------------------------------- list_init ----------------------------   *
*                                                                           *
*****************************************************************************/

void list_init(List *list, void (*destroy)(void *data)) {
```

Example 5-2. Implementation of the Linked List Abstract Datatype (continued)

```c
/***************************************************************************
*                                                                         *
*  Initialize the list.                                                   *
*                                                                         *
***************************************************************************/

list->size = 0;
list->destroy = destroy;
list->head = NULL;
list->tail = NULL;

return;

}

/***************************************************************************
*                                                                         *
*  --------------------------- list_destroy ---------------------------   *
*                                                                         *
***************************************************************************/

void list_destroy(List *list) {

void            *data;

/***************************************************************************
*                                                                         *
*  Remove each element.                                                   *
*                                                                         *
***************************************************************************/

while (list_size(list) > 0) {

   if (list_rem_next(list, NULL, (void **)&data) == 0 && list->destroy !=
      NULL) {

      /***************************************************************************
      *                                                                         *
      *  Call a user-defined function to free dynamically allocated data.       *
      *                                                                         *
      ***************************************************************************/

      list->destroy(data);

   }

}

/***************************************************************************
*                                                                         *
*  No operations are allowed now, but clear the structure as a precaution. *
*                                                                         *
***************************************************************************/
```

Example 5-2. Implementation of the Linked List Abstract Datatype (continued)

```
memset(list, 0, sizeof(List));

return;

}

/***************************************************************************
*                                                                         *
*  --------------------------- list_ins_next ---------------------------  *
*                                                                         *
***************************************************************************/

int list_ins_next(List *list, ListElmt *element, const void *data) {

ListElmt          *new_element;

/***************************************************************************
*                                                                         *
*  Allocate storage for the element.                                      *
*                                                                         *
***************************************************************************/

if ((new_element = (ListElmt *)malloc(sizeof(ListElmt))) == NULL)
   return -1;

/***************************************************************************
*                                                                         *
*  Insert the element into the list.                                      *
*                                                                         *
***************************************************************************/

new_element->data = (void *)data;

if (element == NULL) {

   /***************************************************************************
   *                                                                         *
   *  Handle insertion at the head of the list.                              *
   *                                                                         *
   ***************************************************************************/

   if (list_size(list) == 0)
      list->tail = new_element;

   new_element->next = list->head;
   list->head = new_element;

   }

else {
```

Example 5-2. Implementation of the Linked List Abstract Datatype (continued)

```
/***************************************************************************
*                                                                         *
*  Handle insertion somewhere other than at the head.                     *
*                                                                         *
***************************************************************************/

if (element->next == NULL)
   list->tail = new_element;

new_element->next = element->next;
element->next = new_element;

}

/***************************************************************************
*                                                                         *
*  Adjust the size of the list to account for the inserted element.       *
*                                                                         *
***************************************************************************/

list->size++;

return 0;

}

/***************************************************************************
*                                                                         *
*  --------------------------- list_rem_next ---------------------------  *
*                                                                         *
***************************************************************************/

int list_rem_next(List *list, ListElmt *element, void **data) {

ListElmt          *old_element;

/***************************************************************************
*                                                                         *
*  Do not allow removal from an empty list.                               *
*                                                                         *
***************************************************************************/

if (list_size(list) == 0)
   return -1;

/***************************************************************************
*                                                                         *
*  Remove the element from the list.                                      *
*                                                                         *
***************************************************************************/

if (element == NULL) {
```

Example 5-2. Implementation of the Linked List Abstract Datatype (continued)

```c
/****************************************************************************
*                                                                          *
*  Handle removal from the head of the list.                               *
*                                                                          *
****************************************************************************/

*data = list->head->data;
old_element = list->head;
list->head = list->head->next;

if (list_size(list) == 0)
   list->tail = NULL;

}

else {

/****************************************************************************
*                                                                          *
*  Handle removal from somewhere other than the head.                      *
*                                                                          *
****************************************************************************/

if (element->next == NULL)
   return -1;

*data = element->next->data;
old_element = element->next;
element->next = element->next->next;

if (element->next == NULL)
   list->tail = element;

}

/****************************************************************************
*                                                                          *
*  Free the storage allocated by the abstract datatype.                    *
*                                                                          *
****************************************************************************/

free(old_element);

/****************************************************************************
*                                                                          *
*  Adjust the size of the list to account for the removed element.         *
*                                                                          *
****************************************************************************/

list->size--;

return 0;

}
```

Linked List Example: Frame Management

An interesting application of linked lists is found in the way some systems support *virtual memory*. Virtual memory is a mapping of address space that allows a process (a running program) to execute without being completely in *physical memory*, the real memory of the system. One advantage of this is that a process can make use of an address space that is much larger than that which the physical memory of the system would allow otherwise. Another advantage is that multiple processes can share the memory of the system while running concurrently.

A process running in virtual memory deals with *virtual addresses*. These are addresses that seem like physical addresses to the process, but that the system must translate before using. Address translation takes place using a *page table* and is fast due to dedicated hardware. Each process has its own page table that maps *pages* of its virtual address space to *frames* in physical memory. When a process references a particular virtual address, the appropriate entry in its page table is inspected to determine in which physical frame the page resides (see Figure 5-5). When a process references a virtual address not yet in a frame, a *page fault* occurs and a frame is allocated in physical memory. Why pages of a process are removed from physical memory is another matter. One occasion for removing a page, however, is when a page is accessed infrequently relative to other pages and its frame is needed elsewhere.

This example addresses the management of frames that has just been described. For this, two functions are presented, *alloc_frame* and *free_frame* (see Example 5-3). The *alloc_frame* and *free_frame* functions employ a linked list to maintain the frames that are available to be allocated. The *alloc_frame* function retrieves the number of a free frame from a list of available frames. Given a specific page, this number is placed in the page table to indicate in which physical frame the page is to reside. The *free_frame* function accepts a frame number and places it back into the list of available frames once a page has been removed from physical memory. Both functions assume that before either is called, the operating system has inserted into the list all frames that it wishes to make available. The example for circular lists later in this chapter addresses what happens when *alloc_frame* is called and the list is empty.

A linked list is a good way to manage frames because frame allocation involves frequent insertions and deletions, and these operations are performed at the head of the list. The runtime complexity of both *alloc_frame* and *free_frame* is $O(1)$ because the two functions simply call *list_rem_next* and *list_ins_next* respectively, which are both $O(1)$ operations.

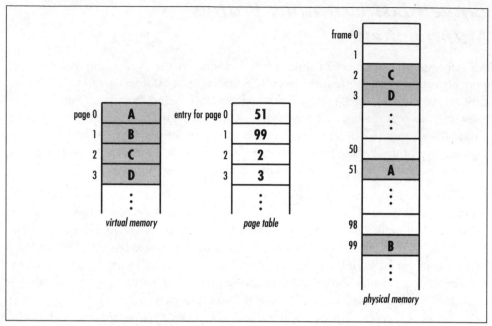

Figure 5-5. A virtual memory system

Example 5-3. Implementation of Functions for Managing Frames

```
/*****************************************************************************
*                                                                           *
*  ----------------------------- frames.c --------------------------------  *
*                                                                           *
*****************************************************************************/

#include <stdlib.h>

#include "frames.h"
#include "list.h"

/*****************************************************************************
*                                                                           *
*  ----------------------------- alloc_frame -----------------------------  *
*                                                                           *
*****************************************************************************/

int alloc_frame(List *frames) {

int                 frame_number,
                    *data;

if (list_size(frames) == 0)
```

Example 5-3. Implementation of Functions for Managing Frames (continued)

```
/*************************************************************************
*                                                                       *
*  Return that there are no frames available.                           *
*                                                                       *
*************************************************************************/

return -1;

else {

   if (list_rem_next(frames, NULL, (void **)&data) != 0)

      /*************************************************************************
      *                                                                       *
      *  Return that a frame could not be retrieved.                          *
      *                                                                       *
      *************************************************************************/

      return -1;

   else {

      /*************************************************************************
      *                                                                       *
      *  Store the number of the available frame.                             *
      *                                                                       *
      *************************************************************************/

      frame_number = *data;
      free(data);

   }

}

return frame_number;

}

/*************************************************************************
*                                                                       *
*  ----------------------------- free_frame -----------------------------  *
*                                                                       *
*************************************************************************/

int free_frame(List *frames, int frame_number) {

int               *data;

/*************************************************************************
*                                                                       *
*  Allocate storage for the frame number.                               *
*                                                                       *
*************************************************************************/
```

Example 5-3. Implementation of Functions for Managing Frames (continued)

```
if ((data = (int *)malloc(sizeof(int))) == NULL)
   return -1;

/**************************************************************************
*                                                                        *
*  Put the frame back in the list of available frames.                   *
*                                                                        *
**************************************************************************/

*data = frame_number;

if (list_ins_next(frames, NULL, data) != 0)
   return -1;

return 0;

}
```

Description of Doubly-Linked Lists

Doubly-linked lists, as their name implies, are composed of elements linked by two pointers. Each element of a doubly-linked list consists of three parts: in addition to the data and the *next* pointer, each element includes a pointer to the previous element, called the *prev* pointer. A doubly-linked list is formed by composing a number of elements so that the *next* pointer of each element points to the element that follows it, and the *prev* pointer points to the element preceding it. To mark the head and tail of the list, we set the *prev* pointer of the first element and the *next* pointer of the last element to NULL.

To traverse backward through a doubly-linked list, we use the *prev* pointers of consecutive elements in the tail-to-head direction. Thus, for the cost of an additional pointer for each element, a doubly-linked list offers greater flexibility than a singly-linked list in moving about the list. This can be useful when we know something about where an element might be stored in the list and can choose wisely how to move to it. For example, one flexibility that doubly-linked lists provide is a more intuitive means of removing an element than singly-linked lists.

Interface for Doubly-Linked Lists

dlist_init

```
void dlist_init(DList *list, void (*destroy)(void *data));
```
Return Value   None.

Description   Initializes the doubly-linked list specified by `list`. This operation must be called for a doubly-linked list before the list can be used with any other operation. The `destroy` argument provides a way to free dynamically allocated data when *dlist_destroy* is called. It works in a manner similar to that described for *list_destroy*. For a doubly-linked list containing data that should not be freed, `destroy` should be set to NULL.

Complexity $O(1)$

dlist_destroy

```
void dlist_destroy(DList *list);
```

Return Value   None.

Description   Destroys the doubly-linked list specified by `list`. No other operations are permitted after calling *dlist_destroy* unless *dlist_init* is called again. The *dlist_destroy* operation removes all elements from a doubly-linked list and calls the function passed as `destroy` to *dlist_init* once for each element as it is removed, provided `destroy` was not set to NULL.

Complexity $O(n)$, where n is the number of elements in the doubly-linked list.

dlist_ins_next

```
int dlist_ins_next(DList *list, DListElmt *element, const void *data);
```

Return Value   0 if inserting the element is successful, or −1 otherwise.

Description   Inserts an element just after `element` in the doubly-linked list specified by `list`. When inserting into an empty list, `element` may point anywhere, but should be NULL to avoid confusion. The new element contains a pointer to `data`, so the memory referenced by `data` should remain valid as long as the element remains in the list. It is the responsibility of the caller to manage the storage associated with `data`.

Complexity $O(1)$

dlist_ins_prev

```
int dlist_ins_prev(DList *list, DListElmt *element, const void *data);
```

Return Value   0 if inserting the element is successful, or −1 otherwise.

Description   Inserts an element just before `element` in the doubly-linked list specified by `list`. When inserting into an empty list, `element` may point anywhere, but should be NULL to avoid confusion. The new element contains a pointer to `data`, so the memory referenced by `data` should remain valid as long as the element remains in the list. It is the responsibility of the caller to manage the storage associated with *data*.

Complexity   O(1)

dlist_remove

```
int dlist_remove(DList *list, DListElmt *element, void **data);
```

Return Value   0 if removing the element is successful, or −1 otherwise.

Description   Removes the element specified as *element* from the doubly-linked list specified by *list*. Upon return, *data* points to the data stored in the element that was removed. It is the responsibility of the caller to manage the storage associated with the data.

Complexity   O(1)

dlist_size

```
int dlist_size(const DList *list);
```

Return Value   Number of elements in the list.

Description   Macro that evaluates to the number of elements in the doubly-linked list specified by *list*.

Complexity   O(1)

dlist_head

```
DListElmt *dlist_head(const DList *list);
```

Return Value   Element at the head of the list.

Description   Macro that evaluates to the element at the head of the doubly-linked list specified by *list*.

Complexity   O(1)

dlist_tail

```
DListElmt *dlist_tail(const DList *list);
```

Return Value   Element at the tail of the list.

Description   Macro that evaluates to the element at the tail of the doubly-linked list specified by *list*.

Complexity   O(1)

dlist_is_head

```
int dlist_is_head(const DListElmt *element);
```

Return Value   1 if the element is at the head of the list, or 0 otherwise.

Description   Macro that determines whether the element specified as `element` is at the head of a doubly-linked list.

Complexity $O(1)$

dlist_is_tail

```
int dlist_is_tail(const DListElmt *element);
```

Return Value   1 if the element is at the tail of the list, or 0 otherwise.

Description   Macro that determines whether the element specified as `element` is at the tail of a doubly-linked list.

Complexity $O(1)$

dlist_data

```
void *dlist_data(const DListElmt *element);
```

Return Value   Data stored in the element.

Description   Macro that evaluates to the data stored in the element of a doubly-linked list specified by `element`.

Complexity $O(1)$

dlist_next

```
DListElmt *dlist_next(const DListElmt *element);
```

Return Value   Element following the specified element.

Description   Macro that evaluates to the element of a doubly-linked list following the element specified by `element`.

Complexity $O(1)$

dlist_prev

```
DListElmt *dlist_prev(const DListElmt *element);
```

Return Value   Element preceding the specified element.

Description   Macro that evaluates to the element of a doubly-linked list preceding the element specified by `element`.

Complexity $O(1)$

Implementation and Analysis of Doubly Linked Lists

Recall that each element of a doubly-linked list consists of three parts: a data member, a pointer to the next element, and a pointer to the previous element. The structure *DListElmt* represents an individual element of a doubly-linked list (see Example 5-4). As you would expect, this structure has three members corresponding to those just mentioned. The structure *DList* is the doubly-linked list data structure (see Example 5-4). This structure has members analogous to the ones used for singly-linked lists.

Example 5-4. Header for the Doubly-Linked List Abstract Datatype

```
/*****************************************************************************
*                                                                           *
*  ---------------------------- dlist.h ----------------------------        *
*                                                                           *
*****************************************************************************/

#ifndef DLIST_H
#define DLIST_H

#include <stdlib.h>

/*****************************************************************************
*                                                                           *
*  Define a structure for doubly-linked list elements.                      *
*                                                                           *
*****************************************************************************/

typedef struct DListElmt_ {

void               *data;
struct DListElmt_  *prev;
struct DListElmt_  *next;

} DListElmt;

/*****************************************************************************
*                                                                           *
*  Define a structure for doubly-linked lists.                              *
*                                                                           *
*****************************************************************************/

typedef struct DList_ {

int                size;

int                (*match)(const void *key1, const void *key2);
void               (*destroy)(void *data);
```

Example 5-4. Header for the Doubly-Linked List Abstract Datatype (continued)

```
DListElmt           *head;
DListElmt           *tail;

} DList;

/***************************************************************************
*                                                                         *
*  ------------------------- Public Interface -------------------------   *
*                                                                         *
***************************************************************************/

void dlist_init(DList *list, void (*destroy)(void *data));

void dlist_destroy(DList *list);

int dlist_ins_next(DList *list, DListElmt *element, const void *data);

int dlist_ins_prev(DList *list, DListElmt *element, const void *data);

int dlist_remove(DList *list, DListElmt *element, void **data);

#define dlist_size(list) ((list)->size)

#define dlist_head(list) ((list)->head)

#define dlist_tail(list) ((list)->tail)

#define dlist_is_head(element) ((element)->prev == NULL ? 1 : 0)

#define dlist_is_tail(element) ((element)->next == NULL ? 1 : 0)

#define dlist_data(element) ((element)->data)

#define dlist_next(element) ((element)->next)

#define dlist_prev(element) ((element)->prev)

#endif
```

dlist_init

The *dlist_init* operation initializes a doubly-linked list so that it can be used in other operations (see Example 5-5). Initialization is the same as with a singly-linked list.

The runtime complexity of *dlist_init* is $O(1)$ because all of the steps in initializing a doubly-linked list run in a constant amount of time.

dlist_destroy

The *dlist_destroy* operation destroys a doubly-linked list (see Example 5-5). Primarily this means removing all elements from the list. The function passed as *destroy* to *dlist_init* is called once for each element as it is removed, provided *destroy* was not set to NULL.

The runtime complexity of *dlist_destroy* is $O(n)$, where n is the number of elements in the list. This is because the $O(1)$ operation *dlist_remove* must be called once for each element.

dlist_ins_next

The *dlist_ins_next* operation inserts an element into a doubly-linked list just after a specified element (see Example 5-5). Inserting an element in a doubly-linked list is similar to inserting one in a singly-linked list. The primary difference is that in addition to managing the **next** pointers, we must manage the **prev** pointers to keep the list linked properly in the reverse direction (see Figure 5-6).

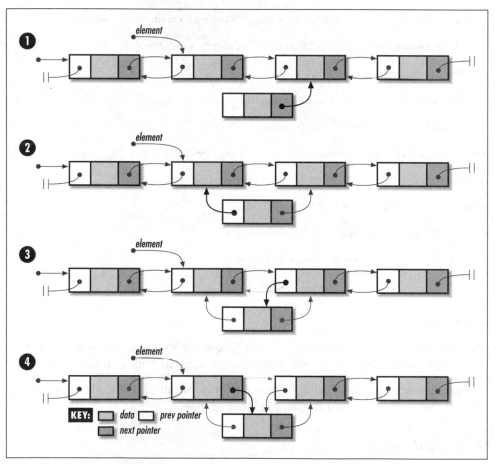

Figure 5-6. Inserting an element into a doubly-linked list with dlist_ins_next

The runtime complexity of *dlist_ins_next* is $O(1)$ because all of the steps in inserting an element into a doubly-linked list run in a constant amount of time.

dlist_ins_prev

The *dlist_ins_prev* operation inserts an element into a doubly-linked list just before a specified element (see Example 5-5). Inserting an element in a doubly-linked list is similar to inserting one in a singly-linked list. As with *dlist_ins_next*, the primary difference is that in addition to managing the next pointers, we must manage the prev pointers to keep the list linked properly in the reverse direction.

The runtime complexity of *dlist_ins_prev* is $O(1)$ because all of the steps in inserting an element into a doubly-linked list run in a constant amount of time.

dlist_remove

The *dlist_remove* operation removes a specified element from a doubly-linked list (see Example 5-5). The primary difference from a singly-linked list is that in addition to managing the next pointers, we must manage the prev pointers to keep the list linked properly in the reverse direction. Another difference is that in a doubly-linked list, it is possible to remove the specified element rather than the one just after it because there is a pointer back to the previous element.

The runtime complexity of *dlist_remove* is $O(1)$ because all of the steps in removing an element from a doubly-linked list run in a constant amount of time.

dlist_size, dlist_head, dlist_tail, dlist_is_head, dlist_is_tail, dlist_data, dlist_next, and dlist_prev

These macros implement some of the simpler doubly-linked list operations (see Example 5-4). Generally, they provide an interface for accessing and testing members of the *DList* and *DListElmt* structures.

The runtime complexity of these operations is $O(1)$ because accessing and testing members of a structure are simple tasks that run in a constant amount of time.

Example 5-5. Implementation of the Doubly-Linked List Abstract Datatype

```
/*****************************************************************************
*                                                                           *
*  ------------------------------- dlist.c -------------------------------   *
*                                                                           *
*****************************************************************************/

#include <stdlib.h>
#include <string.h>
```

Example 5-5. Implementation of the Doubly-Linked List Abstract Datatype (continued)

```c
#include "dlist.h"

/*****************************************************************************
*                                                                           *
*  --------------------------- dlist_init ---------------------------       *
*                                                                           *
*****************************************************************************/

void dlist_init(DList *list, void (*destroy)(void *data)) {

/*****************************************************************************
*                                                                           *
*  Initialize the list.                                                     *
*                                                                           *
*****************************************************************************/

list->size = 0;
list->destroy = destroy;
list->head = NULL;
list->tail = NULL;

return;

}

/*****************************************************************************
*                                                                           *
*  -------------------------- dlist_destroy --------------------------      *
*                                                                           *
*****************************************************************************/

void dlist_destroy(DList *list) {

void            *data;

/*****************************************************************************
*                                                                           *
*  Remove each element.                                                     *
*                                                                           *
*****************************************************************************/

while (dlist_size(list) > 0) {

   if (dlist_remove(list, dlist_tail(list), (void **)&data) == 0 && list->
      destroy != NULL) {

      /*****************************************************************
      *                                                               *
      *  Call a user-defined function to free dynamically allocated data. *
      *                                                               *
      *****************************************************************/

      list->destroy(data);
```

Example 5-5. Implementation of the Doubly-Linked List Abstract Datatype (continued)

```
    }

}

/*****************************************************************************
*                                                                           *
*  No operations are allowed now, but clear the structure as a precaution.  *
*                                                                           *
*****************************************************************************/

memset(list, 0, sizeof(DList));

return;

}

/*****************************************************************************
*                                                                           *
*  -------------------------- dlist_ins_next --------------------------     *
*                                                                           *
*****************************************************************************/

int dlist_ins_next(DList *list, DListElmt *element, const void *data) {

DListElmt          *new_element;

/*****************************************************************************
*                                                                           *
*  Do not allow a NULL element unless the list is empty.                    *
*                                                                           *
*****************************************************************************/

if (element == NULL && dlist_size(list) != 0)
   return -1;

/*****************************************************************************
*                                                                           *
*  Allocate storage for the element.                                        *
*                                                                           *
*****************************************************************************/

if ((new_element = (DListElmt *)malloc(sizeof(DListElmt))) == NULL)
   return -1;

/*****************************************************************************
*                                                                           *
*  Insert the new element into the list.                                    *
*                                                                           *
*****************************************************************************/

new_element->data = (void *)data;
```

Example 5-5. Implementation of the Doubly-Linked List Abstract Datatype (continued)

```
if (dlist_size(list) == 0) {

   /***************************************************************************
   *                                                                         *
   *  Handle insertion when the list is empty.                               *
   *                                                                         *
   ***************************************************************************/

   list->head = new_element;
   list->head->prev = NULL;
   list->head->next = NULL;
   list->tail = new_element;

   }

else {

   /***************************************************************************
   *                                                                         *
   *  Handle insertion when the list is not empty.                           *
   *                                                                         *
   ***************************************************************************/

   new_element->next = element->next;
   new_element->prev = element;

   if (element->next == NULL)
      list->tail = new_element;
   else
      element->next->prev = new_element;

   element->next = new_element;

}

/***************************************************************************
*                                                                         *
*  Adjust the size of the list to account for the inserted element.       *
*                                                                         *
***************************************************************************/

list->size++;

return 0;

}

/***************************************************************************
*                                                                         *
*  -------------------------- dlist_ins_prev -------------------------    *
*                                                                         *
***************************************************************************/

int dlist_ins_prev(DList *list, DListElmt *element, const void *data) {
```

Example 5-5. Implementation of the Doubly-Linked List Abstract Datatype (continued)

```
DListElmt          *new_element;

/***************************************************************************
*                                                                         *
*  Do not allow a NULL element unless the list is empty.                  *
*                                                                         *
***************************************************************************/

if (element == NULL && dlist_size(list) != 0)
   return -1;

/***************************************************************************
*                                                                         *
*  Allocate storage to be managed by the abstract datatype.               *
*                                                                         *
***************************************************************************/

if ((new_element = (DListElmt *)malloc(sizeof(DListElmt))) == NULL)
   return -1;

/***************************************************************************
*                                                                         *
*  Insert the new element into the list.                                  *
*                                                                         *
***************************************************************************/

new_element->data = (void *)data;

if (dlist_size(list) == 0) {

   /***********************************************************************
   *                                                                     *
   *  Handle insertion when the list is empty.                           *
   *                                                                     *
   ***********************************************************************/

   list->head = new_element;
   list->head->prev = NULL;
   list->head->next = NULL;
   list->tail = new_element;

   }


else {

   /***********************************************************************
   *                                                                     *
   *  Handle insertion when the list is not empty.                       *
   *                                                                     *
   ***********************************************************************/

   new_element->next = element;
   new_element->prev = element->prev;
```

Example 5-5. Implementation of the Doubly-Linked List Abstract Datatype (continued)

```
   if (element->prev == NULL)
      list->head = new_element;
   else
      element->prev->next = new_element;

   element->prev = new_element;

}


/*****************************************************************************
*                                                                           *
*  Adjust the size of the list to account for the new element.              *
*                                                                           *
*****************************************************************************/

list->size++;

return 0;

}

/*****************************************************************************
*                                                                           *
*  --------------------------- dlist_remove ---------------------------     *
*                                                                           *
*****************************************************************************/

int dlist_remove(DList *list, DListElmt *element, void **data) {

/*****************************************************************************
*                                                                           *
*  Do not allow a NULL element or removal from an empty list.               *
*                                                                           *
*****************************************************************************/

if (element == NULL || dlist_size(list) == 0)
   return -1;

/*****************************************************************************
*                                                                           *
*  Remove the element from the list.                                        *
*                                                                           *
*****************************************************************************/

*data = element->data;

if (element == list->head) {

   /*************************************************************************
   *                                                                       *
```

Example 5-5. Implementation of the Doubly-Linked List Abstract Datatype (continued)

```
   *   Handle removal from the head of the list.                         *
   *                                                                     *
   ***********************************************************************/

   list->head = element->next;

   if (list->head == NULL)
      list->tail = NULL;
   else
      element->next->prev = NULL;

   }

else {

   /***********************************************************************
   *                                                                     *
   *   Handle removal from other than the head of the list.              *
   *                                                                     *
   ***********************************************************************/

   element->prev->next = element->next;

   if (element->next == NULL)
      list->tail = element->prev;
   else
      element->next->prev = element->prev;

}

/***********************************************************************
*                                                                     *
*   Free the storage allocated by the abstract datatype.              *
*                                                                     *
***********************************************************************/

free(element);

/***********************************************************************
*                                                                     *
*   Adjust the size of the list to account for the removed element.   *
*                                                                     *
***********************************************************************/

list->size--;

return 0;

}
```

Description of Circular Lists

The circular list is another form of linked list that provides additional flexibility in traversing elements. A circular list may be singly-linked or doubly-linked, but its distinguishing feature is that it has no tail. In a circular list, the *next* pointer of the last element points back to its first element rather than to NULL. In the case of a doubly-linked circular list, the *prev* pointer of the first element is set to point to the last element as well.

Whether dealing with a singly-linked or doubly-linked circular list, we never need to worry about reaching an element from which we can traverse no further as we move from element to element. Instead, the traversal simply continues back to the first element, or, in the case of a doubly-linked circular list, back to the last element. Traversing a list in this manner produces a circular pattern (see Figure 5-7), hence its name.

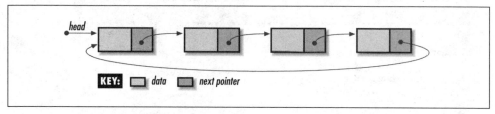

Figure 5-7. Elements linked together to form a circular list

The circular list presented in the following sections is a singly-linked circular list. Therefore, we are concerned only with maintaining a link from the last element back to the first element. In practice, whether to make use of a singly-linked circular list or one that is doubly-linked depends on the same reasoning presented earlier for choosing between singly-linked and doubly-linked lists that are not circular.

Interface for Circular Lists

clist_init

```
void clist_init(CList *list, void (*destroy)(void *data));
```

Return Value   None.

Description   Initializes the circular list specified by `list`. This operation must be called for a circular list before the list can be used with any other operation. The `destroy` argument provides a way to free dynamically allocated data when *clist_destroy* is called. It works in a manner similar to that described for *list_destroy*.

For a circular list containing data that should not be freed, *destroy* should be set to NULL.

Complexity   O(1)

clist_destroy

```
void clist_destroy(CList *list);
```

Return Value   None.

Description   Destroys the circular list specified by *list*. No other operations are permitted after calling *clist_destroy* unless *clist_init* is called again. The *clist_destroy* operation removes all elements from a circular list and calls the function passed as *destroy* to *clist_init* once for each element as it is removed, provided *destroy* was not set to NULL.

Complexity   O(*n*), where *n* is the number of elements in the circular list.

clist_ins_next

```
int clist_ins_next(CList *list, CListElmt *element, const void *data);
```

Return Value   0 if inserting the element is successful, or −1 otherwise.

Description   Inserts an element just after *element* in the circular list specified by *list*. When inserting into an empty list, *element* may point anywhere but should be NULL to avoid confusion. The new element contains a pointer to *data*, so the memory referenced by *data* should remain valid as long as the element remains in the list. It is the responsibility of the caller to manage the storage associated with *data*.

Complexity   O(1)

clist_rem_next

```
int clist_rem_next(CList *list, CListElmt *element, void **data);
```

Return Value   0 if removing the element is successful, or −1 otherwise.

Description   Removes the element just after *element* from the circular list specified by *list*. Upon return, *data* points to the data stored in the element that was removed. It is the responsibility of the caller to manage the storage associated with the data.

Complexity   O(1)

clist_size

```
int clist_size(const CList *list);
```

Return Value   Number of elements in the list.

Description   Macro that evaluates to the number of elements in the circular list specified by *list*.

Complexity $O(1)$

clist_head

```
CListElmt *clist_head(const CList *list);
```

Return Value   Element at the head of the list.

Description   Macro that evaluates to the element at the head of the circular list specified by *list*.

Complexity $O(1)$

clist_data

```
void *clist_data(const CListElmt *element);
```

Return Value   Data stored in the element.

Description   Macro that evaluates to the data stored in the element of a circular list specified by *element*.

Complexity $O(1)$

clist_next

```
CListElmt *clist_next(const CListElmt *element);
```

Return Value   Element following the specified element.

Description   Macro that evaluates to the element of a circular list following the element specified by *element*.

Complexity $O(1)$

Implementation and Analysis
of Circular Lists

As with a singly-linked list, each element of a circular list consists of two parts: a data member and a pointer to the next element. The structure *CListElmt* represents an individual element of a circular list (see Example 5-6). As you would expect, this structure has two members corresponding to those just mentioned. The structure *CList* is the circular list data structure (see Example 5-6). This structure is similar to the one used for singly-linked lists, but it does not contain the *tail* member.

Example 5-6. Header for the Circular List Abstract Datatype

```
/*****************************************************************************
 *                                                                           *
 *   ----------------------------- clist.h ------------------------------    *
 *                                                                           *
 *****************************************************************************/

#ifndef CLIST_H
#define CLIST_H

#include <stdlib.h>

/*****************************************************************************
 *                                                                           *
 *  Define a structure for circular list elements.                           *
 *                                                                           *
 *****************************************************************************/

typedef struct CListElmt_ {

void             *data;
struct CListElmt_  *next;

} CListElmt;

/*****************************************************************************
 *                                                                           *
 *  Define a structure for circular lists.                                   *
 *                                                                           *
 *****************************************************************************/

typedef struct CList_ {

int              size;

int              (*match)(const void *key1, const void *key2);
void             (*destroy)(void *data);

CListElmt        *head;

} CList;

/*****************************************************************************
 *                                                                           *
 *  -------------------------- Public Interface --------------------------   *
 *                                                                           *
 *****************************************************************************/
```

Example 5-6. Header for the Circular List Abstract Datatype (continued)

```
void clist_init(CList *list, void (*destroy)(void *data));

void clist_destroy(CList *list);

int clist_ins_next(CList *list, CListElmt *element, const void *data);

int clist_rem_next(CList *list, CListElmt *element, void **data);

#define clist_size(list) ((list)->size)

#define clist_head(list) ((list)->head)

#define clist_data(element) ((element)->data)

#define clist_next(element) ((element)->next)

#endif
```

clist_init

The *clist_init* operation initializes a circular list so that it can be used in other operations (see Example 5-7). Initialization is the same as with a singly-linked list that is not circular, with the exception that there is no *tail* member to initialize.

The runtime complexity of *clist_init* is O(1) because all of the steps in initializing a circular list run in a constant amount of time.

clist_destroy

The *clist_destroy* operation destroys a circular list (see Example 5-7). Primarily this means removing all elements from the list. The function passed as *destroy* to *clist_init* is called once for each element as it is removed, provided *destroy* was not set to NULL.

The runtime complexity of *clist_destroy* is O(n), where n is the number of elements in the list. This is because the O(1) operation *clist_rem_next* must be called once for each element.

clist_ins_next

The *clist_ins_next* operation inserts an element into a circular list just after a specified element (see Example 5-7). Inserting an element in a singly-linked circular list is similar to inserting one in a singly-linked list that is not circular. The primary difference occurs when we are inserting into an empty list. In this case, we must set the *next* pointer of the inserted element to point back to itself. This allows for the circular traversal of a list containing even just one element. It also ensures the proper insertion of elements in the future.

The runtime complexity of *clist_ins_next* is $O(1)$ because all of the steps in inserting an element into a circular list run in a constant amount of time.

clist_rem_next

The *clist_rem_next* operation removes from a circular list the element just after a specified element (see Example 5-7). Removing an element from a singly-linked circular list is similar to removing an element from one that is not circular.

The runtime complexity of *clist_rem_next* is $O(1)$ because all of the steps in removing an element from a circular list run in a constant amount of time.

clist_size, clist_head, clist_data, and clist_next

These macros implement some of the simpler circular list operations (see Example 5-6). Generally, they provide an interface for accessing and testing members of the *CList* and *CListElmt* structures.

The runtime complexity of these operations is $O(1)$ because accessing and testing members of a structure are simple tasks that run in a constant amount of time.

Example 5-7. Implementation of the Circular List Abstract Datatype

```
/*****************************************************************************
*                                                                           *
*  ----------------------------- clist.c -------------------------------    *
*                                                                           *
*****************************************************************************/

#include <stdlib.h>
#include <string.h>

#include "clist.h"

/*****************************************************************************
*                                                                           *
*  ----------------------------- clist_init -----------------------------   *
*                                                                           *
*****************************************************************************/

void clist_init(CList *list, void (*destroy)(void *data)) {

/*****************************************************************************
*                                                                           *
*  Initialize the list.                                                     *
*                                                                           *
*****************************************************************************/

list->size = 0;
list->destroy = destroy;
list->head = NULL;
```

Example 5-7. Implementation of the Circular List Abstract Datatype (continued)

```c
return;

}

/*****************************************************************************
*                                                                           *
*  -------------------------- clist_destroy ----------------------------    *
*                                                                           *
*****************************************************************************/

void clist_destroy(CList *list) {

void             *data;

/*****************************************************************************
*                                                                           *
*  Remove each element.                                                     *
*                                                                           *
*****************************************************************************/

while (clist_size(list) > 0) {

    if (clist_rem_next(list, list->head, (void **)&data) == 0 && list->destroy
        != NULL) {

        /***********************************************************************
        *                                                                     *
        *  Call a user-defined function to free dynamically allocated data.   *
        *                                                                     *
        ***********************************************************************/

        list->destroy(data);

    }

}

/*****************************************************************************
*                                                                           *
*  No operations are allowed now, but clear the structure as a precaution.  *
*                                                                           *
*****************************************************************************/

memset(list, 0, sizeof(CList));

return;

}

/*****************************************************************************
*                                                                           *
*  -------------------------- clist_ins_next ---------------------------    *
*                                                                           *
*****************************************************************************/
```

Example 5-7. Implementation of the Circular List Abstract Datatype (continued)

```c
int clist_ins_next(CList *list, CListElmt *element, const void *data) {

CListElmt          *new_element;

/***************************************************************************
*                                                                         *
*  Allocate storage for the element.                                      *
*                                                                         *
***************************************************************************/

if ((new_element = (CListElmt *)malloc(sizeof(CListElmt))) == NULL)
   return -1;

/***************************************************************************
*                                                                         *
*  Insert the element into the list.                                      *
*                                                                         *
***************************************************************************/

new_element->data = (void *)data;

if (clist_size(list) == 0) {

   /***************************************************************************
   *                                                                         *
   *  Handle insertion when the list is empty.                               *
   *                                                                         *
   ***************************************************************************/

   new_element->next = new_element;
   list->head = new_element;

   }

else {

   /***************************************************************************
   *                                                                         *
   *  Handle insertion when the list is not empty.                           *
   *                                                                         *
   ***************************************************************************/

   new_element->next = element->next;
   element->next = new_element;

}

/***************************************************************************
*                                                                         *
*  Adjust the size of the list to account for the inserted element.       *
*                                                                         *
***************************************************************************/
```

Example 5-7. Implementation of the Circular List Abstract Datatype (continued)

```c
list->size++;

return 0;

}

/*****************************************************************************
*                                                                           *
*  --------------------------- clist_rem_next ---------------------------    *
*                                                                           *
*****************************************************************************/

int clist_rem_next(CList *list, CListElmt *element, void **data) {

CListElmt          *old_element;

/*****************************************************************************
*                                                                           *
*  Do not allow removal from an empty list.                                 *
*                                                                           *
*****************************************************************************/

if (clist_size(list) == 0)
   return -1;

/*****************************************************************************
*                                                                           *
*  Remove the element from the list.                                        *
*                                                                           *
*****************************************************************************/

*data = element->next->data;

if (element->next == element) {

   /*****************************************************************************
   *                                                                           *
   *  Handle removing the last element.                                        *
   *                                                                           *
   *****************************************************************************/

   old_element = element->next;
   list->head = NULL;

   }

else {

   /*****************************************************************************
   *                                                                           *
   *  Handle removing other than the last element.                             *
   *                                                                           *
   *****************************************************************************/
```

Example 5-7. Implementation of the Circular List Abstract Datatype (continued)

```
    old_element = element->next;
    element->next = element->next->next;

}

/**************************************************************************
*                                                                        *
*  Free the storage allocated by the abstract datatype.                  *
*                                                                        *
**************************************************************************/

free(old_element);

/**************************************************************************
*                                                                        *
*  Adjust the size of the list to account for the removed element.       *
*                                                                        *
**************************************************************************/

list->size--;

return 0;

}
```

Circular List Example: Second-Chance Page Replacement

Earlier we saw how a singly-linked list might be used to manage frame allocation in a virtual memory system. One issue not addressed, however, was how a system allocates new frames when the list of available frames is empty. To deal with this, a system frees a frame by moving a page from physical memory to a disk called a *swap disk*. The system uses a *page-replacement algorithm* to determine which frame is best to free at a given moment. One example of a page-replacement algorithm is the *second-chance algorithm*, sometimes called the *clock algorithm*.

Ideally, it would be great if all pages of a process resided in physical memory at once, but usually this is not possible. Typically, many processes may be running on a system simultaneously, all competing for its physical memory. Sometimes even a single process may have such a large address space that it cannot fit itself into physical memory. Faced with having to replace a page at some point, then, it should seem reasonable that the best page for a system to replace is the one that it will not access for the longest time to come. However, since it can't predict the future, a system sometimes uses an assumption that the past will be a reasonable indication of the future and replaces the page that has been accessed least recently. This is known as *least recently used*, or *LRU*, page replacement.

The second-chance algorithm is one approach to implementing an LRU page-replacement scheme. It works by maintaining a circular list of pages that are currently in physical memory. For simplicity, consider each element in the list to store only a page number and a reference value, which is set to either 1 or 0. In practice, each element contains other information as well. All pages initially have a reference value of 0. Whenever the page is accessed by the system (as in a process reading from or writing to the page, for example), its reference value is set to 1.

When a frame is needed, the system uses the circular list and the reference values it maintains to determine which page should give up its frame. To determine this, it moves through the list until it finds a reference value of 0. As it traverses each page, the system resets the page's reference value from 1 to 0. Once it encounters a 0, it has found a page that has not been accessed by the system since the last cycle through the list; thus, it is the page least recently used. This page is then replaced in physical memory with the new page, and the new page is inserted in place of the old one in the list. If all pages have been accessed since the algorithm was last run, the system ends up making a complete cycle through the list and replaces the page at which it started.

The example here is an implementation of this page-replacement strategy. It uses a function called *replace_page* (see Examples 5-8 and 5-9). The function accepts a single argument called **current**, which points to the element of a circular list containing the page at which to begin searching (see Figure 5-8). As the list is traversed, the algorithm inspects the **reference** member of the **Page** structure stored in each element to determine whether it is 1 or 0. If it is 1, it resets it to 0 and goes to the next page; if it is 0, it has found the page to replace. Eventually, if all pages have been traversed, the circular nature of the list will land the algorithm back on the page at which it began. This time the page's reference value will be 0 (because it was reset when it was first encountered), and it is returned as the page to be replaced. Upon return, **current** points to the page at which the search ended. This becomes the page at which to begin the next time a frame is neededA circular list models this problem nicely because it allows a system to cycle through pages just as the algorithm requires. The runtime complexity of *replace_page* is $O(n)$, where n is the number of pages in the circular list. This is because, in the worst case, the algorithm may need to make a complete cycle through the list to find the page to replace.

Example 5-8. Implementation of Second-Chance Page Replacement

```
#include "clist.h"
#include "page.h"
```

Example 5-8. Implementation of Second-Chance Page Replacement (continued)

```
/***************************************************************************
*                                                                         *
*  --------------------------- replace_page ----------------------------  *
*                                                                         *
***************************************************************************/

int replace_page(CListElmt **current) {

/***************************************************************************
*                                                                         *
*  Circle through the list of pages until one is found to replace.        *
*                                                                         *
***************************************************************************/

while (((Page *)(*current)->data)->reference != 0) {

   ((Page *)(*current)->data)->reference = 0;
   *current = clist_next(*current);

}

return ((Page *)(*current)->data)->number;

}
```

Example 5-9. Header for Second-Chance Page Replacement

```
/***************************************************************************
*                                                                         *
*  ----------------------------- page.h --------------------------------  *
*                                                                         *
***************************************************************************/

#ifndef PAGE_H
#define PAGE_H

#include "clist.h"

/***************************************************************************
*                                                                         *
*  Define a structure for information about pages.                        *
*                                                                         *
***************************************************************************/

typedef struct Page_ {

int             number;
int             reference;

} Page;
```

Example 5-9. Header for Second-Chance Page Replacement (continued)

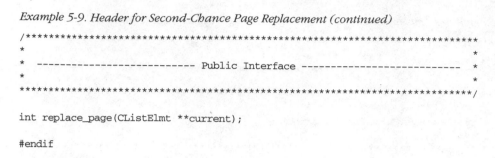

```
int replace_page(CListElmt **current);

#endif
```

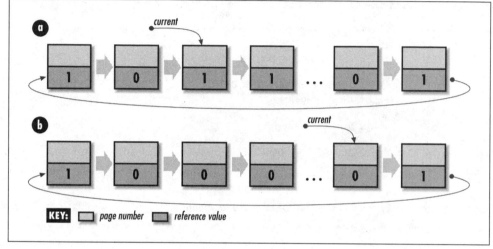

Figure 5-8. Second-chance page-replacement algorithm (a) at the start of a run and (b) after a page has been replaced

Questions and Answers

Q: Some advantages of linked lists over arrays have already been mentioned. However, there are occasions when arrays have advantages over linked lists. When are arrays preferable?

A: Linked lists present advantages over arrays when we expect to insert and remove elements frequently. However, arrays themselves offer some advantages when we expect the number of random accesses to overshadow the number of insertions and deletions. Arrays are strong in this case because their elements are arranged contiguously in memory. This contiguous arrangement allows any element to be accessed in $O(1)$ time by using its index. Recall that to access an element of a linked list, we must have a pointer to the element itself. Getting a pointer to an element can be expensive if we do not know a great deal about the pattern in which the elements will be accessed. In practice, for many applications, we end up traversing at least part of the list.

Arrays are also advantageous when storage is at a premium because they do not require additional pointers to keep their elements "linked" together.

Q: *How do the operations of linked lists for inserting, removing, and accessing elements compare with similar ones for arrays?*

A: Recall that all of the operations presented for each of the linked list variations in this chapter had runtime complexities of $O(1)$, with the exception of the destroy operations. Indeed, this seems tough to beat. What the analyses for linked lists do not show, however, is that for many linked list operations, retrieving a pointer to a specific element in the list can involve a significant cost. For example, if we are not careful, in the worst case we could end up traversing the entire list at a cost of $O(n)$, where n is the number of elements in the list. On the other hand, a well-suited application, such as the frame management example presented in this chapter, may have virtually no overhead for this at all. Therefore, it is important to look at the specifics of the application. With arrays, insertion and removal are both $O(n)$ operations because in the worst case of accessing position 0, all other elements must be moved one slot to adjust for the addition or deletion of the element. Accessing an element in an array is an $O(1)$ operation, provided we know its index.

Q: *Suppose we would like to build a* list_ins_pos *function on top of the linked list implementation in this chapter to insert an element after a specified position, akin to an array. For example, suppose we would like to specify that an element should be inserted after the tenth element instead of providing a pointer to it. What is the runtime complexity of this function?*

A: This function has a runtime complexity of $O(n)$ because generally the only means of knowing when we are at a specific position in a linked list is to start at the head and count the number of elements while moving to it. Here is an application that suffers profoundly from the access problem described in the previous question. That is, the insertion operation itself is $O(1)$, but getting to the required position in the list is $O(n)$.

Q: *Recall that* list_rem_next *removes an element from a singly-linked list after a specified element. Why is no operation provided for singly-linked lists to remove the specified element itself, analogous to the* dlist_remove *operation for doubly-linked lists? (One can ask the same for the circular list implementation.)*

A: In the singly-linked list and circular list implementations, each element does not have a pointer to the one preceding it. Therefore, we cannot set the preceding element's *next* pointer to the element after the one being removed. An alternative approach to the one we selected would be to start at the head element and traverse the list, keeping track of each element preceding the next until the element to be removed is encountered. However, this solution is unattractive because the runtime complexity of removing an element from a singly-linked list or circular list degrades to $O(n)$. Another approach would be to copy the data of the element following the specified element into the one specified and then remove the following element. However, this seemingly benign $O(1)$ approach generates the dangerous side effect of rendering a pointer into the list invalid. This could be a surprise to a developer maintaining a pointer to the element after the one thought to be removed! The approach we selected, then, was to remove the element after the specified one. The disadvantage of this approach is its inconsistency with the *dlist_ remove* operation of the doubly-linked list implementation. However, this is addressed by the naming convention, using *_rem_next* as the suffix for removing an element after the one specified, and *_remove* to indicate that the specified element itself will be removed. In a doubly-linked list, recall that we can remove precisely the element specified because each element has a pointer to the one that precedes it.

Q: *Recall that each of the linked list data structures presented in this chapter has a*
      size member. The `List` and `DList` data structures also contain a `tail` mem-
      ber. Why are each of these members included?

A: By updating these members dynamically as elements are inserted and removed, we avoid the $O(n)$ runtime complexity of traversing the list each time its tail element or size is requested. By maintaining these members, fetching a list's tail element or size becomes an $O(1)$ operation without adding any complexity to the operations for inserting and removing elements.

Q: *Insertion before the head of a list using NULL for the `element` argument is used*
      only in the singly-linked list implementation. Why is this not necessary for
      doubly-linked lists or circular lists?

A: Insertion before the head element of a doubly-linked list is possible using the *prev* pointer of the head element itself. In a circular list, an element is inserted before the head by inserting the element after the last element using *clist_ins_ next*. Remember, in a circular list, the last element points back to the first element.

Related Topics

Doubly-linked circular lists

   Variations of the circular list presented in this chapter, which was singly-linked. Doubly-linked circular lists allow traversals both forward and backward, as well as in a circular fashion.

Linked list arrays

A dynamic approach to multidimensional arrays. Elements maintain additional pointers as well as positional information to keep the array properly linked and accessible.

Multilists

Data structures allowing greater flexibility in how elements are linked together. For example, multiple pointers might be used to form several lists through a set of elements, each representing a separate ordering of the elements.

Cursors

One approach to simulating linked allocation in languages that do not inherently support it. Cursors are useful in FORTRAN and other languages without pointer types.

6

Stacks and Queues

Often it is important to store data so that when it is retrieved later, it is automatically presented in some prescribed order. One common way to retrieve data is in the opposite order as it was stored. For example, consider the data blocks a program maintains to keep track of function calls as it runs. These blocks are called *activation records*. For a set of functions $\{f_1, f_2, f_3\}$ in which f_1 calls f_2 and f_2 calls f_3, a program allocates one activation record each time one of the functions is called. Each record persists until its function returns. Since functions return in the opposite order as they were called, activation records are retrieved and relinquished in the opposite order as they were allocated. Another common way to retrieve data is in the same order as it was stored. For example, this might be useful with a bunch of things to do; often we want to do the first item first and the last item last. Stacks and queues are simple data structures that help in such common situations.

This chapter covers:

Stacks

Efficient data structures for storing and retrieving data in a last-in, first-out, or LIFO, order. This allows us to retrieve data in the opposite order as it was stored.

Queues

Efficient data structures useful for storing and retrieving data in a first-in, first-out, or FIFO, order. This allows us to retrieve data in the same order as it was stored.

Some applications of stacks and queues are:

Semaphores

Programmatic devices for synchronizing access to shared resources. When a process encounters a semaphore, it performs a test to determine whether someone else is currently accessing the resource the semaphore protects. If so, the process blocks and waits until another process signals that the resource is available. Since many processes may be waiting on a resource, some implementations of semaphores use a queue to determine who is next to go.

Event handling (illustrated in this chapter)

A critical part of real-time programming. In real-time systems, events frequently occur when the system is not quite ready to handle them. Therefore, a queue keeps track of events so that they can be processed at a later time in the order they were received.

X Window System

A network-based, graphical window system in which graphics are displayed on servers under the direction of client programs. X is a specific example of a system that does event handling. To manage events in real time, it uses a queue to store events until they can be processed.

Producer-consumer problem

A generalization for modeling cooperating processes wherein one process, the *producer*, writes to a queue shared by another process, the *consumer*, which reads from it. The producer-consumer problem is a classic one to study because many applications can be described in terms of it.

Function calls in C

An essential part of modular programming. When we call a function in a C program, an activation record containing information about the call is pushed onto a stack called the *program stack*. When a function terminates, its activation record is popped off the stack. A stack is the perfect model for this because when functions call one another, they return in the opposite order as they were called.

Abstract stack machines

An abstraction used by compilers and hand-held calculators to evaluate expressions (see the example in Chapter 9, *Trees*).

Description of Stacks

The distinguishing characteristic of a stack is that it stores and retrieves data in a *last-in, first-out*, or *LIFO*, manner. This means that the last element placed on the stack is the first to be removed. A convenient way to think of a stack is as a can of tennis balls. As we place balls in the can, the can is filled up from the bottom to the top. When we remove the balls, the can is emptied from the top to the bottom. Furthermore, if we want a ball from the bottom of the can, we must remove each of the balls above it. In computing, to place an element on the top of a stack, we *push* it; to remove an element from the top, we *pop* it (see Figure 6-1).

Sometimes it is useful to inspect the element at the top of a stack without actually removing it, in which case we *peek* at it.

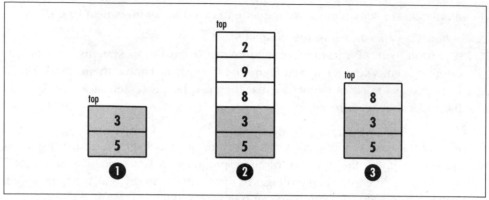

Figure 6-1. A stack (1) with some elements already stacked; (2) after pushing 8, 9, and 2; and (3) after popping 2 and 9

Interface for Stacks

stack_init

```
void stack_init(Stack *stack, void (*destroy)(void *data));
```

Return Value   None.

Description   Initializes the stack specified by ***stack***. This operation must be called for a stack before the stack can be used with any other operation. The ***destroy*** argument provides a way to free dynamically allocated data when *stack_destroy* is called. For example, if the stack contains data dynamically allocated using *malloc*, ***destroy*** should be set to *free* to free the data as the stack is destroyed. For structured data containing several dynamically allocated members, ***destroy*** should be set to a user-defined function that calls *free* for each dynamically allocated member as well as for the structure itself. For a stack containing data that should not be freed, ***destroy*** should be set to NULL.

Complexity $O(1)$

stack_destroy

```
void stack_destroy(Stack *stack);
```

Return Value   None.

Description   Destroys the stack specified by ***stack***. No other operations are permitted after calling *stack_destroy* unless *stack_init* is called again. The *stack_destroy* operation removes all elements from a stack and calls the function passed as *destroy* to *stack_init* once for each element as it is removed, provided *destroy* was not set to NULL.

Complexity $O(n)$, where n is the number of elements in the stack.

stack_push

```
int stack_push(Stack *stack, const void *data);
```

Return Value   0 if pushing the element is successful, or –1 otherwise.

Description   Pushes an element onto the stack specified by *stack*. The new element contains a pointer to *data*, so the memory referenced by *data* should remain valid as long as the element remains in the stack. It is the responsibility of the caller to manage the storage associated with *data*.

Complexity $O(1)$

stack_pop

```
int stack_pop(Stack *stack, void **data);
```

Return Value   0 if popping the element is successful, or –1 otherwise.

Description   Pops an element off the stack specified by *stack*. Upon return, *data* points to the data stored in the element that was popped. It is the responsibility of the caller to manage the storage associated with the data.

Complexity $O(1)$

stack_peek

```
void *stack_peek(const Stack *stack);
```

Return Value   Data stored in the element at the top of the stack, or NULL if the stack is empty.

Description   Macro that evaluates to the data stored in the element at the top of the stack specified by *stack*.

Complexity $O(1)$

stack_size

```
int stack_size(const Stack *stack);
```

Return Value   Number of elements in the stack.

Description   Macro that evaluates to the number of elements in the stack specified by *stack*.

Complexity $O(1)$

Implementation and Analysis of Stacks

The structure *Stack* is the stack data structure. One way to implement a stack is as a linked list. A simple way to do this is to typedef *Stack* to *List* (see Example 6-1). In addition to simplicity, using a typedef has the benefit of making the stack somewhat *polymorphic*. Informally, polymorphism is a principle normally associated with object-oriented languages that allows an object (a variable) of one type to be used in place of another. This means that because the stack is a linked list, and hence has the same properties as a linked list, we can use linked list operations on it in addition to those of a stack. Thus, the stack can behave like a linked list when we want it to.

As an example, suppose we want to traverse the elements of a stack, perhaps so we can display them or determine whether a specific element resides in the stack. To do this, we get the element at the head of the list using *list_head* and traverse the list using *list_next*. Using only stack operations, we would have to pop the elements one at a time, inspect them, and push them onto another stack temporarily. Then, after accessing all of the elements, we would need to rebuild the original stack by popping the elements off the temporary stack and pushing them back onto the original one. This method would be less efficient and undoubtedly would look less than intuitive in a program.

Example 6-1. Header for the Stack Abstract Datatype

```
/*****************************************************************************
*                                                                           *
*  ----------------------------- stack.h -----------------------------      *
*                                                                           *
*****************************************************************************/

#ifndef STACK_H
#define STACK_H

#include <stdlib.h>

#include "list.h"

/*****************************************************************************
*                                                                           *
*  Implement stacks as linked lists.                                        *
*                                                                           *
*****************************************************************************/

typedef List Stack;

/*****************************************************************************
*                                                                           *
*  --------------------------- Public Interface ---------------------------  *
*                                                                           *
*****************************************************************************/
```

Example 6-1. Header for the Stack Abstract Datatype (continued)

```
#define stack_init list_init

#define stack_destroy list_destroy

int stack_push(Stack *stack, const void *data);

int stack_pop(Stack *stack, void **data);

#define stack_peek(stack) ((stack)->head == NULL ? NULL : (stack)->head->data)

#define stack_size list_size

#endif
```

stack_init

The *stack_init* operation initializes a stack so that it can be used in other operations (see Example 6-1). Since a stack is a linked list and requires the same initialization, *stack_init* is defined to *list_init*.

The runtime complexity of *stack_init* is the same as *list_init*, or $O(1)$.

stack_destroy

The *stack_destroy* operation destroys a stack (see Example 6-1). Since a stack is a linked list and requires being destroyed in the same manner, *stack_destroy* is defined to *list_destroy*.

The runtime complexity of *stack_destroy* is the same as *list_destroy*, or $O(n)$, where n is the number of elements in the stack.

stack_push

The *stack_push* operation pushes an element onto the top of a stack by calling *list_ins_next* to insert an element pointing to *data* at the head of the list (see Example 6-2).

The runtime complexity of *stack_push* is the same as *list_ins_next*, or $O(1)$.

stack_pop

The *stack_pop* operation pops an element off the top of a stack by calling *list_rem_next* to remove the element at the head of the list (see Example 6-2). The *list_rem_next* operation sets *data* to point to the data from the element removed.

The runtime complexity of *stack_pop* is the same as *list_rem_next*, or $O(1)$.

stack_peek, stack_size

These macros implement two simple stack operations (see Example 6-1). The *stack_peek* macro provides a way to inspect the element at the top of a stack without actually popping it, and *stack_size* evaluates to the size of a stack. Both of these operations work by accessing members of the **Stack** structure.

The runtime complexity of these operations is $O(1)$ because accessing members of a structure is a simple task that runs in a constant amount of time.

Example 6-2. Implementation of the Stack Abstract Datatype

```
/*****************************************************************************
*                                                                          *
*  ----------------------------- stack.c -----------------------------   *
*                                                                          *
*****************************************************************************/

#include <stdlib.h>

#include "list.h"
#include "stack.h"

/*****************************************************************************
*                                                                          *
*  --------------------------- stack_push ---------------------------   *
*                                                                          *
*****************************************************************************/

int stack_push(Stack *stack, const void *data) {

/*****************************************************************************
*                                                                          *
*  Push the data onto the stack.                                           *
*                                                                          *
*****************************************************************************/

return list_ins_next(stack, NULL, data);

}

/*****************************************************************************
*                                                                          *
*  --------------------------- stack_pop ----------------------------   *
*                                                                          *
*****************************************************************************/

int stack_pop(Stack *stack, void **data) {

/*****************************************************************************
*                                                                          *
*  Pop the data off the stack.                                            *
*                                                                          *
*****************************************************************************/
```

Example 6-2. Implementation of the Stack Abstract Datatype (continued)

```
return list_rem_next(stack, NULL, data);

}
```

Description of Queues

The distinguishing characteristic of a queue is that it stores and retrieves data in a *first-in, first-out,* or *FIFO,* manner. This means that the first element placed in the queue is the first to be removed. A convenient way to think of a queue is as a line at the post office. In fact, anyone who has been to England knows that to form a line there is known colloquially as "queuing up." As the line grows, newcomers join in at the tail. When a clerk becomes available, the person at the head of the line goes next. In computing, to place an element at the tail of a queue, we *enqueue* it; to remove an element from the head, we *dequeue* it (see Figure 6-2). Sometimes it is useful to inspect the element at the head of a queue without actually removing it, in which case we *peek* at it.

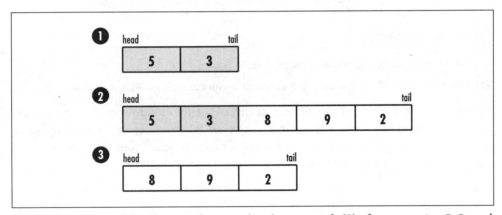

Figure 6-2. A queue (1) with some elements already enqueued; (2) after enqueuing 8, 9, and 2; and (3) after dequeuing 5 and 3

Interface for Queues

queue_init

```
void queue_init(Queue *queue, void (*destroy)(void *data));
```

Return Value   None.

Description   Initializes the queue specified by *queue*. This operation must be called for a queue before the queue can be used with any other operation. The *destroy* argument provides a way to free dynamically allocated data when *queue_destroy* is called. It works in a manner similar to that described for *stack_destroy*. For a queue containing data that should not be freed, *destroy* should be set to NULL.

Complexity   O(1)

queue_destroy

```
void queue_destroy(Queue *queue);
```

Return Value   None.

Description   Destroys the queue specified by *queue*. No other operations are permitted after calling *queue_destroy* unless *queue_init* is called again. The *queue_destroy* operation removes all elements from a queue and calls the function passed as *destroy* to *queue_init* once for each element as it is removed, provided *destroy* was not set to NULL.

Complexity   O(n), where n is the number of elements in the queue.

queue_enqueue

```
int queue_enqueue(Queue *queue, const void *data);
```

Return Value   0 if enqueuing the element is successful, or –1 otherwise.

Description   Enqueues an element at the tail of the queue specified by *queue*. The new element contains a pointer to *data*, so the memory referenced by *data* should remain valid as long as the element remains in the queue. It is the responsibility of the caller to manage the storage associated with *data*.

Complexity   O(1)

queue_dequeue

```
int queue_dequeue(Queue *queue, void **data);
```

Return Value   0 if dequeuing the element is successful, or –1 otherwise.

Description   Dequeues an element from the head of the queue specified by *queue*. Upon return, *data* points to the data stored in the element that was dequeued. It is the responsibility of the caller to manage the storage associated with the data.

Complexity   O(1)

queue_peek

```
void *queue_peek(const Queue *queue);
```

Return Value   Data stored in the element at the head of the queue, or NULL if the queue is empty.

Description   Macro that evaluates to the data stored in the element at the head of the queue specified by *queue*.

Complexity   *O*(1)

queue_size

```
int queue_size(const Queue *queue);
```

Return Value   Number of elements in the queue.

Description   Macro that evaluates to the number of elements in the queue specified by *queue*.

Complexity   *O*(1)

Implementation and Analysis of Queues

The structure *Queue* is the queue data structure. It is implemented as a typedef to *List* (see Example 6-3), just as was described for stacks.

Example 6-3. Header for the Queue Abstract Datatype

```
/*****************************************************************************
*                                                                           *
*   ------------------------------- queue.h -------------------------------  *
*                                                                           *
*****************************************************************************/

#ifndef QUEUE_H
#define QUEUE_H

#include <stdlib.h>

#include "list.h"

/*****************************************************************************
*                                                                           *
*   Implement queues as linked lists.                                       *
*                                                                           *
*****************************************************************************/

typedef List Queue;
```

Example 6-3. Header for the Queue Abstract Datatype (continued)

```
/***************************************************************************
*                                                                         *
*   ------------------------- Public Interface -------------------------   *
*                                                                         *
***************************************************************************/

#define queue_init list_init

#define queue_destroy list_destroy

int queue_enqueue(Queue *queue, const void *data);

int queue_dequeue(Queue *queue, void **data);

#define queue_peek(queue) ((queue)->head == NULL ? NULL : (queue)->head->data)

#define queue_size list_size

#endif
```

queue_init

The *queue_init* operation initializes a queue so that it can be used in other operations (see Example 6-3). Since a queue is a linked list and requires the same initialization, *queue_init* is defined to *list_init*.

The runtime complexity of *queue_init* is the same as *list_init*, or $O(1)$.

queue_destroy

The *queue_destroy* operation destroys a queue (see Example 6-3). Since a queue is
a linked list and requires being destroyed in the same manner, *queue_destroy* is
defined to *list_destroy*.

The runtime complexity of *queue_destroy* is the same as *list_destroy*, or $O(n)$,
where n is the number of elements in the queue.

queue_enqueue

The *queue_enqueue* operation enqueues an element at the tail of a queue by calling *list_ins_next* to insert an element pointing to **data** at the tail of the list (see
Example 6-4).

The runtime complexity of *queue_enqueue* is the same as *list_ins_next*, or $O(1)$.

queue_dequeue

The *queue_dequeue* operation dequeues an element from the head of a queue by
calling *list_rem_next* to remove the element at the head of the list (see

Example 6-4). The *list_rem_next* operation sets **data** to point to the data from the element removed.

The runtime complexity of *queue_dequeue* is the same as *list_rem_next*, or *O*(1).

queue_peek, queue_size

These macros implement two simple queue operations (see Example 6-3). The *queue_peek* macro provides a way to inspect the element at the head of a queue without actually dequeuing it, and *queue_size* evaluates to the size of a queue. Both of these operations work by accessing members of the *Queue* structure.

The runtime complexity of these operations is *O*(1) because accessing members of a structure is a simple task that runs in a constant amount of time.

Example 6-4. Implementation of the Queue Abstract Datatype

```
/*****************************************************************************
*                                                                          *
* ------------------------------ queue.c ------------------------------    *
*                                                                          *
*****************************************************************************/

#include <stdlib.h>

#include "list.h"
#include "queue.h"

/*****************************************************************************
*                                                                          *
* --------------------------- queue_enqueue ---------------------------    *
*                                                                          *
*****************************************************************************/

int queue_enqueue(Queue *queue, const void *data) {

/*****************************************************************************
*                                                                          *
*  Enqueue the data.                                                       *
*                                                                          *
*****************************************************************************/

return list_ins_next(queue, list_tail(queue), data);

}

/*****************************************************************************
*                                                                          *
* --------------------------- queue_dequeue ---------------------------    *
*                                                                          *
*****************************************************************************/
```

Example 6-4. Implementation of the Queue Abstract Datatype (continued)

```
int queue_dequeue(Queue *queue, void **data) {

/***************************************************************************
*                                                                         *
*  Dequeue the data.                                                      *
*                                                                         *
***************************************************************************/

return list_rem_next(queue, NULL, data);

}
```

Queue Example: Event Handling

One popular application of queues is handling events in event-driven applications. Event-driven applications execute largely under the direction of real-time occurrences called *events*. In a graphical user interface developed in Java, X, or Windows, for example, the behavior of an application depends a great deal on key presses, mouse movements, and other events triggered by the user. Other examples of event-driven applications occur frequently in control systems such as those found in aircraft or factory equipment.

In nearly all event-driven applications, events can occur at any moment, so queues play an important role in storing events until an application is ready to deal with them. A queue works well for this because applications handle events more or less in the same order as they occur.

Example 6-5 presents two functions for handling events: *receive_event* and *process_event*. Both functions operate on a queue containing events of type `Event`. `Event` is defined in *event.h*, which is not shown. An application calls *receive_event* to enqueue an event it has been notified about. Exactly how an application is notified of an event varies, but notification often begins with a hardware interrupt. When the application decides it is time to process an event, it calls *process_event*. Inside of *process_event*, an event is dequeued from the event queue and is passed to an application-specific dispatch function. The dispatch function is passed to *process_event* as the parameter `dispatch`. The purpose of the dispatch function is to take the appropriate action to handle the event. There are two approaches `dispatch` can take to do this: it can process the event *synchronously*, so that no other processing is performed until handling the event is completed; or it can process the event *asynchronously*, in which case it starts a separate process to handle the event while the main process moves on. Asynchronous event handling usually is more efficient, but it requires particularly careful coordination between the main and subordinate processes.

The runtime complexity of *receive_event* is $O(1)$ because it simply calls the $O(1)$ queue operation *queue_enqueue*. The runtime complexity of *process_event* depends on the dispatch function it invokes. The rest of *process_event* runs in a constant amount of time.

Example 6-5. Implementation of Functions for Handling Events

```
/*****************************************************************************
*                                                                          *
*  --------------------------- events.c ---------------------------        *
*                                                                          *
*****************************************************************************/

#include <stdlib.h>
#include <string.h>

#include "event.h"
#include "events.h"
#include "queue.h"

/*****************************************************************************
*                                                                          *
*  -------------------------- receive_event --------------------------     *
*                                                                          *
*****************************************************************************/

int receive_event(Queue *events, const Event *event) {

Event              *new_event;

/*****************************************************************************
*                                                                          *
*  Allocate space for the event.                                           *
*                                                                          *
*****************************************************************************/

if ((new_event = (Event *)malloc(sizeof(Event))) == NULL)
   return -1;

/*****************************************************************************
*                                                                          *
*  Make a copy of the event and enqueue it.                                *
*                                                                          *
*****************************************************************************/

memcpy(new_event, event, sizeof(Event));

if (queue_enqueue(events, new_event) != 0)
   return -1;

return 0;

}
```

Example 6-5. Implementation of Functions for Handling Events (continued)

```
/*****************************************************************************
*                                                                           *
*  -------------------------- process_event --------------------------      *
*                                                                           *
*****************************************************************************/

int process_event(Queue *events, int (*dispatch)(Event *event)) {

Event               *event;

if (queue_size(events) == 0)

   /*****************************************************************************
   *                                                                           *
   *  Return that there are no events to dispatch.                             *
   *                                                                           *
   *****************************************************************************/

   return -1;

else {

   if (queue_dequeue(events, (void **)&event) != 0)

      /*****************************************************************************
      *                                                                           *
      *  Return that an event could not be retrieved.                            *
      *                                                                           *
      *****************************************************************************/

      return -1;

   else {

      /*****************************************************************************
      *                                                                           *
      *  Call a user-defined function to dispatch the event.                     *
      *                                                                           *
      *****************************************************************************/

      dispatch(event);
      free(event);

   }

}

return 0;

}
```

Questions and Answers

Q: *If* Stack *and* Queue *are not made typedefs of* List, *what are the implications for the stack and queue abstract datatypes?*

A: Making Stack and Queue both typedefs of List has some nice benefits, but alternative approaches could be chosen to implement these data structures. For example, Stack and Queue could be made their own unique structures consisting of the same members as List. However, this would not allow the use of linked list operations in the implementation. Another approach would be to implement stacks and queues as structures that each contain a linked list member. This would allow the use of linked list operations in the implementation, but it does not model very nicely what stacks and queues really are. That is, stacks and queues do not *have* linked lists as part of them; they *are* linked lists.

Q: *Why is there no* stack_next *macro for stacks and no* queue_next *macro for queues? These operations would have provided a way to traverse the members of a stack or queue, respectively.*

A: By implementing the Stack and Queue data structures as typedefs of List, there is no need for these operations because we can call *list_next*. This is good because traversing the members of a stack or queue is not generally part of the normal behavior of these abstract datatypes. By making a developer use operations of a linked list when a stack or queue needs to act like one, we maintain a pure interface to the stack and queue.

Q: *Sometimes we need to remove an element from a queue out of sequence (i.e., from somewhere other than the head). What would be the sequence of queue operations to do this if in a queue of five requests,* $\langle req_1, \ldots, req_5 \rangle$, *we wish to process* req_1, req_3, *and* req_5 *immediately while leaving* req_2 *and* req_4 *in the queue in order? What would be the sequence of linked list operations to do this if we morph the queue into a linked list?*

A: Using queue operations, we dequeue req_1 for processing, dequeue req_2 and re-enqueue it, dequeue req_3 for processing, dequeue req_4 and re-enqueue it, and dequeue req_5 for processing. Because we re-enqueued req_2 and req_4, the queue now contains only these requests in order. Removing requests out of sequence is more intuitive when we treat the queue as a linked list and apply linked list operations to it. In this case, we simply call *list_next* to traverse the requests one at a time and *list_rem_next* to remove the appropriate requests.

Related Topics

Polymorphism

A principle that allows an object (a variable) of one type to be used in place of another provided the two share some common characteristics. Polymorphism is an important part of object-oriented languages. However, even in languages that do not support it inherently, we can apply certain techniques to provide polymorphic behavior to some degree.

Double-ended queues

Often called *deques* (pronounced "decks") for short. A deque is a more flexible queue that allows insertions and deletions at both its head and tail.

Circular queues

Queues akin to circular lists. As with circular lists, circular queues do not have a tail. Instead, the last element in the queue is linked back to the first element so that the queue can be traversed in a circular fashion.

7

Sets

Sets are collections of distinguishable objects, called *members,* grouped together because they are in some way related. Two important characteristics of sets are that their members are unordered and that no members occur more than once. Sets are an important part of discrete mathematics, an area of mathematics particularly relevant to computing. In computing, we use sets to group data, especially when we plan to correlate it with other data in the future. Some languages, such as Pascal, support sets intrinsically, but C does not. Therefore, this chapter presents a set abstract datatype.

This chapter covers:

Set principles

The fundamental mathematics describing sets. Like other mathematical objects, sets can be described in terms of some definitions, basic operations, and properties.

Sets

Abstract datatypes based on the mathematical concept of a set. Sets are unordered collections of related members in which no members occur more than once.

Some applications of sets are:

Data correlation

Determining interesting relationships between sets of data. For example, the *intersection* of two sets tells which members are present in both sets. The *difference* of two sets tells which members of the first set do not appear in the second set.

Set covering (illustrated in this chapter)

An optimization problem that nicely models many problems of combinatorics and resource selection. For example, imagine trying to form a team from a large set of candidate players, each with a certain set of skills. We might use the set-covering abstraction to form the smallest team possible possessing a certain set of skills overall. That is, for any skill required by the team as a whole, at least one player on the team should possess the skill.

Mathematics with sets

Specifically, combinatorics and probability. Sets have their own principles and rules that computers help apply. Computers are especially useful when working with large sets, which may contain many thousands of members. Operations with sets of this size, like operations in mathematics with large numbers, are very tedious to carry out by hand.

Graphs

Data structures typically used to model problems defined in terms of relationships or connections between objects (see Chapter 11, *Graphs*). The most common way to represent a graph is using *adjacency lists*. An adjacency list contains the vertices adjacent to a single vertex. One way to represent an adjacency list is as a set of adjacent vertices.

Graph algorithms

Algorithms that solve problems modeled by graphs (see Chapter 16, *Graph Algorithms*). Frequently, graph algorithms use sets to group vertices or edges together. For example, Kruskal's algorithm for computing minimum spanning trees (see the related topics at the end of Chapter 16) uses one set to keep track of edges in the minimum spanning tree as it grows. It uses sets of vertices to avoid cycles in the tree.

Relational algebra

The theoretical query language for database systems. Fundamentally, set theory forms the basis for all query languages. For example, suppose we query a database of problem reports at a software company using SQL (Structured Query Language). We query the database for all developers who are working on problems classified with either a status of OPEN, meaning the developer is working on a problem, or WAIT, meaning the developer has not started. Effectively, this query is the union of all records that have either status.

Description of Sets

Sets are unordered collections of related members in which no members occur more than once. Formally, sets are written with braces around them. Thus, if *S* is a set containing the members 1, 2, and 3, then *S* = {1, 2, 3}. Of course, because a set is unordered, this is the same as writing $S = \{3, 2, 1\}$. If a member, m, is in a set, S, then membership is indicated by writing $m \in S$; otherwise, $m \notin S$. For example, in the set $S = \{1, 2, 3\}$, $2 \in S$, but $4 \notin S$. To effectively use sets, we should be familiar with some definitions, basic operations, and properties.

Definitions

1. A set containing no members is the *empty set*. The set of all possible members is the *universe*. (Of course, sometimes the universe is difficult to determine!) In set notation:

   $S = U$ is the universe; $S = \varnothing$ is the empty set

2. Two sets are *equal* if they contain exactly the same members. For example, if $S_1 = \{1, 2, 3\}$, $S_2 = \{3, 2, 1\}$, and $S_3 = \{1, 2, 4\}$, then S_1 is equal to S_2, but S_1 is not equal to S_3. In set notation:

   $S_1 = S_2$ means S_1 and S_2 are equal; $S_1 \neq S_2$ means S_1 and S_2 are not equal

3. One set, S_1, is a *subset* of another set, S_2, if S_2 contains all of the members of S_1. For example, if $S_1 = \{1, 3\}$, $S_2 = \{1, 2, 3\}$, and $S_3 = \{1, 2\}$, then S_1 is a subset of S_2, but S_1 is not a subset of S_3. In set notation,

   $S_1 \subset S_2$ means S_1 is a subset of S_2; $S_1 \not\subset S_2$ means S_1 is not a subset of S_2

Basic Operations

1. The *union* of two sets, S_1 and S_2, is a set, S_u, that contains all of the members of S_1 in addition to all of the members of S_2. For example, if $S_1 = \{1, 2, 3\}$ and $S_2 = \{3, 4\}$, then $S_u = \{1, 2, 3, 4\}$. In set notation:

   $S_1 \cup S_2$ represents the union of S_1 and S_2

2. The *intersection* of two sets, S_1 and S_2, is a set, S_i, that contains only the members that exist in both S_1 and S_2. For example, if $S_1 = \{1, 2, 3\}$ and $S_2 = \{1, 2\}$, then $S_i = \{1, 2\}$. In set notation:

   $S_1 \cap S_2$ represents the intersection of S_1 and S_2

3. The *difference* of two sets, S_1 and S_2, is a set, S_d, that contains all of the members of S_1 except those in S_2. For example, if $S_1 = \{1, 2, 3\}$ and $S_2 = \{3, 4\}$, then $S_d = \{1, 2\}$. In set notation:

   $S_1 - S_2$ represents the difference of S_1 and S_2

Properties

1. The intersection of a set with the empty set is the empty set. The union of a set with the empty set is the original set. This behavior is described by the *empty set laws*:

$$S \cap \emptyset = \emptyset$$
$$S \cup \emptyset = S$$

2. The intersection of a set with itself is the original set. Similarly, the union of a set with itself is the original set. This behavior is described by the *idempotency laws*:

$$S \cap S = S$$
$$S \cup S = S$$

3. The intersection of a set, S_1, with another set, S_2, results in the same set as the intersection of S_2 with S_1. The same is true for the union of two sets. This behavior is described by the *commutative laws*:

$$S_1 \cap S_2 = S_2 \cap S_1$$
$$S_1 \cup S_2 = S_2 \cup S_1$$

4. The intersection of a number of sets can be performed in any order (see Figure 7-1). The same is true for the union of a number of sets. This behavior is described by the *associative laws*:

$$S_1 \cap (S_2 \cap S_3) = (S_1 \cap S_2) \cap S_3$$
$$S_1 \cup (S_2 \cup S_3) = (S_1 \cup S_2) \cup S_3$$

5. The intersection of a set with the union of two others can be carried out in a distributed manner. The same is true for the union of a set with the intersection of two others. This behavior is described by the *distributive laws*:

$$S_1 \cap (S_2 \cup S_3) = (S_1 \cap S_2) \cup (S_1 \cap S_3)$$
$$S_1 \cup (S_2 \cap S_3) = (S_1 \cup S_2) \cap (S_1 \cup S_3)$$

6. The intersection of a set with the union of itself and another results in the original set. The same is true for the union of a set with the intersection of itself and another. This behavior is described by the *absorption laws*:

$$S_1 \cap (S_1 \cup S_2) = S_1$$
$$S_1 \cup (S_1 \cap S_2) = S_1$$

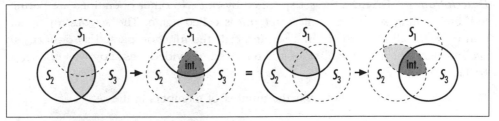

Figure 7-1. The associativity of set intersections (property 4) illustrated using a Venn diagram (see the related topics at the end of the chapter)

7. An interesting result occurs when the difference of one set is taken with either the intersection or union of two others. The resulting behavior is described by *DeMorgan's laws*:

$$S_1 - (S_2 \cup S_3) = (S_1 - S_2) \cap (S_1 - S_3)$$
$$S_1 - (S_2 \cap S_3) = (S_1 - S_2) \cup (S_1 - S_3)$$

Interface for Sets

set_init

```
void set_init(Set *set, int (*match)(const void *key1, const void *key2),
   void (*destroy)(void *data));
```

Return Value   None.

Description   Initializes the set specified by **set**. This operation must be called for a set before the set can be used with any other operation. The **match** argument is a function used by various set operations to determine if two members match. It should return 1 if **key1** is equal to **key2**, and 0 otherwise. The **destroy** argument provides a way to free dynamically allocated data when *set_destroy* is called. For example, if the set contains data dynamically allocated using *malloc*, **destroy** should be set to *free* to free the data as the set is destroyed. For structured data containing several dynamically allocated members, **destroy** should be set to a user-defined function that calls *free* for each dynamically allocated member as well as for the structure itself. For a set containing data that should not be freed, **destroy** should be set to NULL.

Complexity $O(1)$

set_destroy

```
void set_destroy(Set *set);
```

Return Value   None.

Description   Destroys the set specified by **set**. No other operations are permitted after calling *set_destroy* unless *set_init* is called again. The *set_destroy* operation removes all members from a set and calls the function passed as **destroy** to *set_init* once for each member as it is removed, provided **destroy** was not set to NULL.

Complexity $O(n)$, where n is the number of members in the set.

set_insert

```
int set_insert(Set *set, const void *data);
```

Return Value   0 if inserting the member is successful, 1 if the member is already in the set, or –1 otherwise.

Description   Inserts a member into the set specified by **set**. The new member contains a pointer to **data**, so the memory referenced by **data** should remain valid as long as the member remains in the set. It is the responsibility of the caller to manage the storage associated with **data**.

Complexity $O(n)$, where n is the number of members in the set.

set_remove

```
int set_remove(Set *set, void **data);
```

Return Value   0 if removing the member is successful, or –1 otherwise.

Description   Removes the member matching **data** from the set specified by **set**. Upon return, **data** points to the data stored in the member that was removed. It is the responsibility of the caller to manage the storage associated with the data.

Complexity $O(n)$, where n is the number of members in the set.

set_union

```
int set_union(Set *setu, const Set *set1, const Set *set2);
```

Return Value   0 if computing the union is successful, or –1 otherwise.

Description   Builds a set that is the union of **set1** and **set2**. Upon return, **setu** contains the union. Because **setu** points to data in **set1** and **set2**, the data in **set1** and **set2** must remain valid until **setu** is destroyed with *set_destroy*.

Complexity $O(mn)$, where m and n are the number of members in **set1** and **set2**, respectively.

set_intersection

`int set_intersection(Set *seti, const Set *set1, const Set *set2);`

Return Value 0 if computing the intersection is successful, or –1 otherwise.

Description Builds a set that is the intersection of *set1* and *set2*. Upon return, *seti* contains the intersection. Because *seti* points to data in *set1*, the data in *set1* must remain valid until *seti* is destroyed with *set_destroy*.

Complexity $O(mn)$, where m and n are the number of members in *set1* and *set2*, respectively.

set_difference

`int set_difference(Set *setd, const Set *set1, const Set *set2);`

Return Value 0 if computing the difference is successful, or –1 otherwise.

Description Builds a set that is the difference of *set1* and *set2*. Upon return, *setd* contains the difference. Because *setd* points to data in *set1*, the data in *set1* must remain valid until *setd* is destroyed with *set_destroy*.

Complexity $O(mn)$, where m and n are the number of members in *set1* and *set2*, respectively.

set_is_member

`int set_is_member(const Set *set, const void *data);`

Return Value 1 if the member is found, or 0 otherwise.

Description Determines whether the data specified by *data* matches that of a member in the set specified by *set*.

Complexity $O(n)$, where n is the number of members in the set.

set_is_subset

`int set_is_subset(const Set *set1, const Set *set2);`

Return Value 1 if the set is a subset, or 0 otherwise.

Description Determines whether the set specified by *set1* is a subset of the set specified by *set2*.

Complexity $O(mn)$, where m and n are the number of members in *set1* and *set2*, respectively.

set_is_equal

```
int set_is_equal(const Set *set1, const Set *set2);
```

Return Value   1 if the two sets are equal, or 0 otherwise.

Description   Determines whether the set specified by *set1* is equal to the set specified by *set2*.

Complexity $O(mn)$, where m and n are the number of members in *set1* and *set2*, respectively.

set_size

```
int set_size(const Set *set);
```

Return Value   Number of members in the set.

Description   Macro that evaluates to the number of members in the set specified by *set*.

Complexity $O(1)$

Implementation and Analysis of Sets

The structure *Set* is the set data structure. A good way to implement a set is as a linked list. A simple way to do this is to typedef *Set* to *List* (see Example 7-1). In addition to simplicity, using a typedef has the benefit of making the set somewhat polymorphic, just as was described for stacks and queues (see Chapter 6, *Stacks and Queues*). Thus, because the set is a linked list, we can use linked list operations on it when we want it to act like one. The biggest benefit of this with sets is that we can use *list_next* to traverse a set, and *list_rem_next* to remove members without having to identify them by the data they store. Recall that *set_remove* only removes members keyed by their data, which can be a problem when we do not know the members a set contains.

In general, the set operations presented here are somewhat costly, primarily because many of them search for members of one set in another by traversing each member. However, we can improve the running times of these operations by using a more efficient searching technique, such as hashing (see Chapter 8, *Hash Tables*). Nevertheless, the implementation provided here is a general-purpose approach whose performance is adequate for small to medium-sized sets of data.

Example 7-1. Header for the Set Abstract Datatype

```
/*****************************************************************************
*                                                                          *
*  ------------------------------- set.h -------------------------------    *
*                                                                          *
*****************************************************************************/
```

Example 7-1. Header for the Set Abstract Datatype (continued)

```c
#ifndef SET_H
#define SET_H

#include <stdlib.h>

#include "list.h"

/*****************************************************************************
*                                                                           *
*  Implement sets as linked lists.                                          *
*                                                                           *
*****************************************************************************/

typedef List Set;

/*****************************************************************************
*                                                                           *
*  --------------------------- Public Interface ---------------------------  *
*                                                                           *
*****************************************************************************/

void set_init(Set *set, int (*match)(const void *key1, const void *key2),
   void (*destroy)(void *data));

#define set_destroy list_destroy

int set_insert(Set *set, const void *data);

int set_remove(Set *set, void **data);

int set_union(Set *setu, const Set *set1, const Set *set2);

int set_intersection(Set *seti, const Set *set1, const Set *set2);

int set_difference(Set *setd, const Set *set1, const Set *set2);

int set_is_member(const Set *set, const void *data);

int set_is_subset(const Set *set1, const Set *set2);

int set_is_equal(const Set *set1, const Set *set2);

#define set_size(set) ((set)->size)

#endif
```

set_init

The *set_init* operation initializes a set so that it can be used in other operations (see Example 7-2). Since a set is a linked list, *list_init* is called to initialize it. The `match` member is set to `match` by hand because this member is not used by linked lists and is therefore not set by *list_init*.

The runtime complexity of *set_init* is the same as *list_init*, or $O(1)$.

set_destroy

The *set_destroy* operation destroys a set (see Example 7-1). Since a set is a linked list and requires being destroyed in the same manner, *set_destroy* is defined to *list_destroy*.

The runtime complexity of *set_destroy* is the same as *list_destroy*, or $O(n)$, where n is the number of members in the set.

set_insert

The *set_insert* operation inserts a member into a set (see Example 7-2). Since a member must not occur more than once in a set, *set_is_member* is called to make sure that the set does not already contain the new member. As long as the member does not already exist in the set, *list_ins_next* is called to insert the member.

The runtime complexity of *set_insert* is $O(n)$ because *set_is_member* runs in $O(n)$ time, and *list_ins_next* runs in $O(1)$.

set_remove

The *set_remove* operation removes a member from a set by traversing it using *list_next* until `match` determines that the member to be removed has been found (see Example 7-2). The pointer `prev` points just before the member to be removed since this is required by *list_rem_next*. The *list_rem_next* operation sets `data` to point to the data from the member removed.

The runtime complexity of *set_remove* is $O(n)$, where n is the number of elements in the set. This is because, in the worst case, the entire set must be traversed in order to find the member to be removed. This results in n times $O(1)$, the cost of the statements within the loop, for a running time of $O(n)$ overall. Once the member is found, *list_rem_next* removes it in $O(1)$ time.

set_union

The *set_union* operation builds a set, `setu`, which is the union of the sets `set1` and `set2` (see Example 7-2). First, `setu` is initialized by calling *set_init*. Next, the members of `set1` are inserted into `setu` by calling *list_ins_next* repeatedly for each member of `set1`. Finally, the members of `set2` are inserted into `setu` in a similar manner except that *set_is_member* is called before each insertion to ensure that no members are duplicated in `setu`.

The runtime complexity of *set_union* is $O(mn)$, where m is the size of `set1` and n is the size of `set2`. In the first loop, each member of `set1` is traversed and inserted into *setu*, which results in a running time of $O(m)$. In the second loop, each element of *set2* is traversed, which results in n times the cost of the statements within this loop. This loop contains the $O(m)$ operation *set_is_member*. Therefore, the overall complexity of the loop is $O(mn)$. Since the two loops are executed one after another, the complexity of *set_union* is the more expensive of the two, or $O(mn)$.

set_intersection

The *set_intersection* operation builds a set, *seti*, which is the intersection of the sets *set1* and *set2* (see Example 7-2). First, *seti* is initialized by calling *set_init*. Next, for each member of *set1*, *set_is_member* is called to determine whether the member is in *set2*. If so, the member is inserted into *seti*.

The runtime complexity of *set_intersection* is $O(mn)$, where m is the size of *set1* and n is the size of *set2*. This is because for each member in *set1*, the $O(n)$ operation *set_is_member* is called to determine whether the member is in *set2*.

set_difference

The *set_difference* operation builds a set, *setd*, which is the difference of the sets *set1* and *set2* (see Example 7-2). First, *setd* is initialized by calling *set_init*. Next, for each member of *set1*, *set_is_member* is called to determine whether the member is in *set2*. If not, the member is inserted into *setd*.

The runtime complexity of *set_difference* is $O(mn)$, where m is the size of *set1* and n is the size of *set2*. This is because for each member in *set1*, the $O(n)$ operation *set_is_member* is called to determine whether the member is in *set2*.

set_is_member

The *set_is_member* operation determines whether a particular member exists in a set (see Example 7-2). This is accomplished by traversing the set using *list_next* until either a member matching *data* is found or all members are traversed.

The runtime complexity of *set_is_member* is $O(n)$, where n is the number of members in the set. This is because, in the worst case, the entire set must be traversed to find the member for which we are searching.

set_is_subset

The *set_is_subset* operation determines whether one set, *set1*, is a subset of another set, *set2* (see Example 7-2). Since a set that is a subset of another must be the same size or smaller, we begin by comparing sizes. If this test fails, then *set1* is not a subset of *set2*. Otherwise, *set1* is traversed using *list_next* until either a member of *set1* that is not in *set2* is found or all members are traversed. If we find a member of *set1* not in *set2*, then *set1* is not a subset of *set2*. If we end up traversing all members of *set1*, then *set1* is a subset of *set2*.

The runtime complexity of *set_is_subset* is $O(mn)$, where m is the size of *set1* and n is the size of *set2*. This is because for each member in *set1*, the $O(n)$ operation *set_is_member* is called to determine whether the member is in *set2*.

set_is_equal

The *set_is_equal* operation determines whether one set, *set1*, is equal to another set, *set2* (see Example 7-2). Since two sets that are equal must be the same size, we begin by comparing sizes. If the two sets are not the same size, then they are not equal. If the two sets are the same size, we need only return the result of whether *set1* is a subset of *set2*. This is determined by calling *set_is_subset*.

The runtime complexity of *set_is_equal* is $O(mn)$, where m is the size of *set1* and n is the size of *set2*. This is because *set_is_subset* runs in $O(mn)$ time.

set_size

This macro evaluates to the size of a set (see Example 7-1). It works by accessing the *size* member of the *Set* structure.

The runtime complexity of *set_size* is $O(1)$ because accessing a member of a structure is a simple task that runs in a constant amount of time.

Example 7-2. Implementation of the Set Abstract Datatype

```
/*****************************************************************************
 *                                                                          *
 *  ------------------------------- set.c ---------------------------------  *
 *                                                                          *
 *****************************************************************************/

#include <stdlib.h>
#include <string.h>

#include "list.h"
#include "set.h"

/*****************************************************************************
 *                                                                          *
 *  ----------------------------- set_init -----------------------------  *
 *                                                                          *
 *****************************************************************************/

void set_init(Set *set, int (*match)(const void *key1, const void *key2),
   void (*destroy)(void *data)) {
```

Example 7-2. Implementation of the Set Abstract Datatype (continued)

```
/***************************************************************************
*                                                                         *
*  Initialize the set.                                                    *
*                                                                         *
***************************************************************************/

list_init(set, destroy);
set->match = match;

return;

}

/***************************************************************************
*                                                                         *
*  ---------------------------- set_insert ----------------------------   *
*                                                                         *
***************************************************************************/

int set_insert(Set *set, const void *data) {

/***************************************************************************
*                                                                         *
*  Do not allow the insertion of duplicates.                             *
*                                                                         *
***************************************************************************/

if (set_is_member(set, data))
   return 1;

/***************************************************************************
*                                                                         *
*  Insert the data.                                                       *
*                                                                         *
***************************************************************************/

return list_ins_next(set, list_tail(set), data);

}

/***************************************************************************
*                                                                         *
*  ---------------------------- set_remove ----------------------------   *
*                                                                         *
***************************************************************************/

int set_remove(Set *set, void **data) {

ListElmt          *member,
                  *prev;
```

Example 7-2. Implementation of the Set Abstract Datatype (continued)

```
/*****************************************************************************
*                                                                           *
*  Find the member to remove.                                               *
*                                                                           *
*****************************************************************************/

prev = NULL;

for (member = list_head(set); member != NULL; member = list_next(member)) {

   if (set->match(*data, list_data(member)))
      break;

   prev = member;

}

/*****************************************************************************
*                                                                           *
*  Return if the member was not found.                                      *
*                                                                           *
*****************************************************************************/

if (member == NULL)
   return -1;

/*****************************************************************************
*                                                                           *
*  Remove the member.                                                       *
*                                                                           *
*****************************************************************************/

return list_rem_next(set, prev, data);

}

/*****************************************************************************
*                                                                           *
*  ----------------------------- set_union -----------------------------    *
*                                                                           *
*****************************************************************************/

int set_union(Set *setu, const Set *set1, const Set *set2) {

ListElmt           *member;

void               *data;

/*****************************************************************************
*                                                                           *
*  Initialize the set for the union.                                        *
*                                                                           *
*****************************************************************************/
```

Example 7-2. Implementation of the Set Abstract Datatype (continued)

```
set_init(setu, set1->match, NULL);

/***************************************************************************
*                                                                         *
*  Insert the members of the first set.                                   *
*                                                                         *
***************************************************************************/

for (member = list_head(set1); member != NULL; member = list_next(member)) {

   data = list_data(member);

   if (list_ins_next(setu, list_tail(setu), data) != 0) {

      set_destroy(setu);
      return -1;

   }

}

/***************************************************************************
*                                                                         *
*  Insert the members of the second set.                                  *
*                                                                         *
***************************************************************************/

for (member = list_head(set2); member != NULL; member = list_next(member)) {

   if (set_is_member(set1, list_data(member))) {

      /*********************************************************************
      *                                                                   *
      *  Do not allow the insertion of duplicates.                        *
      *                                                                   *
      *********************************************************************/

      continue;

      }

   else {

      data = list_data(member);

      if (list_ins_next(setu, list_tail(setu), data) != 0) {

         set_destroy(setu);
         return -1;

      }

      }
```

Example 7-2. Implementation of the Set Abstract Datatype (continued)

```
}

return 0;

}

/***************************************************************************
*                                                                         *
*  -------------------------- set_intersection --------------------------  *
*                                                                         *
***************************************************************************/

int set_intersection(Set *seti, const Set *set1, const Set *set2) {

ListElmt          *member;

void              *data;

/***************************************************************************
*                                                                         *
*  Initialize the set for the intersection.                               *
*                                                                         *
***************************************************************************/

set_init(seti, set1->match, NULL);

/***************************************************************************
*                                                                         *
*  Insert the members present in both sets.                               *
*                                                                         *
***************************************************************************/

for (member = list_head(set1); member != NULL; member = list_next(member)) {

   if (set_is_member(set2, list_data(member))) {

      data = list_data(member);

      if (list_ins_next(seti, list_tail(seti), data) != 0) {

         set_destroy(seti);
         return -1;

      }

   }

}

return 0;

}
```

Example 7-2. Implementation of the Set Abstract Datatype (continued)

```
/***************************************************************************
*                                                                         *
*  --------------------------- set_difference --------------------------  *
*                                                                         *
***************************************************************************/

int set_difference(Set *setd, const Set *set1, const Set *set2) {

ListElmt          *member;

void              *data;

/***************************************************************************
*                                                                         *
*  Initialize the set for the difference.                                 *
*                                                                         *
***************************************************************************/

set_init(setd, set1->match, NULL);

/***************************************************************************
*                                                                         *
*  Insert the members from set1 not in set2.                              *
*                                                                         *
***************************************************************************/

for (member = list_head(set1); member != NULL; member = list_next(member)) {

   if (!set_is_member(set2, list_data(member))) {

      data = list_data(member);

      if (list_ins_next(setd, list_tail(setd), data) != 0) {

         set_destroy(setd);
         return -1;

      }

   }

}

return 0;

}

/***************************************************************************
*                                                                         *
*  --------------------------- set_is_member ---------------------------  *
*                                                                         *
***************************************************************************/

int set_is_member(const Set *set, const void *data) {
```

Example 7-2. Implementation of the Set Abstract Datatype (continued)

```c
ListElmt            *member;

/*****************************************************************************
*                                                                           *
*  Determine if the data is a member of the set.                            *
*                                                                           *
*****************************************************************************/

for (member = list_head(set); member != NULL; member = list_next(member)) {

   if (set->match(data, list_data(member)))
      return 1;

}

return 0;

}

/*****************************************************************************
*                                                                           *
*  --------------------------- set_is_subset ---------------------------    *
*                                                                           *
*****************************************************************************/

int set_is_subset(const Set *set1, const Set *set2) {

ListElmt            *member;

/*****************************************************************************
*                                                                           *
*  Do a quick test to rule out some cases.                                  *
*                                                                           *
*****************************************************************************/

if (set_size(set1) > set_size(set2))
   return 0;

/*****************************************************************************
*                                                                           *
*  Determine if set1 is a subset of set2.                                   *
*                                                                           *
*****************************************************************************/

for (member = list_head(set1); member != NULL; member = list_next(member)) {

   if (!set_is_member(set2, list_data(member)))
      return 0;

}

return 1;

}
```

Example 7-2. Implementation of the Set Abstract Datatype (continued)

```
/*****************************************************************************
*                                                                           *
*  --------------------------- set_is_equal ---------------------------      *
*                                                                           *
*****************************************************************************/

int set_is_equal(const Set *set1, const Set *set2) {

/*****************************************************************************
*                                                                           *
*  Do a quick test to rule out some cases.                                  *
*                                                                           *
*****************************************************************************/

if (set_size(set1) != set_size(set2))
   return 0;

/*****************************************************************************
*                                                                           *
*  Sets of the same size are equal if they are subsets.                     *
*                                                                           *
*****************************************************************************/

return set_is_subset(set1, set2);

}
```

Set Example: Set Covering

Set covering is an optimization problem that nicely models many problems of combinatorics and resource selection. Here is the idea: given a set S and a set P of subsets A_1 to A_n of S, set C, which is composed of one or more sets from P, is said to *cover* S if each member in S is contained in at least one of the subsets in C; in addition, C contains as few sets from P as possible.

As an example, imagine trying to form a team from a large set of candidate players, each with a certain set of skills. The goal is to form the smallest team possible possessing a certain set of skills overall. That is, for any skill required by the team as a whole, at least one player on the team must possess the skill. Let S be the skills that must be present on the team, and let P be the sets of skills possessed by various candidate players. The players from P that are placed in set C together must cover all of the skills in set S. But remember, we must select as few players as possible.

The algorithm presented here for set covering is an approximation algorithm (see Chapter 1, *Introduction*). It does not always obtain the best solution, but it does come within a logarithmic bound. The algorithm works by repeatedly picking a set from P that covers the most members not yet covered in S. In other words, it tries to cover as much of S as it can as early as it can. Thus, the algorithm is greedy (see Chapter 1). As each set is selected from P, it is removed, and its members are removed from S as well. When there are no members left to cover in S, the cover set C is complete.

Let's look at finding the optimal covering of a set of twelve skills S = {a, b, c, d, e, f, g, h, i, j, k, l} considering a set of seven candidate players P = {A_1, ..., A_7}. The players in P have the following assortments of skills: A_1 = {a, b, c, d}, A_2 = {e, f, g, h, i}, A_3 = {j, k, l}, A_4 = {a, e}, A_5 = {b, f, g}, A_6 = {c, d, g, h, k, l}, and A_7 = {l}. The optimal covering is C = {A_1, A_2, A_3}. The algorithm presented here selects the set C = {A_6, A_2, A_1, A_3} (see Figure 7-2).

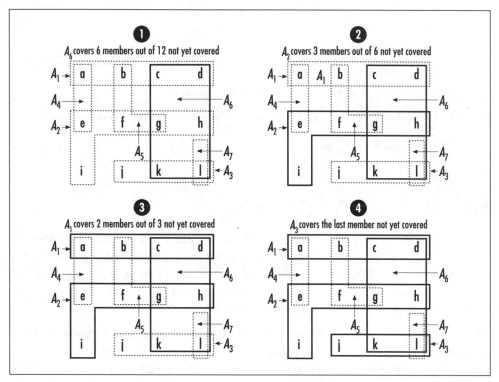

Figure 7-2. A set covering problem

Examples 7-3 and 7-4 present a function, *cover,* that determines a nearly optimal covering of S considering the subsets A_1 to A_n in P. The function has three arguments: **members** is the set S to be covered, **subsets** is the set of subsets in P, and **covering** is the set C returned as the covering. The function modifies all three sets passed to it, so copies should be made before calling the function, if necessary.

To begin, **covering** is initialized by calling *set_init.* The outermost loop iterates as long as there are noncovered members in **members** and the algorithm has not run out of subsets for the covering. Inside this loop, during each iteration, it finds the set in *subsets* that produces the largest intersection with *members*. It then adds this set to the covering and removes its members from *members*. Last in the loop, the selected set is removed from *subsets*. If the outermost loop terminates with *members* not empty, then a complete covering was not possible using the sets in *subsets*. This is also the case if during any iteration none of the sets in *subsets* intersects with *members*. The function *cover* returns 0 if it finds a covering, 1 if a covering is not possible, or −1 otherwise.

The runtime complexity of *cover* is $O(m^3)$, where m is the initial number of members in *members*. This occurs when there is exactly one subset in *subsets* for each member in *members*; consequently, there are m subsets. In this case, *set-intersection* runs in $O(m)$ time because each subset contains only one member to traverse when computing the intersection with *members*. Thus, the inner loop of *cover* is $O(m^2)$ and this loop is executed m times.

Example 7-3. Header for Set Covering

```
/****************************************************************************
*                                                                          *
*   ------------------------------ cover.h ------------------------------   *
*                                                                          *
****************************************************************************/

#ifndef COVER_H
#define COVER_H

#include "set.h"

/****************************************************************************
*                                                                          *
*   Define a structure for subsets identified by a key.                    *
*                                                                          *
****************************************************************************/

typedef struct KSet_ {

void             *key;
Set              set;

} KSet;

/****************************************************************************
*                                                                          *
*   -------------------------- Public Interface --------------------------  *
*                                                                          *
****************************************************************************/

int cover(Set *members, Set *subsets, Set *covering);

#endif
```

Example 7-4. Implementation of a Function for Set Covering

```c
/***************************************************************************
*                                                                         *
*  ----------------------------- cover.c -----------------------------    *
*                                                                         *
***************************************************************************/

#include <stdlib.h>

#include "cover.h"
#include "list.h"
#include "set.h"

/***************************************************************************
*                                                                         *
*  ------------------------------ cover ------------------------------    *
*                                                                         *
***************************************************************************/

int cover(Set *members, Set *subsets, Set *covering) {

Set                intersection;

KSet               *subset;

ListElmt           *member,
                   *max_member;

void               *data;

int                max_size;

/***************************************************************************
*                                                                         *
*  Initialize the covering.                                               *
*                                                                         *
***************************************************************************/

set_init(covering, subsets->match, NULL);

/***************************************************************************
*                                                                         *
*  Continue while there are noncovered members and candidate subsets.     *
*                                                                         *
***************************************************************************/

while (set_size(members) > 0 && set_size(subsets) > 0) {

   /***************************************************************************
   *                                                                         *
   *  Find the subset that covers the most members.                          *
   *                                                                         *
   ***************************************************************************/
```

Example 7-4. Implementation of a Function for Set Covering (continued)

```c
max_size = 0;

for (member = list_head(subsets); member != NULL; member =
   list_next(member)) {

   if (set_intersection(&intersection, &((KSet *)list_data(member))->set,
      members) != 0) {

      return -1;

   }

   if (set_size(&intersection) > max_size) {

      max_member = member;
      max_size = set_size(&intersection);

   }

   set_destroy(&intersection);

}

/***************************************************************************
*                                                                         *
*  A covering is not possible if there was no intersection.               *
*                                                                         *
***************************************************************************/

if (max_size == 0)
   return 1;

/***************************************************************************
*                                                                         *
*  Insert the selected subset into the covering.                          *
*                                                                         *
***************************************************************************/

subset = (KSet *)list_data(max_member);

if (set_insert(covering, subset) != 0)
   return -1;

/***************************************************************************
*                                                                         *
*  Remove each covered member from the set of noncovered members.         *
*                                                                         *
***************************************************************************/

for (member = list_head(&((KSet *)list_data(max_member))->set); member !=
   NULL; member = list_next(member)) {

   data = list_data(member);
```

Example 7-4. Implementation of a Function for Set Covering (continued)

```
        if (set_remove(members, (void**)&data) == 0 && members->destroy != NULL)
           members->destroy(data);

    }

    /**************************************************************************
    *                                                                        *
    *   Remove the subset from the set of candidate subsets.                 *
    *                                                                        *
    **************************************************************************/

    if (set_remove(subsets, (void **)&subset) != 0)
       return -1;

}

/**************************************************************************
*                                                                        *
*   No covering is possible if there are still noncovered members.       *
*                                                                        *
**************************************************************************/

if (set_size(members) > 0)
   return -1;

return 0;

}
```

Questions and Answers

Q: *Instead of implementing* set_is_subset *as shown, how could we use other set operations to determine if one set, S_1, is a subset of another set, S_2? Why is* set_is_subset *provided?*

A: In set notation, if $S_1 \cap S_2 = S_1$, then $S_1 \subset S_2$. Therefore, we could use a combination of the *set_intersection* and *set_is_equal* operations. Whether we implement this operation as shown or use *set_intersection* and *set_is_equal*, its runtime complexity is $O(mn)$, where m is the size of S_1 and n is the size of S_2. However, in the case of calling *set_intersection* and *set_is_equal*, the running time is actually closer to $T(m, n) = 2mn$ because both *set_intersection* and *set_is_equal* run in $T(m, n) = mn$ times some constant. Compare this with the operation *set_is_subset*, which runs closer to $T(m, n) = mn$. Although the complexities of the two methods are the same, calling *set_intersection* and *set_is_equal* requires approximately double the time in practice.

Q: *Instead of implementing* set_is_equal *as shown, how could we use other set operations to determine if one set, S_1, is equal to another set, S_2?*

A: In set notation, if $S_1 - S_2 = \emptyset$ and $S_2 - S_1 = \emptyset$, then $S_1 = S_2$. Therefore, we could implement this, albeit less efficiently, using two calls to *set_difference* and two calls to *set_size*.

Q: *Instead of implementing* set_intersection *as shown, how could we use the* set_difference *operation to compute the intersection of two sets,* S_1 *and* S_2?

A: In set notation, $S_1 \cap S_2 = S_1 - (S_1 - S_2)$. Therefore, we could implement this, albeit less efficiently, using two calls to *set_difference*.

Q: *Why was* list_ins_next *used instead of* set_insert *to insert members into the sets built within* set_union, set_intersection, *and* set_difference?

A: Recall that the running time of *set_insert* is $O(n)$ because it traverses a set to ensure that the member being inserted is not duplicated. Since the *set_union*, *set_intersection*, and *set_difference* operations ensure this already, it is considerably more efficient to call the $O(1)$ operation *list_ins_next* instead.

Q: *Suppose we have three sets,* $S_1 = \{1, 2, 3\}$, $S_2 = \{1, 4, 5\}$, *and* $S_3 = \{1\}$. *What is the result of the set operations* $S_1 \cup S_2$, $S_1 - (S_2 \cap S_3)$, *and* $(S_1 \cap S_2) - S_3$?

A: $S_1 \cup S_2 = \{1, 2, 3, 4, 5\}$, $S_1 - (S_2 \cap S_3) = \{2, 3\}$, and $(S_1 \cap S_2) - S_3 = \emptyset$.

Q: *Using the properties and basic operations presented for sets, simplify* $(((S_1 \cap S_2) \cup (S_1 \cap S_3)) - (S_1 \cap (S_2 \cup S_3))) \cup (S_1 \cap S_2)$.

A: $(((S_1 \cap S_2) \cup (S_1 \cap S_3)) - (S_1 \cap (S_2 \cup S_3))) \cup (S_1 \cap S_2)$

Applying the distributive law produces:

$((S_1 \cap (S_2 \cup S_3)) - (S_1 \cap (S_2 \cup S_3))) \cup (S_1 \cap S_2)$

Applying set difference produces:

$\emptyset \cup (S_1 \cap S_2)$

Applying the empty set law produces:

$S_1 \cap S_2$

Q: *The symmetric difference of two sets consists of those members that are in either of the two sets, but not both. The notation for the symmetric difference of two sets,* S_1 *and* S_2, *is* $S_1 \triangle S_2$. *How could we implement a symmetric difference operation using the set operations presented in this chapter? Could this operation be implemented more efficiently some other way?*

A: In set notation, $S_1 \triangle S_2 = (S_1 - S_2) \cup (S_2 - S_1)$. Therefore, we could implement this operation using two calls to *set_difference* followed by a call to *set_union*. This produces a worst-case running time of $T(m, n) = 3mn$ times some constant, for a complexity of $O(mn)$, where m is the size of S_1 and n is the size of

S_2. For example, consider the sets S_1 = {1, 2, 3} and S_2 = {4, 5, 6}, which represent a worst-case scenario. To compute $S_1 - S_2$, we must search all of S_2 for each member in S_1, which results in the set {1, 2, 3}. Similarly, to compute $S_2 - S_1$, we must search all of S_1 for each member of S_2, which results in the set {4, 5, 6}. Since both sets are the same size as the original sets, sizes m and n, their union is another operation that runs in time proportionate to m times n. However, since we know that the sets produced by $S_1 - S_2$ and $S_2 - S_1$ will not generate any duplicate members between them, we could avoid the use of *set_union* and simply insert each member into the final set by calling the $O(1)$ operation *list_ins_next* once for each member $m + n$ times. This is a better implementation in practice, but it does not change the overall complexity.

Q: A multiset (see the related topics at the end of the chapter) is a type of set that allows members to occur more than once. How would the runtime complexities of inserting and removing members with a multiset compare with the operations for inserting and removing members in this chapter?

A: When inserting a member into a set, in which members may not be duplicated, we must search the entire set to ensure that we do not duplicate a member. This is an $O(n)$ process. Removing a member from a set is $O(n)$ as well because we may have to search the entire set again. In a multiset, inserting a member is considerably more efficient because we do not have to traverse the members looking for duplicates. Therefore, we can insert the new member in $O(1)$ time. In a multiset, removing a member remains an $O(n)$ process because we still must search for the member we want to remove.

Related Topics

Venn diagrams

Graphical representations of sets that help determine the results of set operations visually. For example, a Venn diagram depicting two intersecting sets consists of two slightly overlapping circles. The overlapping regions represent the intersection of the sets.

Bit-vector representation

A representation for sets useful when the universe is small and known. Each member in the universe is represented as a bit in an array. If a member exists in the set, its bit is set to 1; otherwise, its bit is set to 0.

Multisets

Sets in which members may be duplicated. In some problems the restriction of no duplicate members is too strict. A multiset is an alternative type of set for these problems.

8

Hash Tables

Hash tables support one of the most efficient types of searching: *hashing*. Fundamentally, a hash table consists of an array in which data is accessed via a special index called a *key*. The primary idea behind a hash table is to establish a mapping between the set of all possible keys and positions in the array using a *hash function*. A hash function accepts a key and returns its *hash coding*, or *hash value*. Keys vary in type, but hash codings are always integers.

Since both computing a hash value and indexing into an array can be performed in constant time, the beauty of hashing is that we can use it to perform constant-time searches. When a hash function can guarantee that no two keys will generate the same hash coding, the resulting hash table is said to be *directly addressed*. This is ideal, but direct addressing is rarely possible in practice. For example, imagine a phone-mail system in which eight-character names are hashed to find messages for users in the system. If we were to rely on direct addressing, the hash table would contain more than $26^8 = (2.09)10^{11}$ entries, and the majority would be unused since most character combinations are not names.

Typically, the number of entries in a hash table is small relative to the universe of possible keys. Consequently, most hash functions map some keys to the same position in the table. When two keys map to the same position, they *collide*. A good hash function minimizes collisions, but we must still be prepared to deal with them. This chapter presents two types of hash tables that resolve collisions in different ways.

This chapter covers:

Chained hash tables
> Hash tables that store data in *buckets*. Each bucket is a linked list that can grow as large as necessary to accommodate collisions.

Open-addressed hash tables

Hash tables that store data in the table itself instead of in buckets. Collisions are resolved using various methods of probing the table.

Selecting a hash function

The crux of hashing. By distributing keys in a random manner about the table, collisions are minimized. Thus, it is important to select a hash function that accomplishes this.

Collision resolution

Methods of managing when several keys map to the same index. Chained hash tables have an inherent way to resolve collisions. Open-addressed hash tables use various forms of probing.

Some applications of hash tables are:

Database systems

Specifically, those that require efficient random access. Generally, database systems try to optimize between two types of access methods: sequential and random. Hash tables are an important part of efficient random access because they provide a way to locate data in a constant amount of time.

Symbol tables (illustrated in this chapter)

The tables used by compilers to maintain information about symbols from a program. Compilers access information about symbols frequently. Therefore, it is important that symbol tables be implemented very efficiently.

Tagged buffers

A mechanism for storing and retrieving data in a machine-independent manner. Each data member resides at a fixed offset in the buffer. A hash table is stored in the buffer so that the location of each tagged member can be ascertained quickly. One use of a tagged buffer is sending structured data across a network to a machine whose byte ordering and structure alignment may not be the same as the original host's. The buffer handles these concerns as the data is stored and extracted member by member.

Data dictionaries

Data structures that support adding, deleting, and searching for data. Although the operations of a hash table and a data dictionary are similar, other data structures may be used to implement data dictionaries. Using a hash table is particularly efficient.

Associative arrays

Most commonly used in languages that do not support structured types. Associative arrays consist of data arranged so that the nth element of one array corresponds to the nth element of another. Associative arrays are useful for indexing a logical grouping of data by several key fields. A hash table helps to key into each array efficiently.

Description of Chained Hash Tables

A chained hash table fundamentally consists of an array of linked lists. Each list forms a *bucket* in which we place all elements hashing to a specific position in the array (see Figure 8-1). To insert an element, we first pass its key to a hash function in a process called *hashing the key*. This tells us in which bucket the element belongs. We then insert the element at the head of the appropriate list. To look up or remove an element, we hash its key again to find its bucket, then traverse the appropriate list until we find the element we are looking for. Because each bucket is a linked list, a chained hash table is not limited to a fixed number of elements. However, performance degrades if the table becomes too full.

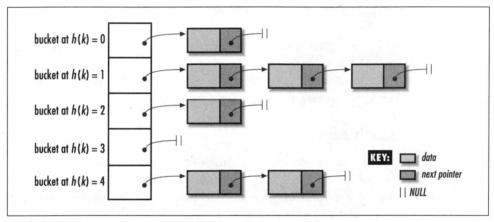

Figure 8-1. A chained hash table with five buckets containing a total of seven elements

Collision Resolution

When two keys hash to the same position in a hash table, they *collide*. Chained hash tables have a simple solution for resolving collisions: elements are simply placed in the bucket where the collision occurs. One problem with this, however, is that if an excessive number of collisions occur at a specific position, a bucket becomes longer and longer. Thus, accessing its elements takes more and more time.

Ideally, we would like all buckets to grow at the same rate so that they remain nearly the same size and as small as possible. In other words, the goal is to distribute elements about the table in as uniform and random a manner as possible. This theoretically perfect situation is known as *uniform hashing*; however, in practice it usually can only be approximated.

Even assuming uniform hashing, performance degrades significantly if we make the number of buckets in the table small relative to the number of elements we plan to insert. In this situation, all of the buckets become longer and longer. Thus, it is important to pay close attention to a hash table's *load factor*. The load factor of a hash table is defined as:

$$\alpha = n/m$$

where *n* is the number of elements in the table and *m* is the number of positions into which elements may be hashed. The load factor of a chained hash table indicates the maximum number of elements we can *expect* to encounter in a bucket, assuming uniform hashing.

For example, in a chained hash table with *m* = 1699 buckets and a total of *n* = 3198 elements, the load factor of the table is α = 3198/1699 = 2. Therefore, in this case, we can expect to encounter no more than two elements while searching any one bucket. When the load factor of a table drops below 1, each position will probably contain no more than one element. Of course, since uniform hashing is only approximated, in actuality we end up encountering somewhat more or less than what the load factor suggests. How close we come to uniform hashing ultimately depends on how well we select our hash function.

Selecting a Hash Function

The goal of a good hash function is to approximate uniform hashing, that is, to spread elements about a hash table in as uniform and random a manner as possible. A hash function *h* is a function we define to map a key *k* to some position *x* in a hash table. *x* is called the *hash coding* of *k*. Formally stated:

$$h(k) = x$$

Generally, most hashing methods assume *k* to be an integer so that it may be easily altered mathematically to make *h* distribute elements throughout the table more uniformly. When *k* is not an integer, we can usually coerce it into one without much difficulty.

Precisely how to coerce a set of keys depends a great deal on the characteristics of the keys themselves. Therefore, it is important to gain as much of a qualitative understanding of them in a particular application as we can. For example, if we were to hash the identifiers found in a program, we might observe that many have similar prefixes and suffixes since developers tend to gravitate toward variables such as *sampleptr*, *simpleptr*, and *sentryptr*. A poor way to coerce these keys would be any method depending strictly on characters at the beginning and end of the keys, since this would result in many of the same integers for *k*. On the other hand, we might try selecting characters from four positions that have the propensity to be somewhat random, permute them in a way that randomizes them further, and stuff them into specific bytes of a four-byte integer. Whatever approach we choose for coercing keys, the most important thing to remember, again, is that a hash function should distribute a set of keys about a hash table in a uniform and random manner.

Division method

Once we have a key k represented as an integer, one of the simplest hashing methods is to map it into one of m positions in a table by taking the remainder of k divided by m. This is called the *division method*. Formally stated:

$$h(k) = k \bmod m$$

Using this method, if the table has $m = 1699$ positions, and we hash the key $k = 25,657$, the hash coding is $25,657 \bmod 1699 = 172$. Typically, we should avoid values for m that are powers of 2. This is because if $m = 2^p$, h becomes just the p lowest-order bits of k. Usually we choose m to be a prime number not too close to a power of 2, while considering storage constraints and load factor.

For example, if we expect to insert around $n = 4500$ elements into a chained hash table, we might choose $m = 1699$, a good prime number between 2^{10} and 2^{11}. This results in a load factor of $\alpha = 4500/1699 \approx 2.6$, which indicates that generally two or three elements will reside in each bucket, assuming uniform hashing.

Multiplication method

An alternative to the division method is to multiply the integer key k by a constant A in the range $0 < A < 1$; extract the fractional part; multiply this value by the number of positions in the table, m; and take the floor of the result. Typically, A is chosen to be 0.618, which is the square root of 5, minus 1, all divided by 2. This method is called the *multiplication method*. Formally stated:

$$h(k) = \lfloor m(kA \bmod 1) \rfloor, \text{ where } A \approx (\sqrt{5} - 1)/2 = 0.618$$

An advantage to this method is that m, the number of positions in the table, is not as critical as in the division method. For example, if the table contains $m = 2000$ positions, and we hash the key $k = 6341$, the hash coding is $\lfloor (2000)((6341)(0.618) \bmod 1) \rfloor = \lfloor (2000)(3918.738 \bmod 1) \rfloor = \lfloor (2000)(0.738) \rfloor = 1476$.

In a chained hash table, if we expect to insert no more than $n = 4500$ elements, we might let $m = 2250$. This results in a load factor of $\alpha = 4500/2250 = 2$, which indicates that no more than two traversals should be required to locate an element in any bucket, assuming uniform hashing. Again, notice how this method of hashing allows more flexibility in choosing m to suit the maximum number of traversals acceptable to us.

Example 8-1 presents a hash function that performs particularly well for strings. It coerces a key into a permuted integer through a series of bit operations. The resulting integer is mapped using the division method. The function was adapted from *Compilers: Principles, Techniques, and Tools* (Reading, MA: Addison-Wesley, 1986), by Alfred V. Aho, Ravi Sethi, and Jeffrey D. Ullman, who attributed it to P. J. Weinberger as a hash function that performed well in hashing strings for his compiler.

Example 8-1. A Hash Function That Performs Well for Strings

```
/*****************************************************************************
*                                                                           *
*  ----------------------------- hashpjw.c -----------------------------    *
*                                                                           *
*****************************************************************************/

#include "hashpjw.h"

/*****************************************************************************
*                                                                           *
*  ------------------------------ hashpjw ------------------------------    *
*                                                                           *
*****************************************************************************/

int hashpjw(const void *key) {

const char        *ptr;

int               val;

/*****************************************************************************
*                                                                           *
*  Hash the key by performing a number of bit operations on it.             *
*                                                                           *
*****************************************************************************/

val = 0;
ptr = key;

while (*ptr != '\0') {

   int tmp;

   val = (val << 4) + (*ptr);

   if (tmp = (val & 0xf0000000)) {

      val = val ^ (tmp >> 24);
      val = val ^ tmp;

   }

   ptr++;

}
```

Example 8-1. A Hash Function That Performs Well for Strings (continued)

```
/**************************************************************************
*                                                                        *
*   In practice, replace PRIME_TBLSIZ with the actual table size.        *
*                                                                        *
**************************************************************************/

return val % PRIME_TBLSIZ;

}
```

Interface for Chained Hash Tables

chtbl_init

```
int chtbl_init(CHTbl *htbl, int buckets, int (*h)(const void *key),
   int (*match)(const void *key1, const void *key2),
   void (*destroy)(void *data));
```

Return Value   0 if initializing the hash table is successful, or –1 otherwise.

Description   Initializes the chained hash table specified by ***htbl***. This operation must be called for a chained hash table before the hash table can be used with any other operation. The number of buckets allocated in the hash table is specified by ***buckets***. The function pointer ***h*** specifies a user-defined hash function for hashing keys. The function pointer ***match*** specifies a user-defined function to determine whether two keys match. It should return 1 if ***key1*** is equal to ***key2***, and 0 otherwise. The ***destroy*** argument provides a way to free dynamically allocated data when *chtbl_destroy* is called. For example, if the hash table contains data dynamically allocated using *malloc*, ***destroy*** should be set to *free* to free the data as the hash table is destroyed. For structured data containing several dynamically allocated members, ***destroy*** should be set to a user-defined function that calls *free* for each dynamically allocated member as well as for the structure itself. For a hash table containing data that should not be freed, ***destroy*** should be set to NULL.

Complexity $O(m)$, where m is the number of buckets in the hash table.

chtbl_destroy

```
void chtbl_destroy(CHTbl *htbl);
```

Return Value   None.

Description   Destroys the chained hash table specified by ***htbl***. No other operations are permitted after calling *chtbl_destroy* unless *chtbl_init* is called again. The *chtbl_destroy* operation removes all elements from a hash table and calls the function passed as *destroy* to *chtbl_init* once for each element as it is removed, provided *destroy* was not set to NULL.

Complexity $O(m)$, where m is the number of buckets in the hash table.

chtbl_insert

```
int chtbl_insert(CHTbl *htbl, const void *data);
```

Return Value   0 if inserting the element is successful, 1 if the element is already in the hash table, or –1 otherwise.

Description   Inserts an element into the chained hash table specified by *htbl*. The new element contains a pointer to *data*, so the memory referenced by *data* should remain valid as long as the element remains in the hash table. It is the responsibility of the caller to manage the storage associated with *data*.

Complexity $O(1)$

chtbl_remove

```
int chtbl_remove(CHTbl *htbl, void **data);
```

Return Value   0 if removing the element is successful, or –1 otherwise.

Description   Removes the element matching *data* from the chained hash table specified by *htbl*. Upon return, *data* points to the data stored in the element that was removed. It is the responsibility of the caller to manage the storage associated with the data.

Complexity $O(1)$

chtbl_lookup

```
int chtbl_lookup(const CHTbl *htbl, void **data);
```

Return Value   0 if the element is found in the hash table, or –1 otherwise.

Description   Determines whether an element matches *data* in the chained hash table specified by *htbl*. If a match is found, *data* points to the matching data in the hash table upon return.

Complexity $O(1)$

chtbl_size

```
int chtbl_size(CHTbl *htbl);
```

Return Value   Number of elements in the hash table.

Description   Macro that evaluates to the number of elements in the chained hash table specified by *htbl*.

Complexity $O(1)$

Implementation and Analysis of Chained Hash Tables

A chained hash table consists of an array of buckets. Each bucket is a linked list containing the elements that hash to a certain position in the table. The structure *CHTbl* is the chained hash table data structure (see Example 8-2). This structure consists of six members: *buckets* is the number of buckets allocated in the table; *h*, *match*, and *destroy* are members used to encapsulate the functions passed to *chtbl_init*; *size* is the number of elements currently in the table; and *table* is the array of buckets.

Example 8-2. Header for the Chained Hash Table Abstract Datatype

```
/*****************************************************************************
*                                                                           *
*   ----------------------------- chtbl.h -----------------------------     *
*                                                                           *
*****************************************************************************/

#ifndef CHTBL_H
#define CHTBL_H

#include <stdlib.h>

#include "list.h"

/*****************************************************************************
*                                                                           *
*  Define a structure for chained hash tables.                              *
*                                                                           *
*****************************************************************************/

typedef struct CHTbl_ {

int             buckets;

int             (*h)(const void *key);
int             (*match)(const void *key1, const void *key2);
void            (*destroy)(void *data);

int             size;
List            *table;

} CHTbl;
```

Example 8-2. Header for the Chained Hash Table Abstract Datatype (continued)

```
/*****************************************************************************
*                                                                           *
*  ------------------------- Public Interface -------------------------     *
*                                                                           *
*****************************************************************************/

int chtbl_init(CHTbl *htbl, int buckets, int (*h)(const void *key), int
   (*match)(const void *key1, const void *key2), void (*destroy)(void *data));

void chtbl_destroy(CHTbl *htbl);

int chtbl_insert(CHTbl *htbl, const void *data);

int chtbl_remove(CHTbl *htbl, void **data);

int chtbl_lookup(const CHTbl *htbl, void **data);

#define chtbl_size(htbl) ((htbl)->size)

#endif
```

chtbl_init

The *chtbl_init* operation initializes a chained hash table so that it can be used in other operations (see Example 8-3). Initializing a chained hash table is a simple operation in which we allocate space for the buckets; initialize each bucket by calling *list_init*; encapsulate the `h`, `match`, and `destroy` functions; and set the `size` member to 0.

The runtime complexity of *chtbl_init* is $O(m)$, where m is the number of buckets in the table. This is because the $O(1)$ operation *list_init* must be called once for each of the m buckets. All other parts of the operation run in a constant amount of time.

chtbl_destroy

The *chtbl_destroy* operation destroys a chained hash table (see Example 8-3). Primarily this means removing the elements from each bucket and freeing the memory *chtbl_init* allocated for the table. The function passed as `destroy` to *chtbl_init* is called once for each element as it is removed, provided `destroy` was not set to NULL.

The runtime complexity of *chtbl_destroy* is $O(m)$, where m is the number of buckets in the table. This is because *list_destroy* is called once for each bucket. In each bucket, we expect to remove a number of elements equal to the load factor of the hash table, which is treated as a small constant.

chtbl_insert

The *chtbl_insert* operation inserts an element into a chained hash table (see Example 8-3). Since a key is not allowed to be inserted into the hash table more than once, *chtbl_lookup* is called to make sure that the table does not already contain the new element. If no element with the same key already exists in the hash table, we hash the key for the new element and insert it into the bucket at the position in the hash table that corresponds to the hash coding. If this is successful, we increment the table size.

Assuming we approximate uniform hashing well, the runtime complexity of *chtbl_insert* is $O(1)$, since *chtbl_lookup*, hashing a key, and inserting an element at the head of a linked list all run in a constant amount of time.

chtbl_remove

The *chtbl_remove* operation removes an element from a chained hash table (see Example 8-3). To remove the element, we hash its key, search the appropriate bucket for an element with a key that matches, and call *list_rem_next* to remove it. The pointer **prev** maintains a pointer to the element before the one to be removed since *list_rem_next* requires this. Recall that *list_rem_next* sets **data** to point to the data removed from the table. If a matching key is not found in the bucket, the element is not in the table. If removing the element is successful, we decrease the table size by 1.

Assuming we approximate uniform hashing well, the runtime complexity of *chtbl_remove* is $O(1)$. This is because we expect to search a number of elements equal to the load factor of the hash table, which is treated as a small constant.

chtbl_lookup

The *chtbl_lookup* operation searches for an element in a chained hash table and returns a pointer to it (see Example 8-3). This operation works much like *chtbl_remove*, except that once the element is found, it is not removed from the table.

Assuming we approximate uniform hashing well, the runtime complexity of *chtbl_lookup* is $O(1)$. This is because we expect to search a number of elements equal to the load factor of the hash table, which is treated as a small constant.

chtbl_size

This macro evaluates to the number of elements in a chained hash table (see Example 8-2). It works by accessing the **size** member of the **CHTbl** structure.

The runtime complexity of *chtbl_size* is $O(1)$ because accessing a member of a structure is a simple task that runs in a constant amount of time.

Example 8-3. Implementation of the Chained Hash Table Abstract Datatype

```
/****************************************************************************
*                                                                          *
*  ---------------------------- chtbl.c ----------------------------       *
*                                                                          *
****************************************************************************/

#include <stdlib.h>
#include <string.h>

#include "list.h"
#include "chtbl.h"

/****************************************************************************
*                                                                          *
*  ---------------------------- chtbl_init ----------------------------    *
*                                                                          *
****************************************************************************/

int chtbl_init(CHTbl *htbl, int buckets, int (*h)(const void *key), int
   (*match)(const void *key1, const void *key2), void (*destroy)(void*data)) {

int                i;

/****************************************************************************
*                                                                          *
*  Allocate space for the hash table.                                      *
*                                                                          *
****************************************************************************/

if ((htbl->table = (List *)malloc(buckets * sizeof(List))) == NULL)
   return -1;

/****************************************************************************
*                                                                          *
*  Initialize the buckets.                                                 *
*                                                                          *
****************************************************************************/

htbl->buckets = buckets;

for (i = 0; i < htbl->buckets; i++)
   list_init(&htbl->table[i], destroy);

/****************************************************************************
*                                                                          *
*  Encapsulate the functions.                                              *
*                                                                          *
****************************************************************************/

htbl->h = h;
htbl->match = match;
htbl->destroy = destroy;
```

Example 8-3. Implementation of the Chained Hash Table Abstract Datatype (continued)

```
/***************************************************************************
*                                                                         *
*  Initialize the number of elements in the table.                        *
*                                                                         *
***************************************************************************/

htbl->size = 0;

return 0;

}

/***************************************************************************
*                                                                         *
*  --------------------------- chtbl_destroy ---------------------------   *
*                                                                         *
***************************************************************************/

void chtbl_destroy(CHTbl *htbl) {

int              i;

/***************************************************************************
*                                                                         *
*  Destroy each bucket.                                                    *
*                                                                         *
***************************************************************************/

for (i = 0; i < htbl->buckets; i++) {

   list_destroy(&htbl->table[i]);

}

/***************************************************************************
*                                                                         *
*  Free the storage allocated for the hash table.                         *
*                                                                         *
***************************************************************************/

free(htbl->table);

/***************************************************************************
*                                                                         *
*  No operations are allowed now, but clear the structure as a precaution. *
*                                                                         *
***************************************************************************/

memset(htbl, 0, sizeof(CHTbl));

return;

}
```

Example 8-3. Implementation of the Chained Hash Table Abstract Datatype (continued)

```c
/***************************************************************************
*                                                                         *
*  --------------------------- chtbl_insert ---------------------------   *
*                                                                         *
***************************************************************************/

int chtbl_insert(CHTbl *htbl, const void *data) {

void            *temp;

int             bucket,
                retval;

/***************************************************************************
*                                                                         *
*  Do nothing if the data is already in the table.                        *
*                                                                         *
***************************************************************************/

temp = (void *)data;

if (chtbl_lookup(htbl, &temp) == 0)
   return 1;

/***************************************************************************
*                                                                         *
*  Hash the key.                                                          *
*                                                                         *
***************************************************************************/

bucket = htbl->h(data) % htbl->buckets;

/***************************************************************************
*                                                                         *
*  Insert the data into the bucket.                                       *
*                                                                         *
***************************************************************************/

if ((retval = list_ins_next(&htbl->table[bucket], NULL, data)) == 0)
   htbl->size++;

return retval;

}

/***************************************************************************
*                                                                         *
*  --------------------------- chtbl_remove ---------------------------   *
*                                                                         *
***************************************************************************/

int chtbl_remove(CHTbl *htbl, void **data) {
```

Example 8-3. Implementation of the Chained Hash Table Abstract Datatype (continued)

```
ListElmt              *element,
                      *prev;

int                   bucket;

/***************************************************************************
*                                                                         *
*  Hash the key.                                                          *
*                                                                         *
***************************************************************************/

bucket = htbl->h(*data) % htbl->buckets;

/***************************************************************************
*                                                                         *
*  Search for the data in the bucket.                                    *
*                                                                         *
***************************************************************************/

prev = NULL;

for (element = list_head(&htbl->table[bucket]); element != NULL; element =
   list_next(element)) {

   if (htbl->match(*data, list_data(element))) {

      /***********************************************************************
      *                                                                    *
      *  Remove the data from the bucket.                                  *
      *                                                                    *
      ***********************************************************************/

      if (list_rem_next(&htbl->table[bucket], prev, data) == 0) {

         htbl->size--;
         return 0;

         }

      else {

         return -1;

      }

   }

   prev = element;

}
```

Example 8-3. Implementation of the Chained Hash Table Abstract Datatype (continued)

```
/***************************************************************************
*                                                                         *
*  Return that the data was not found.                                    *
*                                                                         *
***************************************************************************/

return -1;

}

/***************************************************************************
*                                                                         *
*  --------------------------- chtbl_lookup ---------------------------   *
*                                                                         *
***************************************************************************/

int chtbl_lookup(const CHTbl *htbl, void **data) {

ListElmt          *element;

int               bucket;

/***************************************************************************
*                                                                         *
*  Hash the key.                                                          *
*                                                                         *
***************************************************************************/

bucket = htbl->h(*data) % htbl->buckets;

/***************************************************************************
*                                                                         *
*  Search for the data in the bucket.                                     *
*                                                                         *
***************************************************************************/

for (element = list_head(&htbl->table[bucket]); element != NULL; element =
   list_next(element)) {

   if (htbl->match(*data, list_data(element))) {

      /*********************************************************************
      *                                                                   *
      *  Pass back the data from the table.                               *
      *                                                                   *
      *********************************************************************/

      *data = list_data(element);
      return 0;

   }

}
```

Example 8-3. Implementation of the Chained Hash Table Abstract Datatype (continued)

```
/***************************************************************************
*                                                                         *
*  Return that the data was not found.                                    *
*                                                                         *
***************************************************************************/

return -1;

}
```

Chained Hash Table Example: Symbol Tables

An important application of hash tables is the way compilers maintain information about symbols encountered in a program. Formally, a compiler translates a program written in one language, a *source language* such as C, into another language, which is a set of instructions for the machine on which the program will run. In order to maintain information about the symbols in a program, compilers make use of a data structure called a *symbol table*. Symbol tables are often implemented as hash tables because a compiler must be able to store and retrieve information about symbols very quickly.

Several parts of a compiler access the symbol table during various phases of the compilation process. One part, the *lexical analyzer*, inserts symbols. The lexical analyzer is the part of a compiler charged with grouping characters from the source code into meaningful strings, called *lexemes*. These are translated into syntactic elements, called *tokens*, that are passed on to the *parser*. The parser performs syntactical analysis. As the lexical analyzer encounters symbols in its input stream, it stores information about them into the symbol table. Two important attributes stored by the lexical analyzer are a symbol's lexeme and the type of token the lexeme constitutes (e.g., an identifier or an operator).

The example presented here is a very simple lexical analyzer that analyzes a string of characters and then groups the characters into one of two types of tokens: a token consisting only of digits or a token consisting of something other than digits alone. For simplicity, we assume that tokens are separated in the input stream by a single blank. The lexical analyzer is implemented as a function, *lex* (see Examples 8-4 and 8-5), which a parser calls each time it requires another token.

The function works by first calling the *next_token* function (whose implementation is not shown) to get the next blank-delimited string from the input stream `istream`. If *next_token* returns NULL, there are no more tokens in the input stream. In this case, the function returns `lexit`, which tells the parser that there are no more tokens to be processed. If *next_token* finds a string, some simple analysis is performed to determine what type of token the string represents. Next, the function inserts the lexeme and token type together as a *Symbol* structure into the symbol table, *symtbl*, and returns the token type to the parser. The type *Symbol* is defined in *symbol.h*, which is not included in this example.

A chained hash table is a good way to implement a symbol table because, in addition to being an efficient way to store and retrieve information, we can use it to store a virtually unlimited amount of data. This is important for a compiler since it is difficult to know how many symbols a program will contain before lexical analysis.

The runtime complexity of *lex* is $O(1)$, assuming *next_token* runs in a constant amount of time. This is because *lex* simply calls *chtbl_insert*, which is an $O(1)$ operation.

Example 8-4. Header for a Simple Lexical Analyzer

```
/*****************************************************************************
*                                                                           *
*  ------------------------------- lex.h --------------------------------   *
*                                                                           *
*****************************************************************************/

#ifndef LEX_H
#define LEX_H

#include "chtbl.h"

/*****************************************************************************
*                                                                           *
*  Define the token types recognized by the lexical analyzer.               *
*                                                                           *
*****************************************************************************/

typedef enum Token_ {lexit, error, digit, other} Token;

/*****************************************************************************
*                                                                           *
*  -------------------------- Public Interface --------------------------   *
*                                                                           *
*****************************************************************************/

Token lex(const char *istream, CHTbl *symtbl);

#endif
```

Example 8-5. Implementation of a Simple Lexical Analyzer

```
/*****************************************************************************
*                                                                           *
*  ------------------------------- lex.c --------------------------------   *
*                                                                           *
*****************************************************************************/
```

Example 8-5. Implementation of a Simple Lexical Analyzer (continued)

```c
#include <ctype.h>
#include <stdlib.h>
#include <string.h>

#include "chtbl.h"
#include "lex.h"
#include "symbol.h"

/*****************************************************************************
*                                                                           *
* --------------------------------- lex --------------------------------- *
*                                                                           *
*****************************************************************************/

Token lex(const char *istream, CHTbl *symtbl) {

Token              token;

Symbol             *symbol;

int                length,
                   retval,
                   i;

/*****************************************************************************
*                                                                           *
*  Allocate space for a symbol.                                             *
*                                                                           *
*****************************************************************************/

if ((symbol = (Symbol *)malloc(sizeof(Symbol))) == NULL)
   return error;

/*****************************************************************************
*                                                                           *
*  Process the next token.                                                  *
*                                                                           *
*****************************************************************************/

if ((symbol->lexeme = next_token(istream)) == NULL) {

   /*****************************************************************************
   *                                                                           *
   *  Return that there is no more input.                                      *
   *                                                                           *
   *****************************************************************************/

   free(symbol);
   return lexit;

   }

else {
```

Example 8-5. Implementation of a Simple Lexical Analyzer (continued)

```
/*************************************************************************
*                                                                        *
*  Determine the token type.                                             *
*                                                                        *
*************************************************************************/

symbol->token = digit;
length = strlen(symbol->lexeme);

for (i = 0; i < length; i++) {

   if (!isdigit(symbol->lexeme[i]))
      symbol->token = other;

}

memcpy(&token, &symbol->token, sizeof(Token));

/*************************************************************************
*                                                                        *
*  Insert the symbol into the symbol table.                              *
*                                                                        *
*************************************************************************/

if ((retval = chtbl_insert(symtbl, symbol)) < 0) {

   free(symbol);
   return error;

   }

else if (retval == 1) {

   /*************************************************************************
   *                                                                        *
   *  The symbol is already in the symbol table.                            *
   *                                                                        *
   *************************************************************************/

   free(symbol);

   }

}

/*************************************************************************
*                                                                        *
*  Return the token for the parser.                                      *
*                                                                        *
*************************************************************************/

return token ;

}
```

Description of Open-Addressed Hash Tables

In a chained hash table, elements reside in buckets extending from each position. In an open-addressed hash table, on the other hand, all elements reside in the table itself. This may be important for some applications that rely on the table being a fixed size. Without a way to extend the number of elements at each position, however, an open-addressed hash table needs another way to resolve collisions.

Collision Resolution

Whereas chained hash tables have an inherent means of resolving collisions, open-addressed hash tables must handle them in a different way. The way to resolve collisions in an open-addressed hash table is to *probe* the table. To insert an element, for example, we probe positions until we find an unoccupied one, and insert the element there. To remove or look up an element, we probe positions until the element is located or until we encounter an unoccupied position. If we encounter an unoccupied position before finding the element, or if we end up traversing all of the positions, the element is not in the table.

Of course, the goal is to minimize how many probes we have to perform. Exactly how many positions we end up probing depends primarily on two things: the load factor of the hash table and the degree to which elements are distributed uniformly. Recall that the load factor of a hash table is $\alpha = n/m$, where n is the number of elements and m is the number of positions into which the elements may be hashed. Notice that since an open-addressed hash table cannot contain more elements than the number of positions in the table ($n > m$), its load factor is always less than or equal to 1. This makes sense, since no position can ever contain more than one element.

Assuming uniform hashing, the number of positions we can expect to probe in an open-addressed hash table is:

$$1/(1-\alpha)$$

For an open-addressed hash table that is half full (whose load factor is 0.5), for example, the number of positions we can expect to probe is $1/(1 - 0.5) = 2$. Table 8-1 illustrates how dramatically the expected number of probes increases as the load factor of an open-addressed hash table approaches 1 (or 100%), at which point the table is completely full. In a particularly time-sensitive application, it may be advantageous to increase the size of the hash table to allow extra space for probing.

Table 8-1. Expected Probes as a Result of Load Factor, Assuming Uniform Hashing

Load Factor (%)	Expected Probes
< 50	$1 / (1 - 0.50) < 2$
80	$1 / (1 - 0.80) = 5$
90	$1 / (1 - 0.90) = 10$
95	$1 / (1 - 0.95) = 20$

How close we come to the figures presented in Table 8-1 depends on how closely we approximate uniform hashing. Just as in a chained hash table, this depends on how well we select our hash function. In an open-addressed hash table, however, this also depends on how we probe subsequent positions in the table when collisions occur. Generally, a hash function for probing positions in an open-addressed hash table is defined by:

$$h(k, i) = x$$

where k is a key, i is the number of times the table has been probed thus far, and x is the resulting hash coding. Typically, h makes use of one or more *auxiliary hash functions* selected for the same properties as presented for chained hash tables. However, for an open-addressed hash table, h must possess an additional property: as i increases from 0 to $m - 1$, where m is the number of positions in the hash table, all positions in the table must be visited before any position is visited twice; otherwise, not all positions will be probed.

Linear probing

One simple approach to probing an open-addressed hash table is to probe successive positions in the table. Formally stated, if we let i go between 0 and $m - 1$, where m is the number of positions in the table, a hash function for linear probing is defined as:

$$h(k, i) = (h'(k) + i) \bmod m$$

The function h' is an auxiliary hash function, which is selected like any hash function; that is, so that elements are distributed in a uniform and random manner. For example, we might choose to use the division method of hashing and let $h'(k) = k \bmod m$. In this case, if we hash an element with key $k = 2998$ into a table of size $m = 1000$, the hash codings produced are $(998 + 0) \bmod 1000 = 998$ when $i = 0$, $(998 + 1) \bmod 1000 = 999$ when $i = 1$, $(998 + 2) \bmod 1000 = 0$ when $i = 2$, and so on. Therefore, to insert an element with key $k = 2998$, we would look for an unoccupied position first at position 998, then 999, then 0, and so on.

The advantage of linear probing is that it is simple and there are no constraints on m to ensure that all positions will eventually be probed. Unfortunately, linear probing does not approximate uniform hashing very well. In particular, linear probing suffers from a phenomenon known as *primary clustering*, in which large chains of occupied positions begin to develop as the table becomes more and more full. This results in excessive probing (see Figure 8-2).

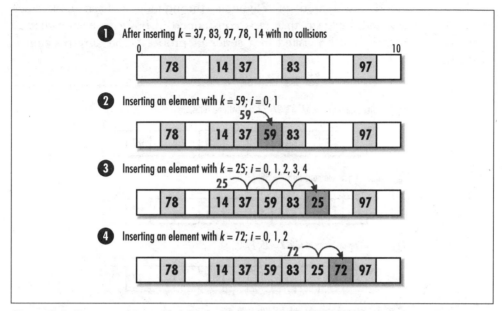

Figure 8-2. Linear probing with h(k, i) = (k mod 11 + i) mod 11

Double hashing

One of the most effective approaches for probing an open-addressed hash table focuses on adding the hash codings of two auxiliary hash functions. Formally stated, if we let i go between 0 and $m - 1$, where m is the number of positions in the table, a hash function for double hashing is defined as:

$$h(k, i) = (h_1(k) + ih_2(k)) \bmod m$$

The functions h_1 and h_2 are auxiliary hash functions, which are selected like any hash function: so that elements are distributed in a uniform and random manner. However, in order to ensure that all positions in the table are visited before any position is visited twice, we must adhere to one of the following procedures: we must select m to be a power of 2 and make h_2 always return an odd value, or we must make m prime and design h_2 so that it always returns a positive integer less than m.

Typically, we let $h_1(k) = k \bmod m$ and $h_2(k) = 1 + (k \bmod m')$, where m' is slightly less than m, say, $m - 1$ or $m - 2$. Using this approach, for example, if the hash table contains $m = 1699$ positions (a prime number) and we hash the key $k = 15,385$, the positions probed are (94 + (0)(113)) mod 1699 = 94 when *i* = 0, and every 113th position after this as *i* increases.

The advantage of double hashing is that it is one of the best forms of probing, producing a good distribution of elements throughout a hash table (see Figure 8-3). The disadvantage is that *m* is constrained in order to ensure that all positions in the table will be visited in a series of probes before any position is probed twice.

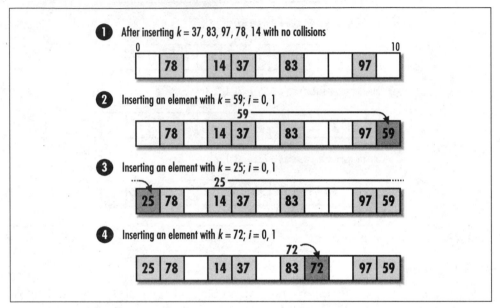

Figure 8-3. Hashing the same keys as Figure 8-2 but with double hashing, where h(k, i) = (k mod 11 + i(1 + k mod 9)) mod 11

Interface for Open-Addressed Hash Tables

ohtbl_init

```
int ohtbl_init(OHTbl *htbl, int positions, int (*h1)(const void *key)
   int (*h2)(const void *key), int (*match)(const void *key1
   const void *key2), void (*destroy)(void *data));
```

Return Value   0 if initializing the hash table is successful, or –1 otherwise.

Description   Initializes the open-addressed hash table specified by *htbl*. This operation must be called for an open-addressed hash table before the hash table can be used with any other operation. The number of positions to be allocated in the hash table is specified by *positions*. The function pointers *h1* and *h2* specify user-defined auxiliary hash functions for double hashing. The function pointer *match* specifies a user-defined function to determine if two keys match. It should perform in a manner similar to that described for *chtbl_init*. The *destroy* argument provides a way to free dynamically allocated data when *ohtbl_destroy* is called. It works in a manner similar to that described for *chtbl_destroy*. For an open-addressed hash table containing data that should not be freed, *destroy* should be set to NULL.

Complexity $O(m)$, where m is the number of positions in the hash table.

ohtbl_destroy

```
void ohtbl_destroy(OHTbl *htbl);
```

Return Value   None.

Description   Destroys the open-addressed hash table specified by *htbl*. No other operations are permitted after calling *ohtbl_destroy* unless *ohtbl_init* is called again. The *ohtbl_destroy* operation removes all elements from a hash table and calls the function passed as *destroy* to *ohtbl_init* once for each element as it is removed, provided *destroy* was not set to NULL.

Complexity $O(m)$, where m is the number of positions in the hash table.

ohtbl_insert

```
int ohtbl_insert(OHTbl *htbl, const void *data);
```

Return Value   0 if inserting the element is successful, 1 if the element is already in the hash table, or −1 otherwise.

Description   Inserts an element into the open-addressed hash table specified by *htbl*. The new element contains a pointer to *data*, so the memory referenced by *data* should remain valid as long as the element remains in the hash table. It is the responsibility of the caller to manage the storage associated with *data*.

Complexity $O(1)$

ohtbl_remove

```
int ohtbl_remove(OHTbl *htbl, void **data);
```

Return Value   0 if removing the element is successful, or −1 otherwise.

Description   Removes the element matching *data* from the open-addressed hash table specified by *htbl*. Upon return, *data* points to the data stored in the element that was removed. It is the responsibility of the caller to manage the storage associated with the data.

Complexity $O(1)$

ohtbl_lookup

```
int ohtbl_lookup(const OHTbl *htbl, void **data);
```

Return Value   0 if the element is found in the hash table, or −1 otherwise.

Description   Determines whether an element matches *data* in the open-addressed hash table specified by *htbl*. If a match is found, upon return *data* points to the matching data in the hash table.

Complexity $O(1)$

ohtbl_size

```
int ohtbl_size(const OHTbl *htbl);
```

Return Value   Number of elements in the hash table.

Description   Macro that evaluates to the number of elements in the open-addressed hash table specified by *htbl*.

Complexity $O(1)$

Implementation and Analysis of Open Addressed Hash Tables

An open-addressed hash table fundamentally consists of a single array. The structure *OHTbl* is the open-addressed hash table data structure (see Example 8-6). This structure consists of eight members: *positions* is the number of positions allocated in the hash table; *vacated* is a pointer that will be initialized to a special storage location to indicate that a particular position in the table has had an element removed from it; *h1*, *h2*, *match*, and *destroy* are members used to encapsulate the functions passed to *ohtbl_init*; *size* is the number of elements currently in the table; and *table* is the array in which the elements are stored.

The *vacated* member requires a bit of discussion. Its purpose is to support the removal of elements. An unoccupied position in an open-addressed hash table usually contains a NULL pointer. However, when we remove an element, we cannot set its data pointer back to NULL because when probing to look up a subsequent element, NULL would indicate that the position is unoccupied and no more probes should be performed. In actuality, one or more elements may have been inserted by probing past the removed element while it was still in the table.

Considering this, we set the data pointer to the *vacated* member of the hash table data structure when we remove an element. The address of *vacated* serves as a special sentinel to indicate that a new element may be inserted at the position. This way, when probing to look up an element, we are assured that a NULL really means to stop probing.

Example 8-6. Header for the Open-Addressed Hash Table Abstract Datatype

```
/*****************************************************************************
*                                                                           *
* ----------------------------- ohtbl.h -------------------------------     *
*                                                                           *
*****************************************************************************/

#ifndef OHTBL_H
#define OHTBL_H

#include <stdlib.h>

/*****************************************************************************
*                                                                           *
*  Define a structure for open-addressed hash tables.                       *
*                                                                           *
*****************************************************************************/

typedef struct OHTbl_ {

int             positions;
void            *vacated;

int             (*h1)(const void *key);
int             (*h2)(const void *key);
int             (*match)(const void *key1, const void *key2);
void            (*destroy)(void *data);

int             size;
void            **table;

} OHTbl;

/*****************************************************************************
*                                                                           *
* -------------------------- Public Interface --------------------------    *
*                                                                           *
*****************************************************************************/

int ohtbl_init(OHTbl *htbl, int positions, int (*h1)(const void *key), int
   (*h2)(const void *key), int (*match)(const void *key1, const void *key2),
   void (*destroy)(void *data));

void ohtbl_destroy(OHTbl *htbl);

int ohtbl_insert(OHTbl *htbl, const void *data);

int ohtbl_remove(OHTbl *htbl, void **data);

int ohtbl_lookup(const OHTbl *htbl, void **data);

#define ohtbl_size(htbl) ((htbl)->size)

#endif
```

ohtbl_init

The *ohtbl_init* operation initializes an open-addressed hash table so that it can be used in other operations (see Example 8-7). Initializing an open-addressed hash table is a simple operation in which we allocate space for the table; initialize the pointer in each position to NULL; encapsulate the *h1*, *h2*, `match` and `destroy` functions; initialize `vacated` to its sentinel address; and set the `size` member to 0.

The runtime complexity of *ohtbl_init* is $O(m)$, where m is the number of positions in the table. This is because the data pointer in each of the m positions must be initialized to NULL, and all other parts of the operation run in a constant amount of time.

ohtbl_destroy

The *ohtbl_destroy* operation destroys an open-addressed hash table (see Example 8-7). Primarily this means freeing the memory *ohtbl_init* allocated for the table. The function passed as `destroy` to *ohtbl_init* is called once for each element as it is removed, provided `destroy` was not set to NULL.

The runtime complexity of *ohtbl_destroy* is $O(m)$, where m is the number of positions in the hash table. This is because we must traverse all positions in the hash table to determine which are occupied. If `destroy` is NULL, *ohtbl_destroy* runs in $O(1)$ time.

ohtbl_insert

The *ohtbl_insert* operation inserts an element into an open-addressed hash table (see Example 8-7). Since an open-addressed hash table has a fixed size, we first ensure that there is room for the new element to be inserted. Also, since a key is not allowed to be inserted into the hash table more than once, we call *ohtbl_lookup* to make sure the table does not already contain the new element.

Once these conditions are met, we use double hashing to probe the table for an unoccupied position. A position in the table is unoccupied if it points either to NULL or the address in `vacated`, a special member of the hash table data structure that indicates that a position has had an element removed from it. Once we find an unoccupied position in the table, we set the pointer at that position to point to the data we wish to insert. After this, we increment the table size.

Assuming we approximate uniform hashing well and the load factor of the hash table is relatively small, the runtime complexity of *ohtbl_insert* is $O(1)$. This is because in order to find an unoccupied position at which to insert the element, we expect to probe $1/(1 - \alpha)$ positions, a number treated as a small constant, where α is the load factor of the hash table.

ohtbl_remove

The *ohtbl_remove* operation removes an element from an open-addressed hash table (see Example 8-7). To remove the element, we use double hashing as in *ohtbl_insert* to locate the position at which the element resides. We continue searching until we locate the element or NULL is found. If we find the element, we set *data* to the data being removed and decrease the table size by 1. Also, we set the position in the table to the *vacated* member of the hash table data structure.

Assuming we approximate uniform hashing well, the runtime complexity of *ohtbl_remove* is $O(1)$. This is because we expect to probe $1/(1 - \alpha)$ positions, a number treated as a small constant, where α is the largest load factor of the hash table since calling *ohtbl_init*. The reason that the performance of this operation depends on the largest load factor and thus does not improve as elements are removed is that we must still probe past vacated positions. The use of the *vacated* member only improves the performance of *ohtbl_insert*.

ohtbl_lookup

The *ohtbl_lookup* operation searches for an element in an open-addressed hash table and returns a pointer to it (see Example 8-7). This operation works similarly to *ohtbl_remove*, except that the element is not removed from the table.

Assuming we approximate uniform hashing well, the runtime complexity of *ohtbl_lookup* is the same as *ohtbl_remove*, or $O(1)$. This is because we expect to probe $1/(1 - \alpha)$ positions, a number treated as a small constant, where α is the largest load factor of the hash table since calling *ohtbl_init*. The reason that performance depends on the largest load factor since calling *ohtbl_init* is the same as described for *ohtbl_remove*.

ohtbl_size

This macro evaluates to the number of elements in an open-addressed hash table (see Example 8-6). It works by accessing the *size* member of the *OHTbl* structure.

The runtime complexity of *ohtbl_size* is $O(1)$ because accessing a member of a structure is a simple task that runs in a constant amount of time.

Example 8-7. Implementation of the Open-Addressed Hash Table Abstract Datatype

```
/*****************************************************************************
*                                                                           *
*  ----------------------------- ohtbl.c -----------------------------      *
*                                                                           *
*****************************************************************************/
```

Example 8-7. Implementation of the Open-Addressed Hash Table
Abstract Datatype (continued)

```
#include <stdlib.h>
#include <string.h>

#include "ohtbl.h"

/***************************************************************************
*                                                                         *
*  Reserve a sentinel memory address for vacated elements.                *
*                                                                         *
***************************************************************************/

static char         vacated;

/***************************************************************************
*                                                                         *
*  ----------------------------- ohtbl_init -----------------------------  *
*                                                                         *
***************************************************************************/

int ohtbl_init(OHTbl *htbl, int positions, int (*h1)(const void *key), int
   (*h2)(const void *key), int (*match)(const void *key1, const void *key2),
   void (*destroy)(void *data)) {

int                 i;

/***************************************************************************
*                                                                         *
*  Allocate space for the hash table.                                     *
*                                                                         *
***************************************************************************/

if ((htbl->table = (void **)malloc(positions * sizeof(void *))) == NULL)
   return -1;

/***************************************************************************
*                                                                         *
*  Initialize each position.                                              *
*                                                                         *
***************************************************************************/

htbl->positions = positions;

for (i = 0; i < htbl->positions; i++)
   htbl->table[i] = NULL;

/***************************************************************************
*                                                                         *
*  Set the vacated member to the sentinel memory address reserved for this. *
*                                                                         *
***************************************************************************/

htbl->vacated = &vacated;
```

Example 8-7. Implementation of the Open-Addressed Hash Table
Abstract Datatype (continued)

```
/***************************************************************************
*                                                                         *
*  Encapsulate the functions.                                             *
*                                                                         *
***************************************************************************/

htbl->h1 = h1;
htbl->h2 = h2;
htbl->match = match;
htbl->destroy = destroy;

/***************************************************************************
*                                                                         *
*  Initialize the number of elements in the table.                        *
*                                                                         *
***************************************************************************/

htbl->size = 0;

return 0;

}

/***************************************************************************
*                                                                         *
*  -------------------------- ohtbl_destroy --------------------------    *
*                                                                         *
***************************************************************************/

void ohtbl_destroy(OHTbl *htbl) {

int              i;

if (htbl->destroy != NULL) {

   /***********************************************************************
   *                                                                     *
   *  Call a user-defined function to free dynamically allocated data.   *
   *                                                                     *
   ***********************************************************************/

   for (i = 0; i < htbl->positions; i++) {

      if (htbl->table[i] != NULL && htbl->table[i] != htbl->vacated)
         htbl->destroy(htbl->table[i]);

   }

}
```

Example 8-7. Implementation of the Open-Addressed Hash Table
Abstract Datatype (continued)

```
/***************************************************************************
*                                                                         *
*  Free the storage allocated for the hash table.                         *
*                                                                         *
***************************************************************************/

free(htbl->table);

/***************************************************************************
*                                                                         *
*  No operations are allowed now, but clear the structure as a precaution. *
*                                                                         *
***************************************************************************/

memset(htbl, 0, sizeof(OHTbl));

return;

}

/***************************************************************************
*                                                                         *
*  --------------------------- ohtbl_insert ---------------------------   *
*                                                                         *
***************************************************************************/

int ohtbl_insert(OHTbl *htbl, const void *data) {

void              *temp;

int               position,
                  i;

/***************************************************************************
*                                                                         *
*  Do not exceed the number of positions in the table.                    *
*                                                                         *
***************************************************************************/

if (htbl->size == htbl->positions)
   return -1;

/***************************************************************************
*                                                                         *
*  Do nothing if the data is already in the table.                        *
*                                                                         *
***************************************************************************/

temp = (void *)data;

if (ohtbl_lookup(htbl, &temp) == 0)
   return 1;
```

Example 8-7. Implementation of the Open-Addressed Hash Table
Abstract Datatype (continued)

```
/***************************************************************************
 *                                                                         *
 *  Use double hashing to hash the key.                                    *
 *                                                                         *
 ***************************************************************************/

for (i = 0; i < htbl->positions; i++) {

   position = (htbl->h1(data) + (i * htbl->h2(data))) % htbl->positions;

   if (htbl->table[position] == NULL || htbl->table[position] == htbl->
      vacated) {

      /***********************************************************************
       *                                                                   *
       *   Insert the data into the table.                                 *
       *                                                                   *
       ***********************************************************************/

      htbl->table[position] = (void *)data;
      htbl->size++;
      return 0;

   }

}

/***************************************************************************
 *                                                                         *
 *  Return that the hash functions were selected incorrectly.              *
 *                                                                         *
 ***************************************************************************/

return -1;

}

/***************************************************************************
 *                                                                         *
 *  --------------------------- ohtbl_remove --------------------------    *
 *                                                                         *
 ***************************************************************************/

int ohtbl_remove(OHTbl *htbl, void **data) {

int              position,
                 i;

/***************************************************************************
 *                                                                         *
 *  Use double hashing to hash the key.                                    *
 *                                                                         *
 ***************************************************************************/
```

*Example 8-7. Implementation of the Open-Addressed Hash Table
Abstract Datatype (continued)*

```
for (i = 0; i < htbl->positions; i++) {

   position = (htbl->h1(*data) + (i * htbl->h2(*data))) % htbl->positions;

   if (htbl->table[position] == NULL) {

      /*************************************************************************
      *                                                                       *
      *  Return that the data was not found.                                  *
      *                                                                       *
      *************************************************************************/

      return -1;

      }

   else if (htbl->table[position] == htbl->vacated) {

      /*************************************************************************
      *                                                                       *
      *  Search beyond vacated positions.                                     *
      *                                                                       *
      *************************************************************************/

      continue;

      }

   else if (htbl->match(htbl->table[position], *data)) {

      /*************************************************************************
      *                                                                       *
      *  Pass back the data from the table.                                   *
      *                                                                       *
      *************************************************************************/

      *data = htbl->table[position];
      htbl->table[position] = htbl->vacated;
      htbl->size--;
      return 0;

      }

   }

/*************************************************************************
*                                                                       *
*  Return that the data was not found.                                  *
*                                                                       *
*************************************************************************/
```

Example 8-7. Implementation of the Open-Addressed Hash Table
Abstract Datatype (continued)

```c
return -1;

}

/***************************************************************************
*                                                                         *
*  --------------------------- ohtbl_lookup ---------------------------    *
*                                                                         *
***************************************************************************/

int ohtbl_lookup(const OHTbl *htbl, void **data) {

int              position,
                 i;

/***************************************************************************
*                                                                         *
*  Use double hashing to hash the key.                                    *
*                                                                         *
***************************************************************************/

for (i = 0; i < htbl->positions; i++) {

   position = (htbl->h1(*data) + (i * htbl->h2(*data))) % htbl->positions;

   if (htbl->table[position] == NULL) {

      /***************************************************************************
      *                                                                         *
      *  Return that the data was not found.                                    *
      *                                                                         *
      ***************************************************************************/

      return -1;

      }

   else if (htbl->match(htbl->table[position], *data)) {

      /***************************************************************************
      *                                                                         *
      *  Pass back the data from the table.                                     *
      *                                                                         *
      ***************************************************************************/

      *data = htbl->table[position];
      return 0;

   }

}
```

Example 8-7. Implementation of the Open-Addressed Hash Table
Abstract Datatype (continued)

```
/****************************************************************************
*                                                                          *
*  Return that the data was not found.                                     *
*                                                                          *
****************************************************************************/

return -1;

}
```

Questions and Answers

Q: *In the implementation of chained hash tables presented in this chapter, the*
actual hash code used for accessing the table is the hash code modulo the table
size. Why is this?

A: This transformation ensures that the hash coding does not position us past the
end of the table. Although the hash function should ensure this itself, it is
worthwhile for the hash table implementation to provide the guarantee as
well, especially since the hash function is provided by the caller. However,
this is not the same reason that the modulo is performed when double hashing a key in an open-addressed hash table. In this case, the process of double
hashing may produce a hash coding that falls outside of the bounds of the
table, even for two auxiliary hash functions each producing hash codings
within the table. This is because the two hash codings are added together.

Q: *Why are hash tables good for random access but not sequential access? For*
example, in a database system in which records are to be accessed in a sequen-
tial fashion, what is the problem with hashing?

A: Hash tables are excellent for random access because each key hashes us precisely to where we need to be in the table to access the data, or at least within
a few steps when a collision occurs. However, hash tables do not support
sequential access. After hashing to some position, we have no way to determine where the next smallest or largest key resides. Compare this with a
linked list containing elements that are sorted. Assuming some initial position
in the list, the next key is easy to determine: we simply look at the next element in the list.

Q: *What is the worst-case performance of searching for an element in a chained*
hash table? How do we ensure that this case will not occur?

A: A chained hash table performs the worst when all elements hash into a single
bucket. In this case, searching for an element is $O(n)$, where n is the number
of elements in the table. A ridiculous hash function that would result in this

performance is $h(k) = c$, where c is some constant within the bounds of the hash table. Selecting a good hash function ensures that this case will not occur. If the hash function approximates uniform hashing well, we can expect to locate an element in constant time.

Q: What is the worst-case performance of searching for an element in an open-addressed hash table? How do we ensure that this case will not occur?

A: The worst-case performance of searching for an element in an open-addressed hash table occurs once the hash table is completely full and the element we are searching for is not in the table. In this case, searching for an element is an $O(m)$ operation, where m is the number of positions in the table. This case can occur with any hash function. To ensure reasonable performance in an open-addressed hash table, we should not let the table become more than 80% full. If we choose a hash function that approximates uniform hashing well, we can expect performance consistent with what is presented in Table 8-1.

Related Topics

Direct-address tables

A simple type of hash table in which there is a one-to-one mapping between all possible keys and positions in the table. Since no two keys map to the same position, there is no need for collision resolution. However, if there are many possible keys, the table will be large. Generally, direct addressing works well when the universe of possible keys is small.

Linear congruential generators

A common class of random number generators. Understanding the principles behind random number generators can help in devising good hash functions.

Quadratic probing

An alternative to linear probing and double hashing for probing an open-addressed hash table. In quadratic probing, the sequence of positions probed is determined using a quadratic-form hash function. In general, quadratic probing performs better than linear probing, but it does not perform as well as double hashing. Quadratic probing results in *secondary clustering*, a form of clustering that is less severe than the primary clustering of linear probing.

Universal hashing

A hashing method in which hashing functions are generated randomly at run-time so that no particular set of keys is likely to produce a bad distribution of elements in the hash table. Because the hash functions are generated randomly, even hashing the same set of keys during different executions may result in different measures of performance.

9

Trees

Picture a family tree, the draw sheet of a tournament, or the roots of a plant; these are all good examples of a tree's organization as a data structure. In computing, a tree consists of elements called *nodes* organized in a hierarchical arrangement. The node at the top of the hierarchy is called the *root*. The nodes directly below the root are its *children*, which in turn usually have children of their own. With the exception of the root, each node in the hierarchy has exactly one *parent*, which is the node directly above it. The number of children a node may parent depends on the type of tree. This number is a tree's *branching factor*, which dictates how fast the tree will branch out as nodes are inserted. This chapter focuses on the *binary tree*, a relatively simple but powerful tree with a branching factor of 2. It also explores *binary search trees*, binary trees organized specifically for searching.

This chapter covers:

Binary trees

> Trees containing nodes with up to two children. The binary tree is a very popular type of tree utilized in a wide variety of problems. It provides the foundation for more sophisticated tree structures as well.

Traversal methods

> Techniques for visiting the nodes of a tree in a specific order. Because the nodes of a tree are organized in a hierarchical fashion, there are several options for traversing them.

Tree balancing

> A process used to keep a tree as short as possible for a given number of nodes. This is especially important in search trees, wherein height influences the overall performance of the tree a great deal.

Binary search trees

Binary trees organized specifically for searching. Binary search trees are good for searching data in which we expect to perform insertions and deletions.

Rotations

Methods for keeping binary search trees balanced. Specifically, this chapter explores AVL rotations, the rotations applied to AVL (Adel'son-Vel'skii and Landis) trees. An AVL tree is one type of balanced binary search tree.

Some applications of trees are:

Huffman coding

A method of data compression that uses a Huffman tree to compress a set of data (see Chapter 14, *Data Compression*). A Huffman tree is a binary tree that determines the best way to assign codes to symbols in the data. Symbols occurring frequently are assigned short codes, whereas symbols occurring less frequently are assigned longer ones.

User interfaces

Examples are graphical user interfaces and interfaces to file systems. In graphical user interfaces, windows take on a hierarchical arrangement forming a tree. Every window, except the top-level window, has one parent from which it is started, and each window may have several children launched from it. Directories in hierarchical file systems have a similar organization.

Database systems

In particular, those that require both efficient sequential and random access while performing frequent insertions and deletions. The *B-tree*, a tree characterized generally as a balanced search tree with a large branching factor, is especially good in this situation (see the related topics at the end of the chapter). Typically the branching factor of a B-tree is optimized so that disk I/O is minimized when accessing records in the database.

Expression processing (illustrated in this chapter)

A task performed frequently by compilers and hand-held calculators. One intuitive way to process arithmetic expressions is with an expression tree, a binary tree containing a hierarchical arrangement of an expression's operators and operands.

Artificial intelligence

A discipline that addresses many problems traditionally difficult for computers, such as logic-based games like chess. Many AI problems are solved using *decision trees*. A decision tree consists of nodes that represent states in a problem. Each node is a point at which a decision must be made to continue. Each branch represents a conclusion derived from a series of decisions. Using various rules of logic, branches that cannot possibly contain desired conclusions are pruned, thus decreasing the time to a solution.

Event schedulers

Applications for scheduling and triggering real-time events. Often real-time systems require looking up and retrieving the latest information associated with events as they are triggered. A binary search tree can help make looking up information efficient.

Priority queues

Data structures that use a binary tree to keep track of which element in a set has the next highest priority (see Chapter 10, *Heaps and Priority Queues*). Priority queues offer a better solution than having to keep a set completely sorted.

Description of Binary Trees

A binary tree is a hierarchical arrangement of nodes, each having up to two nodes immediately below it. The nodes immediately below a node are called its *children*. The node above each child is called its *parent*. Nodes can also have *siblings*, *descendants*, and *ancestors*. As you might expect, the siblings of a node are the other children of its parent. The descendants of a node are all of the nodes branching out below it. The ancestors of a node are all the nodes along the path between it and the root. The performance associated with a tree often is discussed in terms of its *height*, the number of levels in which nodes reside. As we will see, tree terminology is as much familial as it is arboreal (see Figure 9-1).

Each node in a binary tree contains three parts: a data member and two pointers called the *left* and *right* pointers. Using this three-member structure, we form a binary tree by setting the *left* and *right* pointers of each node to point to its children (see Figure 9-2). If a node does not have a child to its left or right, we set the appropriate pointer to NULL, a convenient sentinel that marks the end of a *branch*. A branch is a series of nodes beginning at the root and ending at a *leaf node*. Leaf nodes are the nodes along the fringe of the tree that have no children. Sometimes when working with several trees at once, the trees are said to form a *forest*.

Traversal Methods

Traversing a binary tree means visiting its nodes one at a time in a specific order. Compared with some linked data structures, such as linked lists, how to traverse the nodes of a binary tree may not be immediately apparent. In fact, there are many ways in which we can proceed. Typically, one of four types of traversals is used: *preorder*, *inorder*, *postorder*, or *level order*. The example of expression trees later in this chapter presents recursive implementations of the preorder, inorder, and postorder traversals. For now, let's look at how each traversal works.

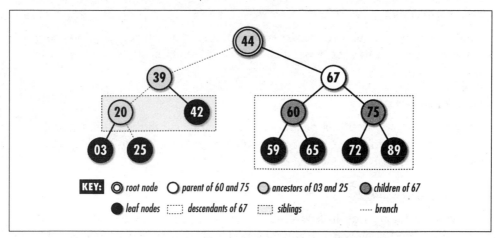

Figure 9-1. Common tree terminology illustrated with a four-level binary tree

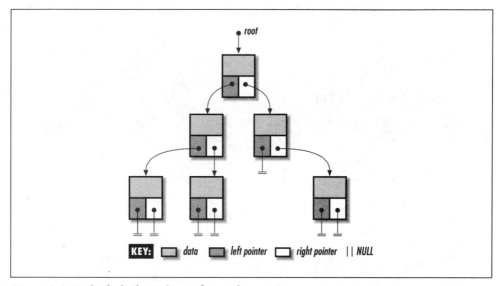

Figure 9-2. Nodes linked together to form a binary tree

Traversing a tree is particularly simple if we think of the tree recursively as being composed of many smaller subtrees. Figure 9-3 illustrates each traversal. Although these traversals are presented in the context of binary trees, each can be generalized to other types of trees as well.

Preorder traversal

To traverse a binary tree in a preorder fashion, visit its root node, then traverse the left subtree of its root node in preorder followed by the right subtree of its root node in preorder. The preorder traversal is a depth-first exploration, like that presented for graphs in Chapter 11, *Graphs*.

Inorder traversal

To traverse a binary tree in an inorder fashion, traverse the left subtree of its root node in inorder, then visit its root node, then traverse the right subtree of its root node in inorder.

Postorder traversal

To traverse a binary tree in a postorder fashion, traverse the left subtree of its root node in postorder followed by the right subtree of its root node in postorder, then visit its root node.Level-order traversal

Level-order traversal

To traverse a binary tree in a level-order fashion, visit its nodes beginning at the root and proceed downward, visiting the nodes at each level from left to right. The level-order traversal is a breadth-first exploration, like that presented for graphs in Chapter 11.

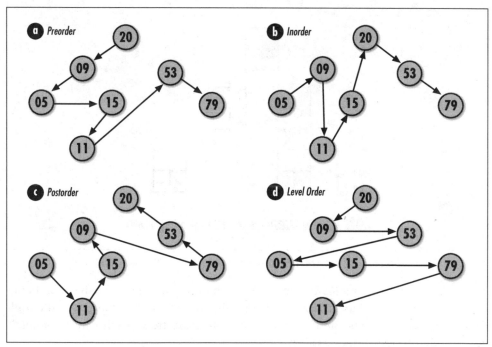

Figure 9-3. Traversing a binary tree in (a) preorder, (b) inorder, (c) postorder, and (d) level order

Tree Balancing

Balancing a tree is the process of keeping it as short as possible for a given number of nodes. This means making sure that one level of the tree is completely full before allowing a node to exist at the next level. Formally, a tree is balanced if all leaf nodes are at the same level or, if not, all leaf nodes are in the last two levels and the second-to-last level is full. For example, the tree in Figure 9-1 is balanced because all leaf nodes are in the third and fourth levels, and the third level is full. On the other hand, the tree in Figure 9-3 is not balanced. A balanced tree is *left-balanced* if all leaves occupy only the leftmost positions in the last level. The tree in Figure 9-4 is a left-balanced tree. We will see one important application of balanced trees when binary search trees are discussed later in this chapter. In Chapter 10 we will see how a left-balanced binary tree helps to implement a heap and priority queue.

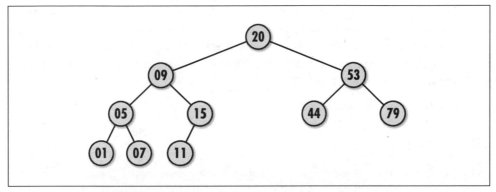

Figure 9-4. A left-balanced binary tree

Interface for Binary Trees

This interface provides basic operations for manipulating binary trees. However, it does not provide operations for inserting and removing individual nodes that are not leaves, because these operations require adjusting other nodes in the tree in some application-specific way to accommodate the node that is inserted or removed.

bitree_init

```
void bitree_init(BiTree *tree, void (*destroy)(void *data));
```

Return Value   None.

Description   Initializes the binary tree specified by *tree*. This operation must be called for a binary tree before the tree can be used with any other operation. The *destroy* argument provides a way to free dynamically allocated data when *bitree_destroy* is called. For example, if the tree contains data dynamically allocated using *malloc*, *destroy* should be set to *free* to free the data as the binary tree is destroyed. For structured data containing several dynamically allocated members, *destroy* should be set to a user-defined function that calls *free* for each dynamically allocated member as well as for the structure itself. For a binary tree containing data that should not be freed, *destroy* should be set to NULL.

Complexity $O(1)$

bitree_destroy

```
void bitree_destroy(BiTree *tree);
```

Return Value   None.

Description   Destroys the binary tree specified by *tree*. No other operations are permitted after calling *bitree_destroy* unless *bitree_init* is called again. The *bitree_destroy* operation removes all nodes from a binary tree and calls the function passed as *destroy* to *bitree_init* once for each node as it is removed, provided *destroy* was not set to NULL.

Complexity $O(n)$, where n is the number of nodes in the binary tree.

bitree_ins_left

```
int bitree_ins_left(BiTree *tree, BiTreeNode *node, const void *data);
```

Return Value   0 if inserting the node is successful, or −1 otherwise.

Description   Inserts a node as the left child of *node* in the binary tree specified by *tree*. If *node* already has a left child, *bitree_ins_left* returns −1. If *node* is NULL, the new node is inserted as the root node. The tree must be empty to insert a node as the root node; otherwise, *bitree_ins_left* returns −1. When successful, the new node contains a pointer to *data*, so the memory referenced by *data* should remain valid as long as the node remains in the binary tree. It is the responsibility of the caller to manage the storage associated with *data*.

Complexity $O(1)$

bitree_ins_right

```
int bitree_ins_right(BiTree *tree, BiTreeNode *node, const void *data);
```

Return Value   0 if inserting the node is successful, or −1 otherwise.

Description   This operation is similar to *bitree_ins_left*, except that it inserts a node as the right child of *node* in the binary tree specified by *tree*.

Complexity $O(1)$

bitree_rem_left

```
void bitree_rem_left(BiTree *tree, BiTreeNode *node);
```

Return Value   None.

Description   Removes the subtree rooted at the left child of *node* from the binary tree specified by *tree*. If *node* is NULL, all nodes in the tree are removed. The function passed as *destroy* to *bitree_init* is called once for each node as it is removed, provided *destroy* was not set to NULL.

Complexity $O(n)$, where n is the number of nodes in the subtree.

bitree_rem_right

```
void bitree_rem_right(BiTree *tree, BiTreeNode *node);
```

Return Value   None.

Description   This operation is similar to *bitree_rem_left*, except that it removes the subtree rooted at the right child of *node* from the binary tree specified by *tree*.

Complexity $O(n)$, where n is the number of nodes in the subtree.

bitree_merge

```
int bitree_merge(BiTree *merge, BiTree *left, BiTree *right, const void *data);
```

Return Value   0 if merging the trees is successful, or −1 otherwise.

Description   Merges the two binary trees specified by *left* and *right* into the single binary tree *merge*. After merging is complete, *merge* contains *data* in its root node, and *left* and *right* are the left and right subtrees of its root. Once the trees have been merged, *left* and *right* are as if *bitree_destroy* had been called on them.

Complexity $O(1)$

bitree_size

```
int bitree_size(const BiTree *tree);
```

Return Value   Number of nodes in the tree.

Description   Macro that evaluates to the number of nodes in the binary tree specified by *tree*.

Complexity $O(1)$

bitree_root

```
BiTreeNode *bitree_root(const BiTree *tree);
```

Return Value   Node at the root of the tree.

Description   Macro that evaluates to the node at the root of the binary tree specified by *tree*.

Complexity $O(1)$

bitree_is_eob

```
int bitree_is_eob(const BiTreeNode *node);
```

Return Value   1 if the node marks the end of a branch, or 0 otherwise.

Description   Macro that determines whether the node specified as *node* marks the end of a branch in a binary tree.

Complexity $O(1)$

bitree_is_leaf

```
int bitree_isleaf(const BiTreeNode *node);
```

Return Value   1 if the node is a leaf node, or 0 otherwise.

Description   Macro that determines whether the node specified as *node* is a leaf node in a binary tree.

Complexity $O(1)$

bitree_data

```
void *bitree_data(const BiTreeNode *node);
```

Return Value   Data stored in the node.

Description   Macro that evaluates to the data stored in the node of a binary tree specified by *node*.

Complexity $O(1)$

bitree_left

```
BiTreeNode *bitree_left(const BiTreeNode *node);
```

Return Value   Left child of the specified node.

Description   Macro that evaluates to the node of a binary tree that is the left child of the node specified by *node*.

Complexity $O(1)$

bitree_right

```
BiTreeNode *bitree_right(const BiTreeNode *node);
```

Return Value   Right child of the specified node.

Description   Macro that evaluates to the node of a binary tree that is the right child of the node specified by *node*.

Complexity   *O*(1)

Implementation and Analysis of Binary Trees

Recall that each node of a binary tree consists of three parts: a data member and two pointers to its children. The structure *BiTreeNode* represents an individual node of a binary tree (see Example 9-1). As you would expect, this structure has three members that correspond to those just mentioned. The structure *BiTree* is the binary tree data structure (see Example 9-1). This structure consists of four members: *size* is the number of nodes in the tree, *compare* is a member not used by binary trees but by datatypes that will be derived later from binary trees, *destroy* is the encapsulated destroy function passed to *bitree_init*, and *root* is a pointer to the top of the node hierarchy.

Example 9-1. Header for the Binary Tree Abstract Datatype

```
/*****************************************************************************
*                                                                           *
*  ------------------------------- bitree.h -------------------------------  *
*                                                                           *
*****************************************************************************/

#ifndef BITREE_H
#define BITREE_H

#include <stdlib.h>

/*****************************************************************************
*                                                                           *
*  Define a structure for binary tree nodes.                                *
*                                                                           *
*****************************************************************************/

typedef struct BiTreeNode_ {

void             *data;
struct BiTreeNode_ *left;
struct BiTreeNode_ *right;

} BiTreeNode;
```

Example 9-1. Header for the Binary Tree Abstract Datatype (continued)

```
/*****************************************************************************
*                                                                           *
*  Define a structure for binary trees.                                     *
*                                                                           *
*****************************************************************************/

typedef struct BiTree_ {

int             size;

int             (*compare)(const void *key1, const void *key2);
void            (*destroy)(void *data);

BiTreeNode      *root;

} BiTree;

/*****************************************************************************
*                                                                           *
*  -------------------------- Public Interface --------------------------   *
*                                                                           *
*****************************************************************************/

void bitree_init(BiTree *tree, void (*destroy)(void *data));

void bitree_destroy(BiTree *tree);

int bitree_ins_left(BiTree *tree, BiTreeNode *node, const void *data);

int bitree_ins_right(BiTree *tree, BiTreeNode *node, const void *data);

void bitree_rem_left(BiTree *tree, BiTreeNode *node);

void bitree_rem_right(BiTree *tree, BiTreeNode *node);

int bitree_merge(BiTree *merge, BiTree *left, BiTree *right, const void *data);

#define bitree_size(tree) ((tree)->size)

#define bitree_root(tree) ((tree)->root)

#define bitree_is_eob(node) ((node) == NULL)

#define bitree_is_leaf(node) ((node)->left == NULL && (node)->right == NULL)

#define bitree_data(node) ((node)->data)

#define bitree_left(node) ((node)->left)

#define bitree_right(node) ((node)->right)

#endif
```

bitree_init

The *bitree_init* operation initializes a binary tree so that it can be used in other operations (see Example 9-2). Initializing a binary tree is a simple operation in which we set the `size` member of the tree to 0, the `destroy` member to `destroy`, and the `root` pointer to NULL.

The runtime complexity of *bitree_init* is $O(1)$ because all of the steps in initializing a binary tree run in a constant amount of time.

bitree_destroy

The *bitree_destroy* operation destroys a binary tree (see Example 9-2). Primarily this means removing all nodes from the tree. The function passed as `destroy` to *bitree_init* is called once for each node as it is removed, provided `destroy` was not set to NULL.

The runtime complexity of *bitree_destroy* is $O(n)$, where n is the number of nodes in the binary tree. This is because *bitree_destroy* simply calls *bitree_rem_left*, which runs in $O(n)$ time, where n is the number of nodes in the tree.

bitree_ins_left

The *bitree_ins_left* operation inserts a node into a binary tree as the left child of a specified node (see Example 9-2). The call sets the new node to point to the data passed by the caller. Linking the new node into the tree is accomplished by setting the `left` pointer of `node` to point to the new node. If `node` is NULL and the tree is empty, we set the `root` member of the tree data structure to the new node. We update the size of the tree by incrementing the `size` member.

The runtime complexity of *bitree_ins_left* is $O(1)$ because all of the steps in inserting a node into a binary tree run in a constant amount of time.

bitree_ins_right

The *bitree_ins_right* operation inserts a node into a binary tree as the right child of a specified node (see Example 9-2). This operation works similarly to *bitree_ins_left*, except that linking the new node into the tree is accomplished by setting the `right` pointer of `node` to point to the new node.

The runtime complexity of *bitree_ins_right* is $O(1)$ because all of the steps in inserting a node into a binary tree run in a constant amount of time.

bitree_rem_left

The *bitree_rem_left* operation removes the subtree rooted at the left child of a specified node (see Example 9-2). Nodes are removed by performing a postorder traversal beginning at the left child of *node*. If *node* is NULL, we begin the traversal at the root node. The function passed as *destroy* to *bitree_init* is called once for each node as it is removed, provided *destroy* was not set to NULL. As each node is removed, we update the *size* member of the tree data structure as well.

The runtime complexity of *bitree_rem_left* is $O(n)$, where n is the number of nodes in the subtree rooted at the left child of *node*. This is because *bitree_rem_left* performs a postorder traversal to visit each of the nodes in the subtree while all other parts of the operation run in a constant amount of time.

bitree_rem_right

The *bitree_rem_right* operation removes the subtree rooted at the right child of a specified node (see Example 9-2). This operation works much like *bitree_rem_left*, except that nodes are removed by performing a postorder traversal beginning at the right child of *node*.

The runtime complexity of *bitree_rem_right* is $O(n)$, where n is the number of nodes in the subtree rooted at the right child of *node*. This is because *bitree_rem_right* performs a postorder traversal to visit each of the nodes in the subtree while all other parts of the operation run in a constant amount of time.

bitree_merge

The *bitree_merge* operation merges two binary trees into a single binary tree (see Example 9-2). First, we initialize **merge** by calling *bitree_merge*. Next, we insert **data** into the merged tree at its root. The merged tree's left and right children are then set to be the root nodes of **left** and **right**, and the size of the tree is adjusted to reflect the sizes of the subtrees. Last, we detach the nodes now in the merged tree from the original trees and set the size of each tree to 0.

The runtime complexity of *bitree_merge* is $O(1)$ because all of the steps in merging two binary trees run in a constant amount of time.

bitree_size, bitree_root, bitree_is_eob, bitree_is_leaf, bitree_data, bitree_left, bitree_right

These macros implement some of the simpler binary tree operations (see Example 9-1). Generally, they provide an interface for accessing and testing members of the *BiTree* and *BiTreeNode* structures.

The runtime complexity of these operations is $O(1)$ because accessing and testing members of a structure are simple tasks that run in a constant amount of time.

Example 9-2. Implementation of the Binary Tree Abstract Datatype

```
/*****************************************************************************
*                                                                           *
*  ----------------------------- bitree.c -----------------------------     *
*                                                                           *
*****************************************************************************/

#include <stdlib.h>
#include <string.h>

#include "bitree.h"

/*****************************************************************************
*                                                                           *
*  ----------------------------- bitree_init -----------------------------  *
*                                                                           *
*****************************************************************************/

void bitree_init(BiTree *tree, void (*destroy)(void *data)) {

/*****************************************************************************
*                                                                           *
*  Initialize the binary tree.                                              *
*                                                                           *
*****************************************************************************/

tree->size = 0;
tree->destroy = destroy;
tree->root = NULL;

return;

}

/*****************************************************************************
*                                                                           *
*  --------------------------- bitree_destroy ---------------------------   *
*                                                                           *
*****************************************************************************/

void bitree_destroy(BiTree *tree) {

/*****************************************************************************
*                                                                           *
*  Remove all the nodes from the tree.                                      *
*                                                                           *
*****************************************************************************/

bitree_rem_left(tree, NULL);

/*****************************************************************************
*                                                                           *
*  No operations are allowed now, but clear the structure as a precaution.  *
*                                                                           *
*****************************************************************************/
```

Example 9-2. Implementation of the Binary Tree Abstract Datatype (continued)

```c
memset(tree, 0, sizeof(BiTree));

return;

}

/*****************************************************************************
*                                                                           *
*  --------------------------- bitree_ins_left ---------------------------   *
*                                                                           *
*****************************************************************************/

int bitree_ins_left(BiTree *tree, BiTreeNode *node, const void *data) {

BiTreeNode          *new_node,
                    **position;

/*****************************************************************************
*                                                                           *
*  Determine where to insert the node.                                      *
*                                                                           *
*****************************************************************************/

if (node == NULL) {

   /*****************************************************************************
   *                                                                           *
   *  Allow insertion at the root only in an empty tree.                       *
   *                                                                           *
   *****************************************************************************/

   if (bitree_size(tree) > 0)
      return -1;

   position = &tree->root;

   }

else {

   /*****************************************************************************
   *                                                                           *
   *  Normally allow insertion only at the end of a branch.                    *
   *                                                                           *
   *****************************************************************************/

   if (bitree_left(node) != NULL)
      return -1;

   position = &node->left;

   }
```

Example 9-2. Implementation of the Binary Tree Abstract Datatype (continued)

```
/***************************************************************************
 *                                                                         *
 *  Allocate storage for the node.                                         *
 *                                                                         *
 ***************************************************************************/

if ((new_node = (BiTreeNode *)malloc(sizeof(BiTreeNode))) == NULL)
   return -1;

/***************************************************************************
 *                                                                         *
 *  Insert the node into the tree.                                         *
 *                                                                         *
 ***************************************************************************/

new_node->data = (void *)data;
new_node->left = NULL;
new_node->right = NULL;
*position = new_node;

/***************************************************************************
 *                                                                         *
 *  Adjust the size of the tree to account for the inserted node.          *
 *                                                                         *
 ***************************************************************************/

tree->size++;

return 0;

}

/***************************************************************************
 *                                                                         *
 *  -------------------------- bitree_ins_right --------------------------  *
 *                                                                         *
 ***************************************************************************/

int bitree_ins_right(BiTree *tree, BiTreeNode *node, const void *data) {

BiTreeNode         *new_node,
                   **position;

/***************************************************************************
 *                                                                         *
 *  Determine where to insert the node.                                    *
 *                                                                         *
 ***************************************************************************/

if (node == NULL) {
```

Example 9-2. Implementation of the Binary Tree Abstract Datatype (continued)

```
/**************************************************************************
*                                                                        *
*  Allow insertion at the root only in an empty tree.                    *
*                                                                        *
**************************************************************************/

if (bitree_size(tree) > 0)
   return -1;

position = &tree->root;

}

else {

/**************************************************************************
*                                                                        *
*  Normally allow insertion only at the end of a branch.                 *
*                                                                        *
**************************************************************************/

if (bitree_right(node) != NULL)
   return -1;

position = &node->right;

}

/**************************************************************************
*                                                                        *
*  Allocate storage for the node.                                        *
*                                                                        *
**************************************************************************/

if ((new_node = (BiTreeNode *)malloc(sizeof(BiTreeNode))) == NULL)
   return -1;

/**************************************************************************
*                                                                        *
*  Insert the node into the tree.                                        *
*                                                                        *
**************************************************************************/

new_node->data = (void *)data;
new_node->left = NULL;
new_node->right = NULL;
*position = new_node;

/**************************************************************************
*                                                                        *
*  Adjust the size of the tree to account for the inserted node.         *
*                                                                        *
**************************************************************************/
```

Example 9-2. Implementation of the Binary Tree Abstract Datatype (continued)

```c
tree->size++;

return 0;

}

/*****************************************************************************
*                                                                           *
*  --------------------------- bitree_rem_left ---------------------------  *
*                                                                           *
*****************************************************************************/

void bitree_rem_left(BiTree *tree, BiTreeNode *node) {

BiTreeNode           **position;

/*****************************************************************************
*                                                                           *
*  Do not allow removal from an empty tree.                                 *
*                                                                           *
*****************************************************************************/

if (bitree_size(tree) == 0)
   return;

/*****************************************************************************
*                                                                           *
*  Determine where to remove nodes.                                         *
*                                                                           *
*****************************************************************************/

if (node == NULL)
   position = &tree->root;
else
   position = &node->left;

/*****************************************************************************
*                                                                           *
*  Remove the nodes.                                                        *
*                                                                           *
*****************************************************************************/

if (*position != NULL) {

   bitree_rem_left(tree, *position);
   bitree_rem_right(tree, *position);

   if (tree->destroy != NULL) {

      /*****************************************************************
      *                                                               *
      *  Call a user-defined function to free dynamically allocated data. *
      *                                                               *
      *****************************************************************/
```

Example 9-2. Implementation of the Binary Tree Abstract Datatype (continued)

```
      tree->destroy((*position)->data);

   }

   free(*position);
   *position = NULL;

   /*************************************************************************
   *                                                                       *
   *  Adjust the size of the tree to account for the removed node.         *
   *                                                                       *
   *************************************************************************/

   tree->size--;

}

return;

}

/****************************************************************************
*                                                                          *
*  -------------------------- bitree_rem_right --------------------------  *
*                                                                          *
****************************************************************************/

void bitree_rem_right(BiTree *tree, BiTreeNode *node) {

BiTreeNode          **position;

/****************************************************************************
*                                                                          *
*  Do not allow removal from an empty tree.                                *
*                                                                          *
****************************************************************************/

if (bitree_size(tree) == 0)
   return;

/****************************************************************************
*                                                                          *
*  Determine where to remove nodes.                                        *
*                                                                          *
****************************************************************************/

if (node == NULL)
   position = &tree->root;
else
   position = &node->right;
```

Example 9-2. Implementation of the Binary Tree Abstract Datatype (continued)

```
/***************************************************************************
*                                                                          *
*  Remove the nodes.                                                       *
*                                                                          *
***************************************************************************/

if (*position != NULL) {

   bitree_rem_left(tree, *position);
   bitree_rem_right(tree, *position);

   if (tree->destroy != NULL) {

      /*********************************************************************
      *                                                                   *
      *  Call a user-defined function to free dynamically allocated data. *
      *                                                                   *
      *********************************************************************/

      tree->destroy((*position)->data);

   }

   free(*position);
   *position = NULL;

   /***********************************************************************
   *                                                                      *
   *  Adjust the size of the tree to account for the removed node.        *
   *                                                                      *
   ***********************************************************************/

   tree->size--;

}

return;

}

/***************************************************************************
*                                                                          *
*  --------------------------- bitree_merge ----------------------------   *
*                                                                          *
***************************************************************************/

int bitree_merge(BiTree *merge, BiTree *left, BiTree *right, const void
   *data) {
```

Example 9-2. Implementation of the Binary Tree Abstract Datatype (continued)

```
/***************************************************************************
*                                                                         *
*  Initialize the merged tree.                                            *
*                                                                         *
***************************************************************************/

bitree_init(merge, left->destroy);

/***************************************************************************
*                                                                         *
*  Insert the data for the root node of the merged tree.                  *
*                                                                         *
***************************************************************************/

if (bitree_ins_left(merge, NULL, data) != 0) {

   bitree_destroy(merge);
   return -1;

}

/***************************************************************************
*                                                                         *
*  Merge the two binary trees into a single binary tree.                  *
*                                                                         *
***************************************************************************/

bitree_root(merge)->left = bitree_root(left);
bitree_root(merge)->right = bitree_root(right);

/***************************************************************************
*                                                                         *
*  Adjust the size of the new binary tree.                                *
*                                                                         *
***************************************************************************/

merge->size = merge->size + bitree_size(left) + bitree_size(right);

/***************************************************************************
*                                                                         *
*  Do not let the original trees access the merged nodes.                 *
*                                                                         *
***************************************************************************/

left->root = NULL;
left->size = 0;
right->root = NULL;
right->size = 0;

return 0;

}
```

Binary Tree Example: Expression Processing

One intuitive way to process arithmetic expressions with a computer is using an *expression tree*. An expression tree is a binary tree consisting of nodes containing two types of objects: *operators* and *terminal values*. Operators are objects that have operands; terminal values are objects that have no operands.

The idea behind an expression tree is simple: the subtrees rooted at the children of each node are the operands of the operator stored in the parent (see Figure 9-5). Operands may be terminal values, or they may be other expressions themselves. Expressions are expanded in subtrees; terminal values reside in leaf nodes. One of the nice things about this idea is how easily an expression tree allows us to translate an expression into one of three common representations: *prefix*, *infix*, and *postfix*. To obtain these representations, we simply traverse the tree using a preorder, inorder, or postorder traversal.

Traversing the tree in Figure 9-5 in preorder, for example, yields the prefix expression × / − 74 10 32 + 23 17. To evaluate a prefix expression, we apply each operator to the two operands that immediately follow it. Thus, the prefix expression just given is evaluated as:

$$(\times (/ (- \ 74 \ 10) 32) (+ \ 23 \ 17)) = 80$$

Infix expressions are the expressions we are most familiar with from mathematics, but they are not well suited to processing by a computer. If we traverse the tree of Figure 9-5 using an inorder traversal, we get the infix expression 74 − 10 / 32 × 23 + 17. Notice that one of the difficulties with infix expressions is that they do not inherently identify in which order operations should be performed, whereas prefix and postfix expressions do. However, we can remedy this situation in an infix expression by parenthesizing each part of the expression as we traverse it in the tree. Fully parenthesized, the previous infix expression is evaluated as:

$$(((74 - 10) / 32) \times (23 + 17)) = 80$$

Postfix expressions are well suited to processing by a computer. If we traverse the tree of Figure 9-5 in postorder, we get the postfix expression 74 10 − 32 / 23 17 + ×. To evaluate a postfix expression, we apply each operator to the two operands immediately preceding it. Thus, the postfix expression just given is evaluated as:

$$(((74 \ 10 \ -) \ 32 \ / \ ) (23 \ 17 +) \times) = 80$$

One reason postfix expressions are well suited to computers is that they are easy to evaluate with an *abstract stack machine*, an abstraction used by compilers and hand-held calculators. To process a postfix expression using an abstract stack

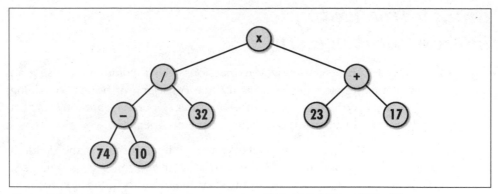

Figure 9-5. An expression tree for the expression ((74 – 10) / 32) × (23 + 17)

machine, we proceed as follows. First, we move from left to right through the expression, pushing values onto the stack until an operator is encountered. Next, the operands required by the operator are popped, the operator is applied to them, and the result is pushed back on the stack. This procedure is repeated until the entire expression has been processed, at which point the value of the expression is the lone item remaining on the stack (see Figure 9-6).

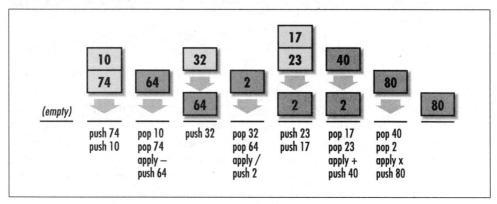

Figure 9-6. An abstract stack machine processing the postfix expression 74 10 – 32 / 23 17 + ×

Example 9-3 illustrates how to produce the prefix, infix, and postfix representations of an expression stored in an expression tree. For this, three functions are provided, *preorder, inorder,* and *postorder,* which traverse a binary tree in preorder, inorder, and postorder, respectively. Each function accepts two arguments: *node* and *list*.

To begin a traversal, we set *node* to the root node of the expression tree we wish to traverse. Successive recursive calls set *node* to the node at the top of the sub-tree about to be traversed. On the initial call to each function, we also pass into *list* an empty linked list already initialized with *list_init*. For each of the traversals, nodes are placed into the list in the order they are encountered. When the initial call in the recursion returns, *list* contains the preorder, inorder, or postorder listing of the nodes, as appropriate. Notice how a recursive implementation of these traversals nicely models the definitions presented earlier in the chapter.

Example 9-3. Implementation of Functions for Traversing a Binary Tree

```
/*****************************************************************************
*                                                                           *
*  --------------------------- traverse.c ---------------------------        *
*                                                                           *
*****************************************************************************/

#include "list.h"
#include "traverse.h"

/*****************************************************************************
*                                                                           *
*  ----------------------------- preorder -----------------------------      *
*                                                                           *
*****************************************************************************/

int preorder(const BiTreeNode *node, List *list) {

/*****************************************************************************
*                                                                           *
*  Load the list with a preorder listing of the tree.                        *
*                                                                           *
*****************************************************************************/

if (!bitree_is_eob(node)) {

   if (list_ins_next(list, list_tail(list), bitree_data(node)) != 0)
      return -1;

   if (!bitree_is_eob(bitree_left(node)))
      if (preorder(bitree_left(node), list) != 0)
         return -1;

   if (!bitree_is_eob(bitree_right(node)))
      if (preorder(bitree_right(node), list) != 0)
         return -1;

}

return 0;

}

/*****************************************************************************
*                                                                           *
*  ----------------------------- inorder ------------------------------      *
*                                                                           *
*****************************************************************************/
```

Example 9-3. Implementation of Functions for Traversing a Binary Tree (continued)

```c
int inorder(const BiTreeNode *node, List *list) {

/*****************************************************************************
*                                                                           *
*  Load the list with an inorder listing of the tree.                       *
*                                                                           *
*****************************************************************************/

if (!bitree_is_eob(node)) {

   if (!bitree_is_eob(bitree_left(node)))
      if (inorder(bitree_left(node), list) != 0)
         return -1;

   if (list_ins_next(list, list_tail(list), bitree_data(node)) != 0)
      return -1;

   if (!bitree_is_eob(bitree_right(node)))
      if (inorder(bitree_right(node), list) != 0)
         return -1;

}

return 0;

}

/*****************************************************************************
*                                                                           *
*  ------------------------------ postorder -----------------------------   *
*                                                                           *
*****************************************************************************/

int postorder(const BiTreeNode *node, List *list) {

/*****************************************************************************
*                                                                           *
*  Load the list with a postorder listing of the tree.                      *
*                                                                           *
*****************************************************************************/

if (!bitree_is_eob(node)) {

   if (!bitree_is_eob(bitree_left(node)))
      if (postorder(bitree_left(node), list) != 0)
         return -1;

   if (!bitree_is_eob(bitree_right(node)))
      if (postorder(bitree_right(node), list) != 0)
         return -1;

   if (list_ins_next(list, list_tail(list), bitree_data(node)) != 0)
      return -1;
```

Example 9-3. Implementation of Functions for Traversing a Binary Tree (continued)

```
}

return 0;

}
```

Description of Binary Search Trees

Binary search trees are binary trees organized specifically for searching. To search for a node in a binary search tree, we start at the root of the tree and descend level by level until we find the node we are looking for. When we encounter a node greater than the desired node, we follow its left pointer. When we encounter a node that is less, we follow its right pointer. For example, to locate 15 in the tree of Figure 9-7, start at the root and move to the left since 15 is less than 20, then to the right since 15 is greater than 09, at which point we find 15. If we reach the end of a branch before locating the desired node, it does not exist.

Of course, the process of searching a binary tree depends on nodes having been inserted in a similar way. Thus, to insert a node, we start at the root of the tree and descend level by level, moving left or right as appropriate. When we reach the end of a branch, we make the insertion. For example, to insert 65 into the tree of Figure 9-7, we start at the root and move to the right since 65 is greater than 20, then to the right again since 65 is greater than 53, and then to the left since 65 is less than 79. This point is the end of a branch, so we insert the key as the left child of 79. Duplicate keys are not allowed.

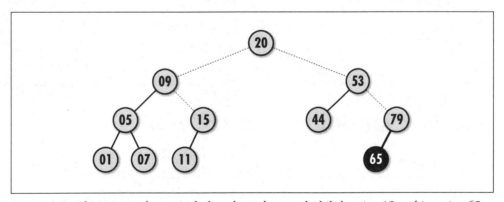

Figure 9-7. A binary search tree, including the paths traced while locating 15 and inserting 65

Binary search trees are efficient structures for searching because in the worst case, we only end up searching the data in one branch, instead of having to search every piece of data. Thus, searching becomes an $O(\lg n)$ operation, where n is the number of nodes in the tree, provided the tree is kept balanced. Recall that keeping a tree balanced means that it will be as short as possible for a given number of nodes. Keeping a binary search tree balanced is important because it means that no branch we search will be exceptionally long.

To understand further the importance of keeping a binary search tree balanced, consider what happens as a binary search tree becomes more and more unbalanced. As this occurs, searching for a node approaches $O(n)$, which is no better than searching from one end of the data to the next. For example, imagine a binary search tree containing 2^{16} words from a dictionary inserted in alphabetical order (see Figure 9-8). In this case, the tree consists of a single branch to the right, and searching for a word could require inspecting as many as 2^{16} words. However, if we insert the words in a random fashion, the tree should end up at least somewhat balanced, and we can expect to traverse closer to $\lg 2^{16} = 16$ words in the worst case. Since normally the order in which nodes are inserted and removed is not something we can control, we cannot rely on this method to keep a tree balanced. Instead, we must take a more proactive approach.

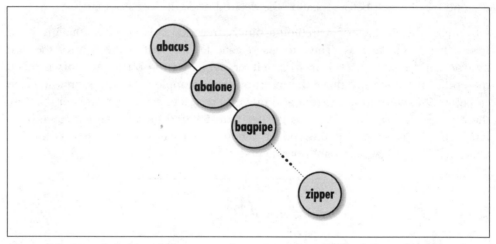

Figure 9-8. A poorly balanced binary search tree consisting of a single branch to the right

Interface for Binary Search Trees

bistree_init

```
void bistree_init(BisTree *tree, void (*compare)(const void *key1,
   const void *key2), void (*destroy)(void *data));
```

Return Value   None.

Description   Initializes the binary search tree specified by *tree*. This operation must be called for a binary search tree before the tree can be used with any other operation. The function pointer *compare* specifies a user-defined function to compare elements. This function should return 1 if *key1* > *key2*, 0 if *key1* = *key2*, and −1 if *key1* < *key2*. The *destroy* argument provides a way to free dynamically allocated data when *bistree_destroy* is called. It works in a manner similar to that described for *bitree_destroy*. For a binary search tree containing data that should not be freed, *destroy* should be set to NULL.

Complexity $O(1)$

bistree_destroy

```
void bistree_destroy(BisTree *tree);
```

Return Value   None.

Description   Destroys the binary search tree specified by *tree*. No other operations are permitted after calling *bistree_destroy* unless *bistree_init* is called again. The *bistree_destroy* operation removes all nodes from a binary search tree and calls the function passed as *destroy* to *bistree_init* once for each node as it is removed, provided *destroy* was not set to NULL.

Complexity $O(n)$, where n is the number of nodes in the binary search tree.

bistree_insert

```
int bistree_insert(BisTree *tree, const void *data);
```

Return Value   0 if inserting the node is successful, 1 if the node is already in the tree, or −1 otherwise.

Description   Inserts a node into the binary search tree specified by *tree*. The new node contains a pointer to *data*, so the memory referenced by *data* should remain valid as long as the node remains in the binary search tree. It is the responsibility of the caller to manage the storage associated with *data*.

Complexity $O(\lg n)$, where n is the number of nodes in the binary search tree.

bistree_remove

```
int bistree_remove(BisTree *tree, const void *data);
```

Return Value   0 if removing the node is successful, or −1 otherwise.

Description   Removes the node matching *data* from the binary search tree specified by *tree*. In actuality, this operation only performs a *lazy removal*, in which the node is simply marked as hidden. Thus, no pointer is returned to the data matching *data*. Furthermore, the data in the tree must remain valid even after it has been removed. Consequently, the size of the binary search tree, as returned by *bistree_size*, does not decrease after removing a node. This approach is explained further in the implementation and analysis section.

Complexity $O(\lg\ n)$, where n is the number of nodes in the binary search tree.

bistree_lookup

```
int bistree_lookup(const BisTree *tree, void **data);
```

Return Value   0 if the data is found in the binary search tree, or –1 otherwise.

Description   Determines whether a node matches **data** in the binary search tree specified as **tree**. If a match is found, **data** points to the matching data in the binary search tree upon return.

Complexity $O(\lg\ n)$, where n is the number of nodes in the binary search tree.

bistree_size

```
int bistree_size(const BisTree *tree);
```

Return Value   Number of nodes in the tree.

Description   Macro that evaluates to the number of nodes in the binary search tree specified by **tree**.

Complexity $O(1)$

Implementation and Analysis of Binary Search Trees

As described earlier, binary search trees perform well only if the tree remains balanced. Unfortunately, keeping a binary search tree balanced is a more difficult problem than it may at first appear. Nevertheless, there are a few clever approaches one can take. One of the best approaches is to implement the tree as an *AVL tree*.

An AVL (Adel'son-Vel'skii and Landis) tree is a special type of binary tree that stores an extra piece of information with each node: its *balance factor*. The balance factor of a node is the height of the subtree rooted at its left child minus the height of the subtree rooted at its right child (see Figure 9-9). As nodes are inserted, an AVL tree adjusts itself so that all balance factors stay +1, –1, or 0. A subtree whose root node has a balance factor of +1 is said to be *left-heavy*. A subtree whose root node has a balance factor of –1 is said to be *right-heavy*. A subtree whose root node has a balance factor of 0 is considered balanced. By keeping its subtrees nearly balanced, an AVL tree stays *approximately* balanced overall.

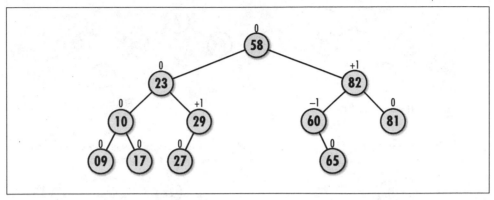

Figure 9-9. An AVL tree, including balance factors

The basic means of searching and inserting nodes in an AVL tree is the same as described earlier. However, when we insert a node into an AVL tree, we have some additional work to do after the node descends to its appropriate position. First, we must account for the change in balance factors that occurs as a result of the insertion. Also, if any balance factor becomes ±2, we must rebalance the tree from that point down, which is done by performing an operation called a *rotation*.

Rotations in AVL Trees

A rotation rebalances part of an AVL tree by rearranging nodes while preserving the relationship wherein the left is smaller than the parent and the parent is smaller than the right, which must be maintained for the tree to remain a binary search tree. After the rotation, the balance factors of all nodes in the rotated sub-tree are +1, −1, or 0.

There are only four types of rotations that ever have to be performed. These are the LL (*left-left*), LR (*left-right*), RR (*right-right*), and RL (*right-left*) rotations. The functions *rotate_left* and *rotate_right*, presented later in Example 9-5, implement each of these rotations. To understand when we need to apply each rotation, let *x* represent the node we have just inserted into its proper location in an AVL tree, and let *A* be the nearest ancestor of *x* whose balance factor has changed to ±2.

LL rotation

We perform an LL, or left-left, rotation when *x* lies in the *left* subtree of the *left* subtree of *A* (see Figure 9-10). Let *left* be the left child of *A*. To perform an LL rotation, we set the left pointer of *A* to the right child of *left*, the right pointer of *left* to *A*, and the pointer referencing *A* to *left*. After the rotation, we set the balance factors of both *A* and *left* to 0. All other balance factors do not change.

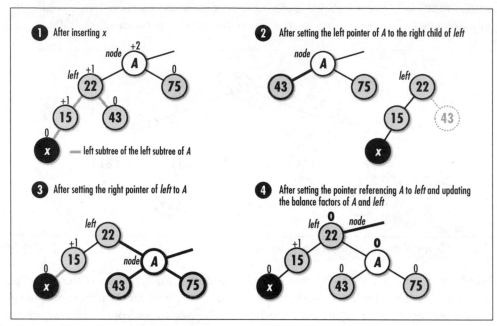

① After inserting *x*

— left subtree of the left subtree of *A*

② After setting the left pointer of *A* to the right child of *left*

③ After setting the right pointer of *left* to *A*

④ After setting the pointer referencing *A* to *left* and updating the balance factors of *A* and *left*

Figure 9-10. An LL rotation in an AVL tree

LR rotation

We perform an LR, or left-right, rotation when *x* lies in the *right* subtree of the *left* subtree of *A* (see Figure 9-11). Let *left* be the left child of *A* and *grandchild* be the right child of *left*. To perform an LR rotation, we set the right child of *left* to the left child of *grandchild*, the left child of *grandchild* to *left*, the left child of *A* to the right child of *grandchild*, the right child of *grandchild* to *A*, and finally the pointer referencing *A* to *grandchild*.

Adjusting the balance factors of nodes after an LR rotation depends on the original balance factor of *grandchild*. Figure 9-12 illustrates the three cases to consider. If the original balance factor of *grandchild* was +1, we set the balance factor of *A* to − 1 and *left* to 0. If the original balance factor of *grandchild* was 0, we set the balance factors of both *A* and *left* to 0. If the original balance factor of *grandchild* was −1, we set the balance factor of *A* to 0 and that of *left* to +1. In all cases, we set the new balance factor of *grandchild* to 0. All other balance factors do not change.

RR rotation

We perform an RR, or right-right, rotation when *x* lies in the *right* subtree of the *right* subtree of *A*. The RR rotation is symmetric to the LL rotation. Let *right* be the right child of *A*. To perform an RR rotation, we set the right pointer of *A* to the left child of *right*, the left pointer of *right* to *A*, and the pointer referencing *A* to *right*. After the rotation, we set the balance factors of both *A* and *left* to 0. All other balance factors do not change.

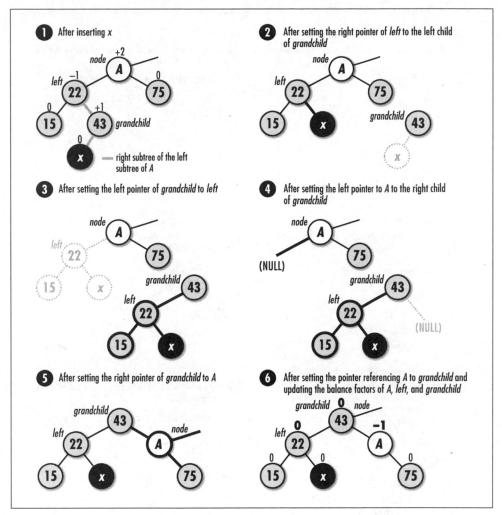

Figure 9-11. An LR rotation in an AVL tree

RL rotation

We perform an RL, or right-left, rotation when x lies in the *left* subtree of the *right* subtree of A. The RL rotation is symmetric to the LR rotation. Let *right* be the right child of A and *grandchild* be the left child of *right*. To perform an RL rotation, we set the left child of *right* to the right child of *grandchild*, the right child of *grandchild* to *right*, the right child of A to the left child of *grandchild*, the left child of *grandchild* to A, and finally the pointer referencing A to *grandchild*.

Adjusting the balance factors of nodes after an RL rotation depends on the original balance factor of *grandchild*. There are three cases to consider. If the original balance factor of *grandchild* was +1, we set the balance factor of A to 0 and that

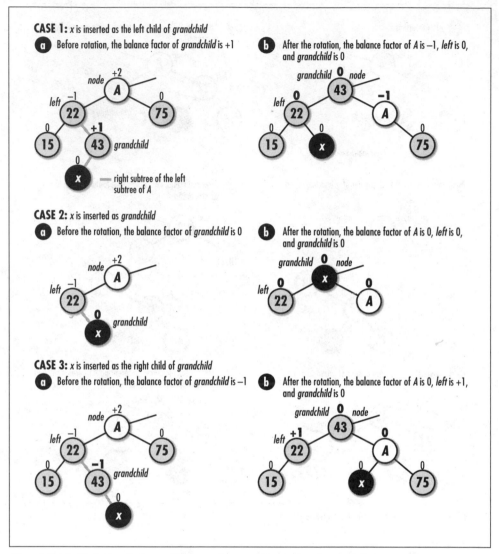

CASE 1: *x* is inserted as the left child of *grandchild*

(a) Before rotation, the balance factor of *grandchild* is +1

(b) After the rotation, the balance factor of *A* is −1, *left* is 0, and *grandchild* is 0

CASE 2: *x* is inserted as *grandchild*

(a) Before the rotation, the balance factor of *grandchild* is 0

(b) After the rotation, the balance factor of *A* is 0, *left* is 0, and *grandchild* is 0

CASE 3: *x* is inserted as the right child of *grandchild*

(a) Before the rotation, the balance factor of *grandchild* is −1

(b) After the rotation, the balance factor of *A* is 0, *left* is +1, and *grandchild* is 0

Figure 9-12. Updating balance factors after an LR rotation in an AVL tree

of *right* to −1. If the original balance factor of *grandchild* was 0, we set the balance factors of both *A* and *left* to 0. If the original balance factor of *grandchild* was −1, we set the balance factor of *A* to +1 and that of *left* to 0. In all cases, we set the new balance factor of *grandchild* to 0. All other balance factors do not change. These adjustments are symmetric to those shown in Figure 9-12 for an LR rotation.

The structure *BisTree* is the binary search tree data structure. A good way to implement a binary search tree is to use the binary tree abstract datatype discussed earlier. Thus, *BisTree* is implemented as a typedef to *BiTree* (see Example 9-4).

In addition to simplicity, using a typedef has the benefit of making the binary search tree somewhat polymorphic, just as described for stacks and queues (see Chapter 6, *Stacks and Queues*). This means that we can use binary tree operations on a binary search tree in addition to those operations defined specifically for binary search trees.

Since keeping a binary search tree balanced requires that each node store more than just the data placed in the tree, a structure, *AvlNode*, is defined for each node to contain (see Example 9-4). An *AvlNode* structure consists of three members: *data* is the data stored in the node, *hidden* is a member used to mark a node when it is removed, and *factor* is the node's balance factor. The implementation presented here also uses identifiers to represent the possible values for balance factors. Example 9-4 equates *AVL_LEFT_HEAVY* to 1, *AVL_BALANCED* to 0, and *AVL_RGT_HEAVY* to −1.

Example 9-4. Header for the Binary Search Tree Abstract Datatype

```
/*****************************************************************************
*                                                                           *
*  ---------------------------- bistree.h ----------------------------      *
*                                                                           *
*****************************************************************************/

#ifndef BISTREE_H
#define BISTREE_H

#include "bitree.h"

/*****************************************************************************
*                                                                           *
*  Define balance factors for AVL trees.                                    *
*                                                                           *
*****************************************************************************/

#define         AVL_LFT_HEAVY         1
#define         AVL_BALANCED          0
#define         AVL_RGT_HEAVY        -1

/*****************************************************************************
*                                                                           *
*  Define a structure for nodes in AVL trees.                               *
*                                                                           *
*****************************************************************************/

typedef struct AvlNode_ {

void            *data;
int             hidden;
int             factor;

} AvlNode;
```

Example 9-4. Header for the Binary Search Tree Abstract Datatype (continued)

```
/**********************************************************************
*                                                                    *
*  Implement binary search trees as binary trees.                    *
*                                                                    *
**********************************************************************/

typedef BiTree BisTree;

/**********************************************************************
*                                                                    *
*  ------------------------- Public Interface ----------------------  *
*                                                                    *
**********************************************************************/

void bistree_init(BisTree *tree, int (*compare)(const void *key1, const void
   *key2), void (*destroy)(void *data));

void bistree_destroy(BisTree *tree);

int bistree_insert(BisTree *tree, const void *data);

int bistree_remove(BisTree *tree, const void *data);

int bistree_lookup(BisTree *tree, void **data);

#define bistree_size(tree) ((tree)->size)

#endif
```

bistree_init

The *bistree_init* operation initializes a binary search tree so that it can be used in other operations (see Example 9-5). Since a binary search tree is a binary tree, we call *bitree_init* to initialize it. The **compare** member is set to **compare** by hand because this member is not used by binary trees and therefore is not set by *bitree_init*.

The runtime complexity of *bistree_init* is the same as *bitree_init*, or $O(1)$.

bistree_destroy

The *bistree_destroy* operation destroys a binary search tree (see Example 9-5). To do this, we employ the support of two additional functions, *destroy_left* and *destroy_right*, which recursively destroy the left and right subtrees beneath a node. These functions work similarly to the *bitree_rem_left* and *bitree_rem_right* functions defined previously for binary trees. Separate functions are required for binary search trees so that we can destroy the data referenced by a node's **AvlNode** structure as well as free the **AvlNode** structure itself.

The runtime complexity of *bistree_destroy* is the same as *bitree_destroy*, or $O(n)$, where n is the number of nodes in the tree.

bistree_insert

The *bistree_insert* operation inserts a node into a binary search tree (see Example 9-5). The operation works by recursively calling *insert* to descend to the point at which the actual insertion should be made. Once we insert the node, we update balance factors on our way back up the tree as the recursion unwinds. If, in so doing, any balance factor reaches ±2, we perform a rotation.

We begin by checking whether we are inserting a node into an empty tree. If this is the case, we simply insert the node and set its balance factor to AVL_BALANCED. Otherwise, we compare the data to be inserted with that of the current node to determine the direction in which to move. We proceed as we described earlier for inserting a node into a binary search tree. When the data we are inserting is less than that of the current node we are traversing, we make a recursive call that moves us to the left. When the data is greater, we make a recursive call that moves us to the right. Once we locate the point at which to make the insertion, we allocate an AvlNode structure and insert it into the tree as the appropriate child of the current node. If the data to be inserted matches that of a node hidden as a result of being removed, we destroy the data currently in the node, insert the new data in its place, and mark the node as no longer hidden. In this case, rebalancing is not required.

Except after replacing a previously hidden node, we next determine how the balance of the tree has been affected so that we can make repairs if necessary. Whether we have inserted the node to the left or right, we set balanced to 0 to indicate that the insertion may have upset the balance of the tree. This causes a switch statement to be executed that adjusts the balance factor of the current node. Adjusting the balance factor of the current node may, in turn, upset the balance factors of nodes higher in the tree. Thus, as we reenter each activation of *insert*, we update the balance factor of the node traversed at that level, provided balanced is still 0. Once we determine that no more updates are required, we set balanced to 0 to inform previous activations of this decision.

The switch statements that determine how to update balance factors also determine when rotations should be performed. The actual function we call to perform the rotation, either *rotate_left* or *rotate_right*, determines the type of rotation to apply: either LL or LR if we call *rotate_left*, or RR or RL if we call *rotate_right*. Since rotations change the balance factors of nodes, each rotation function also adjusts balance factors. The best way to understand the process of updating balance factors and performing rotations is to trace through the example in Figure 9-13.

Earlier it was mentioned that the runtime complexity of inserting a node into a perfectly balanced binary search tree is $O(\lg n)$. However, since an AVL tree keeps

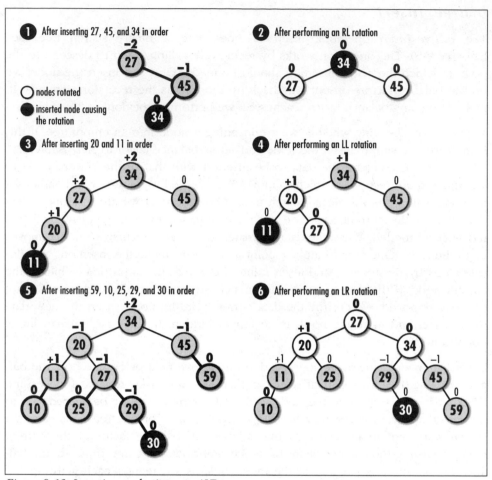

Figure 9-13. Inserting nodes into an AVL tree

itself only approximately balanced, one might wonder how this affects performance. It turns out that the worst-case running time of inserting a node into an AVL tree is $T(n) = 1.5k \lg n$, where k is some constant, n is the number of nodes in the tree, and $T(n) = k \lg n$ is the time to insert a node into a perfectly balanced binary tree. Just as with insertion into a perfectly balanced tree, this results in a runtime complexity of $O(\lg n)$. However, the constant of 1.5 does influence performance somewhat in practice.

bistree_remove

The *bistree_remove* operation removes a node from a binary search tree (see Example 9-5). For this operation, we apply a rather simplistic heuristic termed *lazy removal*, in which we hide nodes instead of actually removing them. To hide a node, we set the *hidden* member of its *AvlNode* structure to 1. If we insert the same data again later, we simply make the node visible again by setting its *hidden* member back to 0 (see *bistree_insert*). In practice, this approach is acceptable if we do not expect to remove many nodes relative to the number we insert. If we plan to remove a large number of nodes, we might consider actually removing the node and adjusting the tree. To locate the node to hide, we recursively call *hide* until we reach the node we are looking for. Once we hide the node, there is no need to rebalance the tree because we did not change its structure. Thus, we set *balanced* to 1.

The analysis of removing a node from an AVL tree is the same as for inserting a node. Thus, the runtime complexity of *bistree_remove* is $O(\lg n)$.

bistree_lookup

The *bistree_lookup* operation searches for a node within a binary search tree and returns a pointer to the data member of its *AvlNode* structure (see Example 9-5). The operation works by calling *lookup* recursively to descend through the tree until the desired node is found. At each level, we first check if we have reached the end of a branch. If we reach the end of a branch, the node we are looking for does not exist. Otherwise, we move to either the left or right in the same manner as described for *bistree_insert*. The recursion terminates once we encounter the desired node, at which point we return 0.

The analysis of searching an AVL tree is the same as for inserting a node. Thus, the runtime complexity of *bistree_lookup* is $O(\lg n)$.

bistree_size

This macro evaluates to the size of a set (see Example 9-4). It works by accessing the *size* member of the *BisTree* structure.

The runtime complexity of *bistree_size* is $O(1)$ because accessing a member of a structure is a simple task that runs in a constant amount of time.

Example 9-5. Implementation of the Binary Search Tree Abstract Datatype

```
/*****************************************************************************
*                                                                           *
*  ---------------------------- bistree.c ----------------------------      *
*                                                                           *
*****************************************************************************/

#include <stdlib.h>
#include <string.h>

#include "bistree.h"
```

Example 9-5. Implementation of the Binary Search Tree Abstract Datatype (continued)

```c
/***************************************************************************
*                                                                         *
*   ----------------------------- rotate_left -----------------------------  *
*                                                                         *
***************************************************************************/

static void rotate_left(BiTreeNode **node) {

BiTreeNode          *left,
                    *grandchild;

left = bitree_left(*node);

if (((AvlNode *)bitree_data(left))->factor == AVL_LFT_HEAVY) {

   /***************************************************************************
   *                                                                         *
   *   Perform an LL rotation.                                               *
   *                                                                         *
   ***************************************************************************/

   bitree_left(*node) = bitree_right(left);
   bitree_right(left) = *node;
   ((AvlNode *)bitree_data(*node))->factor = AVL_BALANCED;
   ((AvlNode *)bitree_data(left))->factor = AVL_BALANCED;
   *node = left;

   }

else {

   /***************************************************************************
   *                                                                         *
   *   Perform an LR rotation.                                               *
   *                                                                         *
   ***************************************************************************/

   grandchild = bitree_right(left);
   bitree_right(left) = bitree_left(grandchild);
   bitree_left(grandchild) = left;
   bitree_left(*node) = bitree_right(grandchild);
   bitree_right(grandchild) = *node;

   switch (((AvlNode *)bitree_data(grandchild))->factor) {

      case AVL_LFT_HEAVY:

      ((AvlNode *)bitree_data(*node))->factor = AVL_RGT_HEAVY;
      ((AvlNode *)bitree_data(left))->factor = AVL_BALANCED;
      break;

      case AVL_BALANCED:
```

Example 9-5. Implementation of the Binary Search Tree Abstract Datatype (continued)

```
      ((AvlNode *)bitree_data(*node))->factor = AVL_BALANCED;
      ((AvlNode *)bitree_data(left))->factor = AVL_BALANCED;
      break;

   case AVL_RGT_HEAVY:

      ((AvlNode *)bitree_data(*node))->factor = AVL_BALANCED;
      ((AvlNode *)bitree_data(left))->factor = AVL_LFT_HEAVY;
      break;

   }

   ((AvlNode *)bitree_data(grandchild))->factor = AVL_BALANCED;
   *node = grandchild;

}

return;

}

/***************************************************************************
*                                                                         *
* ---------------------------- rotate_right ----------------------------- *
*                                                                         *
***************************************************************************/

static void rotate_right(BiTreeNode **node) {

BiTreeNode          *right,
                    *grandchild;

right = bitree_right(*node);

if (((AvlNode *)bitree_data(right))->factor == AVL_RGT_HEAVY) {

   /***********************************************************************
   *                                                                     *
   *   Perform an RR rotation.                                           *
   *                                                                     *
   ***********************************************************************/

   bitree_right(*node) = bitree_left(right);
   bitree_left(right) = *node;
   ((AvlNode *)bitree_data(*node))->factor = AVL_BALANCED;
   ((AvlNode *)bitree_data(right))->factor = AVL_BALANCED;
   *node = right;

   }

else {
```

Example 9-5. Implementation of the Binary Search Tree Abstract Datatype (continued)

```
/***************************************************************************
*                                                                         *
*   Perform an RL rotation.                                               *
*                                                                         *
***************************************************************************/

grandchild = bitree_left(right);
bitree_left(right) = bitree_right(grandchild);
bitree_right(grandchild) = right;
bitree_right(*node) = bitree_left(grandchild);
bitree_left(grandchild) = *node;

switch (((AvlNode *)bitree_data(grandchild))->factor) {

   case AVL_LFT_HEAVY:

   ((AvlNode *)bitree_data(*node))->factor = AVL_BALANCED;
   ((AvlNode *)bitree_data(right))->factor = AVL_RGT_HEAVY;
   break;

   case AVL_BALANCED:

   ((AvlNode *)bitree_data(*node))->factor = AVL_BALANCED;
   ((AvlNode *)bitree_data(right))->factor = AVL_BALANCED;
   break;

   case AVL_RGT_HEAVY:

   ((AvlNode *)bitree_data(*node))->factor = AVL_LFT_HEAVY;
   ((AvlNode *)bitree_data(right))->factor = AVL_BALANCED;
   break;

   }

   ((AvlNode *)bitree_data(grandchild))->factor = AVL_BALANCED;
   *node = grandchild;

}

return;

}

/***************************************************************************
*                                                                         *
*   ---------------------------- destroy_left ----------------------------  *
*                                                                         *
***************************************************************************/

static void destroy_left(BisTree *tree, BiTreeNode *node) {

BiTreeNode          **position;
```

Example 9-5. Implementation of the Binary Search Tree Abstract Datatype (continued)

```c
/***************************************************************************
*                                                                         *
*  Do not allow destruction of an empty tree.                             *
*                                                                         *
***************************************************************************/

if (bitree_size(tree) == 0)
   return;

/***************************************************************************
*                                                                         *
*  Determine where to destroy nodes.                                      *
*                                                                         *
***************************************************************************/

if (node == NULL)
   position = &tree->root;
else
   position = &node->left;

/***************************************************************************
*                                                                         *
*  Destroy the nodes.                                                     *
*                                                                         *
***************************************************************************/

if (*position != NULL) {

   bitree_rem_left(tree, *position);
   bitree_rem_right(tree, *position);

   if (tree->destroy != NULL) {

      /***************************************************************
      *                                                             *
      *  Call a user-defined function to free dynamically allocated data. *
      *                                                             *
      ***************************************************************/

      tree->destroy(((AvlNode *)(*position)->data)->data);

   }

   /***************************************************************************
   *                                                                         *
   *  Free the AVL data in the node, then free the node itself.              *
   *                                                                         *
   ***************************************************************************/

   free((*position)->data);
   free(*position);
   *position = NULL;
```

Example 9-5. Implementation of the Binary Search Tree Abstract Datatype (continued)

```
/***************************************************************************
*                                                                         *
*   Adjust the size of the tree to account for the destroyed node.        *
*                                                                         *
***************************************************************************/

tree->size--;

}

return;

}

/***************************************************************************
*                                                                         *
*   --------------------------- destroy_right ---------------------------  *
*                                                                         *
***************************************************************************/

static void destroy_right(BisTree *tree, BiTreeNode *node) {

BiTreeNode          **position;

/***************************************************************************
*                                                                         *
*   Do not allow destruction of an empty tree.                            *
*                                                                         *
***************************************************************************/

if (bitree_size(tree) == 0)
   return;

/***************************************************************************
*                                                                         *
*   Determine where to destroy nodes.                                     *
*                                                                         *
***************************************************************************/

if (node == NULL)
   position = &tree->root;
else
   position = &node->right;

/***************************************************************************
*                                                                         *
*   Destroy the nodes.                                                    *
*                                                                         *
***************************************************************************/

if (*position != NULL) {
```

Example 9-5. Implementation of the Binary Search Tree Abstract Datatype (continued)

```
    destroy_left(tree, *position);
    destroy_right(tree, *position);

    if (tree->destroy != NULL) {

        /**********************************************************************
        *                                                                    *
        *  Call a user-defined function to free dynamically allocated data.  *
        *                                                                    *
        **********************************************************************/

        tree->destroy(((AvlNode *)(*position)->data)->data);

    }

    /**********************************************************************
    *                                                                    *
    *  Free the AVL data in the node, then free the node itself.         *
    *                                                                    *
    **********************************************************************/

    free((*position)->data);
    free(*position);
    *position = NULL;

    /**********************************************************************
    *                                                                    *
    *  Adjust the size of the tree to account for the destroyed node.    *
    *                                                                    *
    **********************************************************************/

    tree->size--;

}

return;

}

/**********************************************************************
*                                                                    *
*  ------------------------------ insert ------------------------------  *
*                                                                    *
**********************************************************************/

static int insert(BisTree *tree, BiTreeNode **node, const void *data, int
   *balanced) {

AvlNode          *avl_data;

int              cmpval,
                 retval;
```

Example 9-5. Implementation of the Binary Search Tree Abstract Datatype (continued)

```
/***************************************************************************
*                                                                         *
*  Insert the data into the tree.                                         *
*                                                                         *
***************************************************************************/

if (bitree_is_eob(*node)) {

   /***************************************************************************
   *                                                                         *
   *  Handle insertion into an empty tree.                                   *
   *                                                                         *
   ***************************************************************************/

   if ((avl_data = (AvlNode *)malloc(sizeof(AvlNode))) == NULL)
      return -1;

   avl_data->factor = AVL_BALANCED;
   avl_data->hidden = 0;
   avl_data->data = (void *)data;

   return bitree_ins_left(tree, *node, avl_data);

   }

else {

   /***************************************************************************
   *                                                                         *
   *  Handle insertion into a tree that is not empty.                        *
   *                                                                         *
   ***************************************************************************/

   cmpval = tree->compare(data, ((AvlNode *)bitree_data(*node))->data);

   if (cmpval < 0) {

      /***************************************************************************
      *                                                                         *
      *  Move to the left.                                                      *
      *                                                                         *
      ***************************************************************************/

      if (bitree_is_eob(bitree_left(*node))) {

         if ((avl_data = (AvlNode *)malloc(sizeof(AvlNode))) == NULL)
            return -1;

         avl_data->factor = AVL_BALANCED;
         avl_data->hidden = 0;
         avl_data->data = (void *)data;

         if (bitree_ins_left(tree, *node, avl_data) != 0)
            return -1;
```

Example 9-5. Implementation of the Binary Search Tree Abstract Datatype (continued)

```
        *balanced = 0;

        }

    else {

        if ((retval = insert(tree, &bitree_left(*node), data, balanced))
            != 0) {

            return retval;

        }

    }

    /**************************************************************************
     *                                                                        *
     *  Ensure that the tree remains balanced.                                *
     *                                                                        *
     **************************************************************************/

    if (!(*balanced)) {

        switch (((AvlNode *)bitree_data(*node))->factor) {

            case AVL_LFT_HEAVY:

            rotate_left(node);
            *balanced = 1;
            break;

            case AVL_BALANCED:

            ((AvlNode *)bitree_data(*node))->factor = AVL_LFT_HEAVY;
            break;

            case AVL_RGT_HEAVY:

            ((AvlNode *)bitree_data(*node))->factor = AVL_BALANCED;
            *balanced = 1;

        }

    }

    } /* if (cmpval < 0) */

else if (cmpval > 0) {

    /**************************************************************************
     *                                                                        *
     *  Move to the right.                                                    *
     *                                                                        *
     **************************************************************************/
```

Example 9-5. Implementation of the Binary Search Tree Abstract Datatype (continued)

```
    if (bitree_is_eob(bitree_right(*node))) {

       if ((avl_data = (AvlNode *)malloc(sizeof(AvlNode))) == NULL)
          return -1;

       avl_data->factor = AVL_BALANCED;
       avl_data->hidden = 0;
       avl_data->data = (void *)data;

       if (bitree_ins_right(tree, *node, avl_data) != 0)
          return -1;

       *balanced = 0;

       }

    else {

       if ((retval = insert(tree, &bitree_right(*node), data, balanced))
          != 0) {

          return retval;

          }

       }

    /*************************************************************************
    *                                                                       *
    *  Ensure that the tree remains balanced.                               *
    *                                                                       *
    *************************************************************************/

    if (!(*balanced)) {

       switch (((AvlNode *)bitree_data(*node))->factor) {

          case AVL_LFT_HEAVY:

          ((AvlNode *)bitree_data(*node))->factor = AVL_BALANCED;
          *balanced = 1;
          break;

          case AVL_BALANCED:

          ((AvlNode *)bitree_data(*node))->factor = AVL_RGT_HEAVY;
          break;

          case AVL_RGT_HEAVY:

          rotate_right(node);
          *balanced = 1;
```

Example 9-5. Implementation of the Binary Search Tree Abstract Datatype (continued)

```
      }

   }

   } /* if (cmpval > 0) */

else {

   /*****************************************************************
   *                                                               *
   *  Handle finding a copy of the data.                           *
   *                                                               *
   *****************************************************************/

   if (!((AvlNode *)bitree_data(*node))->hidden) {

      /*****************************************************************
      *                                                               *
      *  Do nothing since the data is in the tree and not hidden.     *
      *                                                               *
      *****************************************************************/

      return 1;

      }

   else {

      /*****************************************************************
      *                                                               *
      *  Insert the new data and mark it as not hidden.               *
      *                                                               *
      *****************************************************************/

      if (tree->destroy != NULL) {

         /*****************************************************************
         *                                                               *
         *  Destroy the hidden data since it is being replaced.          *
         *                                                               *
         *****************************************************************/

         tree->destroy(((AvlNode *)bitree_data(*node)) >data);

         }

      ((AvlNode *)bitree_data(*node))->data = (void *)data;
      ((AvlNode *)bitree_data(*node))->hidden = 0;

      /*****************************************************************
      *                                                               *
      *  Do not rebalance because the tree structure is unchanged.    *
      *                                                               *
      *****************************************************************/
```

Example 9-5. Implementation of the Binary Search Tree Abstract Datatype (continued)

```
        *balanced = 1;

    }

   }

}

return 0;

}

/***************************************************************************
*                                                                         *
*  -------------------------------- hide -------------------------------  *
*                                                                         *
***************************************************************************/

static int hide(BisTree *tree, BiTreeNode *node, const void *data) {

int             cmpval,
                retval;

if (bitree_is_eob(node)) {

   /***********************************************************************
   *                                                                     *
   *  Return that the data was not found.                                *
   *                                                                     *
   ***********************************************************************/

   return -1;

}

cmpval = tree->compare(data, ((AvlNode *)bitree_data(node))->data);

if (cmpval < 0) {

   /***********************************************************************
   *                                                                     *
   *  Move to the left.                                                  *
   *                                                                     *
   ***********************************************************************/

   retval = hide(tree, bitree_left(node), data);

   }

else if (cmpval > 0) {
```

Example 9-5. Implementation of the Binary Search Tree Abstract Datatype (continued)

```
/*****************************************************************************
*                                                                           *
*   Move to the right.                                                      *
*                                                                           *
*****************************************************************************/

retval = hide(tree, bitree_right(node), data);

}

else {

/*****************************************************************************
*                                                                           *
*   Mark the node as hidden.                                                *
*                                                                           *
*****************************************************************************/

((AvlNode *)bitree_data(node))->hidden = 1;
retval = 0;

}

return retval;

}
/*****************************************************************************
*                                                                           *
*   ------------------------------ lookup ------------------------------    *
*                                                                           *
*****************************************************************************/

static int lookup(BisTree *tree, BiTreeNode *node, void **data) {

int             cmpval,
                retval;

if (bitree_is_eob(node)) {

/*****************************************************************************
*                                                                           *
*   Return that the data was not found.                                     *
*                                                                           *
*****************************************************************************/

return -1;

}

cmpval = tree->compare(*data, ((AvlNode *)bitree_data(node))->data);

if (cmpval < 0) {
```

Example 9-5. Implementation of the Binary Search Tree Abstract Datatype (continued)

```
/****************************************************************************
*                                                                          *
*  Move to the left.                                                       *
*                                                                          *
****************************************************************************/

retval = lookup(tree, bitree_left(node), data);

}

else if (cmpval > 0) {

/****************************************************************************
*                                                                          *
*  Move to the right.                                                      *
*                                                                          *
****************************************************************************/

retval = lookup(tree, bitree_right(node), data);

}

else {

   if (!((AvlNode *)bitree_data(node))->hidden) {

   /****************************************************************************
   *                                                                          *
   *  Pass back the data from the tree.                                       *
   *                                                                          *
   ****************************************************************************/

   *data = ((AvlNode *)bitree_data(node))->data;
   retval = 0;

   }

   else {

   /****************************************************************************
   *                                                                          *
   *  Return that the data was not found.                                     *
   *                                                                          *
   ****************************************************************************/

   return -1;

   }

}

return retval;

}
```

Example 9-5. Implementation of the Binary Search Tree Abstract Datatype (continued)

```c
/*****************************************************************************
*                                                                           *
*  --------------------------- bistree_init ---------------------------     *
*                                                                           *
*****************************************************************************/

void bistree_init(BisTree *tree, int (*compare)(const void *key1, const void
   *key2), void (*destroy)(void *data)) {

/*****************************************************************************
*                                                                           *
*  Initialize the tree.                                                     *
*                                                                           *
*****************************************************************************/

bitree_init(tree, destroy);
tree->compare = compare;

return;

}

/*****************************************************************************
*                                                                           *
*  --------------------------- bistree_destroy -------------------------    *
*                                                                           *
*****************************************************************************/

void bistree_destroy(BisTree *tree) {

/*****************************************************************************
*                                                                           *
*  Destroy all nodes in the tree.                                           *
*                                                                           *
*****************************************************************************/

destroy_left(tree, NULL);

/*****************************************************************************
*                                                                           *
*  No operations are allowed now, but clear the structure as a precaution.  *
*                                                                           *
*****************************************************************************/

memset(tree, 0, sizeof(BisTree));

return;

}
```

Example 9-5. Implementation of the Binary Search Tree Abstract Datatype (continued)

```
/***************************************************************************
*                                                                         *
*   ------------------------- bistree_insert ------------------------   *
*                                                                         *
***************************************************************************/

int bistree_insert(BisTree *tree, const void *data) {

int                balanced = 0;

return insert(tree, &bitree_root(tree), data, &balanced);

}


/***************************************************************************
*                                                                         *
*   ------------------------- bistree_remove ------------------------   *
*                                                                         *
***************************************************************************/

int bistree_remove(BisTree *tree, const void *data) {

return hide(tree, bitree_root(tree), data);

}


/***************************************************************************
*                                                                         *
*   ------------------------- bistree_lookup ------------------------   *
*                                                                         *
***************************************************************************/

int bistree_lookup(BisTree *tree, void **data) {

return lookup(tree, bitree_root(tree), data);

}
```

Questions and Answers

Q: *Akin to doubly-linked lists, some trees maintain pointers from child nodes back to their parents in addition to the normal pointers from parents to their children. Some trees maintain pointers between sibling nodes as well. Why might we do this?*

A: In general, maintaining additional pointers gives us greater flexibility in how we traverse a tree. For example, maintaining pointers from a parent to its children and from a child to its parent lets us move both up and down through a tree. Maintaining pointers between siblings gives us an easy way to traverse through a node's children without accessing the parent. One benefit of linked siblings is found in *B+-trees,* a type of balanced search tree in which pointers are used to link leaf nodes together. By linking leaf nodes, we effectively form a linked list at the bottom of the tree. This provides an efficient means of looking up a particular key and then retrieving others that either precede or follow it in a sequence. Database systems do this to support efficient random and sequential access simultaneously. Of course, the disadvantage is some overhead and complication in managing the sibling pointers as children are inserted and removed.

Q: *Recall that the example on expression processing used a linked list to return the appropriate ordering of the nodes to the caller. This example illustrates two data structures pointing to the same data. What precautions would we need to take in destroying each instance of these datatypes?*

A: All of the data structures presented in this book follow the convention that only a pointer is maintained to the data inserted into the data structure. There-fore, it is the responsibility of the caller to manage the storage associated with the data itself. In the case of a binary tree and a linked list pointing to the same physical data in memory, it is important that we pass a function to free the data only to one of the initialization operations. The other operation must set *destroy* to NULL. Of course, this approach assumes that the data being shared was dynamically allocated in the first place. If the data structures point to data that was not dynamically allocated, *destroy* should be set to NULL in both initialization operations since there is nothing to free.

Q: *In* bitree_rem_left *and* bitree_rem_right, *why was a postorder traversal used to remove the appropriate subtree? Could a preorder or inorder traversal have been used instead?*

A: It is essential to use a postorder traversal here because a subtree must be removed in its entirety before removing its parent. A preorder traversal ends up removing the parent first, thus freeing the parent and making it impossible to access its children. An inorder traversal also does not work because we still end up removing the parent before its right subtree.

Q: *How do we find the smallest node in a binary search tree? What is the runtime complexity to do this in both an unbalanced and balanced binary search tree, in the worst case? How do we find the largest node in a binary search tree? What are the runtime complexities for this?*

A: The smallest node in a binary search tree is the node that is the furthest to the left. To locate this node, we descend through the tree by following left point-ers until reaching the end of the branch. In an unbalanced binary search tree, this requires $O(n)$ time in the worst case, where n is the number of nodes in the tree. This occurs when the tree consists of a single branch to the left, for example. However, if we keep the tree balanced, no branch will be longer than $\lg n$ nodes. Thus, the runtime complexity of searching for the smallest node in this case is $O(\lg n)$. Finding the largest node is a similar process, except that the largest node is the one that is the furthest to the right in the tree. The runtime complexities for this are the same as for locating the smallest node. If we are interested only in determining the smallest (or largest) element in a set of data repeatedly, we use a priority queue (see Chapter 10).

Q: *When might we choose to make use of a tree with a relatively large branching factor, instead of a binary tree, for example?*

A: Larger branching factors keep a tree shorter for a given number of nodes, provided the tree remains relatively balanced. Therefore, a large branching factor is desirable when an application is particularly sensitive to the height of the tree. Search trees are a good example, although typically the difference in performance attributed to larger branching factors is not that significant when the tree resides in memory. This is one reason that binary trees are most common for searching in memory. However, when searching in the considerably slower world of secondary storage, a larger branching factor can make a substantial difference. In this situation, typically some type of B-tree is used (see the related topics at the end of the chapter).

Q: *In a binary search tree, the successor of some node x is the next largest node after x. For example, in a binary search tree containing the keys 24, 39, 41, 55, 87, 92, the successor of 41 is 55. How do we find the successor of a node in a binary search tree? What is the runtime complexity of this operation?*

A: To determine the successor of some node x in a binary search tree, first we locate x. Next, we follow its right pointer, and then from this node, follow as many left pointers as possible until the end of the branch is reached. The node at the end of this branch is the successor of x. The runtime complexity of locating either x or its successor is $O(\lg n)$.

Q: *In a binary search tree, recall that to insert a node, we trace a specific path to determine the proper point at which to actually insert it. As more and more nodes are inserted into a tree, certain areas within the tree become restricted to certain values. Ultimately, this is why a tree falls out of balance and rotations are performed. In the binary search tree of Figure 9-14, what are the possible values for a node inserted at x?*

A: In Figure 9-14, any node we insert at x must contain a value greater than 44 and less than 49 because any node to the left of 49 must be less than 49. On the other hand, the only way for a node to end up in the right subtree of 44 is to be greater than 44.

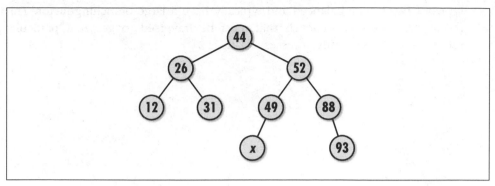

Figure 9-14. A balanced binary search tree

Related Topics

k-ary trees

Trees that have a branching factor of *k*. Branching factors of more than two children per node are useful when modeling certain situations, such as the 1-to-*n* relationship of a parent window and its children in a graphical windowing system, or a directory structure in a file system.

Red-black trees

Binary search trees that keep themselves approximately balanced by maintaining a color with each node, which is either red or black. By enforcing a policy about how nodes can be colored along a branch, red-black trees ensure that no branch will ever become more than twice as long as any other. The worst-case running time of searching a red-black tree is $T(n) = 2k \lg n$, where *n* is the number of nodes in the tree, *k* is some constant, and $T(n) = k \lg n$ is the time to search a perfectly balanced tree.

Tries

Search trees used primarily to search sets of variable-length strings. Conceptually, the nodes at each level in a trie (pronounced "try") represent all characters found at a particular position in the strings being searched. For example, the nodes immediately below the root represent all possible characters in position 1 of the strings, the next level represents all possible characters in position 2, and so forth. Thus, to look up a string, we start at the root and at each level follow the pointer to the node containing the next character in the string we are searching for. This procedure results in search times that are dependent on the size of the search string rather than the number of strings being searched.

B-trees, B+-trees, and B-trees*

Search trees typically used by database systems to improve the performance of accessing data stored on secondary storage devices. Generally, node size is optimized to coincide with the block size of the secondary storage device. All types of B-trees are balanced and typically have a large branching factor. This reduces the number of levels that must be traversed to get at a particular record, thus saving costly accesses to I/O.

10

Heaps and Priority Queues

Many problems rely on being able to determine quickly the largest or smallest element from a set that is undergoing frequent insertions and deletions. One way to approach this problem is to keep a set sorted. This way, the largest or smallest element, depending on whether we sort the data in ascending or descending order, is always the one at the beginning of the set. However, sorting a set over and over again is costly. In addition, because it is not our goal to keep *every* element in order, we end up doing more work than we really need to. To quickly determine only the largest or smallest element, we need only keep this element where we can find it. Heaps and priority queues let us do this in an efficient way.

This chapter covers:

Heaps

> Trees organized so that we can determine the node with the largest value quickly. The cost to preserve this property is less than that of keeping the data sorted. We can also organize a heap so that we can determine the smallest value just as easily.

Priority queues

> Data structures naturally derived from heaps. In a priority queue, data is organized in a heap so that we can determine the node with the next highest priority quickly. The "priority" of an element can mean different things in different problems.

Some applications of heaps and priority queues are:

Sorting

> Specifically, an algorithm called *heapsort*. In heapsort, the data to be sorted begins in a heap. Nodes are extracted from the heap one at a time and placed at the end of a sorted set. As each node is extracted, the next node for the

sorted set percolates to the top of the heap. Heapsort has the same runtime complexity as quicksort (see Chapter 12, *Sorting and Searching*), but a good implementation of quicksort usually beats it by a small constant factor in practice.

Task scheduling

For example, that performed by operating systems to determine which process is next to run on a CPU. Operating systems continually change the priorities of processes. A priority queue is an efficient way to ensure that the highest-priority process is next to get the CPU.

Parcel sorting (illustrated in this chapter)

A process used by delivery companies to prioritize the routing of parcels. As parcels are scanned, high priorities are assigned to those requiring urgent delivery. Parcels that are less urgent are assigned lower priorities. A computer system might use a priority queue as an efficient means of ensuring that the highest priority parcels move through the system the fastest.

Huffman coding

A method of data compression that uses a Huffman tree to assign codes to symbols in the data (see Chapter 14, *Data Compression*). Frequently occurring symbols are assigned short codes, whereas symbols occuring less frequently are assigned longer ones. The Huffman tree is built by merging smaller binary trees two by two. The two trees merged at each step are extracted from a priority queue because we merge the two with the smallest key values.

Load balancing

Often usage statistics are maintained about a number of servers handling similar tasks. As connection requests arrive, a priority queue can be used to determine which server is best able to accommodate a new request.

Description of Heaps

A heap is a tree, usually a binary tree, in which each child node has a smaller value than its parent. Thus, the root node is the largest node in the tree. We may also choose to orient a heap so that each child node has a larger value than its parent. In this case, the root node is the smallest node. Trees like these are *partially ordered* because, although the nodes along every branch have a specific order to them, the nodes at one level are not necessarily ordered with respect to the nodes at another. A heap in which each child is smaller than its parent is *top-heavy*. This is because the largest node is on top (see Figure 10-1). A heap in which each child is larger than its parent is *bottom-heavy*.

Heaps are left-balanced (see Chapter 9, *Trees*), so as nodes are added, the tree grows level by level from left to right. A particularly good way to represent left-balanced binary trees, and therefore heaps, is to store nodes contiguously in an array in the order we would encounter them in a level traversal (see Chapter 9). Assuming a zero-indexed array, this means that the parent of each node at some position i in the array is located at position $\lfloor (i - 1)/2 \rfloor$, where $\lfloor \ \rfloor$ means to ignore the fractional part of $(i - 1)/2$. The left and right children of a node are located at positions $2i + 1$ and $2i + 2$. This organization is especially important for heaps because it allows us to locate a heap's last node quickly: the last node is the right-most node at the deepest level. This is important in implementing certain heap operations.

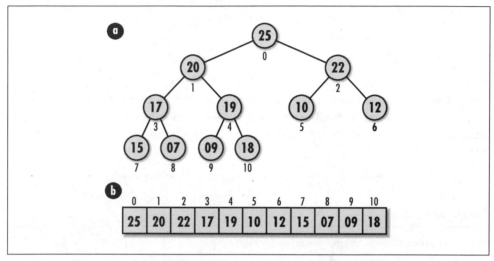

Figure 10-1. A top-heavy heap (a) conceptually and (b) represented in an array

Interface for Heaps

heap_init

```
void heap_init(Heap *heap, int (*compare)(const void *key1, const void *key2)
   void (*destroy)(void *data));
```

Return Value   None.

Description   Initializes the heap specified by *heap*. This operation must be called for a heap before the heap can be used with any other operation. The *compare* argument is a function used by various heap operations to compare nodes when fixing the heap. This function should return 1 if *key1* > *key2*, 0 if *key1* = *key2*, and −1 if *key1* < *key2* for a top-heavy heap. For a bottom-heavy heap, *compare* should reverse the cases that return 1 and −1. The *destroy* argument provides a way to free dynamically allocated data when *heap_destroy* is called. For example, if the heap contains data dynamically allocated using *malloc*, *destroy* should be set to *free* to free the data as the heap is destroyed. For structured data containing several dynamically allocated members, *destroy* should be set to a user-defined function that calls *free* for each dynamically allocated member as well as for the structure itself. For a heap containing data that should not be freed, *destroy* should be set to NULL.

Complexity $O(1)$

heap_destroy

```
void heap_destroy(Heap *heap);
```

Return Value   None.

Description   Destroys the heap specified by *heap*. No other operations are permitted after calling *heap_destroy* unless *heap_init* is called again. The *heap_destroy* operation removes all nodes from a heap and calls the function passed as *destroy* to *heap_init* once for each node as it is removed, provided *destroy* was not set to NULL.

Complexity $O(n)$, where *n* is the number of nodes in the heap.

heap_insert

```
int heap_insert(Heap *heap, const void *data);
```

Return Value   0 if inserting the node is successful, or –1 otherwise.

Description   Inserts a node into the heap specified by *heap*. The new node contains a pointer to *data*, so the memory referenced by *data* should remain valid as long as the node remains in the heap. It is the responsibility of the caller to manage the storage associated with *data*.

Complexity $O(\lg n)$, where *n* is the number of nodes in the heap.

heap_extract

```
int heap_extract(Heap *heap, void **data);
```

Return Value   0 if extracting the node is successful, or –1 otherwise.

Description   Extracts the node at the top of the heap specified by *heap*. Upon return, *data* points to the data stored in the node that was extracted. It is the responsibility of the caller to manage the storage associated with the data.

Complexity $O(\lg n)$, where *n* is the number of nodes in the heap.

heap_size

```
int heap_size(const Heap *heap);
```

Return Value   Number of nodes in the heap.

Description   Macro that evaluates to the number of nodes in the heap specified by *heap*.

Complexity $O(1)$

Implementation and Analysis of Heaps

The heap implemented here is a binary tree whose nodes are arranged hierarchically in an array. The structure *Heap* is the heap data structure (see Example 10-1). This structure consists of four members: *size* is the number of nodes in the heap, *compare* and *destroy* are members used to encapsulate the functions passed to *heap_init*, and *tree* is the array of nodes in the heap.

Example 10-1. Header for the Heap Abstract Datatype

```
/*****************************************************************************
*                                                                           *
*  ------------------------------- heap.h -------------------------------   *
*                                                                           *
*****************************************************************************/

#ifndef HEAP_H
#define HEAP_H

/*****************************************************************************
*                                                                           *
*  Define a structure for heaps.                                            *
*                                                                           *
*****************************************************************************/

typedef struct Heap_ {

int             size;

int             (*compare)(const void *key1, const void *key2);
void            (*destroy)(void *data);

void            **tree;

} Heap;

/*****************************************************************************
*                                                                           *
*  --------------------------- Public Interface ---------------------------  *
*                                                                           *
*****************************************************************************/
```

Example 10-1. Header for the Heap Abstract Datatype (continued)

```
void heap_init(Heap *heap, int (*compare)(const void *key1, const void *key2),
   void (*destroy)(void *data));

void heap_destroy(Heap *heap);

int heap_insert(Heap *heap, const void *data);

int heap_extract(Heap *heap, void **data);

#define heap_size(heap) ((heap)->size)

#endif
```

heap_init

The *heap_init* operation initializes a heap so that it can be used in other operations (see Example 10-2). Initializing a heap is a simple operation in which we set the **size** member of the heap to 0, the **destroy** member to **destroy**, and the **tree** pointer to NULL.

The runtime complexity of *heap_init* is $O(1)$ because all of the steps in initializing a heap run in a constant amount of time.

heap_destroy

The *heap_destroy* operation destroys a heap (see Example 10-2). Primarily this means removing all nodes from the heap. The function passed as **destroy** to *heap_init* is called once for each node as it is removed, provided **destroy** was not set to NULL.

The runtime complexity of *heap_destroy* is $O(n)$, where n is the number of nodes in the heap. This is because we must traverse all nodes in the heap in order to free the data they contain. If **destroy** is NULL, *heap_destroy* runs in $O(1)$ time.

heap_insert

The *heap_insert* operation inserts a node into a heap (see Example 10-2). The call sets the new node to point to the data passed by the caller. To begin, we reallocate storage to enable the tree to accommodate the new node. The actual process of inserting the new node initially places it into the last position in the array. When this causes the heap property to be violated, we must *reheapify* the tree (see Figure 10-2).

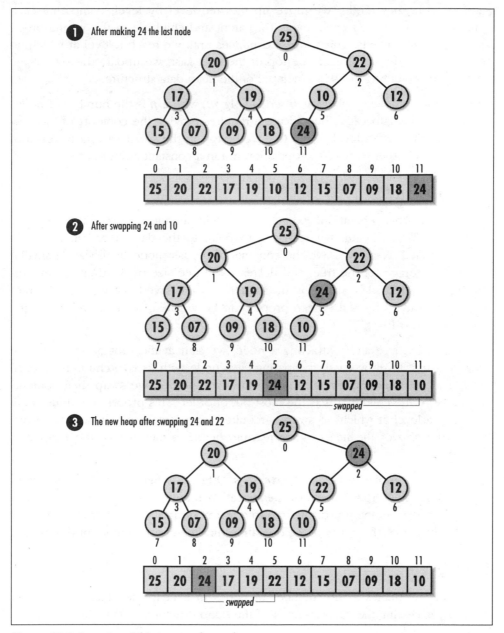

Figure 10-2. Inserting 24 into a top-heavy heap

To reheapify a tree after inserting a node, we need only consider the branch in which the new node has been inserted, since the tree was a heap to begin with.

Starting at the new node, we move up the tree level by level, comparing each child with its parent. At each level, if a parent and child are in the wrong order, we swap their contents. This process continues until we reach a level at which no swap is required, or we reach the top of the tree. Last, we update the size of the heap by incrementing the *size* member of the heap data structure.

The runtime complexity of *heap_insert* is $O(\lg n)$, where n is the number of nodes in the tree. This is because heapification requires moving the contents of the new node from the lowest level of the tree to the top in the worst case, a traversal of $\lg n$ levels. All other parts of the operation run in a constant amount of time.

heap_extract

The *heap_extract* operation extracts the node at the top of a heap (see Example 10-2). To begin, we set *data* to point to the data stored in the node being extracted. Next, we save the contents of the last node, reallocate a smaller amount of storage for the tree, and decrease the tree size by 1. After we are certain this has succeeded, we copy the contents of the saved last node to the root node. When this causes the heap property to be violated, we must reheapify the tree (see Figure 10-3).

To reheapify a tree after extracting a node, we start at the root node and move down the tree level by level, comparing each node with its two children. At each level, if a parent and its children are in the wrong order, we swap their contents and move to the child that was the most out of order. This process continues until we reach a level at which no swap is required, or we reach a leaf node. Last, we update the size of the heap by decreasing the *size* member of the heap data structure by 1.

The runtime complexity of *heap_extract* is $O(\lg n)$, where n is the number of nodes in the tree. This is because heapification requires moving the contents of the root node from the top of the tree to a leaf node in the worst case, a traversal of $\lg n$ levels. All other parts of the operation run in a constant amount of time.

heap_size

This macro evaluates to the number of nodes in a heap (see Example 10-1). It works by accessing the *size* member of the *Heap* structure.

The runtime complexity of *heap_size* is $O(1)$ because accessing a member of a structure is a simple task that runs in a constant amount of time.

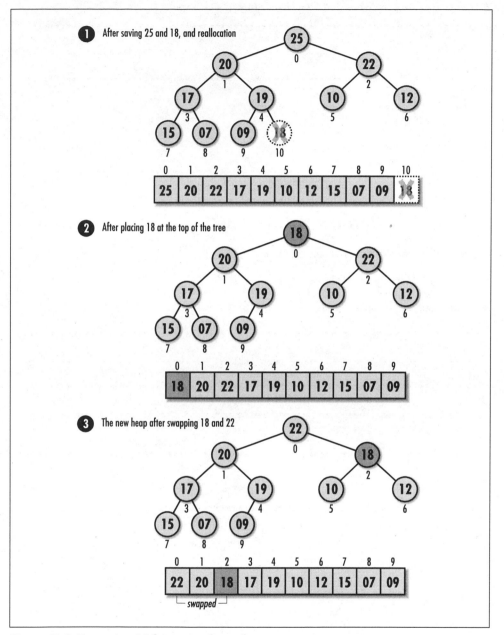

Figure 10-3. Extracting 25 from a top-heavy heap

Example 10-2. Implementation of the Heap Abstract Datatype

```c
/*****************************************************************************
*                                                                           *
*  ------------------------------- heap.c --------------------------------  *
*                                                                           *
*****************************************************************************/

#include <stdlib.h>
#include <string.h>

#include "heap.h"

/*****************************************************************************
*                                                                           *
*  Define private macros used by the heap implementation.                   *
*                                                                           *
*****************************************************************************/

#define heap_parent(npos) ((int)(((npos) - 1) / 2))

#define heap_left(npos) (((npos) * 2) + 1)

#define heap_right(npos) (((npos) * 2) + 2)

/*****************************************************************************
*                                                                           *
*  ----------------------------- heap_init ------------------------------   *
*                                                                           *
*****************************************************************************/

void heap_init(Heap *heap, int (*compare)(const void *key1, const void *key2),
   void (*destroy)(void *data)) {

/*****************************************************************************
*                                                                           *
*  Initialize the heap.                                                     *
*                                                                           *
*****************************************************************************/

heap->size = 0;
heap->compare = compare;
heap->destroy = destroy;
heap->tree = NULL;

return;

}

/*****************************************************************************
*                                                                           *
*  ---------------------------- heap_destroy ----------------------------   *
*                                                                           *
*****************************************************************************/
```

Example 10-2. Implementation of the Heap Abstract Datatype (continued)

```c
void heap_destroy(Heap *heap) {

int              i;

/***************************************************************************
*                                                                         *
*  Remove all the nodes from the heap.                                    *
*                                                                         *
***************************************************************************/

if (heap->destroy != NULL) {

   for (i = 0; i < heap_size(heap); i++) {

      /***************************************************************************
      *                                                                         *
      *  Call a user-defined function to free dynamically allocated data.       *
      *                                                                         *
      ***************************************************************************/

      heap->destroy(heap->tree[i]);

   }

}

/***************************************************************************
*                                                                         *
*  Free the storage allocated for the heap.                               *
*                                                                         *
***************************************************************************/

free(heap->tree);

/***************************************************************************
*                                                                         *
*  No operations are allowed now, but clear the structure as a precaution.*
*                                                                         *
***************************************************************************/

memset(heap, 0, sizeof(Heap));

return;

}

/***************************************************************************
*                                                                         *
*  ----------------------------- heap_insert -----------------------------*
*                                                                         *
***************************************************************************/
```

Example 10-2. Implementation of the Heap Abstract Datatype (continued)

```
int heap_insert(Heap *heap, const void *data) {

void            *temp;

int             ipos,
                ppos;

/***************************************************************************
*                                                                         *
*  Allocate storage for the node.                                         *
*                                                                         *
***************************************************************************/

if ((temp = (void **)realloc(heap->tree, (heap_size(heap) + 1) * sizeof
   (void *))) == NULL) {

   return -1;

   }

else {

   heap->tree = temp;

}

/***************************************************************************
*                                                                         *
*  Insert the node after the last node.                                   *
*                                                                         *
***************************************************************************/

heap->tree[heap_size(heap)] = (void *)data;

/***************************************************************************
*                                                                         *
*  Heapify the tree by pushing the contents of the new node upward.       *
*                                                                         *
***************************************************************************/

ipos = heap_size(heap);
ppos = heap_parent(ipos);

while (ipos > 0 && heap->compare(heap->tree[ppos], heap->tree[ipos]) < 0) {

   /************************************************************************
   *                                                                      *
   *  Swap the contents of the current node and its parent.               *
   *                                                                      *
   ************************************************************************/

   temp = heap->tree[ppos];
   heap->tree[ppos] = heap->tree[ipos];
   heap->tree[ipos] = temp;
```

Example 10-2. Implementation of the Heap Abstract Datatype (continued)

```
/**************************************************************************
 *                                                                        *
 *  Move up one level in the tree to continue heapifying.                 *
 *                                                                        *
 **************************************************************************/

ipos = ppos;
ppos = heap_parent(ipos);

}

/**************************************************************************
 *                                                                        *
 *  Adjust the size of the heap to account for the inserted node.         *
 *                                                                        *
 **************************************************************************/

heap->size++;

return 0;

}

/**************************************************************************
 *                                                                        *
 *  ----------------------------- heap_extract -----------------------------  *
 *                                                                        *
 **************************************************************************/

int heap_extract(Heap *heap, void **data) {

void            *save,
                *temp;

int             ipos,
                lpos,
                rpos,
                mpos;

/**************************************************************************
 *                                                                        *
 *  Do not allow extraction from an empty heap.                           *
 *                                                                        *
 **************************************************************************/

if (heap_size(heap) == 0)
   return -1;

/**************************************************************************
 *                                                                        *
 *  Extract the node at the top of the heap.                              *
 *                                                                        *
 **************************************************************************/
```

Example 10-2. Implementation of the Heap Abstract Datatype (continued)

```c
*data = heap->tree[0];

/***************************************************************************
*                                                                         *
*  Adjust the storage used by the heap.                                   *
*                                                                         *
***************************************************************************/

save = heap->tree[heap_size(heap) - 1];

if (heap_size(heap) - 1 > 0) {

   if ((temp = (void **)realloc(heap->tree, (heap_size(heap) - 1) * sizeof
      (void *))) == NULL) {

      return -1;

      }

   else {

      heap->tree = temp;

   }

   /***************************************************************************
   *                                                                         *
   *  Adjust the size of the heap to account for the extracted node.         *
   *                                                                         *
   ***************************************************************************/

   heap->size--;

   }

else {

   /***************************************************************************
   *                                                                         *
   *  Manage the heap when extracting the last node.                         *
   *                                                                         *
   ***************************************************************************/

   free(heap->tree);
   heap->tree = NULL;
   heap->size = 0;
   return 0;

}
```

Example 10-2. Implementation of the Heap Abstract Datatype (continued)

```
/***************************************************************************
*                                                                         *
*  Copy the last node to the top.                                         *
*                                                                         *
***************************************************************************/

heap->tree[0] = save;

/***************************************************************************
*                                                                         *
*  Heapify the tree by pushing the contents of the new top downward.      *
*                                                                         *
***************************************************************************/

ipos = 0;
lpos = heap_left(ipos);
rpos = heap_right(ipos);

while (1) {

   /***********************************************************************
   *                                                                     *
   *  Select the child to swap with the current node.                    *
   *                                                                     *
   ***********************************************************************/

   lpos = heap_left(ipos);
   rpos = heap_right(ipos);

   if (lpos < heap_size(heap) && heap->compare(heap->tree[lpos], heap->
      tree[ipos]) > 0) {

      mpos = lpos;

      }

   else {

      mpos = ipos;

   }

   if (rpos < heap_size(heap) && heap->compare(heap->tree[rpos], heap->
      tree[mpos]) > 0) {

      mpos = rpos;

   }
```

Example 10-2. Implementation of the Heap Abstract Datatype (continued)

```
/*****************************************************************************
*                                                                           *
*  When mpos is ipos, the heap property has been restored.                  *
*                                                                           *
*****************************************************************************/

if (mpos == ipos) {

   break;

   }

else {

   /*****************************************************************************
   *                                                                           *
   *  Swap the contents of the current node and the selected child.            *
   *                                                                           *
   *****************************************************************************/

   temp = heap->tree[mpos];
   heap->tree[mpos] = heap->tree[ipos];
   heap->tree[ipos] = temp;

   /*****************************************************************************
   *                                                                           *
   *  Move down one level in the tree to continue heapifying.                  *
   *                                                                           *
   *****************************************************************************/

   ipos = mpos;

   }

}

return 0;

}
```

Description of Priority Queues

Priority queues are used to prioritize data. A priority queue consists of elements organized so that the highest priority element can be ascertained efficiently. For example, consider maintaining usage statistics about a number of servers for which you are trying to do load balancing. As connection requests arrive, a priority queue can be used to determine which server is best able to accommodate the new request. In this scenario, the server with least usage is the one that gets the highest priority because it is the best one to service the request.

Interface for Priority Queues

pqueue_init

```
void pqueue_init(PQueue *pqueue, int (*compare)(const void *key1,
   const void *key2), void (*destroy)(void *data));
```

Return Value None.

Description Initializes the priority queue specified by *pqueue*. This operation must be called for a priority queue before it can be used with any other operation. The *compare* argument is a function used by various priority queue operations in maintaining the priority queue's heap property. This function should return 1 if *key1* > *key2*, 0 if *key1* = *key2*, and −1 if *key1* < *key2* for a priority queue in which large keys have a higher priority. For a priority queue in which smaller keys have a higher priority, *compare* should reverse the cases that return 1 and −1. The *destroy* argument provides a way to free dynamically allocated data when *pqueue_destroy* is called. For example, if the priority queue contains data dynamically allocated using *malloc*, *destroy* should be set to *free* to free the data as the priority queue is destroyed. For structured data containing several dynamically allocated members, *destroy* should be set to a user-defined function that calls *free* for each dynamically allocated member as well as for the structure itself. For a priority queue containing data that should not be freed, *destroy* should be set to NULL.

Complexity $O(1)$

pqueue_destroy

```
void pqueue_destroy(PQueue *pqueue);
```

Return Value None.

Description Destroys the priority queue specified by *pqueue*. No other operations are permitted after calling *pqueue_destroy* unless *pqueue_init* is called again. The *pqueue_destroy* operation extracts all elements from a priority queue and calls the function passed as *destroy* to *pqueue_init* once for each element as it is extracted, provided *destroy* was not set to NULL.

Complexity $O(n)$, where n is the number of elements in the priority queue.

pqueue_insert

```
int pqueue_insert(PQueue *pqueue, const void *data);
```

Return Value 0 if inserting the element is successful, or −1 otherwise.

Description   Inserts an element into the priority queue specified by *pqueue*. The new element contains a pointer to *data*, so the memory referenced by *data* should remain valid as long as the element remains in the priority queue. It is the responsibility of the caller to manage the storage associated with *data*.

Complexity $O(\lg n)$, where n is the number of elements in the priority queue.

pqueue_extract

```
int pqueue_extract(PQueue *pqueue, void **data);
```

Return Value   0 if extracting the element is successful, or –1 otherwise.

Description   Extracts the element at the top of the priority queue specified by *pqueue*. Upon return, *data* points to the data stored in the element that was extracted. It is the responsibility of the caller to manage the storage associated with the data.

Complexity $O(\lg n)$, where n is the number of elements in the priority queue.

pqueue_peek

```
void *pqueue_peek(const PQueue *pqueue);
```

Return Value   Highest priority element in the priority queue, or NULL if the priority queue is empty.

Description   Macro that evaluates to the highest priority element in the priority queue specified by *pqueue*.

Complexity $O(1)$

pqueue_size

```
int pqueue_size(const PQueue *pqueue);
```

Return Value   Number of elements in the priority queue.

Description   Macro that evaluates to the number of elements in the priority queue specified by *pqueue*.

Complexity $O(1)$

Implementation and Analysis of Priority Queues

There are several ways to implement a priority queue. Perhaps the most intuitive approach is simply to maintain a sorted set of data. In this approach, the element at the beginning of the sorted set is the one with the highest priority. However, inserting and extracting elements require resorting the set, which is an $O(n)$ process in the worst case, where n is the number of elements. Therefore, a better solution is to keep the set partially ordered using a heap. Recall that the node at the top of a heap is always the one with the highest priority, however this is defined, and that repairing the heap after inserting and extracting data requires only $O(\lg n)$ time.

A simple way to implement a priority queue as a heap is to typedef *PQueue* to *Heap* (see Example 10-3). Since the operations of a priority queue are identical to those of a heap, only an interface is designed for priority queues and the heap datatype serves as the implementation (see Examples 10-2 and 10-3). To do this, each priority queue operation is simply defined to its heap counterpart. The one exception to this is *pqueue_peek*, which has no heap equivalent. This operation works just like *pqueue_extract*, except that the highest priority element is only returned, not removed.

Example 10-3. Header for the Priority Queue Abstract Datatype

```
/*****************************************************************************
*                                                                           *
*   ----------------------------- pqueue.h ------------------------------   *
*                                                                           *
*****************************************************************************/

#ifndef PQUEUE_H
#define PQUEUE_H

#include "heap.h"

/*****************************************************************************
*                                                                           *
*   Implement priority queues as heaps.                                     *
*                                                                           *
*****************************************************************************/

typedef Heap PQueue;

/*****************************************************************************
*                                                                           *
*   -------------------------- Public Interface --------------------------  *
*                                                                           *
*****************************************************************************/

#define pqueue_init heap_init

#define pqueue_destroy heap_destroy

#define pqueue_insert heap_insert
```

Example 10-3. Header for the Priority Queue Abstract Datatype (continued)

```
#define pqueue_extract heap_extract

#define pqueue_peek(pqueue) ((pqueue)->tree == NULL ? NULL : (pqueue)->tree[0])

#define pqueue_size heap_size

#endif
```

Priority Queue Example: Parcel Sorting

Most delivery services offer several options for how fast a parcel can be delivered. Generally, the more a person is willing to pay, the faster the parcel is guaranteed to arrive. Since large delivery services handle millions of parcels each day, prioritizing parcels during the sorting process is important. This is especially true when space associated with a delivery mechanism becomes limited. In this case, parcels with the highest priority must go first. For example, if an airplane is making only one more trip for the day back to a central hub from a busy metropolitan area, all parcels requiring delivery the next day had better be on board.

One way to ensure that parcels heading to a certain destination are processed according to the correct prioritization is to store information about them in a priority queue. The sorting process begins by scanning parcels into the system. As each parcel is scanned, its information is prioritized in the queue so that when parcels begin to move through the system, those with the highest priority will go first.

Example 10-4 presents two functions, *get_parcel* and *put_parcel*, both of which operate on a priority queue containing parcel records of type `Parcel`. `Parcel` is defined in *parcel.h*, which is not shown. A sorter calls *put_parcel* to load information about a parcel into the system. One member of the `Parcel` structure passed to *put_parcel* is a priority code. The *put_parcel* function inserts a parcel into the priority queue, which prioritizes the parcel among the others. When the sorter is ready to move the next parcel through the system, it calls *get_parcel*. The *get_parcel* function fetches the parcel with the next-highest priority so that parcels are processed in the correct order.

A priority queue is a good way to manage parcels because at any moment, we are interested only in the parcel with the next highest priority. Therefore, we can avoid the overhead of keeping parcels completely sorted. The runtime complexities of *get_parcel* and *put_parcel* are both $O(\lg n)$ because the two functions simply call *pqueue_extract* and *pqueue_insert* respectively, which are both $O(\lg n)$ operations.

Example 10-4. Implementation of Functions for Sorting Parcels

```c
/*****************************************************************************
*                                                                           *
*  ----------------------------- parcels.c -----------------------------    *
*                                                                           *
*****************************************************************************/

#include <stdlib.h>
#include <string.h>

#include "parcel.h"
#include "parcels.h"
#include "pqueue.h"

/*****************************************************************************
*                                                                           *
*  ----------------------------- get_parcel -----------------------------   *
*                                                                           *
*****************************************************************************/

int get_parcel(PQueue *parcels, Parcel *parcel) {

Parcel             *data;

if (pqueue_size(parcels) == 0)

   /*************************************************************************
   *                                                                       *
   *  Return that there are no parcels.                                    *
   *                                                                       *
   *************************************************************************/

   return -1;

else {

   if (pqueue_extract(parcels, (void **)&data) != 0)

      /**********************************************************************
      *                                                                    *
      *  Return that a parcel could not be retrieved.                      *
      *                                                                    *
      **********************************************************************/

      return -1;

   else {

      /**********************************************************************
      *                                                                    *
      *  Pass back the highest-priority parcel.                            *
      *                                                                    *
      **********************************************************************/
```

Example 10-4. Implementation of Functions for Sorting Parcels (continued)

```
            memcpy(parcel, data, sizeof(Parcel));
            free(data);

        }

    }

    return 0;

}

/*****************************************************************************
*                                                                           *
*   ----------------------------- put_parcel -----------------------------  *
*                                                                           *
*****************************************************************************/

int put_parcel(PQueue *parcels, const Parcel *parcel) {

Parcel            *data;

/*****************************************************************************
*                                                                           *
*   Allocate storage for the parcel.                                        *
*                                                                           *
*****************************************************************************/

if ((data = (Parcel *)malloc(sizeof(Parcel))) == NULL)
    return -1;

/*****************************************************************************
*                                                                           *
*   Insert the parcel into the priority queue.                              *
*                                                                           *
*****************************************************************************/

memcpy(data, parcel, sizeof(Parcel));

if (pqueue_insert(parcels, data) != 0)
    return -1;

return 0;

}
```

Questions and Answers

Q: *To build a heap from a set of data using the interface presented in this chapter, we call* heap_insert *once for each element in the set. Since* heap_insert *runs in $O(\lg n)$ time, building a heap of n nodes requires $O(n \lg n)$ time. What is an alternative to this approach that runs in $O(n)$ time?*

A: An alternative to calling *heap_insert* repeatedly is to start with an array of nodes that we heapify by pushing data downward just as is done in *heap_insert*. In this approach, we first heapify the tree whose root is at position $\lfloor n/2 \rfloor - 1$, then heapify the tree whose root is at position $\lfloor n/2 \rfloor - 2$, and continue this process until we heapify the tree rooted at position 0. This approach relies on the observation that the nodes at $\lfloor n/2 \rfloor$ to $n - 1$ (in a zero-indexed array) are one-node heaps themselves because they are the leaf nodes. Building a heap in this way is efficient because although there are $\lfloor n/2 \rfloor - 1$ operations that run in $O(\lg n)$ time, a tighter analysis reveals that even in the worst case only half the heapifications require comparing data at more than one level. This results in an $O(n)$ running time overall. On the other hand, when calling *heap_insert* repeatedly, half the heapifications could require traversing all $\lg n$ levels in the worst case. Thus, building a heap in this way runs in $O(n \lg n)$ time.

Q: *Why are* heap_parent, heap_left, *and* heap_right *defined in* heap.c, *whereas the other heap macro,* heap_size, *is defined in* heap.h?

A: The macros *heap_parent*, *heap_left*, and *heap_right* quickly determine the position of a node's parent, left child, and right child in a tree represented in an array. The reason these macros are not defined in *heap.h* is that they are not a part of the public heap interface. That is, a developer using a heap should not be permitted to traverse a heap's nodes indiscriminately. Instead, access to the heap is restricted to those operations defined by the interface published in *heap.h*.

Q: *Recall that left-balanced binary trees are particularly well-suited to arrays. Why is this not true of all binary trees?*

A: Left-balanced binary trees are particularly well-suited to arrays because no nodes go unused between positions 0 and $n - 1$, where n is the number of nodes in the tree. Array representations of binary trees that are not left-balanced, on the other hand, contain gaps of unused nodes. For example, suppose a binary tree of 10 levels is completely full through 9 levels, but in the tenth level only 1 node resides at the far right. In contiguous storage, the node at the far right of the tenth level resides at position $2^{10} - 2 = 1022$ (in a zero-indexed array). The node at the far right of the ninth level resides at position $2^9 - 2 = 510$. This results in $(1022 - 510) - 1 = 511$ empty positions out of the total 1023 positions required to represent the tree. Thus, only 50% of the array is being used.

Q: *Suppose we are using a priority queue to prioritize the order in which tasks are scheduled by an application. If the system continually processes a large number of high-priority tasks, what problems might the system exhibit? How can we correct this?*

A: When high-priority elements are continually being inserted into a priority queue, lower-priority elements may never rise to the top. In a task scheduler, for example, the lower-priority tasks are said to be experiencing *starvation*. To manage this, typically a system employs some mechanism to increase a task's priority gradually as its time in the queue grows. Thus, even in a busy system flooded by high-priority tasks, a low-priority task eventually will obtain a high enough priority to rise to the top. Operating systems frequently use an approach like this to ensure that lower-priority processes are not completely starved of CPU time.

Related Topics

Fibonacci heaps

Collections of heap-ordered trees. Fibonacci heaps are used sometimes in computing minimum spanning trees and finding single-source shortest paths (see Chapter 17, *Geometric Algorithms*).

k-ary heaps

Heaps built from trees with a branching factor of k. Although not as common as heaps that are binary trees, a k-ary heap may be worth considering for some problems.

11

Graphs

Graphs are some of the most flexible data structures in computing. In fact, most other data structures can be represented as graphs, although representing them in this way is usually more complicated. Generally, graphs are used to model problems defined in terms of relationships or connections between objects. Objects in a graph may be tangible entities such as nodes in a network or islands in a river, but they need not be. Often objects are less concrete, such as states in a system or transactions in a database. The same is true for connections and relationships among the objects. Nodes in a network are physically connected, but the connections between states in a system may simply indicate a decision made to get from one state to the next. Whatever the case, graphs model many useful and interesting computational problems.

This chapter covers:

Graphs
> Flexible data structures typically used to model problems defined in terms of relationships or connections between objects. Objects are represented by *vertices*, and the relationships or connections between the objects are represented by *edges* between the vertices.

Search methods
> Techniques for visiting the vertices of a graph in a specific order. Generally, either breadth-first or depth-first searches are used. Many graph algorithms are based on these basic methods of systematically exploring a graph's vertices.

Some applications of graphs are:

Graph algorithms
> Algorithms that solve problems modeled by graphs (see Chapter 16, *Graph Algorithms*). Many graph algorithms solve problems related to connectivity and

routing optimization. For example, Chapter 16 explores algorithms for computing minimum spanning trees, finding shortest paths, and solving the traveling-
salesman problem.

Counting network hops (illustrated in this chapter)

Counting the smallest number of nodes that must be traversed from one node
to reach other nodes in an internet. This information is useful in internets in
which the most significant costs are directly related to the number of nodes
traversed.

Topological sorting (illustrated in this chapter)

A linear ordering of vertices in a directed acyclic graph so that all edges go
from left to right. One of the most common uses of topological sorting is in
determining an acceptable order in which to carry out a number of tasks that
depend on one another.

Graph coloring

A process in which we try to color the vertices of a graph so that no two vertices joined by an edge have the same color. Sometimes we are interested only
in determining the minimum number of colors required to meet this criterion,
which is called the graph's *chromatic number.*

Hamiltonian-cycle problems

Problems in which one works with *hamiltonian cycles*, paths that pass
through every vertex in a graph exactly once before returning to the original
vertex. The traveling-salesman problem (see Chapter 16) is a special case of
hamiltonian-cycle problem. In the traveling-salesman problem, we look for the
hamiltonian cycle with the minimum cost.

Clique problems

Problems in which one works with regions of a graph where every vertex is
connected somehow to every other. Regions with this property are called
cliques. Some clique problems focus on determining the largest clique that a
graph contains. Other clique problems focus on determining whether a graph
contains a clique of a certain size at all.

Conflict serializability

A significant aspect of database optimization. Rather than executing the
instructions of transactions one transaction after another, database systems typically try to reorder a schedule of instructions to obtain a higher degree of
concurrency. However, a serial schedule of instructions cannot be reordered
arbitrarily; a database system must find a schedule that is *conflict serializable.*
A conflict serializable schedule produces the same results as a serial schedule.
To determine if a schedule is conflict serializable, a precedence graph is used
to define relationships among transactions. If the graph does not contain a
cycle, the schedule is conflict serializable.

Description of Graphs

Graphs are composed of two types of elements: *vertices* and *edges*. Vertices represent objects, and edges establish relationships or connections between the objects. In many problems, values, or *weights*, are associated with a graph's edges; however, such problems will not be considered further until Chapter 16.

Graphs may be either *directed* or *undirected*. In a directed graph, edges go from one vertex to another in a specific direction. Pictorially, a directed graph is drawn with circles for its vertices and arrows for its edges (see Figure 11-1a). Sometimes the edges of a directed graph are referred to as *arcs*. In an undirected graph, edges have no direction; thus, its edges are depicted using lines instead of arrows (see Figure 11-1b).

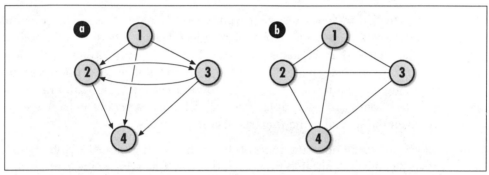

Figure 11-1. Two graphs: (a) a directed graph and (b) an undirected graph

Formally, a graph is a pair $G = (V, E)$, where V is a set of vertices and E is a binary relation on V. In a directed graph, if an edge goes from vertex u to vertex v, E contains the ordered pair (u, v). For example, in Figure 11-1a, $V = \{1, 2, 3, 4\}$ and $E = \{(1, 2), (1, 3), (1, 4), (2, 3), (2, 4), (3, 2), (3, 4)\}$. By convention, parentheses are used instead of braces for sets that represent edges in a graph. In an undirected graph, because an edge (u, v) is the same as (v, u), either edge is listed in E, but not both. Thus, in Figure 11-1b, $V = \{1, 2, 3, 4\}$ and $E = \{(1, 2), (1, 3), (1, 4), (2, 3), (2, 4), (3, 4)\}$. Edges may point back to the same vertex in a directed graph, but not in an undirected graph.

Two important relations in graphs are *adjacency* and *incidence*. Adjacency is a relation between two vertices. If a graph contains the edge (u, v), vertex v is said to be *adjacent to* vertex u. In an undirected graph, this implies that vertex u is also adjacent to vertex v. In other words, the adjacency relation is *symmetric* in an undirected graph. This is not necessarily true in a directed graph. For example, in Figure 11-1a, vertex 2 is adjacent to vertex 1, but vertex 1 is not adjacent to vertex 2. On the other hand, vertices 2 and 3 are adjacent to each other. A graph in which every vertex is adjacent to each other is called *complete*.

Incidence is a relation between a vertex and an edge. In a directed graph, the edge (u, v) is *incident from* or *leaves* vertex u and is *incident to* or *enters* vertex v. Thus, in Figure 11-1a, edge $(1, 2)$ is incident from vertex 1 and incident to vertex 2. In a directed graph, the *in-degree* of a vertex is the number of edges incident to it. Its *out-degree* is the number of edges incident from it. In an undirected graph, the edge (u, v) is *incident on* vertices u and v. In an undirected graph, the *degree* of a vertex is the number of edges incident on it.

Often one talks about *paths* in a graph. A path is a sequence of vertices traversed by following the edges between them. Formally, a path from one vertex u to another vertex u' is a sequence of vertices $\langle v_0, v_1, v_2, \ldots, v_k \rangle$ in which $u = v_0$ and $u' = v_k$, and all (v_{i-1}, v_i) are in E for $i = 1, 2, \ldots, k$. Such a path contains the edges $(v_0, v_1), (v_1, v_2), \ldots, (v_{k-1}, v_k)$ and has a *length* of k. If a path exists from u to u', u' is *reachable* from u. A path is *simple* if it has no repeated vertices.

A *cycle* is a path that includes the same vertex two or more times. That is, in a directed graph, a path is a cycle if one of its edges leaves a vertex and another enters it. Thus, Figure 11-2a contains the cycle {1, 2, 4, 1}. Formally, in a directed graph, a path forms a cycle if $v_0 = v_k$ and the path contains at least one edge. In an undirected graph, a path $\langle v_0, v_1, v_2, \ldots, v_k \rangle$ forms a cycle if $v_0 = v_k$ and no vertices are repeated from v_1 to v_k. Graphs without cycles are *acyclic*. Directed acyclic graphs are given the special name *dag* (see Figure 11-2b).

Connectivity is another important concept in graphs. An undirected graph is *connected* if every vertex is reachable from each other by following some path. If this is true in a directed graph, we say the graph is *strongly connected*. Although an undirected graph may not be connected, it still may contain certain sections that are connected, called *connected components*. If only parts of a directed graph are strongly connected, the parts are *strongly connected components* (see Figure 11-3).

Certain vertices have special significance in keeping a graph or connected component connected. If removing a vertex disconnects a graph or component, the vertex is an *articulation point*. For example, in Figure 11-4, vertices 4 and 5 are articulation points because if either of them is removed, the graph becomes disconnected. Upon removing these vertices, the graph has two connected components, {1, 2, 3} and {6, 7, 8}. Any edge whose removal disconnects a graph is called a *bridge*. A connected graph with no articulation points is *biconnected*. Although a graph may not be biconnected, it still may contain *biconnected components*.

The most common way to represent a graph in a computer is using an *adjacency-list representation*. This consists of a linked list of adjacency-list structures. Each structure in the list contains two members: a vertex and a list of vertices adjacent to the vertex (see Figure 11-5).

In a graph $G = (V, E)$, if two vertices u and v in V form an edge (u, v) in E, vertex v is included in the adjacency list of vertex u. Thus, in a directed graph, the

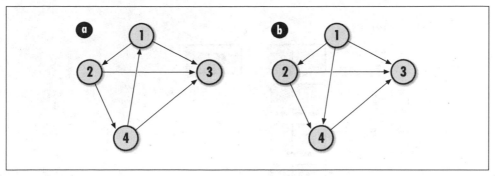

Figure 11-2. Two graphs: (a) a directed graph containing the cycle {1, 2, 4, 1}, and (b) a directed acyclic graph, or dag

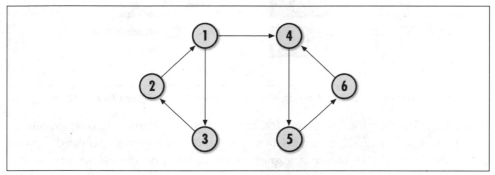

Figure 11-3. A directed graph with two strongly connected components, {1, 2, 3} and {4, 5, 6}

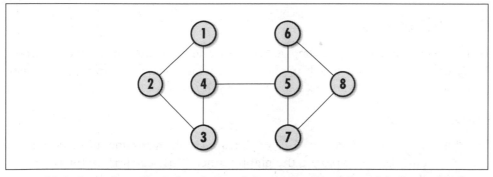

Figure 11-4. An undirected graph with articulation points 4 and 5, and the bridge (4, 5)

total number of vertices in all adjacency lists is the same as the total number of edges. In an undirected graph, since an edge (u, v) implies an edge (v, u), vertex v is included in the adjacency list of vertex u, and vertex u is included in the adjacency list of vertex v. Thus, the total number of vertices in all adjacency lists in this case is twice the total number of edges.

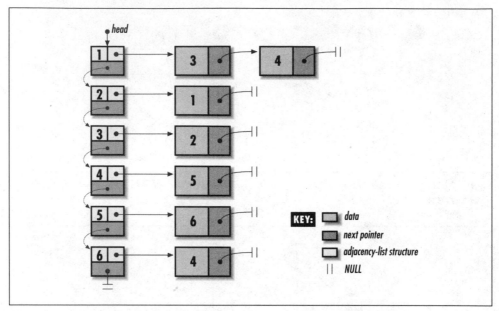

Figure 11-5. An adjacency-list representation of the directed graph from Figure 11-3

Typically, adjacency lists are used for graphs that are *sparse*, that is, graphs in which the number of edges is less than the number of vertices squared. Sparse graphs are common. However, if a graph is *dense*, we may choose to represent it using an *adjacency-matrix representation* (see the related topics at the end of the chapter). Adjacency-matrix representations require $O(VE)$ space.

Search Methods

Searching a graph means visiting its vertices one at a time in a specific order. There are two important search methods from which many important graph algorithms are derived: *breadth-first search* and *depth-first search*.

Breadth-first search

Breadth-first search (see Figure 11-6) explores a graph by visiting all vertices adjacent to a vertex before exploring the graph further. This search is useful in a number of applications, including finding minimum spanning trees and shortest paths (see Chapter 16 and the first example in this chapter).

To begin, we select a start vertex and color it gray. We color all other vertices in the graph white. The start vertex is also placed alone in a queue. The algorithm then proceeds as follows: for each vertex in the queue (initially only the start vertex), we peek at the vertex at the front of the queue and explore each vertex adjacent to it. As each adjacent vertex is explored, its color will be white if it has not

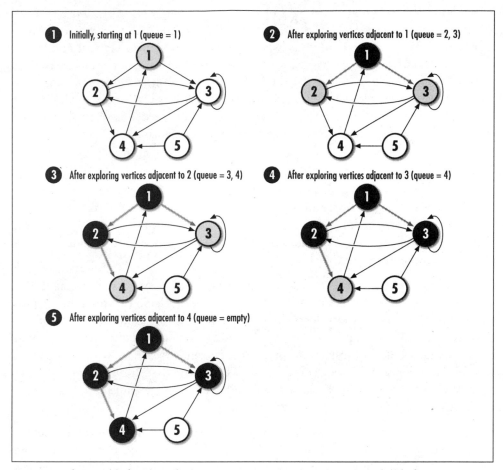

① Initially, starting at 1 (queue = 1)

② After exploring vertices adjacent to 1 (queue = 2, 3)

③ After exploring vertices adjacent to 2 (queue = 3, 4)

④ After exploring vertices adjacent to 3 (queue = 4)

⑤ After exploring vertices adjacent to 4 (queue = empty)

Figure 11-6. Breadth-first search starting at vertex 1; vertex 5 is unreachable from 1

been discovered yet. In this case, we color the vertex gray, indicating it has been discovered, and enqueue it at the end of the queue. If its color is not white, it has already been discovered, and the search proceeds to the next adjacent vertex.

Once all adjacent vertices have been explored, we dequeue the vertex at the front of the queue and color it black, indicating we are finished with it. We continue this process until the queue is empty, at which point all vertices reachable from the start vertex are black. Figure 11-6 illustrates breadth-first search with a directed graph. Breadth-first search works with undirected graphs as well.

In addition to simply visiting vertices, breadth-first search can be used to keep track of useful information. For example, we can record the number of vertices traversed before reaching each vertex, which turns out to be the shortest path to each vertex in graphs whose edges are not weighted. In Figure 11-6, the shortest path from vertex 1 to either vertex 2 or 3 consists of one hop, recorded when we first discover vertex 2 and 3. The shortest path from vertex 1 to vertex 4 consists of two hops: one hop is recorded as we discover vertex 2 from 1, and another is recorded when we discover vertex 4 from 2. We can also use breadth-first search to generate a *breadth-first tree*. A breadth-first tree is the tree formed by maintaining the predecessor of each vertex as we discover it. Since a vertex is discovered only once (when we color it gray), it has exactly one predecessor, or parent. In Figure 11-6, the edges highlighted in gray are branches of the tree.

Depth-first search

Depth-first search (see Figure 11-7) explores a graph by first visiting undiscovered vertices adjacent to the vertex most recently discovered. Thus, the search continually tries to explore as deep as it can. This makes depth-first search useful in a number of applications, including cycle detection and topological sorting (see the second example in this chapter).

To begin, we color every vertex white and select a vertex at which to start. The algorithm then proceeds as follows: first, we color the selected vertex gray to indicate it has been discovered. Then, we select a new vertex from the set of undiscovered vertices adjacent to it, which are white, and repeat the process. When there are no white vertices adjacent to the currently selected vertex, we have searched as deep as possible. Thus, we color the currently selected vertex black to indicate that we are finished with it, and we backtrack to explore the white vertices adjacent to the previously selected vertex.

We continue this process until the vertex we selected as the start vertex has no more white vertices adjacent to it. This process visits only the vertices reachable from the vertex at which we start. Therefore, the entire process must be repeated for each vertex in the graph. For example, in Figure 11-7, vertex 4 would not get visited without this step. When we restart at a vertex that is already black, the search stops immediately, and we move on to the next vertex. Figure 11-7 illustrates depth-first search with a directed graph. Depth-first search works with undirected graphs as well.

In addition to simply visiting vertices, a depth-first search can be used to keep track of some useful information. For example, we can record the times at which each vertex is discovered and finished. Depth-first search also can be used to produce a *depth-first forest*. A depth-first forest is a set of trees, each formed by maintaining the predecessor of each vertex as it is discovered. Since a vertex is discovered only once (when we color it gray), it has exactly one predecessor, or parent. Each tree contains the vertices discovered in searching exactly one connected component. In Figure 11-7, the edges highlighted in gray are branches in the trees.

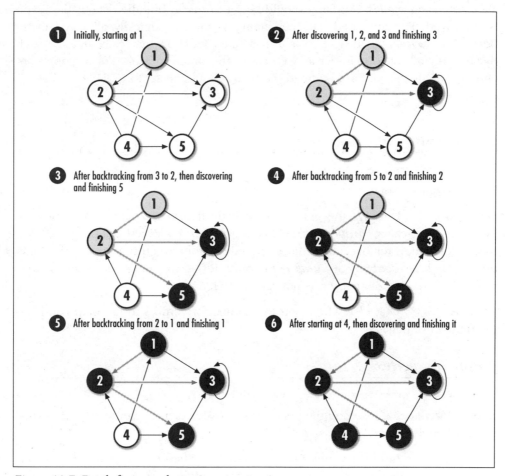

Figure 11-7. Depth-first search starting at vertex 1

Interface for Graphs

graph_init

```
void graph_init(Graph *graph, int (*match)(const void *key1, const void *key2),
   void (*destroy)(void *data));
```

Return Value   None.

Description   Initializes the graph specified by *graph*. This operation must be called for a graph before the graph can be used with any other operation. The *match* argument is a function used by various graph operations to determine if two vertices match. It should return 1 if *key1* is equal to *key2*, and 0 otherwise. The *destroy* argument provides a way to free dynamically allocated data when *graph_destroy* is called. For example, if the graph contains data dynamically allocated using *malloc*, `destroy` should be set to *free* to free the data as the graph is destroyed. For structured data containing several dynamically allocated members, `destroy` should be set to a user-defined function that calls *free* for each dynamically allocated member as well as for the structure itself. For a graph containing data that should not be freed, `destroy` should be set to NULL.

Complexity $O(1)$

graph_destroy

```
void graph_destroy(Graph *graph);
```

Return Value   None.

Description   Destroys the graph specified by `graph`. No other operations are permitted after calling *graph_destroy* unless *graph_init* is called again. The *graph_destroy* operation removes all vertices and edges from a graph and calls the function passed as `destroy` to *graph_init* once for each vertex or edge as it is removed, provided `destroy` was not set to NULL.

Complexity $O(V+E)$, where V is the number of vertices in the graph and E is the number of edges.

graph_ins_vertex

```
int graph_ins_vertex(Graph *graph, const void *data);
```

Return Value   0 if inserting the vertex is successful, 1 if the vertex already exists, or −1 otherwise.

Description   Inserts a vertex into the graph specified by `graph`. The new vertex contains a pointer to `data`, so the memory referenced by `data` should remain valid as long as the vertex remains in the graph. It is the responsibility of the caller to manage the storage associated with `data`.

Complexity $O(V)$, where V is the number of vertices in the graph.

graph_ins_edge

```
int graph_ins_edge(Graph *graph, const void *data1, const void *data2);
```

Return Value   0 if inserting the edge is successful, 1 if the edge already exists, or −1 otherwise.

Description   Inserts an edge from the vertex specified by `data1` to the vertex specified by `data2` in the graph specified by `graph`. Both vertices must have been inserted previously using *graph_ins_vertex*. The new edge is represented with a pointer to `data2` in the adjacency list of the vertex specified by `data1`, so the memory referenced by *data2* should remain valid as long as the edge remains in the graph. It is the responsibility of the caller to manage the storage associated with *data2*. To enter an edge (u, v) in an undirected graph, call this operation twice: once to insert an edge from u to v, and again to insert the implied edge from v to u. This type of representation is common for undirected graphs.

Complexity $O(V)$, where V is the number of vertices in the graph.

graph_rem_vertex

```
int graph_rem_vertex(Graph *graph, void **data);
```

Return Value   0 if removing the vertex is successful, or −1 otherwise.

Description   Removes the vertex matching *data* from the graph specified by *graph*. All edges incident to and from the vertex must have been removed previously using *graph_rem_edge*. Upon return, *data* points to the data stored in the vertex that was removed. It is the responsibility of the caller to manage the storage associated with the data.

Complexity $O(V + E)$, where V is the number of vertices in the graph and E is the number of edges.

graph_rem_edge

```
int graph_rem_edge(Graph *graph, const void *data1, void **data2);
```

Return Value   0 if removing the edge is successful, or −1 otherwise.

Description   Removes the edge from *data1* to *data2* in the graph specified by *graph*. Upon return, *data2* points to the data stored in the adjacency list of the vertex specified by *data1*. It is the responsibility of the caller to manage the storage associated with the data.

Complexity $O(V)$, where V is the number of vertices in the graph.

graph_adjlist

```
int graph_adjlist(const Graph *graph, const void *data, AdjList **adjlist);
```

Return Value   0 if retrieving the adjacency list is successful, or −1 otherwise.

Description   Retrieves vertices that are adjacent to the vertex specified by *data* in *graph*. The adjacent vertices are returned in the form of an *AdjList* structure, a structure containing the vertex matching *data* and a set of vertices adjacent to it. A pointer to the actual adjacency list in the graph is returned, so it must not be manipulated by the caller.

Complexity $O(V)$, where V is the number of vertices in the graph.

graph_is_adjacent

```
int graph_is_adjacent(const Graph *graph, const void *data1, const void *data2);
```

Return Value   1 if the second vertex is adjacent to the first vertex, or 0 otherwise.

Description   Determines whether the vertex specified by *data2* is adjacent to the vertex specified by *data1* in *graph*.

Complexity $O(V)$, where V is the number of vertices in the graph.

graph_adjlists

```
List graph_adjlists(const Graph *graph);
```

Return Value   List of adjacency-list structures.

Description   Macro that evaluates to the list of adjacency-list structures in *graph*. Each element in the list is an *AdjList* structure. The actual list of adjacency-list structures in the graph is returned, so it must not be manipulated by the caller.

Complexity $O(1)$

graph_vcount

```
int graph_vcount(const Graph *graph);
```

Return Value   Number of vertices in the graph.

Description   Macro that evaluates to the number of vertices in the graph specified by *graph*.

Complexity $O(1)$

graph_ecount

```
int graph_ecount(const Graph *graph);
```

Return Value   Number of edges in the graph.

Description   Macro that evaluates to the number of edges in the graph specified by *graph*.

Complexity $O(1)$

Implementation and Analysis of Graphs

An adjacency-list representation of a graph primarily consists of a linked list of adjacency-list structures. Each structure in the list contains two members: a vertex and a list of vertices adjacent to the vertex. In the implementation presented here, an individual adjacency list is represented by the structure *AdjList* (see Example 11-1). As you would expect, this structure has two members that correspond to those just mentioned. Each adjacency list is implemented as a set (see Chapter 7, *Sets*) for reasons discussed in the questions and answers at the end of the chapter. The structure *Graph* is the graph data structure (see Example 11-1). This structure consists of five members: *vcount* is the number of vertices in the graph, *ecount* is the number of edges, *match* and *destroy* are members used to encapsulate the functions passed to *graph_init*, and *adjlists* is the linked list of adjacency-list structures. Example 11-1 also defines an enumerated type for vertex colors, which are often used when working with graphs.

Example 11-1. Header for the Graph Abstract Datatype

```
/*****************************************************************************
*                                                                           *
*  ----------------------------- graph.h -----------------------------      *
*                                                                           *
*****************************************************************************/

#ifndef GRAPH_H
#define GRAPH_H

#include <stdlib.h>

#include "list.h"
#include "set.h"

/*****************************************************************************
*                                                                           *
*  Define a structure for adjacency lists.                                  *
*                                                                           *
*****************************************************************************/

typedef struct AdjList_ {

void              *vertex;
Set               adjacent;

} AdjList;

/*****************************************************************************
*                                                                           *
*  Define a structure for graphs.                                          *
*                                                                           *
*****************************************************************************/

typedef struct Graph_ {

int               vcount;
int               ecount;
```

Example 11-1. Header for the Graph Abstract Datatype (continued)

```
int             (*match)(const void *key1, const void *key2);
void            (*destroy)(void *data);

List            adjlists;

} Graph;

/*****************************************************************************
*                                                                           *
*  Define colors for vertices in graphs.                                    *
*                                                                           *
*****************************************************************************/

typedef enum VertexColor_ {white, gray, black} VertexColor;

/*****************************************************************************
*                                                                           *
*  -------------------------- Public Interface --------------------------   *
*                                                                           *
*****************************************************************************/

void graph_init(Graph *graph, int (*match)(const void *key1, const void
   *key2), void (*destroy)(void *data));

void graph_destroy(Graph *graph);

int graph_ins_vertex(Graph *graph, const void *data);

int graph_ins_edge(Graph *graph, const void *data1, const void *data2);

int graph_rem_vertex(Graph *graph, void **data);

int graph_rem_edge(Graph *graph, void *data1, void **data2);

int graph_adjlist(const Graph *graph, const void *data, AdjList **adjlist);

int graph_is_adjacent(const Graph *graph, const void *data1, const void
   *data2);

#define graph_adjlists(graph) ((graph)->adjlists)

#define graph_vcount(graph) ((graph)->vcount)

#define graph_ecount(graph) ((graph)->ecount)

#endif
```

graph_init

The *graph_init* operation initializes a graph so that it can be used in other operations (see Example 11-2). Initializing a graph is a simple operation in which we set the *vcount* and *ecount* members of the graph to 0, encapsulate the *match* and *destroy* functions, and initialize the list of adjacency-list structures.

The runtime complexity of *graph_init* is $O(1)$ because all of the steps in initializing a graph run in a constant amount of time.

graph_destroy

The *graph_destroy* operation destroys a graph (see Example 11-2). Primarily this means removing each adjacency-list structure, destroying the set of vertices it contains, and freeing the memory allocated to its *vertex* member by calling the function passed as *destroy* to *graph_init*, provided *destroy* was not set to NULL.

The runtime complexity of *graph_destroy* is $O(V + E)$, where V is the number of vertices in the graph and E is the number of edges. This is because we make V calls to the $O(1)$ operation *list_rem_next*, and the total running time of all calls to *set_destroy* is $O(E)$.

graph_ins_vertex

The *graph_ins_vertex* operation inserts a vertex into a graph (see Example 11-2). Specifically, the call inserts an *AdjList* structure into the list of adjacency-list structures and sets its *vertex* member to point to the data passed by the caller. We begin by ensuring that the vertex does not already exist in the list. After this, we insert the vertex by calling *list_ins_next* to insert the *AdjList* structure at the tail of the list. Last, we update the count of vertices in the graph by incrementing the *vcount* member of the graph data structure.

The runtime complexity of *graph_ins_vertex* is $O(V)$, where V is the number of vertices in the graph. This is because searching the list of vertices for a duplicate is an $O(V)$ operation. The call to *list_ins_next* is $O(1)$.

graph_ins_edge

The *graph_ins_edge* operation inserts an edge into a graph (see Example 11-2). To insert an edge from the vertex specified by *data1* to the vertex specified by *data2*, we insert *data2* into the adjacency list of *data1*. We begin by ensuring that both vertices exist in the graph. After this, we insert the vertex specified by *data2* into the adjacency list of *data1* by calling *set_insert*. The call to *set_insert* returns an error if the edge already exists. Last, we update the count of edges in the graph by incrementing the *ecount* member of the graph data structure.

The runtime complexity of *graph_ins_edge* is $O(V)$, where V is the number of vertices in the graph. This is because searching the list of adjacency-list structures and calling *set_insert* are both $O(V)$ operations.

graph_rem_vertex

The *graph_rem_vertex* operation removes a vertex from a graph (see Example 11-2). Specifically, the call removes an `AdjList` structure from the list of adjacency-list structures. We begin by ensuring that the vertex does not exist in any adjacency list, that the vertex does exist in the list of adjacency-list structures, and that the adjacency list of the vertex is empty. After this, we remove the vertex by calling `list_rem_next` to remove the appropriate `AdjList` structure from the list. Last, we update the count of vertices in the graph by decreasing its *vcount* member of the graph data structure by 1.

The runtime complexity of *graph_rem_vertex* is $O(V + E)$, where V is the number of vertices in the graph and E is the number of edges. This is because searching every adjacency list is $O(V + E)$, searching the list of adjacency-list structures is $O(V)$, and calling *list_rem_next* is $O(1)$.

graph_rem_edge

The *graph_rem_edge* operation removes an edge from a graph (see Example 11-2). Specifically, the call removes the vertex specified by *data2* from the adjacency list of *data1*. We begin by ensuring that the first vertex exists in the graph. Once this has been verified, we remove the edge by calling *set_remove* to remove the vertex specified by *data2* from the adjacency list of *data1*. The call to *set_remove* returns an error if *data2* is not in the adjacency list of *data1*. Last, we update the count of edges in the graph by decreasing the *ecount* member of the graph data structure by 1.

The runtime complexity of *graph_rem_edge* is $O(V)$, where V is the number of vertices in the graph. This is because searching the list of adjacency-list structures and calling *set_remove* are both $O(V)$ operations.

graph_adjlist

The *graph_adjlist* operation returns the `AdjList` structure containing the set of vertices adjacent to a specified vertex (see Example 11-2). To do this, we search the list of adjacency-list structures until we find the one that contains the specified vertex.

The runtime complexity of *graph_adjlist* is $O(V)$, where V is the number of vertices in the graph. This is because searching the list of adjacency-list structures runs in $O(V)$ time.

graph_is_adjacent

The *graph_is_adjacent* operation determines whether a specified vertex is adjacent to another (see Example 11-2). To do this, we locate the adjacency-list structure of the vertex specified by *data1* and call *set_is_member* to determine if *data2* is in its adjacency list.

The runtime complexity of *graph_adjlist* is $O(V)$, where V is the number of vertices in the graph. This is because searching the list of adjacency-list structures and calling *set_is_member* are both $O(V)$ operations.

graph_adjlists, graph_vcount, graph_ecount

These macros implement some of the simpler graph operations (see Example 11-1). Generally, they provide an interface for accessing and testing members of the *Graph* structure.

The runtime complexity of these operations is $O(1)$ because accessing members of a structure is a simple task that runs in a constant amount of time.

Example 11-2. Implementation of the Graph Abstract Datatype

```
/***************************************************************************
*                                                                         *
*  ----------------------------- graph.c ----------------------------    *
*                                                                         *
***************************************************************************/

#include <stdlib.h>
#include <string.h>

#include "graph.h"
#include "list.h"
#include "set.h"

/***************************************************************************
*                                                                         *
*  ---------------------------- graph_init ----------------------------   *
*                                                                         *
***************************************************************************/

void graph_init(Graph *graph, int (*match)(const void *key1, const void
   *key2), void (*destroy)(void *data)) {

/***************************************************************************
*                                                                         *
*  Initialize the graph.                                                  *
*                                                                         *
***************************************************************************/

graph->vcount = 0;
graph->ecount = 0;
graph->match = match;
graph->destroy = destroy;
```

Example 11-2. Implementation of the Graph Abstract Datatype (continued)

```
/***************************************************************************
*                                                                         *
*  Initialize the list of adjacency-list structures.                      *
*                                                                         *
***************************************************************************/

list_init(&graph->adjlists, NULL);

return;

}

/***************************************************************************
*                                                                         *
*  --------------------------- graph_destroy ---------------------------  *
*                                                                         *
***************************************************************************/

void graph_destroy(Graph *graph) {

AdjList            *adjlist;

/***************************************************************************
*                                                                         *
*  Remove each adjacency-list structure and destroy its adjacency list.   *
*                                                                         *
***************************************************************************/

while (list_size(&graph->adjlists) > 0) {

   if (list_rem_next(&graph->adjlists, NULL, (void **)&adjlist) == 0) {

      set_destroy(&adjlist->adjacent);

      if (graph->destroy != NULL)
         graph->destroy(adjlist->vertex);

      free(adjlist);

   }

}

/***************************************************************************
*                                                                         *
*  Destroy the list of adjacency-list structures, which is now empty.     *
*                                                                         *
***************************************************************************/

list_destroy(&graph->adjlists);
```

Example 11-2. Implementation of the Graph Abstract Datatype (continued)

```
/***************************************************************************
*                                                                          *
*  No operations are allowed now, but clear the structure as a precaution. *
*                                                                          *
***************************************************************************/

memset(graph, 0, sizeof(Graph));

return;

}

/***************************************************************************
*                                                                          *
*  -------------------------- graph_ins_vertex --------------------------  *
*                                                                          *
***************************************************************************/

int graph_ins_vertex(Graph *graph, const void *data) {

ListElmt          *element;

AdjList           *adjlist;

int               retval;

/***************************************************************************
*                                                                          *
*  Do not allow the insertion of duplicate vertices.                       *
*                                                                          *
***************************************************************************/

for (element = list_head(&graph->adjlists); element != NULL; element =
   list_next(element)) {

   if (graph->match(data, ((AdjList *)list_data(element))->vertex))
      return 1;

}

/***************************************************************************
*                                                                          *
*  Insert the vertex.                                                      *
*                                                                          *
***************************************************************************/

if ((adjlist = (AdjList *)malloc(sizeof(AdjList))) == NULL)
   return -1;

adjlist->vertex = (void *)data;
set_init(&adjlist->adjacent, graph->match, graph->destroy);
```

Example 11-2. Implementation of the Graph Abstract Datatype (continued)

```c
if ((retval = list_ins_next(&graph->adjlists, list_tail(&graph->adjlists),
   adjlist)) != 0) {

   return retval;

}

/*****************************************************************************
*                                                                           *
*  Adjust the vertex count to account for the inserted vertex.              *
*                                                                           *
*****************************************************************************/

graph->vcount++;

return 0;

}

/*****************************************************************************
*                                                                           *
*  --------------------------- graph_ins_edge --------------------------    *
*                                                                           *
*****************************************************************************/

int graph_ins_edge(Graph *graph, const void *data1, const void *data2) {

ListElmt           *element;

int                retval;

/*****************************************************************************
*                                                                           *
*  Do not allow insertion of an edge without both its vertices in the graph. *
*                                                                           *
*****************************************************************************/

for (element = list_head(&graph->adjlists); element != NULL; element =
   list_next(element)) {

   if (graph->match(data2, ((AdjList *)list_data(element))->vertex))
      break;

}

if (element == NULL)
   return -1;

for (element = list_head(&graph->adjlists); element != NULL; element =
   list_next(element)) {

   if (graph->match(data1, ((AdjList *)list_data(element))->vertex))
      break;
```

Example 11-2. Implementation of the Graph Abstract Datatype (continued)

```
}

if (element == NULL)
   return -1;

/****************************************************************************
*                                                                          *
*  Insert the second vertex into the adjacency list of the first vertex.   *
*                                                                          *
****************************************************************************/

if ((retval = set_insert(&((AdjList *)list_data(element))->adjacent, data2))
   != 0) {

   return retval;

}

/****************************************************************************
*                                                                          *
*  Adjust the edge count to account for the inserted edge.                 *
*                                                                          *
****************************************************************************/

graph->ecount++;

return 0;

}

/****************************************************************************
*                                                                          *
*  -------------------------- graph_rem_vertex --------------------------  *
*                                                                          *
****************************************************************************/

int graph_rem_vertex(Graph *graph, void **data) {

ListElmt          *element,
                  *temp,
                  *prev;

AdjList           *adjlist;

int               found;

/****************************************************************************
*                                                                          *
*  Traverse each adjacency list and the vertices it contains.              *
*                                                                          *
****************************************************************************/
```

Example 11-2. Implementation of the Graph Abstract Datatype (continued)

```
prev = NULL;
found = 0;

for (element = list_head(&graph->adjlists); element != NULL; element =
   list_next(element)) {

   /***************************************************************************
   *                                                                         *
   *  Do not allow removal of the vertex if it is in an adjacency list.      *
   *                                                                         *
   ***************************************************************************/

   if (set_is_member(&((AdjList *)list_data(element))->adjacent, *data))
      return -1;

   /***************************************************************************
   *                                                                         *
   *  Keep a pointer to the vertex to be removed.                            *
   *                                                                         *
   ***************************************************************************/

   if (graph->match(*data, ((AdjList *)list_data(element))->vertex)) {

      temp = element;
      found = 1;

   }

   /***************************************************************************
   *                                                                         *
   *  Keep a pointer to the vertex before the vertex to be removed.          *
   *                                                                         *
   ***************************************************************************/

   if (!found)
      prev = element;

}

/***************************************************************************
*                                                                         *
*  Return if the vertex was not found.                                    *
*                                                                         *
***************************************************************************/

if (!found)
   return -1;

/***************************************************************************
*                                                                         *
*  Do not allow removal of the vertex if its adjacency list is not empty. *
*                                                                         *
***************************************************************************/
```

Example 11-2. Implementation of the Graph Abstract Datatype (continued)

```
if (set_size(&((AdjList *)list_data(temp))->adjacent) > 0)
   return -1;

/***************************************************************************
*                                                                         *
*  Remove the vertex.                                                     *
*                                                                         *
***************************************************************************/

if (list_rem_next(&graph->adjlists, prev, (void **)&adjlist) != 0)
   return -1;

/***************************************************************************
*                                                                         *
*  Free the storage allocated by the abstract datatype.                   *
*                                                                         *
***************************************************************************/

*data = adjlist->vertex;
free(adjlist);

/***************************************************************************
*                                                                         *
*  Adjust the vertex count to account for the removed vertex.             *
*                                                                         *
***************************************************************************/

graph->vcount--;

return 0;

}

/***************************************************************************
*                                                                         *
*  -------------------------- graph_rem_edge --------------------------   *
*                                                                         *
***************************************************************************/

int graph_rem_edge(Graph *graph, void *data1, void **data2) {

ListElmt          *element;

/***************************************************************************
*                                                                         *
*  Locate the adjacency list for the first vertex.                        *
*                                                                         *
***************************************************************************/

for (element = list_head(&graph->adjlists); element != NULL; element =
   list_next(element)) {
```

Example 11-2. Implementation of the Graph Abstract Datatype (continued)

```
   if (graph->match(data1, ((AdjList *)list_data(element))->vertex))
      break;

}

if (element == NULL)
   return -1;

/***************************************************************************
*                                                                         *
*  Remove the second vertex from the adjacency list of the first vertex.  *
*                                                                         *
***************************************************************************/

if (set_remove(&((AdjList *)list_data(element))->adjacent, data2) != 0)
   return -1;

/***************************************************************************
*                                                                         *
*  Adjust the edge count to account for the removed edge.                 *
*                                                                         *
***************************************************************************/

graph->ecount--;

return 0;

}

/***************************************************************************
*                                                                         *
*  ---------------------------- graph_adjlist ---------------------------  *
*                                                                         *
***************************************************************************/

int graph_adjlist(const Graph *graph, const void *data, AdjList **adjlist) {

ListElmt           *element,
                   *prev;

/***************************************************************************
*                                                                         *
*  Locate the adjacency list for the vertex.                              *
*                                                                         *
***************************************************************************/

prev = NULL;

for (element = list_head(&graph->adjlists); element != NULL; element =
   list_next(element)) {

   if (graph->match(data, ((AdjList *)list_data(element))->vertex))
      break;
```

Example 11-2. Implementation of the Graph Abstract Datatype (continued)

```
   prev = element;

}

/***************************************************************************
*                                                                         *
*  Return if the vertex was not found.                                    *
*                                                                         *
***************************************************************************/

if (element == NULL)
   return -1;

/***************************************************************************
*                                                                         *
*  Pass back the adjacency list for the vertex.                           *
*                                                                         *
***************************************************************************/

*adjlist = list_data(element);

return 0;

}

/***************************************************************************
*                                                                         *
*  -------------------------- graph_is_adjacent --------------------------  *
*                                                                         *
***************************************************************************/

int graph_is_adjacent(const Graph *graph, const void *data1, const void
   *data2) {

ListElmt          *element,
                  *prev;

/***************************************************************************
*                                                                         *
*  Locate the adjacency list of the first vertex.                         *
*                                                                         *
***************************************************************************/

prev = NULL;

for (element = list_head(&graph->adjlists); element != NULL; element =
   list_next(element)) {

   if (graph->match(data1, ((AdjList *)list_data(element))->vertex))
     break;

   prev = element;

}
```

Example 11-2. Implementation of the Graph Abstract Datatype (continued)

```
/****************************************************************************
*                                                                          *
*   Return if the first vertex was not found.                              *
*                                                                          *
****************************************************************************/

if (element == NULL)
   return 0;

/****************************************************************************
*                                                                          *
*   Return whether the second vertex is in the adjacency list of the first. *
*                                                                          *
****************************************************************************/

return set_is_member(&((AdjList *)list_data(element))->adjacent, data2);

}
```

Graph Example: Counting Network Hops

Graphs play an important part in solving many networking problems. One problem, for example, is determining the best way to get from one node to another in an *internet*, a network of gateways into other networks. One way to model an internet is using an undirected graph in which vertices represent nodes, and edges represent connections between the nodes. With this model, we can use breadth-first search to help determine the smallest number of traversals, or *hops*, between various nodes.

For example, consider the graph in Figure 11-8, which represents an internet of six nodes. Starting at $node_1$, there is more than one way we can reach $node_4$. The paths $\langle node_1, node_2, node_4\rangle$, $\langle node_1, node_3, node_2, node_4\rangle$, and $\langle node_1, node_3, node_5, node_4\rangle$ are all acceptable. Breadth-first search determines the shortest path, $\langle node_1, node_2, node_4\rangle$, which requires two hops.

This example presents a function, *bfs* (see Examples 11-3 and 11-4), that implements breadth-first search. It is used here to determine the smallest number of hops between nodes in an internet. The function has three arguments: **graph** is a graph, which in this problem represents the internet; **start** is the vertex representing the starting point; and **hops** is the list of hop counts that is returned. The function modifies **graph**, so a copy should be made before calling the function, if necessary. Also, vertices returned in **hops** are pointers to the actual vertices from **graph**, so the caller must ensure that the storage in **graph** remains valid as long as **hops** is being accessed. Each vertex in **graph** is a **BfsVertex** structure (see Example 11-3), which has three members: **data** is a pointer to the data associated

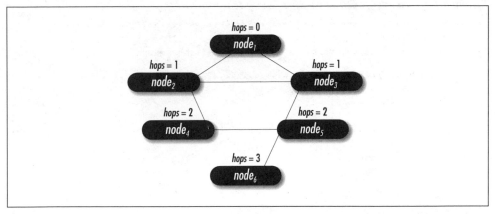

Figure 11-8. Hop counts after performing a breadth-first search on an internet of six nodes

with the vertex, `color` maintains the color of the vertex during the search, and
`hops` maintains the number of hops to the vertex from the start node. The `match`
function for `graph`, which is set by the caller when initializing the graph with
`graph_init`, should compare only the `data` members of `BfsVertex` structures.

The *bfs* function performs breadth-first search as described earlier in this chapter.
To keep track of the minimum number of hops to each vertex, we set the hop
count of each vertex to the hop count of the vertex to which it is adjacent plus 1.
We do this for each vertex as we discover it, and color it gray. Colors and hop
counts for each vertex are maintained by the `BfsVertex` structures in the list of
adjacency-list structures. At the end, we load `hops` with all vertices whose hop
counts are not –1. These are the vertices that were reachable from the start node.

The runtime complexity of *bfs* is $O(V + E)$, where V is the number of vertices in
the graph and E is the number of edges. This is because initializing the colors of
the vertices and ensuring that the start node exists both run in $O(V)$ time, the loop
in which the breadth-first search is performed in $O(V + E)$ time, and loading the
list of hop counts is $O(V)$.

Example 11-3. Header for Breadth-First Search

```
/*****************************************************************************
*                                                                           *
*  ------------------------------- bfs.h -------------------------------     *
*                                                                           *
*****************************************************************************/

#ifndef BFS_H
#define BFS_H

#include "graph.h"
#include "list.h"
```

Example 11-3. Header for Breadth-First Search (continued)

```
/***************************************************************************
*                                                                         *
*  Define a structure for vertices in a breadth-first search.             *
*                                                                         *
***************************************************************************/

typedef struct BfsVertex_ {

void            *data;

VertexColor     color;
int             hops;

} BfsVertex;

/***************************************************************************
*                                                                         *
*  --------------------------- Public Interface --------------------------  *
*                                                                         *
***************************************************************************/

int bfs(Graph *graph, BfsVertex *start, List *hops);

#endif
```

Example 11-4. Implementation of a Function for Breadth-First Search

```
/***************************************************************************
*                                                                         *
*  -------------------------------- bfs.c ---------------------------------  *
*                                                                         *
***************************************************************************/

#include <stdlib.h>

#include "bfs.h"
#include "graph.h"
#include "list.h"
#include "queue.h"

/***************************************************************************
*                                                                         *
*  --------------------------------- bfs ----------------------------------  *
*                                                                         *
***************************************************************************/

int bfs(Graph *graph, BfsVertex *start, List *hops) {

Queue           queue;

AdjList         *adjlist,
                *clr_adjlist;
```

Example 11-4. Implementation of a Function for Breadth-First Search (continued)

```c
BfsVertex           *clr_vertex,
                    *adj_vertex;

ListElmt            *element,
                    *member;

/****************************************************************************
*                                                                          *
*  Initialize all of the vertices in the graph.                            *
*                                                                          *
****************************************************************************/

for (element = list_head(&graph_adjlists(graph)); element != NULL; element =
   list_next(element)) {

   clr_vertex = ((AdjList *)list_data(element))->vertex;

   if (graph->match(clr_vertex, start)) {

      /****************************************************************************
      *                                                                          *
      *  Initialize the start vertex.                                            *
      *                                                                          *
      ****************************************************************************/

      clr_vertex->color = gray;
      clr_vertex->hops = 0;

      }

   else {

      /****************************************************************************
      *                                                                          *
      *  Initialize vertices other than the start vertex.                        *
      *                                                                          *
      ****************************************************************************/

      clr_vertex->color = white;
      clr_vertex->hops = -1;

   }

}

/****************************************************************************
*                                                                          *
*  Initialize the queue with the adjacency list of the start vertex.       *
*                                                                          *
****************************************************************************/

queue_init(&queue, NULL);
```

Example 11-4. Implementation of a Function for Breadth-First Search (continued)

```
if (graph_adjlist(graph, start, &clr_adjlist) != 0) {

   queue_destroy(&queue);
   return -1;

}

if (queue_enqueue(&queue, clr_adjlist) != 0) {

   queue_destroy(&queue);
   return -1;

}

/***************************************************************************
*                                                                         *
*  Perform breadth-first search.                                          *
*                                                                         *
***************************************************************************/

while (queue_size(&queue) > 0) {

   adjlist = queue_peek(&queue);

   /***********************************************************************
   *                                                                     *
   *  Traverse each vertex in the current adjacency list.                *
   *                                                                     *
   ***********************************************************************/

   for (member = list_head(&adjlist->adjacent); member != NULL; member =
      list_next(member)) {

      adj_vertex = list_data(member);

      /*******************************************************************
      *                                                                 *
      *  Determine the color of the next adjacent vertex.               *
      *                                                                 *
      *******************************************************************/

      if (graph_adjlist(graph, adj_vertex, &clr_adjlist) != 0) {

         queue_destroy(&queue);
         return -1;

      }

      clr_vertex = clr_adjlist->vertex;
```

Example 11-4. Implementation of a Function for Breadth-First Search (continued)

```
/***************************************************************************
*                                                                         *
*  Color each white vertex gray and enqueue its adjacency list.           *
*                                                                         *
***************************************************************************/

         if (clr_vertex->color == white) {

            clr_vertex->color = gray;
            clr_vertex->hops = ((BfsVertex *)adjlist->vertex)->hops + 1;

            if (queue_enqueue(&queue, clr_adjlist) != 0) {

               queue_destroy(&queue);
               return -1;

            }

         }

      }

      /***************************************************************************
      *                                                                         *
      *  Dequeue the current adjacency list and color its vertex black.         *
      *                                                                         *
      ***************************************************************************/

      if (queue_dequeue(&queue, (void **)&adjlist) == 0) {

         ((BfsVertex *)adjlist->vertex)->color = black;

         }

      else {

         queue_destroy(&queue);
         return -1;

      }

}

queue_destroy(&queue);

/***************************************************************************
*                                                                         *
*  Pass back the hop count for each vertex in a list.                     *
*                                                                         *
***************************************************************************/

list_init(hops, NULL);
```

Example 11-4. Implementation of a Function for Breadth-First Search (continued)

```
for (element = list_head(&graph_adjlists(graph)); element != NULL; element =
   list_next(element)) {

   /**************************************************************************
   *                                                                        *
   *  Skip vertices that were not visited (those with hop counts of -1).    *
   *                                                                        *
   **************************************************************************/

   clr_vertex = ((AdjList *)list_data(element))->vertex;

   if (clr_vertex->hops != -1) {

      if (list_ins_next(hops, list_tail(hops), clr_vertex) != 0) {

         list_destroy(hops);
         return -1;

      }

   }

}

return, 0;

}
```

Graph Example: Topological Sorting

Sometimes we encounter problems in which we must determine an acceptable ordering by which to carry out tasks that depend on one another. Imagine a set of classes at a university that have prerequisites, or a complicated project in which certain phases must be completed before other phases can begin. To model problems like these, we use a directed graph, called a *precedence graph*, in which vertices represent tasks and edges represent dependencies between them. To show a dependency, we draw an edge from the task that must be completed first to the task that depends on it.

For example, consider the directed acyclic graph in Figure 11-9a, which represents a curriculum of seven courses and their prerequisites: CS100 has no prerequisites, CS200 requires CS100, CS300 requires CS200 and MA100, MA100 has no prerequisites, MA200 requires MA100, MA300 requires CS300 and MA200, and CS150 has no prerequisites and is not a prerequisite itself.

Depth-first search helps to determine an acceptable ordering by performing a *topological sort* on the courses. Topological sorting orders the vertices in a directed acyclic graph so that all edges go from left to right. In the problem involving

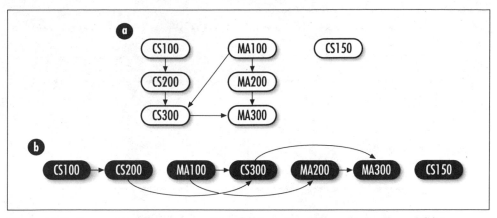

Figure 11-9. Courses and their prerequisites (a) in a directed acrylic graph and (b) in one topological sorting

course prerequisites, this means that all prerequisites will appear to the left of the courses that require them (see Figure 11-9b). Formally, a topological sort of a directed acyclic graph $G = (V, E)$ is a linear ordering of its vertices so that if an edge (u, v) exists in G, then u appears before v in the linear ordering. In many cases, there is more than one ordering that satisfies this.

This example presents a function, *dfs* (see Examples 11-5 and 11-6), that implements depth-first search. It is used here to sort a number of tasks topologically. The function has two arguments: **graph** is a graph, which in this problem represents the tasks to be ordered, and **ordered** is the list of topologically sorted vertices that is returned. The function modifies **graph**, so a copy should be made before calling the function, if necessary. Also, vertices returned in **ordered** are pointers to the actual vertices from **graph**, so the caller must ensure that the storage in **graph** remains valid as long as **ordered** is being accessed. Each vertex in **graph** is a **DfsVertex** structure (see Example 11-5), which has two members: **data** is a pointer to the data associated with the vertex, and **color** maintains the color of the vertex during the search. The **match** function for **graph**, which is set by the caller when initializing the graph with *graph_init*, should compare only the **data** members of **DfsVertex** structures.

The *dfs* function performs depth-first search as described earlier in this chapter. The function *dfs_main* is the actual function that executes the search. The last loop in *dfs* ensures that we end up searching all components of graphs that are not connected, such as the one in Figure 11-9a. As each vertex is finished and colored black in *dfs_main*, it is inserted at the head of **ordered**. At the end, **ordered** contains the topologically sorted list of vertices.

The runtime complexity of *dfs* is $O(V + E)$, where V is the number of vertices in the graph and E is the number of edges. This is because initializing the colors of the vertices runs in $O(V)$ time, and the calls to *dfs_main* run in $O(V + E)$ overall.

Example 11-5. Header for Depth-First Search

```
/***************************************************************************
*                                                                         *
*  ------------------------------ dfs.h ------------------------------    *
*                                                                         *
***************************************************************************/

#ifndef DFS_H
#define DFS_H

#include "graph.h"
#include "list.h"

/***************************************************************************
*                                                                         *
*  Define a structure for vertices in a depth-first search.               *
*                                                                         *
***************************************************************************/

typedef struct DfsVertex_ {

void            *data;

VertexColor     color;

} DfsVertex;

/***************************************************************************
*                                                                         *
*  --------------------------- Public Interface ---------------------------  *
*                                                                         *
***************************************************************************/

int dfs(Graph *graph, List *ordered);

#endif
```

Example 11-6. Implementation of a Function for Depth-First Search

```
/***************************************************************************
*                                                                         *
*  ------------------------------ dfs.c ------------------------------    *
*                                                                         *
***************************************************************************/

#include <stdlib.h>

#include "dfs.h"
#include "graph.h"
#include "list.h"
```

Example 11-6. Implementation of a Function for Depth-First Search (continued)

```
/***************************************************************************
*                                                                         *
* ---------------------------- dfs_main ----------------------------      *
*                                                                         *
***************************************************************************/

static int dfs_main(Graph *graph, AdjList *adjlist, List *ordered) {

AdjList            *clr_adjlist;

DfsVertex          *clr_vertex,
                   *adj_vertex;

ListElmt           *member;

/***************************************************************************
*                                                                         *
* Color the vertex gray and traverse its adjacency list.                  *
*                                                                         *
***************************************************************************/

((DfsVertex *)adjlist->vertex)->color = gray;

for (member = list_head(&adjlist->adjacent); member != NULL; member =
   list_next(member)) {

   /***********************************************************************
   *                                                                     *
   * Determine the color of the next adjacent vertex.                    *
   *                                                                     *
   ***********************************************************************/

   adj_vertex = list_data(member);

   if (graph_adjlist(graph, adj_vertex, &clr_adjlist) != 0)
      return -1;

   clr_vertex = clr_adjlist->vertex;

   /***********************************************************************
   *                                                                     *
   * Move one vertex deeper when the next adjacent vertex is white.      *
   *                                                                     *
   ***********************************************************************/

   if (clr_vertex->color == white) {

      if (dfs_main(graph, clr_adjlist, ordered) != 0)
         return -1;

   }

}
```

Example 11-6. Implementation of a Function for Depth-First Search (continued)

```
/***************************************************************************
*                                                                         *
*  Color the current vertex black and make it first in the list.          *
*                                                                         *
***************************************************************************/

((DfsVertex *)adjlist->vertex)->color = black;

if (list_ins_next(ordered, NULL, (DfsVertex *)adjlist->vertex) != 0)
   return -1;

return 0;

}

/***************************************************************************
*                                                                         *
*  --------------------------------- dfs ---------------------------------  *
*                                                                         *
***************************************************************************/

int dfs(Graph *graph, List *ordered) {

DfsVertex          *vertex;

ListElmt           *element;

/***************************************************************************
*                                                                         *
*  Initialize all of the vertices in the graph.                           *
*                                                                         *
***************************************************************************/

for (element = list_head(&graph_adjlists(graph)); element != NULL; element =
   list_next(element)) {

   vertex = ((AdjList *)list_data(element))->vertex;
   vertex->color = white;

}

/***************************************************************************
*                                                                         *
*  Perform depth-first search.                                            *
*                                                                         *
***************************************************************************/

list_init(ordered, NULL);

for (element = list_head(&graph_adjlists(graph)); element != NULL; element =
   list_next(element)) {
```

Example 11-6. Implementation of a Function for Depth-First Search (continued)

```
/**************************************************************************
 *                                                                        *
 *  Ensure that every component of unconnected graphs is searched.        *
 *                                                                        *
 **************************************************************************/

vertex = ((AdjList *)list_data(element))->vertex;

if (vertex->color == white) {

    if (dfs_main(graph, (AdjList *)list_data(element), ordered) != 0) {

        list_destroy(ordered);
        return -1;

    }

}

}

return 0;

}
```

Questions and Answers

Q: *In the graph implementation presented in this chapter, why is a linked list used for the list of adjacency-list structures but sets are used for the adjacency lists?*

A: Many adjacency-list representations of graphs consist of an array of adjacency lists, with each element in the array corresponding to one vertex in the graph. The implementation in this chapter deviates from this model. First, it uses a linked list in place of the array because the list can dynamically expand and contract as we insert and remove vertices. Second, it uses sets for the adjacency lists because the vertices they contain are not ordered, and the primary operations associated with adjacency lists (inserting and removing vertices, and testing for membership) are well-suited to the set abstract datatype presented earlier. Perhaps the list of adjacency-list structures could have been implemented using a set as well, but this was ruled out because the primary operation here is to locate the adjacency lists of specific vertices. A linked list is better suited to this than a set.

Q: *Suppose we model an internet using a graph (as shown earlier in this chapter) and we determine that the graph contains an articulation point. What are the implications of this?*

A: Graphs have many important uses in network problems. If in a graph model-
     ing an internet we determine that there is an articulation point, the articula-
     tion point represents a single point of failure. Thus, if a system residing at an
     articulation point goes down, other systems are forced into different con-
     nected components and as a result will no longer be able to communicate
     with each other. Therefore, in designing large networks in which connectivity
     is required at all times, it is important that there be no articulation points. We
     can curb this problem by placing redundancies in the network.

Q: *Consider a graph that models a structure of airways, highways in the sky on
     which airplanes are often required to fly. The structure consists of two types of
     elements: navigational facilities, called navaids for short, and airways that
     connect navaids, which are typically within a hundred miles of each other. Air-
     ways may be bidirectional or one-way. At certain times some airways are not
     available for use. Suppose during one of these times we would like to determine
     whether we can still reach a particular destination. How can we determine
     this? What is the runtime complexity of solving this problem?*

A: If we perform breadth-first search from our starting point in the airway struc-
     ture, we can reach any destination if we discover it during the search. Other-
     wise, the destination must reside in a component of the graph that became
     unreachable when an airway was made unavailable. The closed airway consti-
     tutes a bridge in the graph. This problem can be solved in $O(V + E)$ time,
     where V is the number of navaids and E is the number of airways in the struc-
     ture. This is the runtime complexity of breadth-first search.

Q: *Suppose we would like to use a computer to model states in a system. For exam-
     ple, imagine the various states of a traffic-light system at an intersection and
     the decisions the system has to make. How can we use a graph to model this?*

A: Directed graphs are good for modeling state machines, such as the traffic-light
     system mentioned here. In a directed graph, we let vertices represent the vari-
     ous states, and edges represent the decisions made to get from one state to
     another. Edges in the graph are directed because a decision made to get from
     one state to the next does not imply that the decision can be reversed.

Q: *When discussing depth-first search, it was mentioned that sometimes it is use-
     ful to keep track of discovery and finishing times for each vertex. The start time
     of a vertex is a sequence number recorded when the vertex is discovered for the
     first time and we color it gray. The finishing time of a vertex is a sequence
     number recorded when we are finished with the vertex and color it black. In
     the implementation of depth-first search presented in this chapter, these times
     were not recorded. How could we modify the implementation to record them?*

A: Discovery and finishing times recorded during depth-first search are important to some algorithms. To record these times, we use a counter that increments itself each time we color a vertex either gray or black. As a vertex is colored gray, we record the current value of the counter as its discovery time. As a vertex is colored black, we record the current value of the counter as its finishing time. In the implementation presented in this chapter, we could add two members to the *DfsVertex* structure to keep track of these times for each vertex.

Q: *The transpose of a directed graph is a graph with the direction of its edges reversed. Formally, for a directed graph* G = (V, E), *its transpose is indicated as* G^T. *How could we form the transpose of a graph assuming an adjacency-list representation? What is the runtime complexity of this?*

A: To form the transpose G^T of a graph $G = (V, E)$, we traverse the adjacency list of each vertex u in V. As we traverse each list, we make sure that vertex v and u have both been inserted into G^T by calling *graph_ins_vertex* for each vertex. Next, we call *graph_ins_edge* to insert an edge from v to u into G^T. Each call to *graph_ins_vertex* runs in $O(V)$ time. This operation is called $2E$ times, where E is the number of edges in G. Of course, some of these calls will not actually insert the vertex if it was inserted previously. Each call to *graph_ins_edge* runs in $O(V)$ time. This operation is called once for each edge in G as well. Thus, using this approach, the overall time to transpose a graph is $O(VE)$.

Q: *At the start of this chapter, it was mentioned that many data structures can be represented as graphs. How might we think of a binary tree as a graph?*

A: A binary tree is a directed acyclic graph with the following characteristics. Each node has up to two edges incident from it and one edge incident to it, except for the root node, which has only the two edges incident from it. Edges incident from a vertex connect it with its children. The edge incident to a vertex connects its parent to it. Thus, the adjacency list of each vertex contains its children.

Related Topics

Hypergraphs

Graphs similar to undirected graphs but which contain *hyperedges*. Hyperedges are edges that connect an arbitrary number of vertices. In general, most operations and algorithms for graphs, such as the ones described in this chapter, can be adapted to work with hypergraphs as well.

Multigraphs

Graphs similar to undirected graphs but which allow multiple edges between the same two vertices. As with hypergraphs, in general, most operations and algorithms for graphs can be adapted to work with multigraphs as well.

Adjacency-matrix representation

A graph representation that consists of a $V \times V$ matrix, where V is the number of vertices in the graph. If an edge exists between two vertices u and v, we set a flag in position $[u, v]$ in the matrix. An adjacency-matrix representation is typically used for dense graphs, in which the number of edges is close to the number of vertices squared. Although the interface presented in this chapter may appear to reflect the specifics of an adjacency-list representation, there are things we could do to support this interface for an adjacency-matrix representation as well, thus keeping the details of the actual implementation hidden.

III

Algorithms

This part of the book contains six chapters on algorithms. Chapter 12, *Sorting and Searching*, covers various algorithms for sorting, including insertion sort, quicksort, merge sort, counting sort, and radix sort. Chapter 12 also presents binary search. Chapter 13, *Numerical Methods*, covers numerical methods, including algorithms for polynomial interpolation, least-squares estimation, and the solution of equations using Newton's method. Chapter 14, *Data Compression*, presents algorithms for data compression, including Huffman coding and LZ77. Chapter 15, *Data Encryption*, presents algorithms for DES and RSA encryption. Chapter 16, *Graph Algorithms*, covers graph algorithms, including Prim's algorithm for minimum spanning trees, Dijkstra's algorithm for shortest paths, and an algorithm for solving the traveling-salesman problem. Chapter 17, *Geometric Algorithms*, presents geometric algorithms, including methods for testing whether line segments intersect, computing convex hulls, and computing arc lengths on spherical surfaces.

12

Sorting and Searching

Sorting means arranging a set of elements in a prescribed order. Normally a sort is thought of as either *ascending* or *descending*. An ascending sort of the integers {5, 2, 7, 1}, for example, produces {1, 2, 5, 7}, whereas a descending sort produces {7, 5, 2, 1}. In general, sorting serves to organize data so that it is more meaningful. Although the most visible application of sorting is sorting data to display it, often sorting is used to organize data in solving other problems, sometimes as a part of other formal algorithms.

In general, sorting algorithms are divided into two classes: *comparison sorts* and *linear-time sorts*. Comparison sorts rely on comparing elements to place them in the correct order. Surprisingly, not all sorting algorithms rely on making comparisons. For those that do, it is not possible to sort faster than in $O(n \lg n)$ time. Linear-time sorts get their name from sorting in a time proportional to the number of elements being sorted, or $O(n)$. Unfortunately, linear-time sorts rely on certain characteristics in the data, so we cannot always apply them. Some sorts use the same storage that contains the data to store output as the sort proceeds; these are called *in-place sorts*. Others require extra storage for the output data, although they may copy the results back over the original data at the end.

Searching is the ubiquitous task of locating an element in a set of data. The simplest approach to locating an element takes very little thought: we simply scan the set from one end to the other. This is called *linear search*. Generally, it is used with data structures that do not support random access very well, such as linked lists (see Chapter 5, *Linked Lists*). An alternative approach is to use *binary search*, which is presented in this chapter. Other approaches rely on data structures developed specifically for searching, such as hash tables (see Chapter 8, *Hash Tables*) and binary search trees (see Chapter 9, *Trees*). This chapter covers:

Insertion sort

> Although not the most efficient sorting algorithm, insertion sort has the virtue of simplicity and the ability to sort in place. Its best application is for incremental sorting on small sets of data.

Quicksort

> An in-place sorting algorithm widely regarded as the best for sorting in the general case. Its best application is for medium to large sets of data.

Merge sort

> An algorithm with essentially the same performance as quicksort, but with twice its storage requirements. Ironically, its best application is for very large sets of data because it inherently facilitates working with divisions of the original unsorted set.

Counting sort

> A stable, linear-time sorting algorithm that works with integers for which we know the largest value. Its primary use is in implementing radix sort.

Radix sort

> A linear-time sorting algorithm that sorts elements digit by digit. Radix sort is well suited to elements of a fixed size that can be conveniently broken into pieces, expressible as integers.

Binary search

> An effective way to search sorted data in which we do not expect frequent insertions or deletions. Since resorting a set of data is expensive relative to searching it, binary search is best when the data does not change.

Some applications of sorting and searching algorithms are:

Order statistics

> Finding the ith smallest element in a set. One simplistic approach is to select the ith element out of the set once it has been sorted.

Binary search

> An efficient search method that relies on sorted data. Binary search works fundamentally by dividing a sorted set of data repeatedly and inspecting the element in the middle of each division.

Directory listings (illustrated in this chapter)

> Listings of files in a file system that have been organized into groups. Generally, an operating system will sort a directory listing in some manner before displaying it.

Database systems

> Typically, large systems containing vast amounts of data that must be stored and retrieved quickly. The amount of data generally stored in databases makes an efficient and flexible approach to searching the data essential.

Spell checkers (illustrated in this chapter)

Programs that check the spelling of words in text. Validation is performed against words in a dictionary. Since spell checkers frequently deal with long strings of text containing many thousands of words, they must be able to search the set of acceptable words efficiently.

Spreadsheets

An important part of most businesses for managing inventory and financial data. Spreadsheets typically contain diverse data that is more meaningful when sorted.

Description of Insertion Sort

Insertion sort is one of the simplest sorting algorithms. It works like the approach we might use to systematically sort a pile of canceled checks by hand. We begin with a pile of unsorted checks and space for a sorted pile, which initially contains no checks. One at a time, we remove a check from the unsorted pile and, considering its number, insert it at the proper position among the sorted checks. More formally, insertion sort takes one element at a time from an unsorted set and inserts it into a sorted one by scanning the set of sorted elements to determine where the new element belongs. Although at first it may seem that insertion sort would require space for both the sorted and unsorted sets of data independently, it actually sorts in place.

Insertion sort is a simple algorithm, but it is inefficient for large sets of data. This is because determining where each element belongs in the sorted set potentially requires comparing it with every other element in the sorted set thus far. An important virtue of insertion sort, however, is that inserting a single element into a set that is already sorted requires only one scan of the sorted elements, as opposed to a complete run of the algorithm. This makes insertion sort efficient for *incremental sorting*. This situation might occur, for example, in a reservation system of a large hotel. Suppose one display in the system lists all guests, sorted by name, and is updated in real time as new guests check in. Using insertion sort, resorting requires only a single sweep of the data to insert a new name into the list.

Interface for Insertion Sort

issort

```
int issort(void *data, int size, int esize, int (*compare)(const void *key1,
    const void *key2));
```

Return Value   0 if sorting is successful, or −1 otherwise.

Description   Uses insertion sort to sort the array of elements in *data*. The number of elements in *data* is specified by *size*. The size of each element is specified by *esize*. The function pointer *compare* specifies a user-defined function to compare elements. This function should return 1 if *key1* > *key2*, 0 if *key1* = *key2*, and −1 if *key1* < *key2* for an ascending sort. For a descending sort, *compare* should reverse the cases returning 1 and −1. When *issort* returns, *data* contains the sorted elements.

Complexity $O(n^2)$, where *n* is the number of elements to be sorted.

Implementation and Analysis of Insertion Sort

Insertion sort works fundamentally by inserting elements from an unsorted set one at a time into a sorted set. In the implementation presented here, both of these sets reside in *data*, a single block of contiguous storage. Initially, *data* contains the unsorted set consisting of *size* elements. As *issort* runs, *data* gradually becomes consumed by the sorted set until when *issort* returns, *data* is completely sorted. Although this implementation uses contiguous storage, insertion sort can easily be adapted to work with linked lists efficiently, something not all sorts can claim.

Insertion sort revolves around a single nested loop (see Example 12-1). The outer loop, *j*, controls which element from the unsorted set is currently being inserted among the sorted elements. Since the element at the left of the sorted set is always the next to be inserted, we can also think of *j* as the position dividing the sorted and unsorted sets in *data*. For each element at position *j*, an inner loop, *i*, is used to cycle backward through the set of sorted elements until the proper position for the element is found. As we move backward through the set, each element at position *i* is copied one position to the right to make room for the insertion. Once *j* reaches the end of the unsorted set, *data* is sorted (see Figure 12-1).

The runtime complexity of insertion sort focuses on its nested loops. With this in mind, the outer loop has a running time of $T(n) = n − 1$, times some constant amount of time, where *n* is the number of elements being sorted. Examining the inner loop in the worst case, we assume that we will have to go all the way to the left end of the array before inserting each element into the sorted set. Therefore, the inner loop could iterate once for the first element, twice for the second, and so forth until the outer loop terminates. The running time of the nested loop is represented as a summation from 1 to $n − 1$, which results in a running time of $T(n) = (n (n + 1)/2) − n$, times some constant amount of time. (This is from the well-known formula for summing a series from 1 to *n*.) Using the rules of *O*-notation,

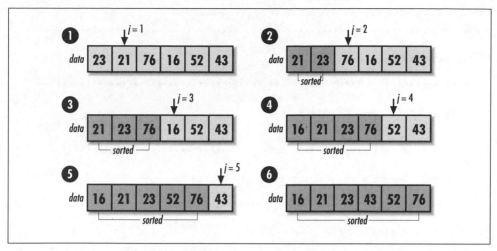

Figure 12-1. Sorting with insertion sort

this simplifies to $O(n^2)$. When we use insertion sort in an incremental sort, its run-time complexity is $O(n)$. Insertion sort sorts in place, so its space requirement is only that occupied by the data to be sorted.

Example 12-1. Implementation of Insertion Sort

```
/*****************************************************************************
*                                                                           *
*  ----------------------------- issort.c -----------------------------     *
*                                                                           *
*****************************************************************************/

#include <stdlib.h>
#include <string.h>

#include "sort.h"

/*****************************************************************************
*                                                                           *
*  ------------------------------ issort ------------------------------     *
*                                                                           *
*****************************************************************************/

int issort(void *data, int size, int esize, int (*compare)(const void *key1,
   const void *key2)) {

char            *a = data;

void            *key;

int             i,
                j;
```

Example 12-1. Implementation of Insertion Sort (continued)

```c
/***************************************************************************
*                                                                         *
*  Allocate storage for the key element.                                  *
*                                                                         *
***************************************************************************/

if ((key = (char *)malloc(esize)) == NULL)
   return -1;

/***************************************************************************
*                                                                         *
*  Repeatedly insert a key element among the sorted elements.             *
*                                                                         *
***************************************************************************/

for (j = 1; j < size; j++) {

   memcpy(key, &a[j * esize], esize);
   i = j - 1;

   /***************************************************************************
   *                                                                         *
   *  Determine the position at which to insert the key element.             *
   *                                                                         *
   ***************************************************************************/

   while (i >= 0 && compare(&a[i * esize], key) > 0) {

      memcpy(&a[(i + 1) * esize], &a[i * esize], esize);
      i--;

   }

   memcpy(&a[(i + 1) * esize], key, esize);

}

/***************************************************************************
*                                                                         *
*  Free the storage allocated for sorting.                                *
*                                                                         *
***************************************************************************/

free(key);

return 0;

}
```

Description of Quicksort

Quicksort is a divide-and-conquer sorting algorithm (see Chapter 1, *Introduction*). It is widely regarded as the best for general use. Like insertion sort, it is a comparison sort that sorts in place, but its efficiency makes it a better choice for medium to large sets of data.

Returning to the example of sorting a pile of canceled checks by hand, we begin with an unsorted pile that we partition in two. In one pile we place all checks numbered less than or equal to what we think may be the median value, and in the other pile we place the checks greater than this. Once we have the two piles, we divide each of them in the same manner, and we repeat the process until we end up with one check in every pile. At this point, the checks are sorted.

Since quicksort is a divide-and-conquer algorithm, it is helpful to consider it more formally in terms of the three steps common to all divide-and-conquer algorithms:

1. Divide: partition the data into two partitions around a partition value.

2. Conquer: sort the two partitions by recursively applying quicksort to them.

3. Combine: do nothing since the partitions are sorted after the previous step.

Considering its popularity, it may be surprising that the worst case of quicksort is no better than the worst case of insertion sort. However, with a little care we can make the worst case of quicksort so unlikely that we can actually count on the algorithm performing to its average case, which is considerably better. The key to reliably achieving quicksort's average-case performance lies in how we choose the partition value in the divide step.

Quicksort performs badly when we choose partition values that continually force the majority of the elements into one partition. Instead, we need to partition the elements in as *balanced* a manner as possible. For example, partitioning around 10 in the set {15, 20, 18, 51, 36, 10, 77, 43} results in the unbalanced partitions of {10} and {20, 18, 51, 36, 15, 77, 43}. On the other hand, partitioning around 36 results in the more balanced partitions of {15, 20, 18, 10} and {36, 51, 77, 43}.

One approach that works well in choosing partition values is to select them randomly. Statistically, this prevents any particular set of data from eliciting bad behavior, even if we try to bog down the algorithm intentionally. We can improve partitioning further by randomly choosing three elements and selecting their median as the partition value. This is called the *median-of-three method*, which virtually guarantees average-case performance. Because this approach to partitioning relies on the statistical properties of random numbers to help the performance of quicksort overall, quicksort is a good example of a randomized algorithm (see Chapter 1).

Interface for Quicksort

qksort

```
int qksort(void *data, int size, int esize, int i, int k, int (*compare)
   (const void *key1, const void *key2));
```

Return Value   0 if sorting is successful, or −1 otherwise.

Description   Uses quicksort to sort the array of elements in *data*. The number of elements in *data* is specified by *size*. The size of each element is specified by *esize*. The arguments *i* and *k* define the current partition being sorted and initially should be 0 and *size* − 1, respectively. The function pointer *compare* specifies a user-defined function to compare elements. It should perform in a manner similar to that described for *issort*. When *qksort* returns, *data* contains the sorted elements.

Complexity $O(n \lg n)$, where *n* is the number of elements to be sorted.

Implementation and Analysis of Quicksort

Quicksort works fundamentally by recursively partitioning an unsorted set of elements until all partitions contain a single element. In the implementation presented here, *data* initially contains the unsorted set of *size* elements stored in a single block of contiguous storage. Quicksort sorts in place, so all partitioning is performed in *data* as well. When *qksort* returns, *data* is completely sorted.

As we have seen, an important part of quicksort is how we partition the data. This task is performed in the function *partition* (see Example 12-2). This function partitions the elements between positions *i* and *k* in *data*, where *i* is less than *k*.

We begin by selecting a partition value using the median-of-three method mentioned earlier. Once the partition value has been selected, we move from *k* to the left in *data* until we find an element that is less than or equal to it. This element belongs in the left partition. Next, we move from *i* to the right until we find an element that is greater than or equal to the partition value. This element belongs in the right partition. Once two elements are found in the wrong partition, they are swapped. We continue in this way until *i* and *k* cross. (You may want to consider how we know that if any one element is in the wrong partition, there is always one that can be swapped with it.) Once *i* and *k* cross, all elements to the left of the partition value are less than or equal to it, and all elements to the right are greater (see Figure 12-2).

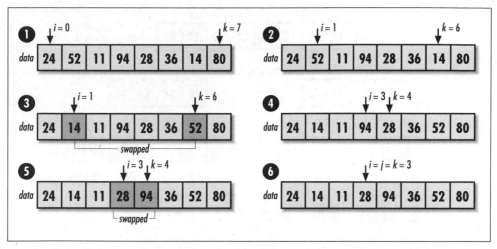

Figure 12-2. Partitioning around 28

Now we look at how the recursion proceeds in *qksort* (see Example 12-2). On the initial call to *qksort*, *i* is set to 0 and *k* is set to *size* – 1. We begin by calling *partition* to partition **data** between positions *i* and *k*. When *partition* returns, *j* is assigned the position of the element that defines where the elements between *i* and *k* are partitioned. Next, we call *qksort* recursively for the left partition, which is from position *i* to *j*. Sorting left partitions continues recursively until an activation of *qksort* is passed a partition containing a single element. In this activation, *i* will not be less than *k*, so the call terminates. In the previous activation of *qksort*, this causes an iteration to the right partition, from position *j* + 1 to *k*. Overall, we continue in this way until the first activation of *qksort* terminates, at which point the data is completely sorted (see Figure 12-3).

The analysis of quicksort centers around its average-case performance, which is widely accepted as its metric. Even though the worst case of quicksort is no better than that of insertion sort, $O(n^2)$, quicksort reliably performs much closer to its average-case running time, $O(n \lg n)$, where *n* is the number of elements being sorted.

Determining the runtime complexity for the average case of quicksort depends on the assumption that there will be an even distribution of balanced and unbalanced partitions. This assumption is reasonable if the median-of-three method for partitioning is used. In this case, as we repeatedly partition the array, it is helpful to picture the tree shown in Figure 12-3, which has a height of $(\lg n) + 1$. Since for the top lg *n* levels of the tree, we must traverse all *n* elements in order to form the partitions of the next level, quicksort runs in time $O(n \lg n)$. Quicksort sorts in place, so its space requirement is only that occupied by the data to be sorted.

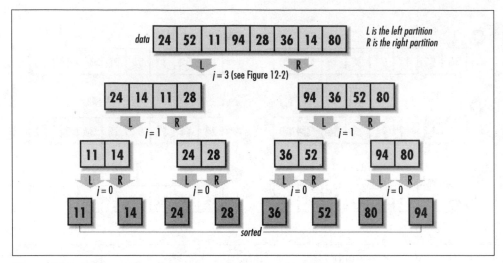

Figure 12-3. Sorting with quicksort assuming optimal partitioning

Example 12-2. Implementation of Quicksort

```
/*****************************************************************************
*                                                                           *
*  ----------------------------- qksort.c -----------------------------     *
*                                                                           *
*****************************************************************************/

#include <stdlib.h>
#include <string.h>

#include "sort.h"

/*****************************************************************************
*                                                                           *
*  ----------------------------- compare_int -----------------------------  *
*                                                                           *
*****************************************************************************/

static int compare_int(const void *int1, const void *int2) {

/*****************************************************************************
*                                                                           *
*  Compare two integers (used during median-of-three partitioning).         *
*                                                                           *
*****************************************************************************/

if (*(const int *)int1 > *(const int *)int2)
   return 1;
else if (*(const int *)int1 < *(const int *)int2)
   return -1;
else
   return 0;

}
```

Example 12-2. Implementation of Quicksort (continued)

```
/****************************************************************************
*                                                                          *
*  ---------------------------- partition ----------------------------     *
*                                                                          *
****************************************************************************/

static int partition(void *data, int esize, int i, int k, int (*compare)
   (const void *key1, const void *key2)) {

char             *a = data;

void             *pval,
                 *temp;

int              r[3];

/****************************************************************************
*                                                                          *
*  Allocate storage for the partition value and swapping.                  *
*                                                                          *
****************************************************************************/

if ((pval = malloc(esize)) == NULL)
   return -1;

if ((temp = malloc(esize)) == NULL) {

   free(pval);
   return -1;

}

/****************************************************************************
*                                                                          *
*  Use the median-of-three method to find the partition value.            *
*                                                                          *
****************************************************************************/

r[0] = (rand() % (k - i + 1)) + i;
r[1] = (rand() % (k - i + 1)) + i;
r[2] = (rand() % (k - i + 1)) + i;
issort(r, 3, sizeof(int), compare_int);
memcpy(pval, &a[r[1] * esize], esize);

/****************************************************************************
*                                                                          *
*  Create two partitions around the partition value.                      *
*                                                                          *
****************************************************************************/

i--;
k++;
```

Example 12-2. Implementation of Quicksort (continued)

```
while (1) {

   /*****************************************************************************
   *                                                                           *
   *  Move left until an element is found in the wrong partition.              *
   *                                                                           *
   *****************************************************************************/

   do {

      k--;

   } while (compare(&a[k * esize], pval) > 0);

   /*****************************************************************************
   *                                                                           *
   *  Move right until an element is found in the wrong partition.             *
   *                                                                           *
   *****************************************************************************/

   do {

      i++;

   } while (compare(&a[i * esize], pval) < 0);

   if (i >= k) {

      /**************************************************************************
      *                                                                        *
      *  Stop partitioning when the left and right counters cross.             *
      *                                                                        *
      **************************************************************************/

      break;

      }

   else {

      /**************************************************************************
      *                                                                        *
      *  Swap the elements now under the left and right counters.              *
      *                                                                        *
      **************************************************************************/

      memcpy(temp, &a[i * esize], esize);
      memcpy(&a[i * esize], &a[k * esize], esize);
      memcpy(&a[k * esize], temp, esize);

   }

}
```

Example 12-2. Implementation of Quicksort (continued)

```
/*****************************************************************************
*                                                                           *
*  Free the storage allocated for partitioning.                            *
*                                                                           *
*****************************************************************************/

free(pval);
free(temp);

/*****************************************************************************
*                                                                           *
*  Return the position dividing the two partitions.                        *
*                                                                           *
*****************************************************************************/

return k;

}

/*****************************************************************************
*                                                                           *
*  ------------------------------ qksort ------------------------------    *
*                                                                           *
*****************************************************************************/

int qksort(void *data, int size, int esize, int i, int k, int (*compare)
   (const void *key1, const void *key2)) {

int            j;

/*****************************************************************************
*                                                                           *
*  Stop the recursion when it is not possible to partition further.        *
*                                                                           *
*****************************************************************************/

while (i < k) {

   /*****************************************************************************
   *                                                                           *
   *  Determine where to partition the elements.                              *
   *                                                                           *
   *****************************************************************************/

   if ((j = partition(data, esize, i, k, compare)) < 0)
      return -1;

   /*****************************************************************************
   *                                                                           *
   *  Recursively sort the left partition.                                    *
   *                                                                           *
   *****************************************************************************/
```

Example 12-2. Implementation of Quicksort (continued)

```
    if (qksort(data, size, esize, i, j, compare) < 0)
      return -1;

    /*************************************************************************
    *                                                                       *
    *  Iterate and sort the right partition.                                *
    *                                                                       *
    *************************************************************************/

    i = j + 1;

  }

  return 0;

}
```

Quicksort Example: Directory Listings

In a hierarchical file system, files are typically organized conceptually into directories. For any directory, we may want to see a list of the files and subdirectories the directory contains. In Unix, we do this with the *ls* command, for example. At the command prompt in Windows, we do this with the *dir* command.

This section presents a function called *directls*, which implements the same basic functionality that *ls* provides. It uses the system call *readdir* to create a listing of the directory specified in `path` (see Examples 12-3 and 12-4). Just as *ls* does in the default case, *directls* sorts the listing by name. Because we allocate the listing using *realloc* as we build it, it is the responsibility of the caller to free it with *free* once it is no longer needed.

The runtime complexity of *directls* is $O(n \lg n)$, where n is the number of entries in the directory being listed. This is because retrieving n directory entries is an operation that runs in $O(n)$ time overall, while the subsequent call to *qksort* sorts the entries in $O(n \lg n)$ time.

Example 12-3. Header for Getting Directory Listings

```
/*************************************************************************
*                                                                       *
*  ---------------------------- directls.h ----------------------------  *
*                                                                       *
*************************************************************************/

#ifndef DIRECTLS_H
#define DIRECTLS_H

#include <dirent.h>
```

Example 12-3. Header for Getting Directory Listings (continued)

```
/****************************************************************************
 *                                                                          *
 *  Define a structure for directory entries.                              *
 *                                                                          *
 ****************************************************************************/

typedef struct Directory_ {

char              name[MAXNAMLEN + 1];

} Directory;

/****************************************************************************
 *                                                                          *
 *  -------------------------- Public Interface --------------------------  *
 *                                                                          *
 ****************************************************************************/

int directory(const char *path, Directory **dir);

#endif
```

Example 12-4. Implementation of a Function for Getting Directory Listings

```
/****************************************************************************
 *                                                                          *
 *  ---------------------------- directls.c ----------------------------    *
 *                                                                          *
 ****************************************************************************/

#include <dirent.h>
#include <stdio.h>
#include <stdlib.h>
#include <string.h>

#include "directls.h"
#include "sort.h"

/****************************************************************************
 *                                                                          *
 *  ---------------------------- compare_dir ----------------------------   *
 *                                                                          *
 ****************************************************************************/

static int compare_dir(const void *key1, const void *key2) {

int              retval;

if ((retval = strcmp(((const Directory *)key1)->name, ((const Directory *)
   key2)->name)) > 0)
   return 1;
else if (retval < 0)
   return -1;
```

Example 12-4. Implementation of a Function for Getting Directory Listings (continued)

```
else
   return 0;

}

/***************************************************************************
 *                                                                         *
 *   ----------------------------- directls -----------------------------  *
 *                                                                         *
 ***************************************************************************/

int directls(const char *path, Directory **dir) {

DIR              *dirptr;

Directory        *temp;

struct dirent    *curdir;

int              count,
                 i;

/***************************************************************************
 *                                                                         *
 *   Open the directory.                                                   *
 *                                                                         *
 ***************************************************************************/

if ((dirptr = opendir(path)) == NULL)
   return -1;

/***************************************************************************
 *                                                                         *
 *   Get the directory entries.                                            *
 *                                                                         *
 ***************************************************************************/

*dir = NULL;
count = 0;

while ((curdir = readdir(dirptr)) != NULL) {

   count++;

   if ((temp = (Directory *)realloc(*dir, count * sizeof(Directory))) ==
       NULL) {

      free(*dir);
      return -1;

   }

   else {
```

Example 12-4. Implementation of a Function for Getting Directory Listings (continued)

```
    *dir = temp;

  }

  strcpy(((*dir)[count - 1]).name, curdir->d_name);

}

closedir(dirptr);

/***************************************************************************
*                                                                         *
*  Sort the directory entries by name.                                    *
*                                                                         *
***************************************************************************/

if (qksort(*dir, count, sizeof(Directory), 0, count - 1, compare_dir) != 0)
   return -1;

/***************************************************************************
*                                                                         *
*  Return the number of directory entries.                                *
*                                                                         *
***************************************************************************/

return count;

}
```

Description of Merge Sort

Merge sort is another example of a divide-and-conquer sorting algorithm (see Chapter 1). Like quicksort, it relies on making comparisons between elements to sort them. However, it does not sort in place.

Returning once again to the example of sorting a pile of canceled checks by hand, we begin with an unsorted pile that we divide in half. Next, we divide each of the resulting two piles in half and continue this process until we end up with one check in every pile. Once all piles contain a single check, we merge the piles two by two so that each new pile is a sorted combination of the two that were merged. Merging continues until we end up with one big pile again. At this point, the checks are sorted.

As with quicksort, since merge sort is a divide-and-conquer algorithm, it is helpful to consider it more formally in terms of the three steps common to all divide-and-conquer algorithms:

1. Divide: we divide the data in half.

2. Conquer: we sort the two divisions by recursively applying merge sort to them.

3. Combine: we merge the two divisions into a single sorted set.

The distinguishing component of merge sort is its merging process. This is the process that takes two sorted sets and merges them into a single sorted one. As we will see, merging two sorted sets is efficient because we need only make one pass through each set. This fact, combined with the predictable way the algorithm divides the data, makes merge sort *in all cases* as good as the average case of quicksort.

Unfortunately, the space requirement of merge sort presents a drawback. Because merging cannot be performed in place, merge sort requires twice the space of the unsorted data. This significantly reduces its desirability in the general case since we can expect to sort just as fast using quicksort, without the extra storage requirement. However, merge sort is nevertheless valuable for very large sets of data because it divides the data in predictable ways. This allows us to divide the data into more manageable pieces ourselves, use merge sort to sort them, and then perform as many merges as necessary without having to keep the entire set of data in memory all at once.

Interface for Merge Sort

mgsort

```
int mgsort(void *data, int size, int esize, int i, int k, int (*compare)
   (const void *key1, const void *key2));
```

Return Value   0 if sorting is successful, or −1 otherwise.

Description   Uses merge sort to sort the array of elements in *data*. The number of elements in *data* is specified by *size*. The size of each element is specified by *esize*. The arguments *i* and *k* define the current division being sorted and initially should be 0 and *size* − 1, respectively. The function pointer *compare* specifies a user-defined function to compare elements. It should perform in a manner similar to that described for *issort*. When *mgsort* returns, *data* contains the sorted elements.

Complexity $O(n \lg n)$, where n is the number of elements to be sorted.

Implementation and Analysis of Merge Sort

Merge sort works fundamentally by recursively dividing an unsorted set of elements into single-element divisions and merging the divisions repeatedly until a single set is reproduced. In the implementation presented here, *data* initially contains the unsorted set of *size* elements stored in a single block of contiguous storage. Since merging is not performed in place, *mgsort* allocates additional storage for the merges. Before *mgsort* returns, the final merged set is copied back into `data`.

As we have seen, an important part of merge sort is the process of merging two sorted sets into a single sorted one. This task is performed by the function *merge* (see Example 12-5), which merges the sets defined from position *i* to *j* and from *j* + 1 to *k* in `data` into a single sorted one from *i* to *k*.

Initially, `ipos` and `jpos` point to the beginning of each sorted set. Merging continues as long as there are still elements in at least one of the sets. While this is true, we proceed as follows. If one set has no elements remaining to be merged, we place all elements remaining in the other set into the merged set. Otherwise, we look at which set contains the next element that should be placed in the merged set to keep it properly ordered, place that element in the merged set, and increment `ipos` or `jpos` to the next element depending on from which set the element came (see Figure 12-4).

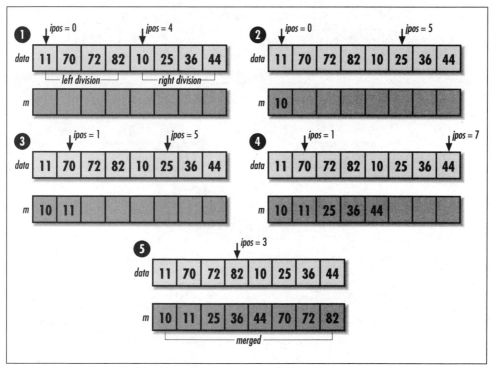

Figure 12-4. Merging two sorted sets

Now we look at how the recursion proceeds in *mgsort* (see Example 12-5). On the initial call to *mgsort*, *i* is set to 0 and *k* is set to `size` − 1. We begin by dividing `data` so that *j* is set to the position of the middle element. Next, we call *mgsort* for the left division, which is from position i to j. We continue dividing left divisions recursively until an activation of *mgsort* is passed a division containing a single element. In this activation, i will not be less than k, so the call terminates. In the previous activation of *mgsort*, this causes *mgsort* to be invoked on the right division of the data, from position $j + 1$ to k. Once this call returns, we merge the two sets. Overall, we continue in this way until the last activation of *mgsort* performs its merge, at which point the data is completely sorted (see Figure 12-5).

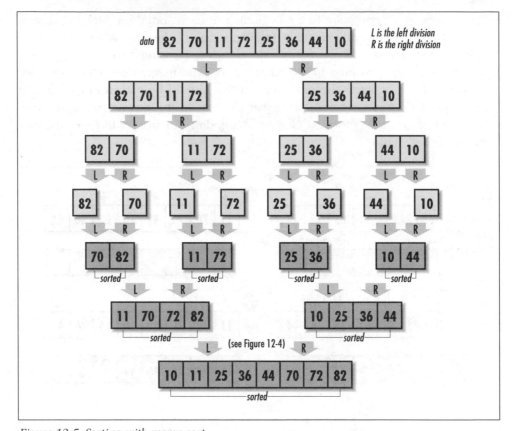

Figure 12-5. Sorting with merge sort

An analysis of merge sort is simplified when we realize that the algorithm is very predictable. If we divide a set of data repeatedly in half as shown in Figure 12-5, lg n levels of divisions are required before all sets contain one element, where n is the number of elements being sorted. For two sorted sets of p and q elements, merging runs in $O(p + q)$ time because a single pass must be made through each set to produce a merged one. Since for each of the lg n levels of divisions we end up traversing all n elements to merge the sets at that level, merge sort runs in time $O(n \lg n)$. Because we cannot merge elements in place, merge sort requires twice the space occupied by the data to be sorted.

Example 12-5. Implementation of Merge Sort

```c
/*****************************************************************************
*                                                                           *
*  --------------------------------- mgsort.c --------------------------------  *
*                                                                           *
*****************************************************************************/

#include <stdlib.h>
#include <string.h>

#include "sort.h"

/*****************************************************************************
*                                                                           *
*  --------------------------------- merge --------------------------------  *
*                                                                           *
*****************************************************************************/

static int merge(void *data, int esize, int i, int j, int k, int (*compare)
   (const void *key1, const void *key2)) {

char              *a = data,
                  *m;

int               ipos,
                  jpos,
                  mpos;

/*****************************************************************************
*                                                                           *
*  Initialize the counters used in merging.                                 *
*                                                                           *
*****************************************************************************/

ipos = i;
jpos = j + 1;
mpos = 0;

/*****************************************************************************
*                                                                           *
*  Allocate storage for the merged elements.                                *
*                                                                           *
*****************************************************************************/

if ((m = (char *)malloc(esize * ((k - i) + 1))) == NULL)
   return -1;

/*****************************************************************************
*                                                                           *
*  Continue while either division has elements to merge.                    *
*                                                                           *
*****************************************************************************/

while (ipos <= j || jpos <= k) {
```

Example 12-5. Implementation of Merge Sort (continued)

```
if (ipos > j) {

   /**********************************************************************
   *                                                                     *
   *  The left division has no more elements to merge.                   *
   *                                                                     *
   **********************************************************************/

   while (jpos <= k) {

      memcpy(&m[mpos * esize], &a[jpos * esize], esize);
      jpos++;
      mpos++;

   }

   continue;

   }

else if (jpos > k) {

   /**********************************************************************
   *                                                                     *
   *  The right division has no more elements to merge.                  *
   *                                                                     *
   **********************************************************************/

   while (ipos <= j) {

      memcpy(&m[mpos * esize], &a[ipos * esize], esize);
      ipos++;
      mpos++;

   }

   continue;

}

/**********************************************************************
*                                                                     *
*  Append the next ordered element to the merged elements.            *
*                                                                     *
**********************************************************************/

if (compare(&a[ipos * esize], &a[jpos * esize]) < 0) {

   memcpy(&m[mpos * esize], &a[ipos * esize], esize);
   ipos++;
   mpos++;

   }
```

Example 12-5. Implementation of Merge Sort (continued)

```
   else {

      memcpy(&m[mpos * esize], &a[jpos * esize], esize);
      jpos++;
      mpos++;

   }

}

/***************************************************************************
*                                                                         *
*  Prepare to pass back the merged data.                                  *
*                                                                         *
***************************************************************************/

memcpy(&a[i * esize], m, esize * ((k - i) + 1));

/***************************************************************************
*                                                                         *
*  Free the storage allocated for merging.                                *
*                                                                         *
***************************************************************************/

free(m);

return 0;

}

/***************************************************************************
*                                                                         *
*  ------------------------------ mgsort ------------------------------   *
*                                                                         *
***************************************************************************/

int mgsort(void *data, int size, int esize, int i, int k, int (*compare)
   (const void *key1, const void *key2)) {

int               j;

/***************************************************************************
*                                                                         *
*  Stop the recursion when no more divisions can be made.                 *
*                                                                         *
***************************************************************************/

if (i < k) {

   /***********************************************************************
   *                                                                     *
   *  Determine where to divide the elements.                            *
   *                                                                     *
   ***********************************************************************/
```

Example 12-5. Implementation of Merge Sort (continued)

```
j = (int)(((i + k - 1)) / 2);

/**************************************************************************
*                                                                        *
*  Recursively sort the two divisions.                                   *
*                                                                        *
**************************************************************************/

if (mgsort(data, size, esize, i, j, compare) < 0)
   return -1;

if (mgsort(data, size, esize, j + 1, k, compare) < 0)
   return -1;

/**************************************************************************
*                                                                        *
*  Merge the two sorted divisions into a single sorted set.              *
*                                                                        *
**************************************************************************/

if (merge(data, esize, i, j, k, compare) < 0)
   return -1;

}

return 0;

}
```

Description of Counting Sort

Counting sort is an efficient, linear-time sorting algorithm that works by counting how many times each element of a set occurs to determine how the set should be ordered. By avoiding the comparisons that have been a part of the sorting methods presented thus far, counting sort improves on the $O(n \lg n)$ runtime bound of comparison sorts.

Counting sort does have some limitations. The most significant is that it works only with integers or data that can be expressed in some integer form. This is because counting sort makes use of an array of counts indexed by the integer elements themselves to keep track of how many times each one occurs. For example, if the integer 3 occurs in the data four times, 4 will be stored initially at position 3 in the array of counts. Also, we must know the largest integer in the set in order to allocate enough space for the counts.

Aside from being fast, an important virtue of counting sort is that it is *stable*. Stable sorts leave elements that have equal values in the same order as they appear in the original set. This is an important attribute in some cases, as we will see with radix sort.

Interface for Counting Sort

ctsort

```
int ctsort(int *data, int size, int k);
```

Return Value   0 if sorting is successful, or −1 otherwise.

Description   Uses counting sort to sort the array of integers in *data*. The number of integers in *data* is specified by *size*. The argument *k* specifies the maximum integer in *data*. When *ctsort* returns, *data* contains the sorted integers.

Complexity $O(n + k)$, where *n* is the number of integers to be sorted and *k* is the maximum integer in the unsorted set.

Implementation and Analysis of Counting Sort

Counting sort works fundamentally by counting how many times integer elements occur in an unsorted set to determine how the set should be ordered. In the implementation presented here, *data* initially contains the unsorted set of *size* integer elements stored in a single block of contiguous storage. Additional storage is allocated to store the sorted data temporarily. Before *ctsort* returns, the sorted set is copied back into *data*.

After allocating storage, we begin by counting the occurrences of each element in *data* (see Example 12-6). These are placed in an array of counts, *counts*, indexed by the integer elements themselves (see Figure 12-6, step 1b). Once the occurrences of each element in *data* have been counted, we adjust the counts to reflect the number of elements that will come before each element in the sorted set. We do this by adding the count of each element in the array to the count of the element that follows it (see Figure 12-6, step 1c). Effectively, *counts* then contains the offsets at which each element belongs in the sorted set, *temp*.

To complete the sort, we place each element in *temp* at its designated offset (see Figure 12-6, steps 2a–f). The count for each element is decreased by 1 as *temp* is updated so that integers appearing more than once in *data* appear more than once in *temp* as well.

The runtime complexity of counting sort is $O(n + k)$, where *n* is the number of integers in the data and *k* is the largest integer value in the set being sorted. This is

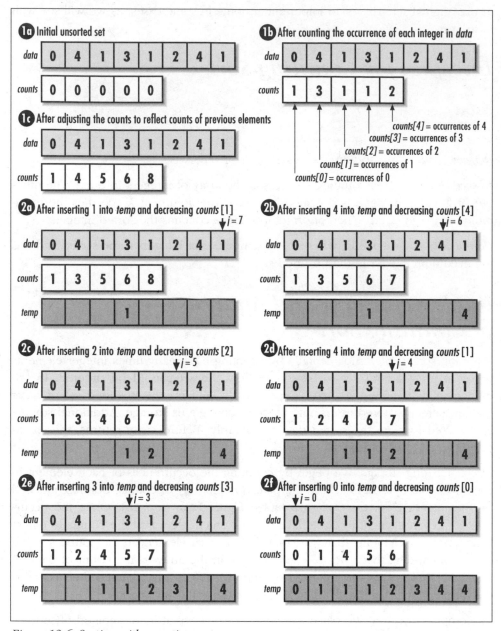

Figure 12-6. Sorting with counting sort

because counting sort consists of three loops, two that run in time proportional to *n*, and one that runs in time proportional to *k*. For space, counting sort requires two arrays of size *n* and an array of size *k*.

Example 12-6. Implementation of Counting Sort

```c
/*****************************************************************************
*                                                                           *
*  ------------------------------- ctsort.c ------------------------------  *
*                                                                           *
*****************************************************************************/

#include <stdlib.h>
#include <string.h>

#include "sort.h"

/*****************************************************************************
*                                                                           *
*  -------------------------------- ctsort -------------------------------  *
*                                                                           *
*****************************************************************************/

int ctsort(int *data, int size, int k) {

int             *counts,
                *temp;

int             i,
                j;

/*****************************************************************************
*                                                                           *
*  Allocate storage for the counts.                                         *
*                                                                           *
*****************************************************************************/

if ((counts = (int *)malloc(k * sizeof(int))) == NULL)
   return -1;

/*****************************************************************************
*                                                                           *
*  Allocate storage for the sorted elements.                                *
*                                                                           *
*****************************************************************************/

if ((temp = (int *)malloc(size * sizeof(int))) == NULL)
   return -1;

/*****************************************************************************
*                                                                           *
*  Initialize the counts.                                                   *
*                                                                           *
*****************************************************************************/

for (i = 0; i < k; i++)
   counts[i] = 0;
```

Example 12-6. Implementation of Counting Sort (continued)

```
/***************************************************************************
*                                                                         *
*  Count the occurrences of each element.                                 *
*                                                                         *
***************************************************************************/

for (j = 0; j < size; j++)
   counts[data[j]] = counts[data[j]] + 1;

/***************************************************************************
*                                                                         *
*  Adjust each count to reflect the counts before it.                     *
*                                                                         *
***************************************************************************/

for (i = 1; i < k; i++)
   counts[i] = counts[i] + counts[i - 1];

/***************************************************************************
*                                                                         *
*  Use the counts to position each element where it belongs.              *
*                                                                         *
***************************************************************************/

for (j = size - 1; j >= 0; j--) {

   temp[counts[data[j]] - 1] = data[j];
   counts[data[j]] = counts[data[j]] - 1;

}

/***************************************************************************
*                                                                         *
*  Prepare to pass back the sorted data.                                  *
*                                                                         *
***************************************************************************/

memcpy(data, temp, size * sizeof(int));

/***************************************************************************
*                                                                         *
*  Free the storage allocated for sorting.                                *
*                                                                         *
***************************************************************************/

free(counts);
free(temp);

return 0;

}
```

Description of Radix Sort

Radix sort is another efficient, linear-time sorting algorithm. It works by sorting data in pieces called *digits*, one digit at a time, from the digit in the least significant position to the most significant. Using radix sort to sort the set of radix-10 numbers {15, 12, 49, 16, 36, 40}, for example, produces {40, 12, 15, 16, 36, 49} after sorting on the least significant digit, and {12, 15, 16, 36, 40, 49} after sorting on the most significant digit.

It is very important that radix sort use a stable sort for sorting on the digit values in each position. This is because once an element has been assigned a place according to the digit value in a less significant position, its place must not change unless sorting on one of the more significant digits requires it. For example, in the set given earlier, when 12 and 15 were sorted on the digits in the most significant position, since both integers contained a "1," a nonstable sort may not have left them in the order they were placed when sorted by their least significant digit. A stable sort ensures that these two are not reordered. Radix sort uses counting sort because, aside from being stable, it runs in linear time, and for any radix, we know the largest integer any digit may be.

Radix sort is not limited to sorting data keyed by integers, as long as we can divide the elements into integer pieces. For example, we might sort a set of strings as radix-2^8 values. Or we might sort a set of 64-bit integers as four-digit, radix-2^{16} values. Exactly what value we choose as a radix depends on the data itself and minimizing $pn + pk$ considering space constraints, where p is the number of digit positions in each element, n is the number of elements, and k is the radix (the number of possible digit values in any position). Generally, we try to keep k close to and no more than n.

Interface for Radix Sort

rxsort

```
int rxsort(int *data, int size, int p, int k);
```

Return Value   0 if sorting is successful, or –1 otherwise.

Description   Uses radix sort to sort the array of integers in *data*. The number of integers in *data* is specified by *size*. The argument *p* specifies the number of digit positions in each integer. The argument *k* specifies the radix. When *rxsort* returns, *data* contains the sorted integers.

Complexity $O(pn + pk)$, where n is the number of integers to be sorted, k is the radix, and p is the number of digit positions.

Implementation and Analysis of Radix Sort

Radix sort works fundamentally by applying counting sort one position at a time to a set of data. In the implementation presented here, *data* initially contains the unsorted set of *size* integer elements stored in a single block of contiguous storage. When *rxsort* returns, *data* is completely sorted.

If we understand counting sort, the operation of radix sort is simple. A single loop governs the position on which we are currently sorting (see Example 12-7). Position by position, we apply counting sort to shuffle and reshuffle the elements, beginning with the least significant position. Once we have shuffled the elements by the digits in the most significant position, sorting is complete (see Figure 12-7). A simple approach involving exponentiation and modular arithmetic is used to obtain each digit value. This works well for integers. Different types of data require different approaches. Some approaches may require considering machine-specific details, such as byte ordering and word alignment.

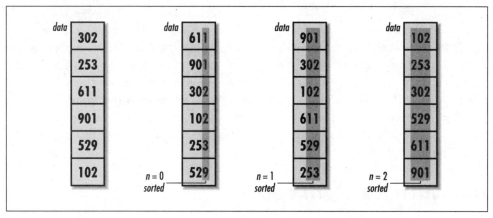

Figure 12-7. Sorting integers as radix-10 numbers with radix sort

Not surprisingly, the runtime complexity of radix sort depends on the stable sorting algorithm chosen to sort the digits. Because radix sort applies counting sort once for each of the p positions of digits in the data, radix sort runs in p times the runtime complexity of counting sort, or $O(pn + pk)$. Its space requirement is the same as for counting sort: two arrays of size n and an array of size k.

Example 12-7. Implementation of Radix Sort

```
/**************************************************************************
*                                                                        *
*  --------------------------------- rxsort.c ---------------------------  *
*                                                                        *
**************************************************************************/
```

Example 12-7. Implementation of Radix Sort (continued)

```c
#include <limits.h>
#include <math.h>
#include <stdlib.h>
#include <string.h>

#include "sort.h"

/*****************************************************************************
*                                                                           *
*  ----------------------------- rxsort -----------------------------       *
*                                                                           *
*****************************************************************************/

int rxsort(int *data, int size, int p, int k) {

int               *counts,
                  *temp;

int               index,
                  pval,
                  i,
                  j,
                  n;

/*****************************************************************************
*                                                                           *
*  Allocate storage for the counts.                                         *
*                                                                           *
*****************************************************************************/

if ((counts = (int *)malloc(k * sizeof(int))) == NULL)
   return -1;

/*****************************************************************************
*                                                                           *
*  Allocate storage for the sorted elements.                                *
*                                                                           *
*****************************************************************************/

if ((temp = (int *)malloc(size * sizeof(int))) == NULL)
   return -1;

/*****************************************************************************
*                                                                           *
*  Sort from the least significant position to the most significant.        *
*                                                                           *
*****************************************************************************/

for (n = 0; n < p; n++) {
```

Example 12-7. Implementation of Radix Sort (continued)

```
/***************************************************************************
 *                                                                         *
 *  Initialize the counts.                                                 *
 *                                                                         *
 ***************************************************************************/

for (i = 0; i < k; i++)
   counts[i] = 0;

/***************************************************************************
 *                                                                         *
 *  Calculate the position value.                                          *
 *                                                                         *
 ***************************************************************************/

pval = (int)pow((double)k, (double)n);

/***************************************************************************
 *                                                                         *
 *  Count the occurrences of each digit value.                            *
 *                                                                         *
 ***************************************************************************/

for (j = 0; j < size; j++) {

   index = (int)(data[j] / pval) % k;
   counts[index] = counts[index] + 1;

}

/***************************************************************************
 *                                                                         *
 *  Adjust each count to reflect the counts before it.                     *
 *                                                                         *
 ***************************************************************************/

for (i = 1; i < k; i++)
   counts[i] = counts[i] + counts[i - 1];

/***************************************************************************
 *                                                                         *
 *  Use the counts to position each element where it belongs.              *
 *                                                                         *
 ***************************************************************************/

for (j = size - 1; j >= 0; j--) {

   index = (int)(data[j] / pval) % k;
   temp[counts[index] - 1] = data[j];
   counts[index] = counts[index] - 1;

}
```

Example 12-7. Implementation of Radix Sort (continued)

```
/*****************************************************************************
*                                                                           *
*  Prepare to pass back the data as sorted thus far.                        *
*                                                                           *
*****************************************************************************/

memcpy(data, temp, size * sizeof(int));

}

/*****************************************************************************
*                                                                           *
*  Free the storage allocated for sorting.                                  *
*                                                                           *
*****************************************************************************/

free(counts);
free(temp);

return 0;

}
```

Description of Binary Search

Binary search is a technique for searching that works similarly to how we might systematically guess numbers in a guessing game. For example, suppose someone tells us to guess a number between 0 and 99. The consistently best approach is to begin with 49, the number in the middle of 0 and 99. If 49 is too high, we try 24, the number in the middle of the lower half of 0 to 99 (0 to 48). Otherwise, if 49 is too low, we try 74, the number in the middle of the upper half of 0 to 99 (50 to 99). We repeat this process for each narrowed range until we guess right.

Binary search begins with a set of data that is sorted. To start the search, we inspect the middle element of the sorted set. If the element is greater than the one we are looking for, we let the lower half of the set be the new set to search. Otherwise, if the element is less, we let the upper half be the new set. We repeat this process on each smaller set until we either locate the element we are looking for or cannot divide the set any further.

Binary search works with any type of data provided we can establish an ordering among the elements. It is a simple algorithm, but as you might suspect, its reliance on sorted data makes it inefficient for sets in which there are frequent insertions and deletions. This is because for each insertion or deletion, we must ensure that the set stays sorted for the search to work properly. Keeping a set sorted is expensive relative to searching it. Also, elements must be in contiguous storage. Thus, binary search is best utilized when the set to be searched is relatively static.

Interface for Binary Search

bisearch

```
int bisearch(void *sorted, void *target, int size, int esize,
   int (*compare)(const void *key1, const void *key2);
```

Return Value   Index of the target if found, or −1 otherwise.

Description   Uses binary search to locate *target* in *sorted*, a sorted array of elements. The number of elements in *sorted* is specified by *size*. The size of each element is specified by *esize*. The function pointer *compare* specifies a user-defined function to compare elements. This function should return 1 if *key1* > *key2*, 0 if *key1* = *key2*, and −1 if *key1* < *key2*.

Complexity $O(\lg n)$, where n is the number of elements to be searched.

Implementation and Analysis of Binary Search

Binary search works fundamentally by dividing a sorted set of data repeatedly and inspecting the element in the middle of each division. In the implementation presented here, the sorted set of data resides in *sorted*, a single block of contiguous storage. The argument *target* is the data we are searching for.

This implementation revolves around a single loop controlled by the variables *left* and *right*, which define the boundaries of the current set in which we are focusing our search (see Example 12-8). Initially, we set *left* and *right* to 0 and *size* − 1, respectively. During each iteration of the loop, we set *middle* to the middle element of the set defined by *left* and *right*. If the element at *middle* is less than the target, we move the left index to one element after *middle*. Thus, the next set searched is the upper half of the current set. If the element at *middle* is greater than the target, we move the right index to one element before *middle*. Thus, the next set searched is the lower half of the current set. As the search continues, *left* moves from left to right, and *right* moves from right to left. The search terminates once we encounter the target at *middle*, or when *left* and *right* cross, if the target is not found. Figure 12-8 illustrates this process.

The runtime complexity of binary search depends on the maximum number of divisions possible during the searching process. For a set of n elements, we can perform up to $\lg n$ divisions. For binary search, this represents the number of inspections that we could end up performing in the worst case: when the target is not found, for example. Therefore, the runtime complexity of binary search is $O(\lg n)$.

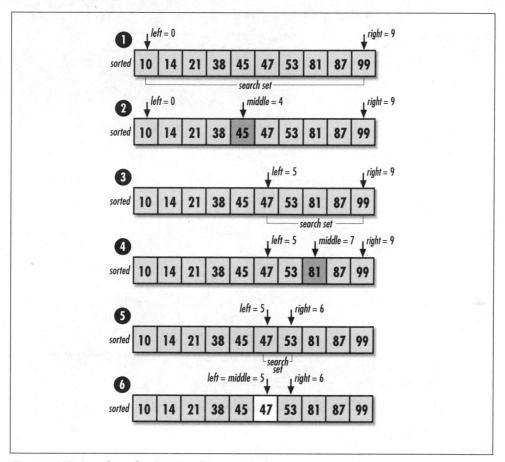

Figure 12-8. Searching for 47 using binary search

Example 12-8. Implementation of Binary Search

```
/*****************************************************************************
*                                                                           *
*  ----------------------------- bisearch.c -----------------------------   *
*                                                                           *
*****************************************************************************/

#include <stdlib.h>
#include <string.h>

#include "search.h"

/*****************************************************************************
*                                                                           *
*  ----------------------------- bisearch -----------------------------     *
*                                                                           *
*****************************************************************************/
```

Example 12-8. Implementation of Binary Search (continued)

```c
int bisearch(void *sorted, const void *target, int size, int esize, int
   (*compare)(const void *key1, const void *key2)) {

int             left,
                middle,
                right;

/*****************************************************************************
*                                                                           *
*  Continue searching until the left and right indices cross.               *
*                                                                           *
*****************************************************************************/

left = 0;
right = size - 1;

while (left <= right) {

   middle = (left + right) / 2;

   switch (compare(((char *)sorted + (esize * middle)), target)) {

      case -1:

      /*********************************************************************
      *                                                                   *
      *  Prepare to search to the right of the middle index.              *
      *                                                                   *
      *********************************************************************/

      left = middle + 1;
      break;

      case 1:

      /*********************************************************************
      *                                                                   *
      *  Prepare to search to the left of the middle index.               *
      *                                                                   *
      *********************************************************************/

      right = middle - 1;
      break;

      case 0:

      /*********************************************************************
      *                                                                   *
      *  Return the exact index where the data has been found.            *
      *                                                                   *
      *********************************************************************/

      return middle;
```

Example 12-8. Implementation of Binary Search (continued)

```
    }

}

/*****************************************************************************
*                                                                           *
*  Return that the data was not found.                                      *
*                                                                           *
*****************************************************************************/

return -1;

}
```

Binary Search Example: Spell Checking

Using spell checkers has become an expected part of preparing all types of documents. From a computing standpoint, a basic spell checker works simply by checking words in a string of text against a dictionary. The dictionary contains the set of acceptable words.

The example presented here consists of a function, *spell* (see Examples 12-9 and 12-10), that checks the spelling of words from a string of text one word at a time. The function accepts three arguments: `dictionary` is a sorted array of acceptable strings, `size` is the number of strings in the dictionary, and **word** is the word to check. The function calls *bisearch* to look up **word** in `dictionary`. If it finds the word, it is spelled correctly.

The runtime complexity of *spell* is $O(\lg n)$, the same time as *bisearch*, where n is the number of words in `dictionary`. The runtime complexity of checking an entire document is $O(m \lg n)$, where m is the number of words in the text to validate and n is the number of words in the dictionary.

Example 12-9. Header for Spell Checking

```
/*****************************************************************************
*                                                                           *
*  -------------------------------- spell.h --------------------------------  *
*                                                                           *
*****************************************************************************/

#ifndef SPELL_H
#define SPELL_H

/*****************************************************************************
*                                                                           *
*  Define the maximum size for words in the dictionary.                     *
*                                                                           *
*****************************************************************************/
```

Example 12-9. Header for Spell Checking (continued)

```
#define          SPELL_SIZE           31

/***************************************************************************
 *                                                                         *
 * ------------------------- Public Interface ------------------------     *
 *                                                                         *
 ***************************************************************************/

int spell(char (*dictionary)[SPELL_SIZE], int size, const char *word);

#endif
```

Example 12-10. Implementation of a Function for Spell Checking

```
/***************************************************************************
 *                                                                         *
 * ----------------------------- spell.c ------------------------------     *
 *                                                                         *
 ***************************************************************************/

#include <string.h>

#include "search.h"
#include "spell.h"

/***************************************************************************
 *                                                                         *
 * --------------------------- compare_str ----------------------------     *
 *                                                                         *
 ***************************************************************************/

static int compare_str(const void *str1, const void *str2) {

int              retval;

if ((retval = strcmp((const char *)str1, (const char *)str2)) > 0)
   return 1;
else if (retval < 0)
   return -1;
else
   return 0;

}

/***************************************************************************
 *                                                                         *
 * ----------------------------- spell --------------------------------     *
 *                                                                         *
 ***************************************************************************/

int spell(char (*dictionary)[SPELL_SIZE], int size, const char *word) {
```

Example 12-10. Implementation of a Function for Spell Checking (continued)

```
/*****************************************************************************
*                                                                           *
*  Look up the word.                                                        *
*                                                                           *
*****************************************************************************/

if (bisearch(dictionary, word, size, SPELL_SIZE, compare_str) >= 0)
   return 1;
else
   return 0;

}
```

Questions and Answers

Q: Suppose we need to sort all of the customer records for a worldwide investment firm by name. The data is so large it cannot be fit into memory all at once. Which sorting algorithm should we use?

A: Merge sort. Aside from running efficiently in $O(n \lg n)$ time, the predictable way that merge sort divides and merges the data lets us easily manage the data ourselves to efficiently bring it in and out of secondary storage.

Q: Suppose we are maintaining a list of sorted elements in a user interface. The list is relatively small and the elements are being entered by a user one at a time. Which sorting algorithm should we use?

A: Insertion sort. The runtime complexity of insertion sort when inserting a single element into a list that is already sorted is $O(n)$.

Q: Suppose we need to sort 10 million 80-character strings representing DNA information from a biological study. Which sorting algorithm should we use?

A: Radix sort. However, precisely how radix sort performs in relation to other sorting algorithms depends on the radix value we choose and our space constraints. An important consideration in selecting radix sort is that the elements in the data are a fixed size and can be broken into integer pieces.

Q: Suppose we need to sort 10,000 C structures containing information about the flight schedule for an airline. Which sorting algorithm should we use?

A: Quicksort. It is the best general-case sorting algorithm and is excellent for medium to large sets of data.

Q: Recall that the interfaces to qksort *and* mgsort *require that* i *and* k *be passed by the caller. Why is this, and how could we avoid it in practice?*

A: The arguments *i* and *k* are necessary to define smaller and smaller subsets of the data while recursing. An alternative to the caller providing these is to place

each function in a *wrapper*. Wrappers generally provide cleaner public interfaces to functions that are otherwise cumbersome to call directly. Wrapping
qksort, for example, gives us the opportunity to alleviate making the caller
pass *i* and *k*, since we know that initially these always should be set to 0 and
$size - 1$. Wrapping *qksort* also gives us the opportunity to encapsulate a call
to *srand*, which seeds the random number generator and prevents certain
inputs from consistently eliciting bad behavior. This is something like what the
standard library function *qsort* actually does. A wrapper might be implemented for *qksort* in Unix as shown below:

```
#include <unistd.h>
#include <stdlib.h>

#include "sort.h"

int qsrt(void *data, int size, int esize, int (*compare)(const void *key1,
   const void *key2)) {

srand(getpid());

return qksort(data, size, esize, 0, size - 1, compare);

}
```

Q: *In* rxsort, *recall that counting sort is implemented explicitly rather than by calling* ctsort. *Why might this have been done?*

A: Because radix sort works by considering only a single digit of the elements at
a time, our counting sort implementation would have had to accept additional
parameters to tell it which digit to consider as well as how to obtain each digit
value. Recall that modular arithmetic was used in the implementation presented in this chapter, but other techniques might be more appropriate for
some data. For example, for long strings we might choose to offset two bytes
at a time into the string to form digits. Accounting for these application-specific considerations in counting sort would have complicated it substantially.
Therefore, a slightly modified form of counting sort was included in the radix
sort implementation.

Q: *Suppose we have 2^{20} 128-bit elements that we would like to sort. What would be
the efficiency of sorting these using quicksort? What would be the efficiency of
sorting these as radix-2^{16} numbers using radix sort? Which approach would be
better? Suppose we have 2^{10} 128-bit elements rather than 2^{20} elements. How do
quicksort and radix sort compare in this case?*

A: Sorting with quicksort requires $O(n \lg n) = (2^{20})(20) = (2.10)(10^7)$ times some
constant amount of time. Considering the elements as radix-2^{16} numbers, the
number of digit positions, *p*, is 8, and the number of possible digit values, *k*, is

2^{16}. Therefore, sorting with radix sort requires $O(pn + pk) = (8)(2^{20}) + (8)(2^{16})$ $= (8.91)(10^6)$ times some constant amount of time. If the space requirements of radix sort are acceptable, radix sort is more than twice as efficient as quicksort. In the second case, sorting with quicksort requires $O(n \lg n) = (2^{10})(10)$ $= 10,240$ times some constant amount of time. Radix sort requires $O(pn + pk)$ $= (8)(2^{10}) + (8)(2^{16}) = 532,480$ times some constant amount of time, or 50 times as much time as quicksort! Here is an example of why k is typically chosen to be close to and no more than n. Had we used a radix of 2^8, radix sort would have required $O(pn + pk) = (16)(2^8) + (16)(2^8) = 8160$ times some constant amount of time, and would have been slightly better than quicksort. However, it is worth noting that the space requirement of radix sort may negate small benefits in time in many cases.

Q: *In a sorted set, the successor of some node* x *is the next largest node after* x. *For example, in a sorted set containing the keys 24, 39, 41, 55, 87, 92, the successor of 41 is 55. How do we find the successor of an element* x *using binary search? What is the runtime complexity of this operation?*

A: In a sorted set, to determine the successor of some element x using binary search, first we locate x. Next, we simply move one element to the right. The runtime complexity of locating either x or its successor is $O(\lg n)$.

Related Topics

Bubble sort

> An inefficient $O(n^2)$ sorting algorithm that works by exchanging neighboring elements to propagate one element at a time to its correct position in the sorted set.

Tournament sort

> An $O(n \lg n)$ algorithm that requires three times the space of the data. It works by pairing up elements to promote a "winner" as the next element to be placed in the sorted set.

Heapsort

> An efficient sorting algorithm that uses a heap (see Chapter 10, *Heaps and Priority Queues*) to build a sorted set. Heapsort runs in $O(n \lg n)$ and sorts in place. However, a good implementation of quicksort generally beats it by a small constant factor.

Introsort

> A sorting algorithm that behaves like quicksort, but detects when it would be better to switch to heapsort. By doing this, in some cases it gains a slight performance advantage over quicksort.

Bucket sort

A linear-time sorting algorithm on average for data that is uniformly randomly distributed. It works by distributing the data into several buckets and sorting the buckets to produce a sorted set.

13

Numerical Methods

Numerical methods are algorithms in *numerical analysis*. Numerical analysis is the study of problems in which numbers and approximation play an especially significant role. Computers are particularly well-suited to problems in numerical analysis because many such problems, while essentially involving common mathematical operations, require a lot of them. In the early days of computing, scientists monopolized computers with problems like this, which were far too intensive to be carried out by hand. Even today, problems in numerical analysis still occupy a good part of the cycles of some of the largest computers in the world. Hence, numerical analysis is a vast subject, and many numerical methods are as complicated and specific as the mathematical problems they solve. This chapter presents three numerical methods that are relatively simple but applicable to a wide variety of problems. This chapter covers:

Polynomial interpolation

A method of approximating values of a function for which values are known at only a few points. Fundamental to this method is the construction of an interpolating polynomial $p_n(z)$ of degree $\leq n$, where $n + 1$ is the number of points for which values are known.

Least-squares estimation

A method of determining estimators b_1 and b_0 for a function $y(x) = b_1 x + b_0$ so that $y(x)$ is a best-fit line through a set of n points $(x_0, y_0), \ldots, (x_{n-1}, y_{n-1})$. A best-fit line using least-squares estimation minimizes the sum of squared vertical distances between each point (x_i, y_i), $i = 0, \ldots, n - 1$, and a corresponding point $(x_i, y(x_i))$ along $y(x)$.

Solution of equations

The process of finding roots of equations having the form $f(x) = 0$. Whereas for some equations it is possible to determine exact roots, a great deal of the time a method of approximation must be used.

Some applications of numerical methods are:

Linear regression models

> Statistical models in which there is a linear-form relationship between an independent variable x and a variable y that depends on it. Least-squares estimators help to predict values of y for values of x we have not observed experimentally.

Curve fitting

> The process of fitting a curve to a number of points. If the points for which we have values are located at meaningful places on the curve we are trying to fit, and we know values at enough points, interpolation helps us draw a smooth curve.

Scatter plots

> Statistical tools that help ascertain the relationship between an independent variable x and a variable y that depends on it. Using least-squares estimators to draw a best-fit line through a linear-form scatter plot helps with this.

Approximating functions

> The process of determining the value of a function at points for which exact values are not known. This can be done by constructing an interpolating polynomial of the appropriate degree.

Function tables

> Tables containing values of computationally expensive functions or models of complicated physical phenomena. Often it is too costly to compute and store values of a function with the granularity required at some later time. Thus, we store a limited number of points and interpolate between them.

Scientific computing

> An area in which solving equations is one of the most fundamental problems routinely performed.

Description of Polynomial Interpolation

There are many problems that can be described in terms of a function. However, often this function is not known, and we must infer what we can about it from only a small number of points. To do this, we *interpolate* between the points. For example, in Figure 13-1, the known points along $f(x)$ are $x_0, \ldots, x_8$, shown by circular black dots. Interpolation helps us get a good idea of the value of the function at points z_0, z_1, and z_2, shown by white squares. This section presents polynomial interpolation.

Fundamental to polynomial interpolation is the construction of a special polynomial called an *interpolating polynomial*. To appreciate the significance of this

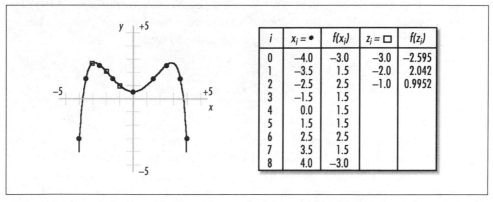

i	$x_i = \bullet$	$f(x_i)$	$z_i = \square$	$f(z_i)$
0	−4.0	−3.0	−3.0	−2.595
1	−3.5	1.5	−2.0	2.042
2	−2.5	2.5	−1.0	0.9952
3	−1.5	1.5		
4	0.0	1.5		
5	1.5	1.5		
6	2.5	2.5		
7	3.5	1.5		
8	4.0	−3.0		

Figure 13-1. Interpolation with nine points to find the value of a function at other points

polynomial, let's look at some principles of polynomials in general. First, a polynomial is a function of the form:

$$p(x) = a_0 + a_1 x + a_2 x^2 + \ldots + a_n x^n$$

where $a_0, \ldots, a_n$ are coefficients. Polynomials of this form are said to have degree n, provided a_n is nonzero. This is the *power form* of a polynomial, which is especially common in mathematical discussions. However, other forms of polynomials are more convenient in certain contexts. For example, a form particularly relevant to polynomial interpolation is the *Newton form*:

$$p(x) = a_0 + a_1(x - c_1) + a_2(x - c_1)(x - c_2) + \ldots + a_n(x - c_1)(x - c_2) \ldots (x - c_n)$$

where $a_0, \ldots, a_n$ are coefficients and $c_1, \ldots, c_n$ are centers. Notice how when $c_1, \ldots, c_n$ are all 0, the Newton form of a polynomial reduces to the power form above.

Constructing an Interpolating Polynomial

Now that we understand a bit about polynomials, let's look at how to construct the polynomial that interpolates a function $f(x)$. To interpolate $f(x)$, a polynomial $p_n(z)$ of degree $\leq n$ is constructed using $n + 1$ points, $x_0, \ldots, x_n$, known along $f(x)$. The points $x_0, \ldots, x_n$ are called *interpolation points*. Using $p_n(z)$, we approximate the value of $f(x)$ at $x=z$. Interpolation requires that point z be on the interval $[x_0, x_n]$. $p_n(z)$ is constructed using the formula:

$$p_n(z) = f[x_0] + f[x_0, x_1](z - x_0) + f[x_0, x_1, x_2](z - x_0)(z - x_1)$$
$$+ \ldots + f[x_0, \ldots, x_n](z - x_0)(z - x_1) \ldots (z - x_{n-1})$$

where $x_0, \ldots, x_n$ are the points along $f(x)$ for which values are known, and $f[x_0]$, $\ldots, f[x_0, \ldots, x_n]$ are *divided differences*, which are derived from $x_0, \ldots, x_n$ and the values of $f(x)$ at these points. This is called the *Newton formula for interpolating polynomials*. Notice its similarities with the Newton form of polynomials in general. Divided differences are computed using the formula:

$$f[x_i, \ldots, x_j] = \begin{cases} f(x_i) & \text{if } i = j \\ \dfrac{f[x_{i+1}, \ldots, x_j] - f[x_i, \ldots, x_{j-1}]}{x_j - x_i} & \text{if } i < j \end{cases}$$

Notice that this formula shows that for divided differences when $i < k$ we must have computed other divided differences beforehand. For example, to compute $f[x_0, x_1, x_2, x_3]$, values are required for $f[x_1, x_2, x_3]$ and $f[x_0, x_1, x_2]$ in the numerator. Fortunately, we can use a *divided-difference table* to help compute divided differences in a systematic manner (see Figure 13-2).

A divided-difference table consists of several rows. The top row stores $x_0, \ldots, x_n$. The second row stores values for $f[x_0], \ldots, f[x_n]$. To compute each divided difference in the remainder of the table, we draw a diagonal from each divided difference back to $f[x_i]$ and $f[x_j]$ (shown as dotted lines for $f[x_1, x_2, x_3]$ in Figure 13-2). To get x_i and x_j in the denominator, we then proceed straight up from $f[x_i]$ and $f[x_j]$. The two divided differences in the numerator are those immediately above the one being computed. When the table is complete, the coefficients for the interpolating polynomial are the divided differences at the far left of each row, beginning with the second row (shown in light gray in Figure 13-2).

Evaluating an Interpolating Polynomial

Once we have determined the coefficients of the interpolating polynomial $p_n(z)$, we evaluate the polynomial once for each point at which we would like to know the value of f. For example, say we know the values of f at four points: $x_0 = -3.0$, $f(x_0) = -5.0$; $x_1 = -2.0$, $f(x_1) = -1.1$; $x_2 = 2.0$, $f(x_2) = 1.9$; and $x_3 = 3.0$, $f(x_3) = 4.8$; and we would like to know the value of f at $z_0 = -2.5$, $z_1 = 0.0$, $z_2 = 1.0$, and $z_3 = 2.5$. Since we know four points along f, the interpolating polynomial will have a degree of 3. Figure 13-3 is the divided-difference table for determining the coefficients of $p_3(z)$.

Once we have obtained the coefficients from the divided-difference table, we construct $p_3(z)$ using the Newton formula for interpolating polynomials presented earlier. Using the coefficients from Figure 13-3, the interpolating polynomial is:

$$p_3(z) = -5.0 + 3.9(z + 3.0) + (-0.63)(z + 3.0)(z + 2.0) + 0.1767(z + 3.0)(z + 2.0)(z - 2.0)$$

Next, we evaluate this polynomial once at each point z. For example, at $z_0 = -2.5$ we perform the following calculation:

$$p_3(-2.5) = -5.0 + 3.9(0.5) + (-0.63)(0.5)(-0.5) + 0.1767(0.5)(-0.5)(-4.5) = -2.694$$

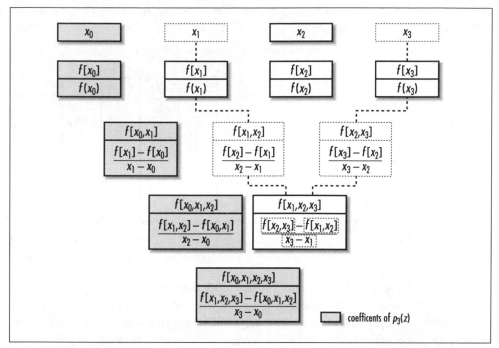

Figure 13-2. A divided-difference table for determining the coefficients of an interpolating polynomial of degree 3

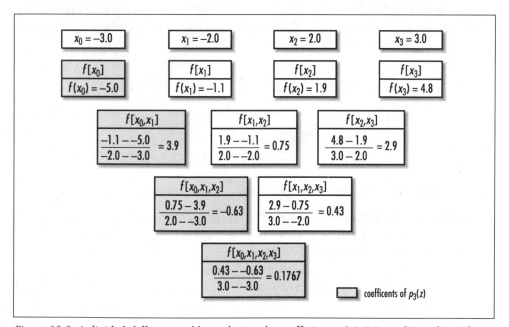

Figure 13-3. A divided-difference table producing the coefficients −5.0, 3.9, −0.63, and 0.1767

The value of f at z_1, z_2, and z_3 is determined in a similar manner. The results are tabulated and plotted in Figure 13-4.

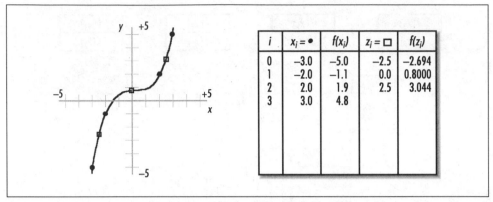

i	$x_i =$ ●	$f(x_i)$	$z_i =$ □	$f(z_i)$
0	−3.0	−5.0	−2.5	−2.694
1	−2.0	−1.1	0.0	0.8000
2	2.0	1.9	2.5	3.044
3	3.0	4.8		

Figure 13-4. Interpolating a function $f(x)$ using the polynomial $p_3(z)$ presented in the text

Now that we have an understanding of how to interpolate a function, it is important to briefly mention the subject of error. As with any approximation method, it is important to understand that an interpolating polynomial usually has some amount of error associated with it. To minimize this error, qualitatively speaking, we must construct an interpolating polynomial using enough points along $f(x)$, and ones properly spaced, so that the resulting polynomial gives an accurate impression of the function's character. Naturally, quantitative methods do exist for bounding the error associated with interpolation, but this book will not address them (see the related topics at the end of the chapter).

Interface for Polynomial Interpolation

interpol

```
int interpol (const double *x, const double *fx, int n, double *z, double *pz,
    int m);
```

Return Value   0 if interpolating is successful, or −1 otherwise.

Description   Determines the value of a function at specified points using polynomial interpolation. Points at which values are known are specified by the caller in *x*. The known values of the function at each point in *x* are specified in *fx*. Points at which values are to be determined are specified in *z*. The values calculated for the points passed in *z* are returned in *pz*. The number of values in *x* and *fx* is specified as *n*. The number of points in *z* (and thus returned in *pz*) is specified as *m*. It is the responsibility of the caller to manage the storage associated with *x*, *fx*, *z*, and *pz*.

Complexity $O(mn^2)$, where *m* is the number of values to determine and *n* is
the number of points at which values are known.

Implementation and Analysis
of Polynomial Interpolation

Polynomial interpolation works fundamentally by determining the value of an
interpolating polynomial at a number of desired points. To obtain this polynomial, first we must determine its coefficients by computing divided differences.

The *interpol* operation begins by allocating space for the divided differences as
well as for the coefficients to be determined (see Example 13-1). Note that since
the entries in each row in a divided-difference table depend only on the entries
computed in the row before it (see Figures 13-2 and 13-3), we do not have to
keep all of the table around at once. Thus, we allocate space only for the largest
row, which has *n* entries. Next, we initialize the first row in the table with the values in *fx*. This is so that we are ready to compute what equates to the third row
of the divided-difference table. (Nothing needs to be done for the first two rows
because these entries are already stored in *x* and *fx*.) The final initialization step is
to store the value of *fx[0]* in *coeff[0]* since this is the first coefficient of the
interpolating polynomial.

The process of computing divided differences revolves around a single nested
loop, which uses the formula for divided differences discussed earlier in the chapter. In terms of Figures 13-2 and 13-3, the outer loop, *k*, counts the number of
rows for which entries must be computed (excluding the rows for *x* and *fx*). The
inner loop, *i*, controls which entry is being computed in the current row. As we
complete the entries in each row, the value in *table[0]* becomes the next coefficient for the interpolating polynomial. Thus, we store this value in *coeff[k]*.
Once we have determined all coefficients for the interpolating polynomial, we
evaluate the polynomial at each point in *z*. The results are stored in *pz*.

The runtime complexity of *interpol* is $O(mn^2)$, where *m* is the number of values in
z (and values returned in *pz*), and *n* is the number of values in *x* (and *fx*). The
factor n^2 comes from the following. For each iteration of the loop controlled by *j*,
we multiply one factor more than the previous term into the current term. Thus,
when *j* is 1, *term* requires one multiplication; when *j* is 2, *term* requires two
multiplications, and so forth until when *j* is $n - 1$, *term* requires $n - 1$ multiplications. Effectively, this becomes a summation from 1 to $n - 1$, which results in a
running time of $T(n) = (n\ (n + 1)/2) - n$, times some constant amount of time.
(This is from the well-known formula for summing an arithmetic series from 1 to
n.) In *O*-notation, this simplifies to $O(n^2)$. The factor *m* in $O(mn^2)$ comes from
evaluating the interpolating polynomial once for each point in *z*. The first nested

loop, in which divided differences are computed, is $O(n^2)$. Thus, this term is not significant relative to mn^2, which has the additional factor m.

Example 13-1. Implementation of Polynomial Interpolation

```
/*****************************************************************************
*                                                                           *
*  --------------------------- interpol.c ---------------------------------*
*                                                                           *
*****************************************************************************/

#include <stdlib.h>
#include <string.h>

#include "nummeths.h"

/*****************************************************************************
*                                                                           *
*  --------------------------- interpol --------------------------------   *
*                                                                           *
*****************************************************************************/

int interpol(const double *x, const double *fx, int n, double *z, double
   *pz, int m) {

double           term,
                 *table,
                 *coeff;

int              i,
                 j,
                 k;

/*****************************************************************************
*                                                                           *
*  Allocate storage for the divided-difference table and coefficients.      *
*                                                                           *
*****************************************************************************/

if ((table = (double *)malloc(sizeof(double) * n)) == NULL)
   return -1;

if ((coeff = (double *)malloc(sizeof(double) * n)) == NULL) {

   free(table);
   return -1;

}

/*****************************************************************************
*                                                                           *
*  Initialize the coefficients.                                             *
*                                                                           *
*****************************************************************************/
```

Example 13-1. Implementation of Polynomial Interpolation (continued)

```
memcpy(table, fx, sizeof(double) * n);

/***************************************************************************
 *                                                                         *
 *  Determine the coefficients of the interpolating polynomial.            *
 *                                                                         *
 ***************************************************************************/

coeff[0] = table[0];

for (k = 1; k < n; k++) {

   for (i = 0; i < n - k; i++) {

      j = i + k;
      table[i] = (table[i + 1] - table[i]) / (x[j] - x[i]);

   }

   coeff[k] = table[0];

}

free(table);

/***************************************************************************
 *                                                                         *
 *  Evaluate the interpolating polynomial at the specified points.         *
 *                                                                         *
 ***************************************************************************/

for (k = 0; k < m; k++) {

   pz[k] = coeff[0];

   for (j = 1; j < n; j++) {

      term = coeff[j];

      for (i = 0; i < j; i++)
         term = term * (z[k] - x[i]);

      pz[k] = pz[k] + term;

   }

}

free(coeff);

return 0;

}
```

Description of Least-Squares Estimation

Least-squares estimation determines estimators b_1 and b_0 for a function $y(x) = b_1 x + b_0$ so that $y(x)$ is a *best-fit line* through a set of n points $(x_0, y_0), \ldots, (x_{n-1}, y_{n-1})$. A best-fit line using least-squares estimation minimizes the sum of squared vertical distances between each point (x_i, y_i), $i = 0, \ldots, n-1$ and a corresponding point $(x_i, y(x_i))$ along $y(x)$. This is one way of defining a line so that each point (x_i, y_i) is as close as possible to it.

Perhaps the most important application of least-squares estimation is to make inferences about a linear-form relationship between two variables. Given an independent variable x and a variable y that depends on it, estimators b_1 and b_0 allow us to calculate the expected value of y at values of x for which we have not actually observed y. This is particularly meaningful when x and y are related by a *statistical relationship*, which is an inexact relationship. For example, imagine how the number of new employees hired each month at a consulting firm is related to the number of hours the firm bills. Generally, as the firm hires more employees, it will bill more hours. However, there is not an exact number of hours it bills for a given number of employees. Contrast this with a *functional relationship*, which is exact. For example, a functional relationship might be one between the amount of money the firm charges for a project and the time the project requires. This relationship is exact if we assume that given a project of a certain length, there is an exact amount of money the firm will charge.

To understand how least-squares estimation works, recall that the distance r between two points (x_1, y_1) and (x_2, y_2) is defined as:

$$r = \sqrt{(x_2 - x_1)^2 + (y_2 - y_1)^2}$$

Since the points (x_i, y_i) and $(x_i, y(x_i))$ have the same x-coordinate, the line between them is vertical. Consequently, this formula tells us that the distance between these points is simply the difference in y-coordinates, or $|y_i - y(x_i)|$. This difference is called the *deviation* of y_i at x_i.

Consider for a moment why the squared deviations are used to compute b_1 and b_0, and not simply the deviations themselves. The reason is primarily anachronistic. When we minimize the sum of the errors, we end up with simultaneous equations that are linear. Before computers, these were the easiest to solve. Another justification can be made on the basis of probability theory. Simply stated, the probability that b_1 and b_0 are optimal for the observed values of (x_i, y_i) is proportional to a negative exponential containing the sum of all $(y_i - y(x_i))^2$. Thus, when we minimize the summation of squared deviations, we maximize the probability that b_1 and b_0 are good estimators as well. Yet another justification is that by squaring the deviations, more emphasis is given to larger deviations. Since in a normal distribution there are fewer instances of large deviations, this gives more weight to the deviations that occur less frequently.

To compute b_1 and b_0, we use the following formulas, where x and y are the coordinates of n points. These are derived from the simultaneous equations we mentioned above but did not show. The Σ (sigma) symbol in the formulas is used as a concise way of saying "sum all."

$$b_1 = \frac{n\sum x_i y_i - \sum x_i \sum y_i}{n\sum x_i^2 - \left(\sum x_i\right)^2},\ b_0 = \frac{\sum y_i - b_1 \sum x_i}{n}$$

Figure 13-5 illustrates computing b_1 and b_0 for a set of $n = 9$ points (x_0, y_0), ..., (x_8, y_8). The results of the calculations that need to be performed appear in the table. Using the values from the table, b_1 and b_0 are calculated using:

$$b_1 = \frac{(9)(35.75)-(-0.5)(-0.5)}{(9)(64.75)-(-0.5)^2} = 0.5519,\ b_0 = \frac{(-0.5)-0.5519(-0.5)}{9} = 0.0249$$

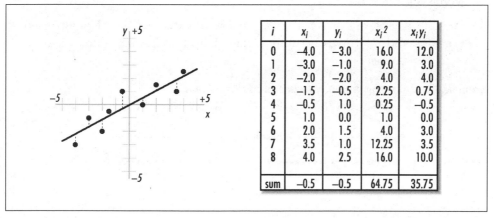

i	x_i	y_i	x_i^2	$x_i y_i$
0	−4.0	−3.0	16.0	12.0
1	−3.0	−1.0	9.0	3.0
2	−2.0	−2.0	4.0	4.0
3	−1.5	−0.5	2.25	0.75
4	−0.5	1.0	0.25	−0.5
5	1.0	0.0	1.0	0.0
6	2.0	1.5	4.0	3.0
7	3.5	1.0	12.25	3.5
8	4.0	2.5	16.0	10.0
sum	−0.5	−0.5	64.75	35.75

Figure 13-5. Least-squares estimation and the best-fit line that results

Substituting these values into $y(x) = b_1 x + b_0$ yields $y(x) = 0.5519x - 0.0249$. Figure 13-5 plots this line with the points used to determine it. From the standpoint of least-squares estimation, no other line is a better fit for the data than this one.

Interface for Least-Squares Estimation

lsqe

```
void lsqe(const double *x, const double *y, int n, double *b1, double *b0);
```

Return Value   None.

Description   Uses least-squares estimation to obtain b_1 and b_0 in $y(x) = b_1x + b_0$ so that $y(x)$ is a best-fit line through a set of points. The x-coordinates of the points are specified in *x*. The *y*-coordinates are specified in *y*. The number of points is specified in *n*. The operation returns the appropriate values in *b1* and *b0*.

Complexity $O(n)$, where n is the number of points used in determining b_1 and b_0.

Implementation and Analysis of Least-Squares Estimation

The implementation of least-squares estimation presented here requires us to do little more than compute a few summations and apply the results to the formulas presented earlier. The operation begins by summing all values for x_i in *sumx*, all values for y_i in *sumy*, all values of x_i^2 in *sumx2*, and all values of x_iy_i in *sumxy* (see Example 13-2). Once we have completed this, we compute b_1 and b_0 using the formulas presented earlier.

The runtime complexity of *lsqe* is $O(n)$, where n is the number of points used to determine b_1 and b_0. This is because a single loop that iterates n times is used to compute the summations.

Example 13-2. Implementation of Least-Squares Estimation

```
/*****************************************************************************
*                                                                           *
*  ------------------------------- lsqe.c ---------------------------------  *
*                                                                           *
*****************************************************************************/

#include <math.h>

#include "nummeths.h"

/*****************************************************************************
*                                                                           *
*  -------------------------------- lsqe ---------------------------------   *
*                                                                           *
*****************************************************************************/

void lsqe(const double *x, const double *y, int n, double *b1, double *b0) {

double          sumx,
                sumy,
                sumx2,
                sumxy;

int             i;
```

Example 13-2. Implementation of Least-Squares Estimation (continued)

```
/******************************************************************************
*                                                                            *
*  Compute the required summations.                                          *
*                                                                            *
******************************************************************************/

sumx = 0.0;
sumy = 0.0;
sumx2 = 0.0;
sumxy = 0.0;

for (i = 0; i < n; i++) {

   sumx = sumx + x[i];
   sumy = sumy + y[i];
   sumx2 = sumx2 + pow(x[i], 2.0);
   sumxy = sumxy + (x[i] * y[i]);

}

/******************************************************************************
*                                                                            *
*  Compute the least-squares estimators.                                     *
*                                                                            *
******************************************************************************/

*b1 = (sumxy - ((sumx * sumy)/(double)n)) / (sumx2-(pow(sumx,2.0)/(double)n));
*b0 = (sumy - ((*b1) * sumx)) / (double)n;

return;

}
```

Description of the Solution of Equations

One of the most fundamental problems in scientific computing is solving equations of the form $f(x) = 0$. This is often referred to as finding the *roots*, or *zeros*, of $f(x)$. Here, we are interested in the real roots of $f(x)$, as opposed to any complex roots it might have. Specifically, we will focus on finding real roots when $f(x)$ is a polynomial.

Finding Roots with Newton's Method

Although factoring and applying formulas are simple ways to determine the roots of polynomial equations, a great majority of the time polynomials are of a large enough degree and sufficiently complicated that we must turn to some method of approximation. One of the best approaches is *Newton's method*. Fundamentally, Newton's method looks for a root of $f(x)$ by moving closer and closer to it through a series of iterations. We begin by choosing an initial value $x = x_0$ that we think is near the root we are interested in. Then, we iterate using the formula:

$$x_{i+1} = x_i - \frac{f(x_i)}{f'(x_i)}$$

until x_{i+1} is a satisfactory approximation. In this formula, $f(x)$ is the polynomial for which we are trying to find a root, and $f'(x)$ is the *derivative* of $f(x)$.

Computing the Derivative of a Polynomial

The derivative of a function is fundamental to calculus and can be described in many ways. For now, let's simply look at a formulaic description, specifically for polynomials. To compute the derivative of a polynomial, we apply to each of its terms one of two formulas:

$$\frac{d}{dx}k = 0, \frac{d}{dx}kx^r = krx^{r-1}$$

where k is a constant, r is a rational number, and x is an unknown. The symbol d/dx means "derivative of," where x is the variable in the polynomial. For each term that is a constant, we apply the first formula; otherwise, we apply the second. For example, suppose we have the function:

$$f(x) = x^3 + 5x^2 + 3x + 4$$

In order to compute $f'(x)$, the derivative of $f(x)$, we apply the second formula to the first three terms of the polynomial, and the first formula to the last term, as follows:

$$f'(x) = (1)(3)x^{(3-1)} + (5)(2)x^{(2-1)} + (3)(1)x^{(1-1)} + 0 = 3x^2 + 10x + 3$$

Sometimes it is necessary to compute higher-order derivatives as well, which are derivatives of derivatives. For example, the second derivative of $f(x)$, written $f''(x)$, is the derivative of $f'(x)$. Similarly, the third derivative of $f(x)$, written $f'''(x)$, is the derivative of $f''(x)$, and so forth. Thus, to compute the second derivative of $f(x)$ in the previous equation, we compute the derivative of $f'(x)$, as follows:

$$f''(x) = (3)(2)x^{(2-1)} + (10)(1)x^{(1-1)} + 0 = 6x + 10$$

Understanding the First and Second Derivative

Now let's look at what derivatives really mean. To use Newton's method properly, it is important to understand the meaning of the first and second derivative in particular.

The value of the first derivative of $f(x)$ at some point $x = x_0$ indicates the *slope* of $f(x)$ at point x_0; that is, whether $f(x)$ is increasing (sloping upward from left to right) or decreasing (sloping downward). If the value of the derivative is positive, $f(x)$ is increasing; if the value is negative, $f(x)$ is decreasing; if the value is zero, $f(x)$ is neither increasing nor decreasing. The magnitude of the value indicates how fast $f(x)$ is increasing or decreasing. For example, Figure 13-6a depicts a function whose value increases within the shaded regions; thus, these are the regions where the first derivative is positive. The plot of the first derivative crosses the x-axis at the points where the slope of $f(x)$ changes sign.

The value of the second derivative of $f(x)$ at some point $x = x_0$ indicates the *concavity* of $f(x)$ at point x_0, that is, whether the function is opening upward or downward. The magnitude of the value indicates how extreme the concavity is. In Figures 13-6a and 13-6c, the dotted line indicates the point at which the concavity of the function changes sign. This is the point at which the plot of the second derivative crosses the x-axis.

Another way to think of the value of the derivative of $f(x)$ at some point $x = c$ is as the slope of the line tangent to $f(x)$ at c, expressed in point-slope form. The point-slope form of a line is:

$$y - f(c) = f'(c)(x - c)$$

Thus, if $f(x) = x^3 - x^2 - 3x + 1.8$ as shown in Figure 13-6a, the equation of the line tangent to $f(x)$ at $c = 1.5$ as can be determined as follows. Figure 13-6d is a plot of this line along with $f(x)$.

$$y - ((1.5)^3 - (1.5)^2 - 3(1.5) + 1.8) = (3(1.5)^2 - 2(1.5) - 3)(x - (1.5))$$
$$y + 1.575 = 0.75(x - 1.5)$$

Selecting an Initial Point for Newton's Method

Now that we understand a little about derivatives, let's return to Newton's method. Paramount to Newton's method is the proper selection of an initial iteration point x_0. In order for Newton's method to converge to the root we are looking for, the initial iteration point must be "near enough" and on the correct side of the root we are seeking. There are two rules that must be followed to achieve this:

1. Determine an interval [a, b] for x_0 where *one and only one* root exists. To do this, choose a and b so that the signs of $f(a)$ and $f(b)$ are not the same and $f'(x)$ does not change sign. If $f(a)$ and $f(b)$ have different signs, the interval contains *at least one* root. If the sign of $f'(x)$ does not change on [a, b], the interval contains *only one* root because the function can only increase or decrease on the interval.

2. Choose either $x_0 = a$ or $x_0 = b$ so that $f(x_0)$ has the same sign as $f''(x)$ on the interval [a, b]. This also implies that $f''(x)$ does not change sign on the interval. Recall that the second derivative of $f(x)$ is an indication of concavity. If

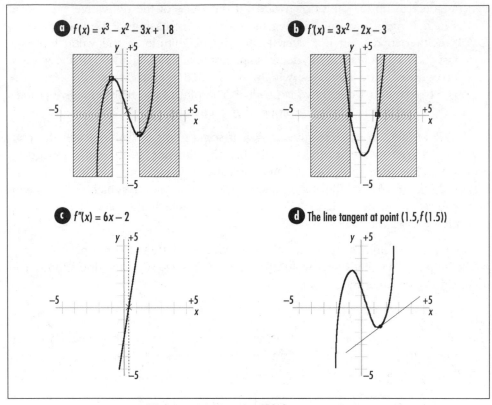

Figure 13-6. The meaning of the first and second derivatives of f(x)

$f''(x)$ does not change sign and x_0 is chosen so that $f(x_0)$ has the same sign as $f''(x)$, each successive iteration of Newton's method will converge closer to the root on the interval $[a, b]$ (see Figure 13-7).

In each of the four parts of Figure 13-7, $f(x)$ is shown as a heavy line, and a and b are shown as vertical dotted lines. If $f(a)$ matches the criteria just given, iteration begins at a and tangent lines slope from a toward the root to which we would like to converge. If $f(b)$ matches the criteria above, iteration begins at b and tangent lines slope from b toward the root to which we would like to converge.

How Newton's Method Works

As an example, suppose we would like to find the roots of $f(x) = x^3 - x^2 - 3x + 1.8$. Figure 13-8 illustrates that this function appears to have three roots: one on the interval $[-2, -1]$, another on the interval $[0, -1]$, and a third on the interval $[2, 3]$. Once we have an idea of the number and location of a function's roots, we test each interval against the rules for selecting an initial iteration point. To do this, we need to know the following:

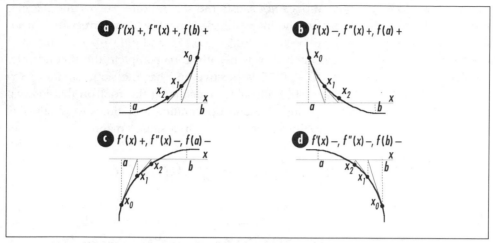

Figure 13-7. Convergence of Newton's method

$$f(x) = x^3 - x^2 - 3x + 1.8, \; f'(x) = 3x^2 - 2x - 3, \; f''(x) = 6x - 2$$

Using this information, we see that the interval [–2, –1] satisfies the first rule because $f(-2) = -4.2$ and $f(-1) = 2.8$, and $f'(x)$ does not change sign on the interval: it is always positive. Considering this, we know there is, in fact, one and only one root on the interval [–2, –1]. To satisfy the second rule, we see that $f''(x)$ does not change sign on the interval: it is negative. We select $x_0 = -2$ as the initial iteration point since $f(-2) = -4.2$ is also negative. Figure 13-8 illustrates calculating the root on this interval to within 0.0001 of its actual value. We end up iterating five times to obtain this approximation.

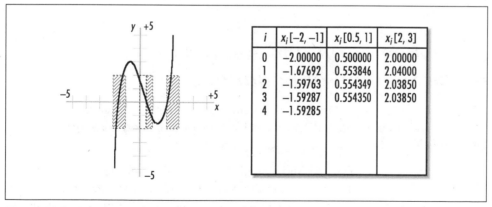

i	$x_i[-2, -1]$	$x_i[0.5, 1]$	$x_i[2, 3]$
0	−2.00000	0.500000	2.00000
1	−1.67692	0.553846	2.04000
2	−1.59763	0.554349	2.03850
3	−1.59287	0.554350	2.03850
4	−1.59285		

Figure 13-8. Calculating the three real roots of $f(x) = x^3 - x^2 - 3x + 1.8 = 0$ to within 0.0001 of their actual values

Moving to the root on the interval [0, 1], we see that the first rule is satisfied just as for the previous interval. However, the sign of $f''(x)$ is not constant on this interval; therefore, the interval does not satisfy the second rule. Suspecting that the root is closer to 1 than 0, we try the interval [0.5, 1] next, which corrects the problem. The first rule is satisfied because $f(0.5) = 0.175$ and $f(1) = -1.2$, and $f'(x)$ does not change sign on the interval: it is negative. To complete the second rule, we select $x_0 = 0.5$ since $f(0.5) = 0.175$ is positive and has the same sign as $f''(x)$ over the interval [0.5, 1]. Figure 13-8 illustrates calculating the root on this interval to within 0.0001 of its actual value. We end up iterating four times to obtain this approximation. Calculating the third root proceeds in a similar manner.

Interface for the Solution of Equations

root

```
int root(double (*f)(double x), double (*g)(double x), double *x, int *n,
    double delta)
```

Return Value   0 if a root is found, −1 otherwise.

Description   Computes the root of f to which Newton's method converges given an initial iteration point. This point is specified in *x[0]*. The derivative of f is specified in *g*. The argument *n* is the maximum number of iterations to perform. The argument *delta* is the difference between successive approximations at which to stop iterating. Upon return, successive values of *x* calculated during the iteration process are returned in the *x* array. Upon return, *n* contains the number of values in array *x*. It is the responsibility of the caller to manage the storage associated with *x*.

Complexity $O(n)$, where n is the maximum number of iterations the caller wishes to perform.

Implementation and Analysis of the Solution of Equations

Recall that solving an equation of the form $f(x) = 0$ means finding its roots. The *root* operation locates the real root to which Newton's method converges given an initial iteration point.

The *root* operation revolves around a single loop (see Example 13-3), which calculates successive approximations using the Newton iteration formula. In the implementation presented here, *f* is the function for which we are approximating the root, and *g* is the derivative of *f*. After each iteration, we determine whether the current approximation of the root is satisfactory. An approximation is deemed satisfactory when the difference between it and that of the previous iteration is less than *delta*. If after *n* iterations a satisfactory root still has not been found, *root* terminates.

The runtime complexity of *root* is $O(n)$, where n is the maximum number of iterations the caller wishes to perform. The worst case occurs when we do not find the root we are looking for.

Example 13-3. Implementation for the Solution of Equations

```c
/*****************************************************************************
*                                                                           *
*  ------------------------------- root.c -------------------------------   *
*                                                                           *
*****************************************************************************/

#include <math.h>

#include "nummeths.h"

/*****************************************************************************
*                                                                           *
*  -------------------------------- root --------------------------------   *
*                                                                           *
*****************************************************************************/

int root(double (*f)(double x), double (*g)(double x), double *x, int *n,
   double delta) {

int              satisfied,
                 i;

/*****************************************************************************
*                                                                           *
*  Use Newton's method to find a root of f.                                 *
*                                                                           *
*****************************************************************************/

i = 0;
satisfied = 0;

while (!satisfied && i + 1 < *n) {

   /*************************************************************************
   *                                                                       *
   *  Determine the next iteration of x.                                   *
   *                                                                       *
   *************************************************************************/

   x[i + 1] = x[i] - (f(x[i]) / g(x[i]));

   /*************************************************************************
   *                                                                       *
   *  Determine whether the desired approximation has been obtained.       *
   *                                                                       *
   *************************************************************************/
```

Example 13-3. Implementation for the Solution of Equations (continued)

```
    if (fabs(x[i + 1] - x[i]) < delta)
        satisfied = 1;

    /************************************************************************
     *                                                                      *
     *  Prepare for the next iteration.                                     *
     *                                                                      *
     ************************************************************************/

    i++;

}

/****************************************************************************
 *                                                                          *
 *  Even without iterating, indicate that one value has been stored in x.   *
 *                                                                          *
 ****************************************************************************/

if (i == 0)
    *n = 1;
else
    *n = i + 1;

/****************************************************************************
 *                                                                          *
 *  Return whether a root was found or the maximum iterations were reached. *
 *                                                                          *
 ****************************************************************************/

if (satisfied)
    return 0;
else
    return -1;

}
```

Questions and Answers

Q: *In the discussion of polynomial interpolation, we stated that we need to choose
enough points to give an accurate impression of the function we are interpolating. What happens if we do not use enough points?*

A: Interpolating a function with not enough points, or poorly placed points, leads
to an interpolating polynomial that does not accurately reflect the function we
think we are interpolating. A simple example is interpolating a quadratic polynomial (a parabola when plotted) with only two points. Interpolation with two
points results in a line, which is far from a parabola!

Q: *Using the guidelines presented in this chapter, how many interpolation points
should we use to interpolate the function $f(x) = x^5 + 2.8x^3 - 3.3x^2 - x + 4.1$?*

A: When interpolating a function that we know is a polynomial itself, we can get a good impression of the function by using $n + 1$ well-placed points, where n is the degree of the polynomial. In this example, the polynomial has a degree of 5, so we should use six well-placed interpolation points. This results in an interpolating polynomial that has the same degree as $f(x)$.

Q: *Recall that to approximate a root of an equation using Newton's method, we select an interval* [a, b] *on which the root exists and iterate closer and closer to it. What if we choose this interval much larger than needed, but in such a way that both rules mentioned in this chapter are still satisfied?*

A: The discussion of Newton's method mentioned two rules that must be satisfied in order to guarantee the algorithm's success: we need to determine an interval $[a, b]$ where one and only one root exists; and we need to choose x_0, the initial iteration point, so that $f(x_0)$ has the same sign as $f''(x)$ over the interval. Provided these rules are satisfied, the interval $[a, b]$ can be as large as we would like to make it. However, Newton's method will require more iterations to converge if we use an interval that is excessively large. Therefore, typically a relatively small interval convenient to the problem should be chosen.

Q: *In the implementation of* root, *what symptoms might we notice if we have violated one the rules of Newton's method that guarantee convergence?*

A: If we follow the rules presented in this chapter, Newton's method guarantees convergence to the root that exists on the interval $[a, b]$ containing the initial iteration point, x_0. Various symptoms help to determine when we have violated these rules. For example, successive approximations that appear to be diverging instead of converging indicate a problem. Another symptom is convergence to a root other than the one we expect. For example, suppose we think there is a root near -2 (perhaps by plotting the function), but we end up finding a root near 9. In order to relay these symptoms back to the caller, *root* returns both an array of the approximations obtained in successive iterations of Newton's method and an array of values for $f(x)$ computed using the approximations. Normally, successive values for $f(x)$ should approach 0. The parameter n of the *root* operation provides a way to keep a divergent series from running too long.

Related Topics

Error approximation

An important part of more substantial work with numerical methods. Numerical analysis is replete with approximation methods, and inherent in any approximation is some amount of error. Often it is important to quantify this.

Derivatives of functions

A fundamental part of calculus. The numerical methods presented in this chapter required only a primitive understanding of derivatives. However, for many numerical methods, a more complete understanding of derivatives and calculus is essential.

Muller's method

An algorithm for finding both the real and complex roots of equations. Complex roots are *complex numbers*, which result from taking the square root of negative numbers. This chapter focused on finding real roots.

14

Data Compression

Data compression is the process of reducing the number of bits used to represent data. It is one of the most significant results of *information theory*, an area of mathematics that addresses various ways to manage and manipulate information. Data compression entails two processes: in one process the data is compressed, or *encoded*, to reduce its size; in a second process it is uncompressed, or *decoded*, to return it to its original state.

To understand why data compression is possible, we must first understand that all data can be characterized by some informational content, called its *entropy* (a term borrowed from thermodynamics). Compression is possible because most data is represented with more bits than its entropy suggests is optimal. To gauge the effectiveness of compression, we look at the ratio of the size of the compressed data divided by its original size, and subtract this from 1. This value is known as the data's *compression ratio*.

In the broadest sense, data compression methods are divided into two classes: *lossy* and *lossless*. In lossy compression we accept a certain loss of accuracy in exchange for greater compression ratios. This is acceptable in some applications, such as graphics and sound processing, provided the degradation is managed carefully. However, frequently we use lossless compression, which ensures that an exact copy of the original data is reproduced when uncompressed.

This chapter focuses on lossless compression, for which there are two general approaches: *minimum redundancy coding* and *dictionary-based methods*. Minimum redundancy coding achieves compression by encoding symbols that occur with great frequency using fewer bits than for those that occur less often. Dictionary-based methods encode data in terms of tokens that take the place of redundant phrases. Example 14-1 is a header for the compression methods presented in this chapter.

This chapter covers:

Bit operations

An important part of data compression because most methods require operating on data one bit at a time to some degree. C provides a number of bitwise operators that can be used to implement an extended class of bit operations.

Huffman coding

One of the oldest and most elegant forms of compression based on minimum redundancy coding. Fundamental to Huffman coding is the construction of a Huffman tree, which is used both to encode and decode the data. Huffman coding is not the most effective form of compression, but it runs fast both when compressing and uncompressing data.

LZ77 (Lempel-Ziv-1977)

One of the fundamental methods of dictionary-based compression. LZ77 uses a sliding window and a look-ahead buffer to encode symbols in terms of phrases encountered earlier in the data. LZ77 generally results in better compression ratios than Huffman coding, but with longer compression times. However, uncompressing data is generally very fast.

Some applications of lossless data compression are:

Software distribution

The process of delivering software on various media. When distributing software on physical media, such as compact discs or magnetic tapes and diskettes, reducing the amount of storage required can produce considerable cost savings in mass distributions.

Archiving

Collecting groups of files into organized libraries. Typically, archives contain large amounts of data. Thus, after creating archives, frequently we compress them.

Mobile computing

An area of computing in which devices typically have limited amounts of memory and secondary storage. Mobile computing generally refers to computing with small, portable devices such as advanced programmable calculators, electronic organizers, and other personal computing devices.

Optimized networking (illustrated in this chapter)

Compression is used especially when sending large amounts of data across wide-area networks. Bandwidth at certain points along wide-area networks is often limited. Although compressing and uncompressing data does require time, in many network applications the cost is well justified.

Embedded applications

An area of computing similar to mobile computing in that devices typically have somewhat limited amounts of memory and secondary storage. Examples of embedded applications are lab instruments, avionics (aircraft electronics), VCRs, home stereos, and other pieces of equipment built around microcontrollers.

Database systems

Typically, large systems that can be optimized by reducing their size to some extent. Databases may be compressed at the record or file level.

Online manuals

Manuals that are accessed directly on a computer. Online manuals are typically of considerable size, but many sections are not accessed on a regular basis. Therefore, it is common to store them in a compressed form and uncompress sections only as they are needed.

Example 14-1. Header for Data Compression

```
/****************************************************************************
*                                                                          *
*  --------------------------- compress.h ---------------------------      *
*                                                                          *
****************************************************************************/

#ifndef COMPRESS_H
#define COMPRESS_H

#include "bitree.h"

/****************************************************************************
*                                                                          *
*  Define a structure for nodes of Huffman trees.                          *
*                                                                          *
****************************************************************************/

typedef struct HuffNode_ {

unsigned char       symbol;
int                 freq;

} HuffNode;

/****************************************************************************
*                                                                          *
*  Define a structure for entries in Huffman code tables.                  *
*                                                                          *
****************************************************************************/

typedef struct HuffCode_ {

unsigned char       used;
unsigned short      code;
unsigned char       size;

} HuffCode;
```

Example 14-1. Header for Data Compression (continued)

```
/***************************************************************************
 *                                                                         *
 *  Define the number of bits required for LZ77 token members.             *
 *                                                                         *
 ***************************************************************************/

#define          LZ77_TYPE_BITS        1
#define          LZ77_WINOFF_BITS      12
#define          LZ77_BUFLEN_BITS      5
#define          LZ77_NEXT_BITS        8


/***************************************************************************
 *                                                                         *
 *  Define the size of the sliding window and the look-ahead buffer for    *
 *  LZ77. Each must be less than or equal to 2 raised to LZ77_WINOFF_BITS   *
 *  and LZ77_BUFLEN_BITS respectively.                                     *
 *                                                                         *
 ***************************************************************************/

#define          LZ77_WINDOW_SIZE      4096
#define          LZ77_BUFFER_SIZE      32


/***************************************************************************
 *                                                                         *
 *  Define the number of bits for LZ77 phrase tokens.                      *
 *                                                                         *
 ***************************************************************************/

#define          LZ77_PHRASE_BITS      (LZ77_TYPE_BITS+LZ77_WINOFF_BITS\
                                        +LZ77_NEXT_BITS+LZ77_BUFLEN_BITS)


/***************************************************************************
 *                                                                         *
 *  Define the number of bits for LZ77 symbol tokens.                      *
 *                                                                         *
 ***************************************************************************/

#define          LZ77_SYMBOL_BITS      (LZ77_TYPE_BITS+LZ77_NEXT_BITS)


/***************************************************************************
 *                                                                         *
 *  -------------------------- Public Interface --------------------------  *
 *                                                                         *
 ***************************************************************************/

int huffman_compress(const unsigned char *original, unsigned char
   **compressed, int size);

int huffman_uncompress(const unsigned char *compressed, unsigned char
   **original);

int lz77_compress(const unsigned char *original, unsigned char **compressed,
   int size);
```

Example 14-1. Header for Data Compression (continued)

```
int lz77_uncompress(const unsigned char *compressed, unsigned char
   **original);
```

```
#endif
```

Description of Bit Operations

When compressing and uncompressing data, often we need to perform operations on less than a single byte. Therefore, before discussing various methods of data compression, it is important to become familiar with some basic operations for working with data one bit at a time. These operations are necessary because bit operators in C work only with intrinsic integral operands, which are small. The operations presented in this section work with buffers containing any number of bits. Note that the set of operations presented here is rather incomplete. Specifically, only those that are used in this chapter and in Chapter 15, *Data Encryption*, are defined.

Interface for Bit Operations

bit_get

```
int bit_get(const unsigned char *bits, int pos);
```

Return Value   State of the desired bit: 1 or 0.

Description   Gets the state of the bit at position *pos* in the buffer *bits*. The leftmost position in the buffer is 0. The state returned is either 1 or 0.

Complexity $O(1)$

bit_set

```
void bit_set(unsigned char *bits, int pos, int state);
```

Return Value   None.

Description   Sets the state of the bit at position *pos* in the buffer *bits* to the value specified by *state*. The leftmost position in the buffer is 0. The state must be 1 or 0.

Complexity $O(1)$

bit_xor

```
void bit_xor(const unsigned char *bits1, const unsigned char *bits2,
   unsigned char *bitsx, int size);
```

Return Value   None.

Description   Computes the bitwise XOR (exclusive OR) of the two buffers *bits1* and *bits2*, each containing *size* bits, and returns the result in *bitsx*. The bitwise XOR of two binary operands yields 0 in each position i of the result where in position i of the operands the bits are the same, and 1 in each position where the bits are different. For example, $11010 \oplus 01011 = 10001$ ($\oplus$ denotes XOR). It is the responsibility of the caller to manage the storage required by *bitsx*.

Complexity $O(\beta)$, where β is the number of bits in each buffer.

bit_rot_left

```
void bit_rot_left(unsigned char *bits, int size, int count);
```

Return Value   None.

Description   Rotates the buffer *bits*, containing *size* bits, to the left *count* bits. After the operation, the leftmost *count* bits become the *count* rightmost bits in the buffer, and all other bits are shifted accordingly.

Complexity $O(n\beta)$, where n is the number of bits rotated to the left and β is the number of bits in the buffer.

Implementation and Analysis of Bit Operations

Each bit operation works with a buffer of data defined as a pointer to an unsigned character. This pointer points to as many bytes as are required to represent the number of bits in the buffer. If the number of bits in the buffer is not a multiple of 8, some bits in the final byte are not used.

bit_get

The *bit_get* operation gets the state of a bit in a buffer (see Example 14-2). To do this, we determine in which byte the desired bit resides and then use a mask to get the specific bit from that byte. The bit set to 1 in *mask* determines which bit will be read from the byte. We use a loop to shift this bit into the proper position. We fetch the desired bit by indexing to the appropriate byte in *bits* and applying the mask.

The runtime complexity of *bit_get* is $O(1)$. This is because all of the steps in getting the state of a bit in a buffer run in a constant amount of time.

bit_set

The *bit_set* operation sets the state of a bit in a buffer (see Example 14-2). This operation works similarly to *bit_get*, except that it uses the mask to set the state of the specified bit rather than to get it.

The runtime complexity of *bit_set* is $O(1)$. This is because all of the steps in getting the state of a bit in a buffer run in a constant amount of time.

bit_xor

The *bit_xor* operation computes the bitwise XOR (exclusive OR) of two buffers, `bits1` and `bits2`, and places the result in another buffer, `bitsx` (see Example 14-2). To do this, we compare the bit in position *i* of `bits1` with the bit in position *i* of `bits2`. If the bits are the same, we set the bit in position *i* of `bitsx` to 0; otherwise, we set the bit in position *i* of `bitsx` to 1. This process continues for as many bits are in each buffer, as specified by `size`.

The runtime complexity of *bit_xor* is $O(\beta)$, where β is the number of bits in each buffer. This is because the loop in the operation iterates once for each bit.

bit_rot_left

The *bit_rot_left* operation rotates a buffer a specified number of bits to the left (see Example 14-2). We begin by saving the leftmost bit of the leftmost byte and then shifting each byte one bit to the left. As we shift each byte, we set the rightmost bit of the preceding byte to the bit shifted off the left of the current byte. Once we have shifted the last byte, we set its rightmost bit to the bit shifted off the first byte. This process is repeated as many times as the number of bits to be rotated.

The runtime complexity of *bit_rot_left* is $O(n\beta)$, where *n* is the number of bits rotated to the left and β is the number of bits in the buffer. This is because for each rotation, $(\beta/8) + 1$ shifts are performed to the left.

Example 14-2. Implementation of Bit Operations

```
/*****************************************************************************
*                                                                           *
*  -------------------------------- bit.c --------------------------------  *
*                                                                           *
*****************************************************************************/

#include <string.h>

#include "bit.h"
```

Example 14-2. Implementation of Bit Operations (continued)

```
/*****************************************************************************
*                                                                           *
*  ------------------------------- bit_get ------------------------------   *
*                                                                           *
*****************************************************************************/

int bit_get(const unsigned char *bits, int pos) {

unsigned char      mask;

int                i;

/*****************************************************************************
*                                                                           *
*  Set a mask for the bit to get.                                           *
*                                                                           *
*****************************************************************************/

mask = 0x80;

for (i = 0; i < (pos % 8); i++)
   mask = mask >> 1;

/*****************************************************************************
*                                                                           *
*  Get the bit.                                                             *
*                                                                           *
*****************************************************************************/

return (((mask & bits[(int)(pos / 8)]) == mask) ? 1 : 0);

}

/*****************************************************************************
*                                                                           *
*  ------------------------------- bit_set ------------------------------   *
*                                                                           *
*****************************************************************************/

void bit_set(unsigned char *bits, int pos, int state) {

unsigned char      mask;

int                i;

/*****************************************************************************
*                                                                           *
*  Set a mask for the bit to set.                                           *
*                                                                           *
*****************************************************************************/

mask = 0x80;
```

Example 14-2. Implementation of Bit Operations (continued)

```c
for (i = 0; i < (pos % 8); i++)
   mask = mask >> 1;

/***************************************************************************
*                                                                         *
*  Set the bit.                                                           *
*                                                                         *
***************************************************************************/

if (state)
   bits[pos / 8] = bits[pos / 8] | mask;
else
   bits[pos / 8] = bits[pos / 8] & (~mask);

return;

}

/***************************************************************************
*                                                                         *
*  ------------------------------ bit_xor ------------------------------  *
*                                                                         *
***************************************************************************/

void bit_xor(const unsigned char *bits1, const unsigned char *bits2, unsigned
   char *bitsx, int size) {

int              i;

/***************************************************************************
*                                                                         *
*  Compute the bitwise XOR (exclusive OR) of the two buffers.             *
*                                                                         *
***************************************************************************/

for (i = 0; i < size; i++) {

   if (bit_get(bits1, i) != bit_get(bits2, i))
      bit_set(bitsx, i, 1);
   else
      bit_set(bitsx, i, 0);

}

return;

}

/***************************************************************************
*                                                                         *
*  --------------------------- bit_rot_left ---------------------------   *
*                                                                         *
***************************************************************************/
```

Example 14-2. Implementation of Bit Operations (continued)

```
void bit_rot_left(unsigned char *bits, int size, int count) {

int             fbit,
                lbit,
                i,
                j;

/***************************************************************************
*                                                                          *
*  Rotate the buffer to the left the specified number of bits.             *
*                                                                          *
***************************************************************************/

if (size > 0) {

   for (j = 0; j < count; j++) {

      for (i = 0; i < (size / 8); i++) {

         /*********************************************************************
         *                                                                   *
         *  Get the bit about to be shifted off the current byte.            *
         *                                                                   *
         *********************************************************************/

         lbit = bit_get(&bits[i], 0);

         if (i == 0) {

            /******************************************************************
            *                                                                *
            *  Save the bit shifted off the first byte for later.            *
            *                                                                *
            ******************************************************************/

            fbit = lbit;

            }

         else {

            /******************************************************************
            *                                                                *
            *  Set the rightmost bit of the previous byte to the leftmost    *
            *  bit about to be shifted off the current byte.                 *
            *                                                                *
            ******************************************************************/

            bit_set(&bits[i - 1], 7, lbit);

            }
```

Example 14-2. Implementation of Bit Operations (continued)

```
/*********************************************************************
*                                                                   *
*   Shift the current byte to the left.                             *
*                                                                   *
*********************************************************************/

        bits[i] = bits[i] << 1;

    }

/*********************************************************************
*                                                                   *
*   Set the rightmost bit of the buffer to the bit shifted off the  *
*   first byte.                                                      *
*                                                                   *
*********************************************************************/

    bit_set(bits, size - 1, fbit);

   }

}

return;

}
```

Description of Huffman Coding

One of the oldest and most elegant forms of data compression is Huffman coding, an algorithm based on minimum redundancy coding. Minimum redundancy coding suggests that if we know how often different symbols occur in a set of data, we can represent the symbols in a way that makes the data require less space. The idea is to encode symbols that occur more frequently with fewer bits than those that occur less frequently. It is important to realize that a symbol is not necessarily a character of text: a symbol can be any amount of data we choose, but it is often one byte's worth.

Entropy and Minimum Redundancy

To begin, let's revisit the concept of entropy introduced at the beginning of the chapter. Recall that every set of data has some informational content, which is called its entropy. The entropy of a set of data is the sum of the entropies of each of its symbols. The entropy S of a symbol z is defined as:

$$S_z = -\lg P_z$$

where P_z is the probability of z being found in the data. If it is known exactly how many times z occurs, P_z is referred to as the *frequency* of z. As an example, if z occurs 8 times in 32 symbols, or one-fourth of the time, the entropy of z is:

   $-\lg(1/4) = 2$ bits

This means that using any more than two bits to represent z is more than we need. If we consider that normally we represent a symbol using eight bits (one byte), we see that compression here has the potential to improve the representation a great deal.

Table 14-1 presents an example of calculating the entropy of some data containing 72 instances of five different symbols. To do this, we sum the entropies contributed by each symbol. Using "U" as an example, the total entropy for a symbol is computed as follows. Since "U" occurs 12 times out of the 72 total, each instance of "U" has an entropy that is calculated as:

   $-\lg(12/72) = 2.584963$ bits

Consequently, because "U" occurs 12 times in the data, its contribution to the entropy of the data is calculated as:

   $(2.584963)(12) = 31.01955$ bits

In order to calculate the overall entropy of the data, we sum the total entropies contributed by each symbol. To do this for the data in Table 14-1, we have:

   $31.01955 + 36.00000 + 23.53799 + 33.94552 + 36.95994 = 161.46300$ bits

If using 8 bits to represent each symbol yields a data size of $(72)(8) = 576$ bits, we should be able to compress this data, in theory, by up to:

   $1 - (161.463000/576) = 72.0\%$

Table 14-1. The Entropy of a Set of Data Containing 72 Instances of 5 Different Symbols

Symbol	Probability	Entropy of Each Instance	Total Entropy
U	12/72	2.584963	31.01955
V	18/72	2.000000	36.00000
W	7/72	3.362570	23.53799
X	15/72	2.263034	33.94552
Y	20/72	1.847997	36.95994

Building a Huffman Tree

Huffman coding presents a way to approximate the optimal representation of data based on its entropy. It works by building a data structure called a *Huffman tree,* which is a binary tree (see Chapter 9, *Trees*) organized to generate *Huffman codes*. Huffman codes are the codes assigned to symbols in the data to achieve compression. However, Huffman codes result in compression that only approximates the data's entropy because, as you may have noticed in Table 14-1, the entropies of symbols often come out to be fractions of bits. Since the actual number of bits used in Huffman codes cannot be fractions in practice, some codes end up with slightly too many bits to be optimal.

Figure 14-1 illustrates the process of building a Huffman tree from the data in Table 14-1. Building a Huffman tree proceeds from its leaf nodes upward. To begin, we place each symbol and its frequency in its own tree (see Figure 14-1, step 1). Next, we merge the two trees whose root nodes have the smallest frequencies and store the sum of the frequencies in the new tree's root (see Figure 14-1, step 2). This process is then repeated until we end up with a single tree (see Figure 14-1, step 5), which is the final Huffman tree. The root node of this tree contains the total number of symbols in the data, and its leaf nodes contain the original symbols and their frequencies. Because Huffman coding continually seeks out the two trees that appear to be the best to merge at any given time, it is a good example of a greedy algorithm (see Chapter 1, *Introduction*).

Compressing and Uncompressing Data

Building a Huffman tree is part of both compressing and uncompressing data. To compress data using a Huffman tree, given a specific symbol, we start at the root of the tree and trace a path to the symbol's leaf. As we descend along the path, whenever we move to the left, we append 0 to the current code; whenever we move to the right, we append 1. Thus, in Figure 14-1, step 6, to determine the Huffman code for "U" we move to the right (1), then to the left (10), and then to the right again (101). The Huffman codes for all of the symbols in the figure are:

U = 101, V = 01, W = 100, X = 00, Y = 11

To uncompress data using a Huffman tree, we read the compressed data bit by bit. Starting at the tree's root, whenever we encounter 0 in the data, we move to the left in the tree; whenever we encounter 1, we move to the right. Once we reach a leaf node, we generate the symbol it contains, move back to the root of the tree, and repeat the process until we exhaust the compressed data. Uncompressing data in this manner is possible because Huffman codes are *prefix free*, which means that no code is a prefix of any other. This ensures that once we encounter a sequence of bits that matches a code, there is no ambiguity as to the symbol it represents. For example, notice that 01, the code for "V," is not a prefix of any of the other codes. Thus, as soon as we encounter 01 in the compressed data, we know that the code must represent "V."

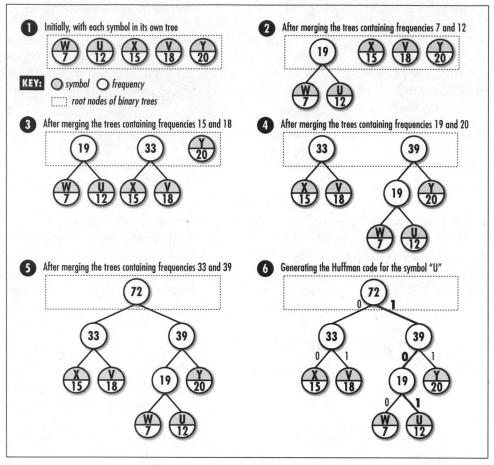

Figure 14-1. Building a Huffman tree from the symbols and frequencies in Table 14-1

Effectiveness of Huffman Coding

To determine the reduced size of data compressed using Huffman coding, we calculate the product of each symbol's frequency times the number of bits in its Huffman code, then add them together. Thus, to calculate the compressed size of the data presented in Table 14-1 and Figure 14-1, we have:

$$(12)(3) + (18)(2) + (7)(3) + (15)(2) + (20)(2) = 163 \text{ bits}$$

Assuming that without compression each of the 72 symbols would be represented with 8 bits, for a total data size of 576 bits, we end up with the following compression ratio:

$$1 - (163/576) = 71.7\%$$

Once again, considering the fact that we cannot take into account fractional bits in Huffman coding, in many cases this value will not be quite as good as the data's entropy suggests, although in this case it is very close.

In general, Huffman coding is not the most effective form of compression, but it runs fast both when compressing and uncompressing data. Generally, the most time-consuming aspect of compressing data with Huffman coding is the need to scan the data twice: once to gather frequencies, and a second time actually to compress the data. Uncompressing the data is particularly efficient because decoding the sequence of bits for each symbol requires only a brief scan of the Huffman tree, which is bounded.

Interface for Huffman Coding

huffman_compress

```
int huffman_compress(const unsigned char *original, unsigned char **compressed,
   int size);
```

Return Value   Number of bytes in the compressed data if compressing the data is successful, or −1 otherwise.

Description   Uses Huffman coding to compress a buffer of data specified by *original*, which contains *size* bytes. The compressed data is written to a buffer returned in *compressed* Since the amount of storage required in *compressed* is unknown to the caller, *huffman_compress* dynamically allocates the necessary storage using *malloc*. It is the responsibility of the caller to free this storage using *free* when it is no longer needed.

Complexity $O(n)$, where n is the number of symbols in the original data.

huffman_uncompress

```
int huffman_uncompress(const unsigned char *compressed, unsigned
   char **original);
```

Return Value   Number of bytes in the restored data if uncompressing the data is successful, or −1 otherwise.

Description   Uses Huffman coding to uncompress a buffer of data specified by *compressed* It is assumed that the buffer contains data previously compressed with *huffman_compress*. The restored data is written to a buffer returned in *original*. Since the amount of storage required in *original* may not be known to the caller, *huffman_uncompress* dynamically allocates the necessary storage using *malloc*. It is the responsibility of the caller to free this storage using *free* when it is no longer needed.

Complexity $O(n)$, where n is the number of symbols in the original data.

Implementation and Analysis of Huffman Coding

With Huffman coding, we try to compress data by encoding symbols as Huffman codes generated in a Huffman tree. To uncompress the data, we rebuild the Huffman tree used in the compression process and convert each code back to the symbol it represents. In the implementation presented here, a symbol in the original data is one byte.

huffman_compress

The *huffman_compress* operation (see Example 14-3) compresses data using Huffman coding. It begins by scanning the data to determine the frequency of each symbol. The frequencies are placed in an array, **freqs**. After scanning the data, the frequencies are scaled so that each can be represented in a single byte. This is done by determining the maximum number of times any symbol occurs in the data and adjusting the other frequencies accordingly. Since symbols that do not occur in the data should be the only ones with frequencies of 0, we perform a simple test to ensure that any nonzero frequencies that scale to less than 1 end up being set to 1 instead of 0.

Once we have determined and scaled the frequencies, we call *build_tree* to build the Huffman tree. The *build_tree* function begins by inserting into a priority queue one binary tree for each symbol occurring at least once in the data. Nodes in the trees are **HuffNode** structures (see Example 14-1). This structure consists of two members: **symbol** is a symbol from the data (used only in leaf nodes), and **freq** is a frequency. Each tree initially contains only a single node, which stores one symbol and its scaled frequency as recorded and scaled in the **freqs** array.

To build the Huffman tree, we use a loop to perform **size** – 1 merges of the trees within the priority queue. On each iteration, we call *pqueue_extract* twice to extract the two binary trees whose root nodes have the smallest frequencies. We then sum the frequencies, merge the trees into a new one, store the sum of the frequencies in the new tree's root, and insert the new tree back into the priority queue. We continue this process until, after **size** – 1 iterations, the only tree remaining in the priority queue is the final Huffman tree.

Using the Huffman tree built in the previous step, we call *build_table* to build a table of the Huffman codes assigned to every symbol. Each entry in the table is a **HuffCode** structure. This structure consists of three members: **used** is a flag set to 1 or 0 indicating whether the entry has a code stored in it, **code** is the Huffman code stored in the entry, and **size** is the number of bits the code contains. Each code is a short integer because it can be proven (although this is not shown here) that when all frequencies are scaled to fit within one byte, no code will be longer than 16 bits.

We build the table by traversing the Huffman tree using a preorder traversal (see Chapter 9). In each activation of *build_table*, *code* keeps track of the current Huffman code being generated, and *size* maintains the number of bits it contains. As we traverse the tree, each time we move to the left, we append 0 to the code; each time we move to the right, we append 1. Once we encounter a leaf node, we store the Huffman code into the table of codes at the appropriate entry. As we store each code, we call the network function *htons* as a convenient way to ensure that the code is stored in big-endian format. This is the format required when we actually generate the compressed data in the next step as well as when we uncompress it.

While generating the compressed data, we use *ipos* to keep track of the current byte being processed in the original data, and *opos* to keep track of the current bit we are writing to the buffer of compressed data. To begin, we write a header that will help to rebuild the Huffman tree in *huffman_uncompress*. The header contains a four-byte value for the number of symbols about to be encoded followed by the scaled frequencies of all 256 possible symbols, including those that are 0. Finally, to encode the data, we read one symbol at a time, look up its Huffman code in the table, and write each code to the compressed buffer. We allocate space for each byte in the compressed buffer as we need it.

The runtime complexity of *huffman_compress* is $O(n)$, where n is the number of symbols in the original data. Only two parts of the algorithm depend on the size of the data: the part in which we determine the frequency of each symbol, and the part in which we read the data so we can compress it. Each of these runs in $O(n)$ time. The time to build the Huffman tree does not affect the complexity of *huffman_compress* because the running time of this process depends only on the number of different symbols in the data, which in this implementation is a constant, 256.

huffman_uncompress

The *huffman_uncompress* operation (see Example 14-3) uncompresses data compressed with *huffman_compress*. This operation begins by reading the header prepended to the compressed data. Recall that the first four bytes of the header contain the number of encoded symbols. This value is stored in *size*. The next 256 bytes contain the scaled frequencies for all symbols.

Using the information stored in the header, we call *build_tree* to rebuild the Huffman tree used in compressing the data. Once we have rebuilt the tree, the next step is to generate the buffer of restored data. To do this, we read the compressed data bit by bit. Starting at the root of the Huffman tree, whenever we encounter a bit that is 0 in the data, we move to the left; whenever we encounter a bit that is 1, we move to the right. Once we encounter a leaf node, we have obtained the Huffman code for a symbol. The decoded symbol resides in the leaf. Thus, we write this symbol to the buffer of restored data. After writing the symbol, we reposition ourselves at the root of the tree and repeat the process. We use *ipos* to keep track of the current bit being processed in the compressed data, and *opos* to keep track of the current byte we are writing to the buffer of restored data. Once *opos* reaches *size*, we have regenerated all of the symbols from the original data.

The runtime complexity of *huffman_uncompress* is $O(n)$, where n is the number of symbols in the original data. This is because for each of the n symbols we decode, the number of levels we must descend in the Huffman tree is a bounded constant that depends on the number of different symbols in the data: in this implementation, 256. The time to build the Huffman tree does not affect the complexity of *huffman_uncompress* because this process depends only on the number of different symbols in the data.

Example 14-3. Implementation of Huffman Coding

```
/*****************************************************************************
*                                                                           *
*  ---------------------------- huffman.c ----------------------------      *
*                                                                           *
*****************************************************************************/

#include <limits.h>
#include <netinet/in.h>
#include <stdlib.h>
#include <string.h>

#include "bit.h"
#include "bitree.h"
#include "compress.h"
#include "pqueue.h"

/*****************************************************************************
*                                                                           *
*  -------------------------- compare_freq --------------------------       *
*                                                                           *
*****************************************************************************/

static int compare_freq(const void *tree1, const void *tree2) {

HuffNode          *root1,
                  *root2;
```

Example 14-3. Implementation of Huffman Coding (continued)

```
/***************************************************************************
*                                                                         *
*  Compare the frequencies stored in the root nodes of two binary trees.  *
*                                                                         *
***************************************************************************/

root1 = (HuffNode *)bitree_data(bitree_root((const BiTree *)tree1));
root2 = (HuffNode *)bitree_data(bitree_root((const BiTree *)tree2));

if (root1->freq < root2->freq)
   return 1;
else if (root1->freq > root2->freq)
   return -1;
else
   return 0;

}

/***************************************************************************
*                                                                         *
*  --------------------------- destroy_tree ---------------------------   *
*                                                                         *
***************************************************************************/

static void destroy_tree(void *tree) {

/***************************************************************************
*                                                                         *
*  Destroy and free one binary tree from the priority queue of trees.     *
*                                                                         *
***************************************************************************/

bitree_destroy(tree);
free(tree);

return;

}

/***************************************************************************
*                                                                         *
*  --------------------------- build_tree ---------------------------     *
*                                                                         *
***************************************************************************/

static int build_tree(int *freqs, BiTree **tree) {

BiTree           *init,
                 *merge,
                 *left,
                 *right;

PQueue           pqueue;
```

Example 14-3. Implementation of Huffman Coding (continued)

```
HuffNode            *data;

int                 size,
                    c;

/***************************************************************************
*                                                                         *
*  Initialize the priority queue of binary trees.                         *
*                                                                         *
***************************************************************************/

*tree = NULL;

pqueue_init(&pqueue, compare_freq, destroy_tree);

for (c = 0; c <= UCHAR_MAX; c++) {

   if (freqs[c] != 0) {

      /***************************************************************************
      *                                                                         *
      *  Set up a binary tree for the current symbol and its frequency.         *
      *                                                                         *
      ***************************************************************************/

      if ((init = (BiTree *)malloc(sizeof(BiTree))) == NULL) {

         pqueue_destroy(&pqueue);
         return -1;

      }

      bitree_init(init, free);

      if ((data = (HuffNode *)malloc(sizeof(HuffNode))) == NULL) {

         pqueue_destroy(&pqueue);
         return -1;

      }

      data->symbol = c;
      data->freq = freqs[c];

      if (bitree_ins_left(init, NULL, data) != 0) {

         free(data);
         bitree_destroy(init);
         free(init);
         pqueue_destroy(&pqueue);
         return -1;

      }
```

Example 14-3. Implementation of Huffman Coding (continued)

```
    /********************************************************************
    *                                                                  *
    *  Insert the binary tree into the priority queue.                 *
    *                                                                  *
    ********************************************************************/

    if (pqueue_insert(&pqueue, init) != 0) {

        bitree_destroy(init);
        free(init);
        pqueue_destroy(&pqueue);
        return -1;

    }

}

}

/********************************************************************
*                                                                  *
*  Build a Huffman tree by merging trees in the priority queue.    *
*                                                                  *
********************************************************************/

size = pqueue_size(&pqueue);

for (c = 1; c <= size - 1; c++) {

    /********************************************************************
    *                                                                  *
    *  Allocate storage for the next merged tree.                      *
    *                                                                  *
    ********************************************************************/

    if ((merge = (BiTree *)malloc(sizeof(BiTree))) == NULL) {

        pqueue_destroy(&pqueue);
        return -1;

    }

    /********************************************************************
    *                                                                  *
    *  Extract the two trees whose root nodes have the smallest frequencies.  *
    *                                                                  *
    ********************************************************************/

    if (pqueue_extract(&pqueue, (void **)&left) != 0) {

        pqueue_destroy(&pqueue);
        free(merge);
        return -1;
```

Example 14-3. Implementation of Huffman Coding (continued)

```
    }

    if (pqueue_extract(&pqueue, (void **)&right) != 0) {

        pqueue_destroy(&pqueue);
        free(merge);
        return -1;

    }

    /*************************************************************************
    *                                                                       *
    *  Allocate storage for the data in the root node of the merged tree.   *
    *                                                                       *
    *************************************************************************/

    if ((data = (HuffNode *)malloc(sizeof(HuffNode))) == NULL) {

        pqueue_destroy(&pqueue);
        free(merge);
        return -1;

    }

    memset(data, 0, sizeof(HuffNode));

    /*************************************************************************
    *                                                                       *
    *  Sum the frequencies in the root nodes of the trees being merged.     *
    *                                                                       *
    *************************************************************************/

    data->freq = ((HuffNode *)bitree_data(bitree_root(left)))->freq +
        ((HuffNode *)bitree_data(bitree_root(right)))->freq;

    /*************************************************************************
    *                                                                       *
    *  Merge the two trees.                                                 *
    *                                                                       *
    *************************************************************************/

    if (bitree_merge(merge, left, right, data) != 0) {

        pqueue_destroy(&pqueue);
        free(merge);
        return -1;

    }

    /*************************************************************************
    *                                                                       *
    *  Insert the merged tree into the priority queue and free the others.  *
    *                                                                       *
    *************************************************************************/
```

Example 14-3. Implementation of Huffman Coding (continued)

```
   if (pqueue_insert(&pqueue, merge) != 0) {

      pqueue_destroy(&pqueue);
      bitree_destroy(merge);
      free(merge);
      return -1;

   }

   free(left);
   free(right);

}

/*****************************************************************************
*                                                                           *
*  The last tree in the priority queue is the Huffman tree.                 *
*                                                                           *
*****************************************************************************/

if (pqueue_extract(&pqueue, (void **)tree) != 0) {

   pqueue_destroy(&pqueue);
   return -1;

   }

else {

   pqueue_destroy(&pqueue);

}

return 0;

}

/*****************************************************************************
*                                                                           *
*  ---------------------------- build_table ----------------------------    *
*                                                                           *
*****************************************************************************/

static void build_table(BiTreeNode *node, unsigned short code, unsigned char
   size, HuffCode *table) {

if (!bitree_is_eob(node)) {

   if (!bitree_is_eob(bitree_left(node))) {
```

Example 14-3. Implementation of Huffman Coding (continued)

```
/*************************************************************************
*                                                                       *
*  Move to the left and append 0 to the current code.                   *
*                                                                       *
*************************************************************************/

build_table(bitree_left(node), code << 1, size + 1, table);

}

if (!bitree_is_eob(bitree_right(node))) {

/*************************************************************************
*                                                                       *
*  Move to the right and append 1 to the current code.                  *
*                                                                       *
*************************************************************************/

build_table(bitree_right(node), (code << 1) | 0x0001, size + 1, table);

}

if (bitree_is_eob(bitree_left(node))&&bitree_is_eob(bitree_right(node))) {

/*************************************************************************
*                                                                       *
*  Ensure that the current code is in big-endian format.                *
*                                                                       *
*************************************************************************/

code = htons(code);

/*************************************************************************
*                                                                       *
*  Assign the current code to the symbol in the leaf node.              *
*                                                                       *
*************************************************************************/

table[((HuffNode *)bitree_data(node))->symbol].used = 1;
table[((HuffNode *)bitree_data(node))->symbol].code = code;
table[((HuffNode *)bitree_data(node))->symbol].size = size;

}

}

return;

}
```

Example 14-3. Implementation of Huffman Coding (continued)

```
/***************************************************************************
*                                                                         *
*  ------------------------- huffman_compress -------------------------   *
*                                                                         *
***************************************************************************/

int huffman_compress(const unsigned char *original, unsigned char
   **compressed, int size) {

BiTree            *tree;
HuffCode          table[UCHAR_MAX + 1];

int               freqs[UCHAR_MAX + 1],
                  max,
                  scale,
                  hsize,
                  ipos,
                  opos,
                  cpos,
                  c,
                  i;

unsigned char     *comp,
                  *temp;

/***************************************************************************
*                                                                         *
*  Initially, there is no buffer of compressed data.                      *
*                                                                         *
***************************************************************************/

*compressed = NULL;

/***************************************************************************
*                                                                         *
*  Get the frequency of each symbol in the original data.                 *
*                                                                         *
***************************************************************************/

for (c = 0; c <= UCHAR_MAX; c++)
   freqs[c] = 0;

ipos = 0;

if (size > 0) {

   while (ipos < size) {

      freqs[original[ipos]]++;
      ipos++;

   }

}
```

Example 14-3. Implementation of Huffman Coding (continued)

```
/*****************************************************************************
*                                                                           *
*  Scale the frequencies to fit into one byte.                              *
*                                                                           *
*****************************************************************************/

max = UCHAR_MAX;

for (c = 0; c <= UCHAR_MAX; c++) {

   if (freqs[c] > max)
      max = freqs[c];

}

for (c = 0; c <= UCHAR_MAX; c++) {

   scale = (int)(freqs[c] / ((double)max / (double)UCHAR_MAX));

   if (scale == 0 && freqs[c] != 0)
      freqs[c] = 1;
   else
      freqs[c] = scale;

}

/*****************************************************************************
*                                                                           *
*  Build the Huffman tree and table of codes for the data.                  *
*                                                                           *
*****************************************************************************/

if (build_tree(freqs, &tree) != 0)
   return -1;

for (c = 0; c <= UCHAR_MAX; c++)
   memset(&table[c], 0, sizeof(HuffCode));

build_table(bitree_root(tree), 0x0000, 0, table);

bitree_destroy(tree);
free(tree);

/*****************************************************************************
*                                                                           *
*  Write the header information.                                            *
*                                                                           *
*****************************************************************************/

hsize = sizeof(int) + (UCHAR_MAX + 1);

if ((comp = (unsigned char *)malloc(hsize)) == NULL)
   return -1;
```

Example 14-3. Implementation of Huffman Coding (continued)

```
memcpy(comp, &size, sizeof(int));

for (c = 0; c <= UCHAR_MAX; c++)
   comp[sizeof(int) + c] = (unsigned char)freqs[c];

/***************************************************************************
*                                                                         *
*  Compress the data.                                                     *
*                                                                         *
***************************************************************************/

ipos = 0;
opos = hsize * 8;

while (ipos < size) {

   /***********************************************************************
   *                                                                     *
   *  Get the next symbol in the original data.                          *
   *                                                                     *
   ***********************************************************************/

   c = original[ipos];

   /***********************************************************************
   *                                                                     *
   *  Write the code for the symbol to the buffer of compressed data.    *
   *                                                                     *
   ***********************************************************************/

   for (i = 0; i < table[c].size; i++) {

      if (opos % 8 == 0) {

         /*****************************************************************
         *                                                               *
         *  Allocate another byte for the buffer of compressed data.     *
         *                                                               *
         *****************************************************************/

         if ((temp = (unsigned char *)realloc(comp,(opos / 8) + 1)) == NULL) {

            free(comp);
            return -1;

         }

         comp = temp;

      }
```

Example 14-3. Implementation of Huffman Coding (continued)

```
        cpos = (sizeof(short) * 8) - table[c].size + i;
        bit_set(comp, opos, bit_get((unsigned char *)&table[c].code, cpos));
        opos++;

    }

    ipos++;

}

/***************************************************************************
*                                                                         *
*  Point to the buffer of compressed data.                                *
*                                                                         *
***************************************************************************/

*compressed = comp;

/***************************************************************************
*                                                                         *
*  Return the number of bytes in the compressed data.                     *
*                                                                         *
***************************************************************************/

return ((opos - 1) / 8) + 1;

}

/***************************************************************************
*                                                                         *
*  ------------------------ huffman_uncompress -------------------------  *
*                                                                         *
***************************************************************************/

int huffman_uncompress(const unsigned char *compressed, unsigned char
   **original) {

BiTree            *tree;
BiTreeNode        *node;

int               freqs[UCHAR_MAX + 1],
                  hsize,
                  size,
                  ipos,
                  opos,
                  state,
                  c;

unsigned char     *orig,
                  *temp;
```

Example 14-3. Implementation of Huffman Coding (continued)

```c
/*****************************************************************************
*                                                                           *
*  Initially there is no buffer of original data.                          *
*                                                                           *
*****************************************************************************/

*original = orig = NULL;

/*****************************************************************************
*                                                                           *
*  Get the header information from the buffer of compressed data.           *
*                                                                           *
*****************************************************************************/

hsize = sizeof(int) + (UCHAR_MAX + 1);
memcpy(&size, compressed, sizeof(int));

for (c = 0; c <= UCHAR_MAX; c++)
   freqs[c] = compressed[sizeof(int) + c];

/*****************************************************************************
*                                                                           *
*  Rebuild the Huffman tree used previously to compress the data.           *
*                                                                           *
*****************************************************************************/

if (build_tree(freqs, &tree) != 0)
   return -1;

/*****************************************************************************
*                                                                           *
*  Uncompress the data.                                                     *
*                                                                           *
*****************************************************************************/

ipos = hsize * 8;
opos = 0;
node = bitree_root(tree);

while (opos < size) {

   /*****************************************************************************
   *                                                                           *
   *  Get the next bit in the compressed data.                                 *
   *                                                                           *
   *****************************************************************************/

   state = bit_get(compressed, ipos);
   ipos++;

   if (state == 0) {
```

Example 14-3. Implementation of Huffman Coding (continued)

```
/*************************************************************************
*                                                                       *
*  Move to the left.                                                    *
*                                                                       *
*************************************************************************/

if (bitree_is_eob(node) || bitree_is_eob(bitree_left(node))) {

   bitree_destroy(tree);
   free(tree);
   return -1;

   }

else
   node = bitree_left(node);

}

else {

   /*************************************************************************
   *                                                                       *
   *  Move to the right.                                                   *
   *                                                                       *
   *************************************************************************/

   if (bitree_is_eob(node) || bitree_is_eob(bitree_right(node))) {

      bitree_destroy(tree);
      free(tree);
      return -1;

      }

   else
      node = bitree_right(node);

}

if (bitree_is_eob(bitree_left(node))&&bitree_is_eob(bitree_right(node))) {

   /*************************************************************************
   *                                                                       *
   *  Write the symbol in the leaf node to the buffer of original data.   *
   *                                                                       *
   *************************************************************************/

   if (opos > 0) {

      if ((temp = (unsigned char *)realloc(orig, opos + 1)) == NULL) {
```

Example 14-3. Implementation of Huffman Coding (continued)

```
            bitree_destroy(tree);
            free(tree);
            free(orig);
            return -1;

         }

      orig = temp;

      }

   else {

      if ((orig = (unsigned char *)malloc(1)) == NULL) {

         bitree_destroy(tree);
         free(tree);
         return -1;

      }

   }

   orig[opos] = ((HuffNode *)bitree_data(node))->symbol;
   opos++;

   /**************************************************************************
   *                                                                        *
   *  Move back to the top of the tree.                                     *
   *                                                                        *
   **************************************************************************/

   node = bitree_root(tree);

   }

}

bitree_destroy(tree);
free(tree);

/*****************************************************************************
*                                                                           *
*  Point to the buffer of original data.                                    *
*                                                                           *
*****************************************************************************/

*original = orig;

/*****************************************************************************
*                                                                           *
*  Return the number of bytes in the original data.                         *
*                                                                           *
*****************************************************************************/
```

Example 14-3. Implementation of Huffman Coding (continued)

```
return opos;

}
```

Huffman Coding Example:
Optimized Networking

Transferring data across a network can be a time-consuming process, particularly across slow wide-area networks. One approach to managing this problem is to compress the data before sending it and then uncompress it when it is received. Although sometimes the time spent compressing and uncompressing data may not be worth the savings in time across the network, in many network applications this cost is well justified. This example presents two functions, *send_comp* and *recv_comp* (see Example 14-4), that send and receive data in a compressed format.

The *send_comp* function sends data by first compressing it and then calling the standard socket function *send*. To send the data, *send_comp* requires four arguments: **s** is a socket descriptor for which a connection has already been established, **data** is the buffer of data to send, **size** is the size of the data, and **flags** is the normal **flags** argument passed to *send*. To begin the sending process, we compress the data in **data** by calling *huffman_compress*. Next, we send the size of the compressed data, as returned by *huffman_compress*, so that space can be allocated on the receiving end. This is part of a simple protocol we establish with the receiver. Last, we send the compressed data itself and then free it as the interface to *huffman_compress* suggests.

The *recv_comp* function uses the standard socket function *recv* to receive data sent by *send_comp*. To receive the data, *recv_comp* requires four arguments: **s** is a socket descriptor for which a connection has already been established, **data** is a pointer that *recv_comp* will set to the uncompressed data, **size** is the size of the data as set by *recv_comp* on return, and **flags** is the normal **flags** argument passed to *recv*. To begin the receiving process, we receive the size of the data and allocate a buffer. Next, we receive the compressed data and call *huffman_uncompress* to uncompress it. Since *huffman_uncompress* dynamically allocates space for the uncompressed data using *malloc*, and *recv_comp* returns this pointer, it is the responsibility of the caller of *recv_comp* to call *free* when the data is no longer needed. Last, we free the buffer we allocated to receive the data.

The runtime complexities of *send_comp* and *recv_comp* are both $O(n)$, where n is the number of symbols sent or received. These complexities are both $O(n)$ because the two functions call *huffman_compress* and *huffman_uncompress* respectively, which are both $O(n)$ operations.

Example 14-4. Implementation of Functions for Optimized Networking

```c
/*****************************************************************************
*                                                                           *
* --------------------------- transfer.c ----------------------------       *
*                                                                           *
*****************************************************************************/

#include <sys/types.h>
#include <sys/socket.h>

#include "compress.h"
#include "transfer.h"

/*****************************************************************************
*                                                                           *
* --------------------------- send_comp -----------------------------       *
*                                                                           *
*****************************************************************************/

int send_comp(int s, const unsigned char *data, int size, int flags) {

unsigned char      *compressed;

int                size_comp;

/*****************************************************************************
*                                                                           *
*  Compress the data.                                                       *
*                                                                           *
*****************************************************************************/

if ((size_comp = huffman_compress(data, &compressed, size)) < 0)
   return -1;

/*****************************************************************************
*                                                                           *
*  Send the compressed data preceded by its size.                          *
*                                                                           *
*****************************************************************************/

if (send(s, (char *)&size_comp, sizeof(int), flags) != sizeof(int))
   return -1;

if (send(s, (char *)compressed, size_comp, flags) != size_comp)
   return -1;

/*****************************************************************************
*                                                                           *
*  Free the buffer of compressed data.                                     *
*                                                                           *
*****************************************************************************/

free(compressed);
```

Example 14-4. Implementation of Functions for Optimized Networking (continued)

```
return 0;

}

/***************************************************************************
*                                                                         *
*  ----------------------------- recv_comp -----------------------------  *
*                                                                         *
***************************************************************************/

int recv_comp(int s, unsigned char **data, int *size, int flags) {

unsigned char       *compressed;

int                 size_comp;

/***************************************************************************
*                                                                         *
*  Receive the compressed data preceded by its size.                      *
*                                                                         *
***************************************************************************/

if (recv(s, (char *)&size_comp, sizeof(int), flags) != sizeof(int))
   return -1;

if ((compressed = (unsigned char *)malloc(size_comp)) == NULL)
   return -1;

if (recv(s, (char *)compressed, size_comp, flags) != size_comp) {

   free(compressed);
   return -1;

}

/***************************************************************************
*                                                                         *
*  Uncompress the data.                                                   *
*                                                                         *
***************************************************************************/

if ((*size = huffman_uncompress(compressed, data)) < 0)
   return -1;

/***************************************************************************
*                                                                         *
*  Free the buffer of compressed data.                                    *
*                                                                         *
***************************************************************************/

free(compressed);
```

Example 14-4. Implementation of Functions for Optimized Networking (continued)

```
return 0;

}
```

Description of LZ77

LZ77 (Lempel-Ziv-1977) is a simple but surprisingly effective form of data compression that takes an entirely different approach from Huffman coding. LZ77 is a dictionary-based method, which means that it tries to compress data by encoding long strings of symbols, called *phrases*, as small tokens that reference entries in a dictionary. Compression is achieved by using relatively small tokens in place of longer phrases that appear several times in the data. As with Huffman coding, it is important to realize that a symbol is not necessarily a character of text: a symbol can be any amount of data we choose, but it is often one byte's worth.

Maintaining a Dictionary of Phrases

Different dictionary-based compression methods use various approaches for maintaining their dictionaries. LZ77 uses a *look-ahead buffer* and a *sliding window*. LZ77 works by first loading a portion of the data into the look-ahead buffer. To understand how the look-ahead buffer stores phrases that effectively form a dictionary, picture the buffer as a sequence of symbols $s_1, \ldots, s_n$, and P_b as a set of phrases constructed from the symbols. From the sequence $s_1, \ldots, s_n$, we form n phrases, defined as:

$$P_b = \{(s_1), (s_1, s_2), \ldots, (s_1, \ldots, s_n)\}$$

This means that if the look-ahead buffer contains the symbols (A, B, D), for example, the phrases in the buffer are {(A), (A, B), (A, B, D)}. Once data passes through the look-ahead buffer, it moves into the sliding window and becomes part of the dictionary. To understand how phrases are represented in the sliding window, consider the window to be a sequence of symbols $s_1, \ldots, s_m$, and P_w to be a set of phrases constructed from these symbols. From the sequence $s_1, \ldots, s_m$, we form the set of phrases as follows:

$$P_w = \{p_1, p_2, \ldots, p_m\}, \text{ where } p_i = \{(s_i), (s_i, s_{i+1}), \ldots, (s_i, s_{i+1}, \ldots, s_m)\}$$

Thus, if the sliding window contains the symbols (A, B, C), the phrases in the window, and hence the dictionary, are {(A), (A, B), (A, B, C), (B), (B, C), (C)}. The main idea behind LZ77 is to look continually for the longest phrase in the look-ahead buffer that matches a phrase currently in the dictionary. In the look-ahead buffer and sliding window just described, the longest match is the two-symbol phrase (A, B).

Compressing and Uncompressing Data

As we compress the data, two situations can exist between the look-ahead buffer and the sliding window at any given moment: there can either be a phrase of some length that matches, or there may be no match at all. When there is at least one match, we encode the longest match as a *phrase token*. Phrase tokens contain three pieces of information: the offset in the sliding window where the match begins, the number of symbols in the match, and the first symbol in the look-ahead buffer after the match. When there is no match, we encode the unmatched symbol as a *symbol token*. Symbol tokens simply contain the unmatched symbol itself, so no compression is accomplished. In fact, we will see that symbol tokens actually contain one bit more than the symbol itself, so a slight expansion occurs.

Once the appropriate token has been generated that encodes some number of symbols *n*, we shift *n* symbols out one end of the sliding window and replace them at the other end by the same number of symbols shifted out of the look-ahead buffer. Next, we refill the look-ahead buffer. This process keeps the sliding window up to date with only the most recent phrases. The exact number of phrases maintained by the sliding window and look-ahead buffer depends on their size.

Figure 14-2 illustrates the compression of a string using LZ77 with a sliding window of 8 bytes and a look-ahead buffer of 4 bytes. In practice, typical sizes for sliding windows are around 4K (4096 bytes). Look-ahead buffers are generally less than 100 bytes.

We uncompress data by decoding tokens and keeping the sliding window updated in a manner analogous to the compression process. As we decode each token, we copy the symbols that the token encodes into the sliding window. Whenever we encounter a phrase token, we consult the appropriate offset in the sliding window and look up the phrase of the specified length that we find there. Whenever we encounter a symbol token, we generate the single symbol stored in the token itself. Figure 14-3 illustrates uncompressing the data compressed in Figure 14-2.

Effectiveness of LZ77

The amount of compression achieved using LZ77 depends on a number of factors, such as the size chosen for the sliding window, the size set for the look-ahead buffer, and the entropy of the data itself. Ultimately, the amount of compression depends on the number of phrases we are able to match and their lengths. In most cases, LZ77 results in better compression ratios than Huffman coding, but compression times are considerably slower.

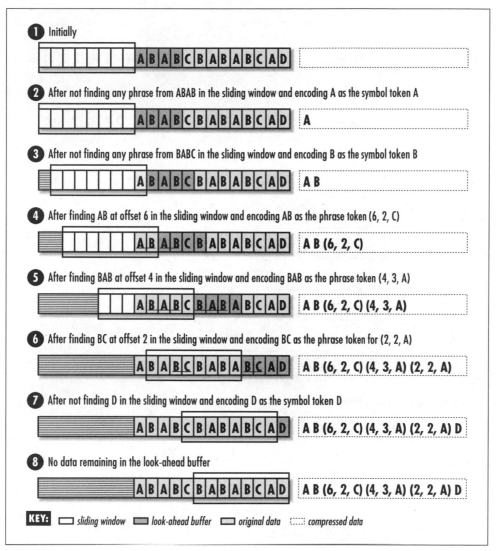

Figure 14-2. Compressing the string ABABCBABABCAD using LZ77

Compressing data with LZ77 is time-consuming because we spend a lot of time searching the sliding window for matching phrases. However, in general, uncompressing data with LZ77 is even faster than ucompressing data with Huffman coding. Uncompressing data with LZ77 is fast because each token tells us exactly where to read symbols out of the buffer. In fact, we end up reading from the sliding window only as many symbols as in the original data.

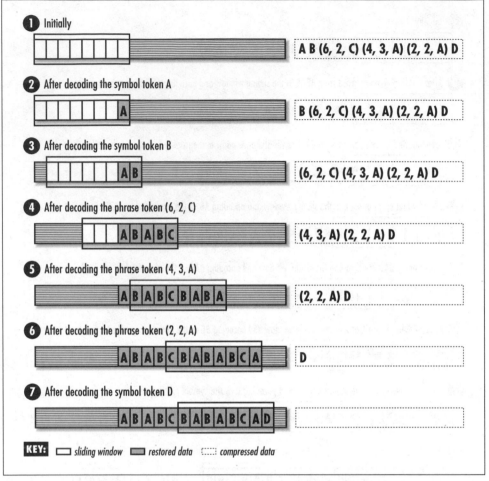

Figure 14-3. Uncompressing the string compressed in Figure 14-2 using LZ77

Interface for LZ77

lz77_compress

```
int lz77_compress(const unsigned char *original, unsigned char **compressed,
   int size);
```

Return Value   Number of bytes in the compressed data if compressing the data is successful, or −1 otherwise.

Description   Uses LZ77 to compress a buffer of data specified by *original*, which contains *size* bytes. The compressed data is written to a buffer returned in *compressed.* Since the amount of storage required in *compressed* is unknown to the caller, *lz77_compress* dynamically allocates the necessary storage using *malloc*. It is the responsibility of the caller to free this storage using *free* when it is no longer needed.

Complexity $O(n)$, where n is the number of symbols in the original data.

lz77_uncompress

```
int lz77_uncompress(const unsigned char *compressed, unsigned char **original);
```

Return Value   Number of bytes in the restored data if uncompressing the data is successful, or −1 otherwise.

Description   Uses LZ77 to uncompress a buffer of data specified by *compressed*. It is assumed that the buffer contains data previously compressed with *lz77_compress*. The restored data is written to a buffer returned in *original*. Since the amount of storage required in *original* may not be known to the caller, *lz77_uncompress* dynamically allocates the necessary storage using *malloc*. It is the responsibility of the caller to free this storage using *free* when it is no longer needed.

Complexity $O(n)$, where n is the number of symbols in the original data.

Implementation and Analysis of LZ77

With LZ77, we try to compress data by encoding phrases from a look-ahead buffer as tokens referencing phrases in a sliding window. To uncompress the data, we decode each token into the phrase or symbol it represents. To do this, we must continually update the sliding window so that at any one time it looks the same as it did during the compression process. In the implementation presented here, a symbol in the original data is one byte.

lz77_compress

The *lz77_compress* operation (see Example 14-5) compresses data using LZ77. It begins by writing the number of symbols in the data to the buffer of compressed data and initializing the sliding window and look-ahead buffer. The look-ahead buffer is then loaded with symbols.

Compression takes place inside of a loop that iterates until there are no more symbols to process. We use *ipos* to keep track of the current byte being processed in the original data, and *opos* to keep track of the current bit we are writing to the buffer of compressed data. During each iteration of the loop, we call *compare_win* to determine the longest phrase in the look-ahead buffer that matches one in the sliding window. The *compare_win* function returns the length of the longest match.

When a match is found, *compare_win* sets `offset` to the position of the match in the sliding window and *next* to the symbol in the look-ahead buffer immediately after the match. In this case, we write a phrase token to the compressed data (see Figure 14-4a). Phrase tokens in the implementation presented here require 12 bits for offsets because the size of the sliding window is 4K (4096 bytes). Phrase tokens require 5 bits for lengths because no match will exceed the length of the look-ahead buffer, which is 32 bytes. If a match is not found, *compare_win* returns 0 and sets *next* to the unmatched symbol at the start of the look-ahead buffer. In this case, we write a symbol token to the compressed data (see Figure 14-4b). Whether we write a phrase or symbol token to the compressed data, before actually writing the token, we call the network function *htonl* as a convenient way to ensure that the token is in big-endian format. This is the format required when we actually store the compressed data as well as when we uncompress it.

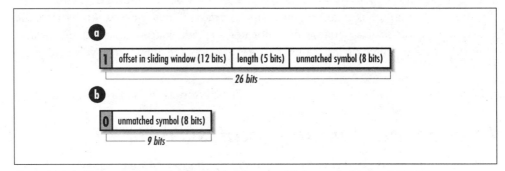

Figure 14-4. The structure of (a) a phrase token and (b) a symbol token in LZ77

Once we write the appropriate token to the buffer of compressed data, we adjust the sliding window and the look-ahead buffer. To move the data through the sliding window, we shift data in from the right side of the window and out the left. We do the same for the look-ahead buffer. The number of bytes we move is equal to the number of symbols we encode in the token.

The runtime complexity of *lz77_compress* is $O(n)$, where n is the number of symbols in the original data. This is because for each of the n/c tokens in which the data is encoded, where $1/c$ is a constant factor that represents how efficiently symbols are encoded in phrase tokens, we call *compare_win* once. The *compare_win* function runs in a constant amount of time because the size of the sliding window and look-ahead buffer are both constant. However, these constants are large and contribute significantly to the overall running time of *lz77_compress*. Thus, the runtime complexity of *lz77_compress* is $O(n)$, but its actual running time is greatly affected by constant factors. This explains the generally slow performance of LZ77 when compressing data.

lz77_uncompress

The *lz77_uncompress* operation (see Figure 14-4) uncompresses data previously compressed with *lz77_compress*. It begins by reading the number of symbols in the compressed data and initializing the sliding window and look-ahead buffer.

Uncompressing the data takes place inside a loop that iterates until there are no more symbols to process. We use *ipos* to keep track of the current bit being processed in the compressed data, and *opos* to keep track of the current byte we are writing to the buffer of restored data. During each iteration of the loop, we first read one bit from the compressed data to determine the type of token we are about to decode.

At the start of interpreting a token, if the first bit read is 1, we have encountered a phrase token. Thus, we read each of its members, look up the phrase in the sliding window, and write the phrase to the buffer of restored data. As we look up each phrase, we call the network function *ntohl* to ensure that the byte ordering of its offset and length in the window are correct for the system. This step is required because both the offset and length are in big-endian format when read from the compressed data. The look-ahead buffer is used as a convenient place to temporarily store the data before copying it into the sliding window. Last, we write the unmatched symbol encoded by the token. If the first bit read for the token is 0, we have encountered a symbol token. In this case, we write the one unmatched symbol it encodes to the buffer of restored data.

Once we write the decoded data to the buffer of restored data, we adjust the sliding window. To move the data through the sliding window, we shift the decoded data in from the right side of the window and out the left. The number of bytes we move is equal to the number of symbols we decode from the token.

The runtime complexity of *lz77_uncompress* is $O(n)$, where n is the number of symbols in the original data. This is because for each of the n/c tokens in which the data is encoded, where $1/c$ is a constant factor that represents how efficiently symbols are encoded in phrase tokens, we perform the constant-time operation of copying symbols from the sliding window to the buffer of restored data. Thus, the runtime complexity of *lz77_uncompress* is $O(n)$. Its lack of significant constant factors explains its generally superior performance to *huffman_uncompress* and its vast improvement in actual running time over *lz77_compress*.

Example 14-5. Implementation of LZ77

Example 14-5. Implementation of LZ77 (continued)

```c
#include <netinet/in.h>
#include <stdlib.h>
#include <string.h>

#include "bit.h"
#include "compress.h"

/*****************************************************************************
*                                                                            *
* ---------------------------- compare_win ----------------------------      *
*                                                                            *
*****************************************************************************/

static int compare_win(const unsigned char *window, const unsigned char
   *buffer, int *offset, unsigned char *next) {

int               match,
                  longest,
                  i,
                  j,
                  k;

/*****************************************************************************
*                                                                            *
*  Initialize the offset, although it is valid only once a match is found.   *
*                                                                            *
*****************************************************************************/

*offset = 0;

/*****************************************************************************
*                                                                            *
*  If no match is found, prepare to return 0 and the next symbol in the      *
*  look-ahead buffer.                                                        *
*                                                                            *
*****************************************************************************/

longest = 0;
*next = buffer[0];

/*****************************************************************************
*                                                                            *
*  Look for the best match in the look-ahead buffer and sliding window.      *
*                                                                            *
*****************************************************************************/

for (k = 0; k < LZ77_WINDOW_SIZE; k++) {

   i = k;
   j = 0;
   match = 0;
```

Example 14-5. Implementation of LZ77 (continued)

```
/***************************************************************************
 *                                                                         *
 *  Determine how many symbols match in the sliding window at offset k.    *
 *                                                                         *
 ***************************************************************************/

while (i < LZ77_WINDOW_SIZE && j < LZ77_BUFFER_SIZE - 1) {

    if (window[i] != buffer[j])
       break;

    match++;
    i++;
    j++;

}

/***************************************************************************
 *                                                                         *
 *  Keep track of the offset, length, and next symbol for the best match.  *
 *                                                                         *
 ***************************************************************************/

if (match > longest) {

    *offset = k;
    longest = match;
    *next = buffer[j];

}

}

return longest;

}

/***************************************************************************
 *                                                                         *
 *  -------------------------- lz77_compress ---------------------------   *
 *                                                                         *
 ***************************************************************************/

int lz77_compress(const unsigned char *original, unsigned char **compressed,
   int size) {

unsigned char      window[LZ77_WINDOW_SIZE],
                   buffer[LZ77_BUFFER_SIZE],
                   *comp,
                   *temp,
                   next;
```

Example 14-5. Implementation of LZ77 (continued)

```
int              offset,
                 length,
                 remaining,
                 hsize,
                 ipos,
                 opos,
                 tpos,
                 i;

/*****************************************************************************
*                                                                           *
*  Make the pointer to the compressed data not valid until later.           *
*                                                                           *
*****************************************************************************/

*compressed = NULL;

/*****************************************************************************
*                                                                           *
*  Write the header information.                                            *
*                                                                           *
*****************************************************************************/

hsize = sizeof(int);

if ((comp = (unsigned char *)malloc(hsize)) == NULL)
   return -1;

memcpy(comp, &size, sizeof(int));

/*****************************************************************************
*                                                                           *
*  Initialize the sliding window and the look-ahead buffer.                 *
*                                                                           *
*****************************************************************************/

memset(window, 0, LZ77_WINDOW_SIZE);
memset(buffer, 0, LZ77_BUFFER_SIZE);

/*****************************************************************************
*                                                                           *
*  Load the look-ahead buffer.                                              *
*                                                                           *
*****************************************************************************/

ipos = 0;

for (i = 0; i < LZ77_BUFFER_SIZE && ipos < size; i++) {

   buffer[i] = original[ipos];
   ipos++;

}
```

Example 14-5. Implementation of LZ77 (continued)

```
/****************************************************************************
*                                                                          *
*  Compress the data.                                                      *
*                                                                          *
****************************************************************************/

opos = hsize * 8;
remaining = size;

while (remaining > 0) {

   if ((length = compare_win(window, buffer, &offset, &next)) != 0) {

      /*********************************************************************
      *                                                                   *
      *  Encode a phrase token.                                           *
      *                                                                   *
      *********************************************************************/

      token = 0x00000001 << (LZ77_PHRASE_BITS - 1);

      /*********************************************************************
      *                                                                   *
      *  Set the offset where the match was found in the sliding window.  *
      *                                                                   *
      *********************************************************************/

      token = token | (offset << (LZ77_PHRASE_BITS - LZ77_TYPE_BITS -
         LZ77_WINOFF_BITS));

      /*********************************************************************
      *                                                                   *
      *  Set the length of the match.                                     *
      *                                                                   *
      *********************************************************************/

      token = token | (length << (LZ77_PHRASE_BITS - LZ77_TYPE_BITS -
         LZ77_WINOFF_BITS - LZ77_BUFLEN_BITS));

      /*********************************************************************
      *                                                                   *
      *  Set the next symbol in the look-ahead buffer after the match.    *
      *                                                                   *
      *********************************************************************/

      token = token | next;

      /*********************************************************************
      *                                                                   *
      *  Set the number of bits in the token.                             *
      *                                                                   *
      *********************************************************************/
```

Example 14-5. Implementation of LZ77 (continued)

```
      tbits = LZ77_PHRASE_BITS;

   }

   else {

      /**********************************************************************
      *                                                                     *
      *  Encode a symbol token.                                             *
      *                                                                     *
      **********************************************************************/

      token = 0x00000000;

      /**********************************************************************
      *                                                                     *
      *  Set the unmatched symbol.                                          *
      *                                                                     *
      **********************************************************************/

      token = token | next;

      /**********************************************************************
      *                                                                     *
      *  Set the number of bits in the token.                              *
      *                                                                     *
      **********************************************************************/

      tbits = LZ77_SYMBOL_BITS;

   }

   /**********************************************************************
   *                                                                     *
   *  Ensure that the token is in big-endian format.                    *
   *                                                                     *
   **********************************************************************/

   token = htonl(token);

   /**********************************************************************
   *                                                                     *
   *  Write the token to the buffer of compressed data.                 *
   *                                                                     *
   **********************************************************************/

   for (i = 0; i < tbits; i++) {

      if (opos % 8 == 0) {
```

Example 14-5. Implementation of LZ77 (continued)

```
           /*****************************************************************
            *                                                              *
            *  Allocate another byte for the buffer of compressed data.    *
            *                                                              * .
            *****************************************************************/

           if ((temp = (unsigned char *)realloc(comp,(opos / 8) + 1)) == NULL) {

              free(comp);
              return -1;

           }

           comp = temp;

        }

        tpos = (sizeof(unsigned long) * 8) - tbits + i;
        bit_set(comp, opos, bit_get((unsigned char *)&token, tpos));
        opos++;

     }

/*****************************************************************
 *                                                              *
 *  Adjust the phrase length to account for the unmatched symbol. *
 *                                                              *
 *****************************************************************/

length++;

/*****************************************************************
 *                                                              *
 *  Copy data from the look-ahead buffer to the sliding window. *
 *                                                              *
 *****************************************************************/

memmove(&window[0], &window[length], LZ77_WINDOW_SIZE - length);
memmove(&window[LZ77_WINDOW_SIZE - length], &buffer[0], length);

/*****************************************************************
 *                                                              *
 *  Read more data into the look-ahead buffer.                  *
 *                                                              *
 *****************************************************************/

memmove(&buffer[0], &buffer[length], LZ77_BUFFER_SIZE - length);

for (i = LZ77_BUFFER_SIZE - length; i<LZ77_BUFFER_SIZE && ipos<size; i++) {

   buffer[i] = original[ipos];
   ipos++;

}
```

Example 14-5. Implementation of LZ77 (continued)

```
/*****************************************************************************
*                                                                           *
*  Adjust the total symbols remaining by the phrase length.                 *
*                                                                           *
*****************************************************************************/

remaining = remaining - length;

}

/*****************************************************************************
*                                                                           *
*  Point to the buffer of compressed data.                                  *
*                                                                           *
*****************************************************************************/

*compressed = comp;

/*****************************************************************************
*                                                                           *
*  Return the number of bytes in the compressed data.                       *
*                                                                           *
*****************************************************************************/

return ((opos - 1) / 8) + 1;

}

/*****************************************************************************
*                                                                           *
*  --------------------------- lz77_uncompress ---------------------------  *
*                                                                           *
*****************************************************************************/

int lz77_uncompress(const unsigned char *compressed, unsigned char
   **original) {

unsigned char        window[LZ77_WINDOW_SIZE],
                     buffer[LZ77_BUFFER_SIZE],
                     *orig,
                     *temp,
                     next;

int                  offset,
                     length,
                     remaining,
                     hsize,
                     size,
                     ipos,
                     opos,
                     tpos,
                     state,
                     i;
```

Example 14-5. Implementation of LZ77 (continued)

```
/***************************************************************************
 *                                                                         *
 *  Make the pointer to the original data not valid until later.           *
 *                                                                         *
 ***************************************************************************/

*original = orig = NULL;

/***************************************************************************
 *                                                                         *
 *  Get the header information.                                            *
 *                                                                         *
 ***************************************************************************/

hsize = sizeof(int);
memcpy(&size, compressed, sizeof(int));

/***************************************************************************
 *                                                                         *
 *  Initialize the sliding window and the look-ahead buffer.               *
 *                                                                         *
 ***************************************************************************/

memset(window, 0, LZ77_WINDOW_SIZE);
memset(buffer, 0, LZ77_BUFFER_SIZE);

/***************************************************************************
 *                                                                         *
 *  Uncompress the data.                                                   *
 *                                                                         *
 ***************************************************************************/

ipos = hsize * 8;
opos = 0;
remaining = size;

while (remaining > 0) {

   /***************************************************************************
    *                                                                         *
    *  Get the next bit in the compressed data.                               *
    *                                                                         *
    ***************************************************************************/

   state = bit_get(compressed, ipos);
   ipos++;

   if (state == 1) {
```

Example 14-5. Implementation of LZ77 (continued)

```
/*****************************************************************************
*                                                                           *
*  Handle processing a phrase token.                                        *
*                                                                           *
*****************************************************************************/

memset(&offset, 0, sizeof(int));

for (i = 0; i < LZ77_WINOFF_BITS; i++) {

   tpos = (sizeof(int) * 8) - LZ77_WINOFF_BITS + i;
   bit_set((unsigned char *)&offset, tpos, bit_get(compressed, ipos));
   ipos++;

}

memset(&length, 0, sizeof(int));

for (i = 0; i < LZ77_BUFLEN_BITS; i++) {

   tpos = (sizeof(int) * 8) - LZ77_BUFLEN_BITS + i;
   bit_set((unsigned char *)&length, tpos, bit_get(compressed, ipos));
   ipos++;

}

next = 0x00;

for (i = 0; i < LZ77_NEXT_BITS; i++) {

   tpos = (sizeof(unsigned char) * 8) - LZ77_NEXT_BITS + i;
   bit_set((unsigned char *)&next, tpos, bit_get(compressed, ipos));
   ipos++;

}

/*****************************************************************************
*                                                                           *
*  Ensure that the offset and length have the correct byte ordering         *
*  for the system.                                                          *
*                                                                           *
*****************************************************************************/

offset = ntohl(offset);
length = ntohl(length);

/*****************************************************************************
*                                                                           *
*  Write the phrase from the window to the buffer of original data.         *
*                                                                           *
*****************************************************************************/

i = 0;
```

Example 14-5. Implementation of LZ77 (continued)

```
if (opos > 0) {

   if ((temp = (unsigned char *)realloc(orig, opos+length+1)) == NULL) {

      free(orig);
      return -1;

   }

   orig = temp;

}

else {

   if ((orig = (unsigned char *)malloc(length + 1)) == NULL)
      return -1;

}

while (i < length && remaining > 0) {

   orig[opos] = window[offset + i];
   opos++;

   /*****************************************************************
   *                                                               *
   *  Record each symbol in the look-ahead buffer until ready to   *
   *  update the sliding window.                                   *
   *                                                               *
   *****************************************************************/

   buffer[i] = window[offset + i];
   i++;

   /*****************************************************************
   *                                                               *
   *  Adjust the total symbols remaining to account for each symbol *
   *  consumed.                                                    *
   *                                                               *
   *****************************************************************/

   remaining--;

}

/*****************************************************************
*                                                               *
*  Write the unmatched symbol to the buffer of original data.   *
*                                                               *
*****************************************************************/
```

Example 14-5. Implementation of LZ77 (continued)

```
    if (remaining > 0) {

       orig[opos] = next;
       opos++;

       /********************************************************************
       *                                                                  *
       *  Also record this symbol in the look-ahead buffer.               *
       *                                                                  *
       ********************************************************************/

       buffer[i] = next;

       /********************************************************************
       *                                                                  *
       *  Adjust the total symbols remaining to account for the unmatched *
       *  symbol.                                                         *
       *                                                                  *
       ********************************************************************/

       remaining--;

    }

    /********************************************************************
    *                                                                  *
    *  Adjust the phrase length to account for the unmatched symbol.   *
    *                                                                  *
    ********************************************************************/

    length++;

    }

 else {

    /********************************************************************
    *                                                                  *
    *  Handle processing a symbol token.                               *
    *                                                                  *
    ********************************************************************/

    next = 0x00;

    for (i = 0; i < LZ77_NEXT_BITS; i++) {

       tpos = (sizeof(unsigned char) * 8) - LZ77_NEXT_BITS + i;
       bit_set((unsigned char *)&next, tpos, bit_get(compressed, ipos));
       ipos++;

    }
```

Example 14-5. Implementation of LZ77 (continued)

```
/***********************************************************************
*                                                                     *
*  Write the symbol to the buffer of original data.                   *
*                                                                     *
***********************************************************************/

if (opos > 0) {

   if ((temp = (unsigned char *)realloc(orig, opos + 1)) == NULL) {

      free(orig);
      return -1;

   }

   orig = temp;

}

else {

   if ((orig = (unsigned char *)malloc(1)) == NULL)
      return -1;

}

orig[opos] = next;
opos++;

/***********************************************************************
*                                                                     *
*  Record the symbol in the look-ahead buffer until ready to update   *
*  the sliding window.                                                *
*                                                                     *
***********************************************************************/

if (remaining > 0)
   buffer[0] = next;

/***********************************************************************
*                                                                     *
*  Adjust the total symbols remaining to account for the unmatched    *
*  symbol.                                                            *
*                                                                     *
***********************************************************************/

remaining--;

/***********************************************************************
*                                                                     *
*  Set the phrase length to account for the unmatched symbol.         *
*                                                                     *
***********************************************************************/
```

Example 14-5. Implementation of LZ77 (continued)

```
    length = 1;

}

/*****************************************************************************
*                                                                           *
*  Copy the look-ahead buffer into the sliding window.                      *
*                                                                           *
*****************************************************************************/

memmove(&window[0], &window[length], LZ77_WINDOW_SIZE - length);
memmove(&window[LZ77_WINDOW_SIZE - length], &buffer[0], length);

}

/*****************************************************************************
*                                                                           *
*  Point to the buffer of original data.                                    *
*                                                                           *
*****************************************************************************/

*original = orig;

/*****************************************************************************
*                                                                           *
*  Return the number of bytes in the original data.                         *
*                                                                           *
*****************************************************************************/

return opos;

}
```

Questions and Answers

Q: *There are certain cases where compressing data may generate poor results. When might we encounter this with Huffman coding?*

A: Effective compression with Huffman coding depends on symbols occurring in the data at varying frequencies. If all possible symbols occur at nearly the same frequency, poor compression results. Huffman coding also performs poorly when used to compress small amounts of data. In this case, the space required by the table in the header negates the compression achieved in the data. Fortunately, these limitations are not normally a problem because the symbols in most data are not uniformly distributed, and we are usually not interested in compressing small amounts of data.

Q: *Just as with Huffman coding, there are certain cases in which LZ77 achieves poor compression. What are some of these cases?*

A: Effective compression with LZ77 depends on being able to encode many sequences of symbols using phrase tokens. If we generate a large number of symbol tokens and only a few phrase tokens representing predominantly short phrases, poor compression results. An excessive number of symbol tokens may even cause the compressed data to be larger than the original data itself. This occurs when the sliding window is made too small to take advantage of recurring phrases effectively.

Q: *In the implementation of both Huffman coding and LZ77 presented in this chapter, the end of the compressed data is recognized by counting symbols. This means we must store a symbol count along with the compressed data itself. What is another approach to recognizing the end of the data? What impact would this have on each implementation?*

A: When uncompressing data, we must have a way to determine exactly where the data ends. An alternative to storing a symbol count is to encode a special end-of-data symbol. In the implementations in this chapter, this would mean encoding 257 symbols instead of 256. To account for this with Huffman coding, we need only make the symbol member of the *HuffNode* structure a short integer instead of an unsigned character. Thus, the size of the compressed data is affected very little. On the other hand, in the implementation of LZ77, without substantial changes to the way we interpret tokens, we would need to store an extra bit with each token to represent the 257 possible symbols. Thus, the size of the compressed data would increase, making this method less effective than simply counting symbols.

Q: *With LZ77, what factors must be balanced in selecting the size of the sliding window? What factors must be balanced in selecting the size of the look-ahead buffer?*

A: Recall that the implementation of LZ77 presented in this chapter used a sliding window 4K (4096 bytes) in size and a look-ahead buffer of 32 bytes, which are common choices. The size of the sliding window determines how far back in the data we search for matching phrases. Generally, it is a good idea to search quite far back to allow a good opportunity for matches. However, we must balance this against the time it takes to search through the sliding window. Also, we must balance this against the space penalty of using more bits for offsets in phrase tokens. The size we choose for the look-ahead buffer determines the maximum length of phrases we can match. If the data has many long phrases that are duplicated, choosing a buffer size that is too small results in multiple phrase tokens where we might otherwise get just one. However, we must balance this against the space penalty of using more bits for lengths in phrase tokens.

Q: *In Huffman coding, how might we decrease the space required by the header at the front of compressed data? Are there any problems associated with this?*

A: Recall that in the implementation of Huffman coding presented in this chapter a header was prepended to the compressed data. This header contained a table of 256 entries, one entry for each possible symbol. If several symbols have frequencies of 0, this is somewhat wasteful. For example, when compressing ASCII text, many symbols are not used, so their frequencies are 0. A better approach to storing the table in this case is to use *count runs*. A count run consists of the value of a starting symbol c followed by a length l. It tells us that the next l entries in the table will be entries for the symbols c, $c + 1$, ..., $c + l - 1$. In many cases, this reduces the size of the table. However, when the table is nearly full to begin with, it actually increases the table size slightly.

Q: *One of the most costly aspects of LZ77 is scanning the sliding window for matching phrases. How can we improve the performance of this?*

A: LZ77 looks for matching phrases by comparing portions of the sliding window to portions of the look-ahead buffer essentially symbol by symbol. A more effective approach is to replace the sliding window with some type of data structure for efficient searching. For example, we might use a hash table (see Chapter 8, *Hash Tables*) or a binary search tree (see Chapter 9) to store phrases encountered earlier. In fact, this is the approach employed by several more efficient variations of LZ77 (see the related topics at the end of the chapter).

Q: *Considering the performance differences and compression normally achieved by Huffman coding and LZ77, when might we use one over the other?*

A: LZ77 generally results in better compression than Huffman coding, but with a significant performance penalty during the compression process. One situation in which this might not pose a problem is the distribution of large software packages. LZ77 works well here because the data only needs to be compressed once (at the production facility), and clients benefit from the considerably faster operation of uncompressing the data. On the other hand, suppose we are sending large amounts of data across a network interactively and would like to compress it before each transmission. In this case, for every transmission, we must compress data on one end of the connection and uncompress it on the other. Therefore, it is best to use Huffman coding. We may not achieve as much compression as with LZ77, but compressing and uncompressing together are faster.

Related Topics

Lossy compression

A broad class of approaches to data compression that do not produce an exact copy of the original data when the data is uncompressed. Lossy compression is useful primarily in graphics and sound applications, where a certain loss of accuracy is acceptable in exchange for greater compression ratios, provided the degradation is carefully managed.

Statistical modeling

The engine behind data compression methods based on minimum redundancy coding. This chapter worked with an *order-0 model*, which simply determines the probability of any one symbol occurring in the data. Higher-order models look at the probabilities associated with combinations of symbols to get a more accurate determination of the data's entropy. For example, if we encounter the symbol "Q" in text data, in many languages the probability is high that the next symbol will be "U." Higher-order models take considerations like this into account.

Shannon-Fano coding

The first form of minimum redundancy coding. Interestingly, it came about in the 1940s, apart from computers, as a result of experiments in information theory during World War II. Shannon-Fano coding is similar to Huffman coding, but it builds its tree from the top down instead of the bottom up.

Adaptive Huffman coding

A variation of Huffman coding that does not require that the table of frequencies be passed along with the compressed data. Instead, a statistical model is *adapted* as the data is compressed and uncompressed. The main benefit of adaptive Huffman coding is in using statistical models greater than the order-0 model described earlier. An order-0 model does not require much space, but the substantial space requirements of higher-order models make prepending a table impractical.

Arithmetic coding

A popular method of data compression that addresses the inaccuracies in Huffman coding brought about by entropies that are fractional values of bits. Arithmetic coding avoids this by encoding data as a single, very long floating-point value that can be uniquely decoded.

LZ78 (Lempel-Ziv-1978) and LZW (Lempel-Ziv-Welch) compression

Variations of LZ77 that use more effective methods than a sliding window to keep track of previously seen phrases. Generally, each method uses some type of data structure for efficient searching, such as a hash table (Chapter 8), a binary tree (see Chapter 9), or a trie (see the related topics at the end of Chapter 9), and applies some unique approach to optimizing the process of encoding and decoding phrases.

15

Data Encryption

Data encryption, or *cryptography*, is the science of secrecy. Its purpose is to keep information in the hands of those who should have it and out of the hands of those who should not. Considering such a statement, it probably comes as no surprise that cryptographic algorithms, called *ciphers*, historically have had profound political, social, and ethical implications. Data encryption, like data compression, is another product of *information theory*, an area of mathematics that addresses various ways to manage and manipulate information. Data encryption entails two processes: in one process we *encipher* recognizable data, called *plaintext*, into an unrecognizable form, called *ciphertext*; in a second process we *decipher* the ciphertext back into the original plaintext. The main idea behind a cipher is that the transformation from ciphertext to plaintext should be easy if we are allowed to read the data, yet impractical if we are not.

Ciphers use a special piece of information, called a *key*, for security. Once a key has been used to encipher some data, only someone who knows the correct key can decipher it. In fact, a fundamental characteristic of any good cipher is that its security revolves around a key, or even several. Furthermore, the security of a good cipher does not rely on keeping the cipher's algorithm a secret. This idea is similar to the security offered by a safe: even though everyone knows how a safe works, we cannot get inside without the combination that opens the door.

One way to classify modern ciphers is by how they use keys. In this regard, a cipher is either *symmetric* or *asymmetric*. In symmetric ciphers, the same key is used both to encipher and decipher data. Consequently, anyone who knows the key is able to encipher data as well as decipher it. In asymmetric ciphers, usually called *public-key ciphers*, the key used to encipher data is different from the key used to decipher it. The key used to encipher data is called the *public key*; the key used to decipher data is called the *private key*. The public and private keys work together so that only a specific private key deciphers the data enciphered using a specific public key. Thus, just because a party knows how to encipher data does not necessarily mean it can decipher data; it must possess the correct private key. Example 15-1 is a header for the ciphers presented in this chapter.

This chapter covers:

DES (Data Encryption Standard)

One of the most popular symmetric ciphers. Today it is considered reasonably secure, but increases in the speed of computers continue to make this method less and less secure over time. DES is considered a very efficient cipher, even when implemented in software.

RSA (Rivest-Shamir-Adleman)

One of the most popular public-key ciphers. RSA is considered very secure. However, it is much slower than DES. Thus, it is often used to encrypt smaller amounts of data, such as keys for other types of encryption, and digital signatures.

Some applications of data encryption are:

Digital cash

A means of conducting financial transactions so that they can be authenticated but not traced. Transactions must be authenticated so that parties involved in the transaction are not cheated. They must be untraceable so that the privacy of each party is protected. In practice, these are difficult requirements to support in tandem without special protocols.

Authentication servers

Servers charged with solving the problem of two parties at different ends of a network talking securely. The parties must be able to exchange keys while at the same time being sure that they are talking to one another rather than an impostor. Authentication servers accomplish this with a variety of protocols that rely on encryption.

Electronic mail

Data in email is typically sent across insecure channels, such as the Internet. The widespread use and abuse of the Internet has made encrypting sensitive electronic messages especially important in recent years.

National security

Matters of diplomacy and national defense. Historically, encryption has played a critical role in a great number of military matters. Embassies constantly transmit and receive sensitive diplomatic information, which must be kept secret, using encryption. National security has long been the main argument cited by the U.S. government for treating encryption technologies much like munitions, with strict controls over exportation.

Digital signatures

A method of validating to whom data really belongs, much like signing a name to a document. One method of creating a digital signature is with a public-key cipher. To do this, party *A* enciphers some data using its private key and sends it to another party *B*. *B*, thinking the data is from *A*, validates this by deciphering the data with *A*'s public key. If this deciphers the data, the data must be from *A*.

Computerized elections

A futuristic concept in which voting must be secure. Secure voting has several interesting requirements, many of which require varying degrees of secrecy. For example, no one should be able to determine for whom someone else voted, but it may be important to know whether someone voted at all.

Smart cards

Small plastic cards containing miniature computers and small amounts of memory. Typically, smart cards are used for various forms of credit, such as in paying for phone calls, train rides, or postage stamps. Other smart cards provide access to computers and open doors to buildings. Smart cards use encryption because they can do potentially powerful things like alter bank accounts and provide access to secure environments.

Example 15-1. Header for Data Encryption

```
/*****************************************************************************
 *                                                                           *
 *  ----------------------------- encrypt.h -----------------------------    *
 *                                                                           *
 *****************************************************************************/

#ifndef ENCRYPT_H
#define ENCRYPT_H

/*****************************************************************************
 *                                                                           *
 *  In a secure implementation, Huge should be at least 400 decimal digits,  *
 *  instead of the 10 below (ULONG_MAX = 4294967295).                        *
 *                                                                           *
 *****************************************************************************/

typedef unsigned long Huge;

/*****************************************************************************
 *                                                                           *
 *  Define a structure for RSA public keys.                                  *
 *                                                                           *
 *****************************************************************************/

typedef struct RsaPubKey_ {
```

Example 15-1. Header for Data Encryption (continued)

```
Huge              e;
Huge              n;

} RsaPubKey;

/****************************************************************************
*                                                                          *
*  Define a structure for RSA private keys.                                *
*                                                                          *
****************************************************************************/

typedef struct RsaPriKey_ {

Huge              d;
Huge              n;

} RsaPriKey;

/****************************************************************************
*                                                                          *
*  ------------------------- Public Interface -------------------------    *
*                                                                          *
****************************************************************************/

void des_encipher(const unsigned char *plaintext, unsigned char *ciphertext,
   const unsigned char *key);

void des_decipher(const unsigned char *ciphertext, unsigned char *plaintext,
   const unsigned char *key);

void rsa_encipher(Huge plaintext, Huge *ciphertext, RsaPubKey pubkey);

void rsa_decipher(Huge ciphertext, Huge *plaintext, RsaPriKey prikey);

#endif
```

Description of DES

DES (Data Encryption Standard) is one of the most popular symmetric ciphers. DES is symmetric because it uses a single key both to encipher and decipher data. This is useful in situations in which parties that encipher data are allowed to decipher data as well. DES is a *block cipher*, which means that it processes data in fixed-size sections called *blocks*. The block size of DES is 64 bits. If the amount of data to be encrypted is not an even multiple of 64 bits, it is padded in some application-specific way.

DES is considered reasonably secure, and it runs fast, even in software. However, as with many ciphers, the security of DES has never been proven publicly. Nevertheless, the algorithm has stood up to years of cryptanalysis, which does suggest a certain level of confidence. Even so, as computing speeds continue to increase, DES becomes less and less secure. Today, its security is challenged regularly in contests that offer cash prizes to those who can crack messages encrypted with DES the fastest.

At its essence, the security of DES revolves around smoke and mirrors, or in cryptographic lingo, the principles of *confusion and diffusion*. The goal of confusion is to hide any relationship between the plaintext, the ciphertext, and the key. The goal of diffusion is to spread the effect of bits in the plaintext and the key over as much of the ciphertext as possible. Together, these make cryptanalysis very difficult.

With DES, we encipher a block of plaintext by performing a series of permutations and substitutions on it. Exactly how the permutations and substitutions affect the original plaintext is essentially a function of 16 subkeys, K_1, K_2, . . ., K_{16}, derived from a starting key, K_0, which is the key we provide. To encipher a block of plaintext, each subkey is applied to the data in order (K_1, K_2, . . ., K_{16}) using a series of operations repeated 16 times, once for each key. Each iteration is called a *round*. Deciphering a block of ciphertext uses the same process but with the keys applied in reverse order (K_{16}, K_{15}, . . ., K_1).

Computing Subkeys

The first step in DES is to compute the 16 subkeys from the initial key. Figure 15-1 illustrates this process. DES uses a key that is 56 bits; however, the key we provide is a 64-bit value. This is so that in hardware implementations every eighth bit can be used for parity checking. In software, the extra bits are simply ignored. To obtain the 56-bit key, we perform a *key transformation* as shown in Table 15-1. To interpret this table, read from left to right, top to bottom. Each position p in the table contains the position of the bit from the initial key that occupies position p in the transformed key. For example, using Table 15-1, bit 57 of the initial key becomes bit 1 of the transformed key, bit 49 becomes bit 2, and so forth. The convention is to number bits from left to right starting at 1.

Table 15-1. The Key Transformation in DES

57,	49,	41,	33,	25,	17,	9,	1,	58,	50,	42,	34,	26,	18,
10,	2,	59,	51,	43,	35,	27,	19,	11,	3,	60,	52,	44,	36,
63,	55,	47,	39,	31,	23,	15,	7,	62,	54,	46,	38,	30,	22,
14,	6,	61,	53,	45,	37,	29,	21,	13,	5,	28,	20,	12,	4

After transforming the key to 56 bits, we compute the subkeys. To do this, we first divide the 56-bit key into two 28-bit blocks. Next, for each subkey, we rotate both blocks an amount that depends on the round in which the subkey will be used

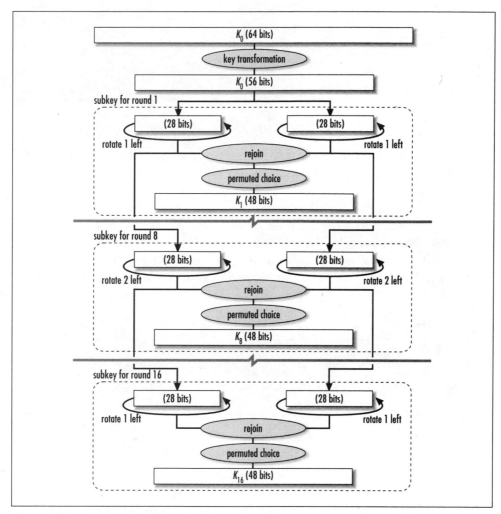

Figure 15-1. Computing subkeys in DES

(see Table 15-2), then rejoin the blocks. After this, we reduce the 56-bit subkey formed from the rejoined blocks to 48 bits by permuting it as shown in Table 15-3. (This table is read like Table 15-1.) Note that Table 15-3 contains two fewer columns because 8 bits are discarded. This permutation is called the *permuted choice*. This process is repeated once for each of the 16 subkeys. All together, the goal here is to ensure that we apply different bits from the initial key to the data in each round.

Table 15-2. The Number of Rotations per Round for DES Subkeys

Round	1	2	3	4	5	6	7	8	9	10	11	12	13	14	15	16
Rotations	1	1	2	2	2	2	2	2	1	2	2	2	2	2	2	1

Table 15-3. The Permuted Choice for DES Subkeys

14,	17,	11,	24,	1,	5,	3,	28,	15,	6,	21,	10,
23,	19,	12,	4,	26,	8,	16,	7,	27,	20,	13,	2,
41,	52,	31,	37,	47,	55,	30,	40,	51,	45,	33,	48,
44,	49,	39,	56,	34,	53,	46,	42,	50,	36,	29,	32

Enciphering and Deciphering Data Blocks

Once we have prepared the subkeys, we are ready to encipher or decipher data blocks. Figure 15-2 illustrates this process. We begin by permuting the 64-bit data block as shown in Table 15-4. (This table is read like Table 15-1.) This permutation is aptly named the *initial permutation*. It does not enhance the security of DES, but is believed to have been added to make data easier to load into DES chips before the advent of 16-bit and 32-bit buses. Although anachronistic, the permutation should still be performed in order to comply with the DES standard. After the initial permutation, the 64-bit data block is divided into two 32-bit blocks, L_0 and R_0.

Table 15-4. The Initial Permutation for Data Blocks in DES

58,	50,	42,	34,	26,	18,	10,	2,	60,	52,	44,	36,	28,	20,	12,	4,
62,	54,	46,	38,	30,	22,	14,	6,	64,	56,	48,	40,	32,	24,	16,	8,
57,	49,	41,	33,	25,	17,	9,	1,	59,	51,	43,	35,	27,	19,	11,	3,
61,	53,	45,	37,	29,	21,	13,	5,	63,	55,	47,	39,	31,	23,	15,	7

After completing the initial permutation, the data block moves through a series of operations that are repeated for 16 rounds. The goal of each round i is to compute L_i and R_i, which are used by the next round, until we finally end up with the data block $R_{16}L_{16}$. We begin each round with L_{i-1} and R_{i-1}, and expand R_{i-1} from 32 to 48 bits using the *expansion permutation*, as shown in Table 15-5. (This table is read like Table 15-1.) The primary purpose of this permutation is to create an *avalanche effect* when enciphering data. This makes one bit in the data block affect more bits in the step to follow, and thus produces diffusion. Once the expansion permutation is complete, we compute the XOR (denoted $\oplus$) of the 48-bit result and K_i, the subkey for the round. This produces an intermediate 48-bit result, which is called R_{int}. If we let E be the expansion permutation, the operations thus far in the round can be expressed as:

$$R_{int} = E(R_{i-1}) \oplus K_i$$

Next, R_{int} undergoes eight substitutions performed using eight separate *S-boxes*. Each S-box j takes a six-bit block from position $6j$ to $6j + 6$ in R_{int} and looks up a

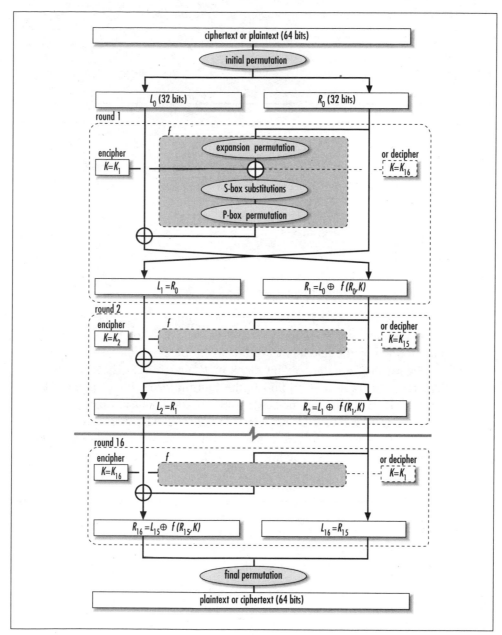

Figure 15-2. Enciphering and deciphering data blocks in DES

four-bit value for it in a table (see Table 15-6). This value is written to a buffer at position $4j$ (see Figure 15-3).

Table 15-5. The Expansion Permutation for Data Blocks in DES

32,	1,	2,	3,	4,	5,	4,	5,	6,	7,	8,	9,
8,	9,	10,	11,	12,	13,	12,	13,	14,	15,	16,	17,
16,	17,	18,	19,	20,	21,	20,	21,	22,	23,	24,	25,
24,	25,	26,	27,	28,	29,	28,	29,	30,	31,	32,	1

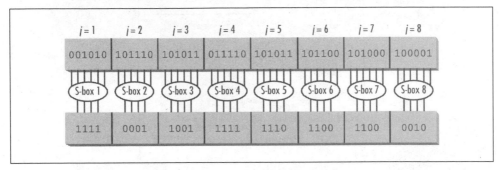

Figure 15-3. Eight S-box substitutions for a data block in DES

To read Table 15-6, find S-box j, look up the row number having the two-bit value formed by the first and last bit of the six-bit block, and find the column having the four-bit value formed by the middle bits of the six-bit block (both zero-indexed). For example, in Figure 15-2, the third six-bit block in R_{int} is 101011. Therefore, we consult the third S-box in Table 15-6 to find 9, the four-bit value found in row 11_2 = 3 and column 0101_2 = 5 (both zero-indexed). S-boxes add confusion to the data, and more than anything else give DES its security. Consequently, they have also long been the source of great scrutiny. Some groups even suspect that they may include a back door by their designers. No one knows, or at least admits to knowing.

Table 15-6. The S-Box Substitutions for Data Blocks in DES

S-Box 1															
14,	4,	13,	1,	2,	15,	11,	8,	3,	10,	6,	12,	5,	9,	0,	7,
0,	15,	7,	4,	14,	2,	13,	1,	10,	6,	12,	11,	9,	5,	3,	8,
4,	1,	14,	8,	13,	6,	2,	11,	15,	12,	9,	7,	3,	10,	5,	0,
15,	12,	8,	2,	4,	9,	1,	7,	5,	11,	3,	14,	10,	0,	6,	13
S-Box 2															
15,	1,	8,	14,	6,	11,	3,	4,	9,	7,	2,	13,	12,	0,	5,	10,
3,	13,	4,	7,	15,	2,	8,	14,	12,	0,	1,	10,	6,	9,	11,	5,
0,	14,	7,	11,	10,	4,	13,	1,	5,	8,	12,	6,	9,	3,	2,	15,
13,	8,	10,	1,	3,	15,	4,	2,	11,	6,	7,	12,	0,	5,	14,	9

Table 15-6. The S-Box Substitutions for Data Blocks in DES (continued)

S-Box 3

10,	0,	9,	14,	6,	3,	15,	5,	1,	13,	12,	7,	11,	4,	2,	8,
13,	7,	0,	9,	3,	4,	6,	10,	2,	8,	5,	14,	12,	11,	15,	1,
13,	6,	4,	9,	8,	15,	3,	0,	11,	1,	2,	12,	5,	10,	14,	7,
1,	10,	13,	0,	6,	9,	8,	7,	4,	15,	14,	3,	11,	5,	2,	12

S-Box 4

7,	13,	14,	3,	0,	6,	9,	10,	1,	2,	8,	5,	11,	12,	4,	15,
13,	8,	11,	5,	6,	15,	0,	3,	4,	7,	2,	12,	1,	10,	14,	9,
10,	6,	9,	0,	12,	11,	7,	13,	15,	1,	3,	14,	5,	2,	8,	4,
3,	15,	0,	6,	10,	1,	13,	8,	9,	4,	5,	11,	12,	7,	2,	14

S-Box 5

2,	12,	4,	1,	7,	10,	11,	6,	8,	5,	3,	15,	13,	0,	14,	9,
14,	11,	2,	12,	4,	7,	13,	1,	5,	0,	15,	10,	3,	9,	8,	6,
4,	2,	1,	11,	10,	13,	7,	8,	15,	9,	12,	5,	6,	3,	0,	14,
11,	8,	12,	7,	1,	14,	2,	13,	6,	15,	0,	9,	10,	4,	5,	3

S-Box 6

12,	1,	10,	15,	9,	2,	6,	8,	0,	13,	3,	4,	14,	7,	5,	11,
10,	15,	4,	2,	7,	12,	9,	5,	6,	1,	13,	14,	0,	11,	3,	8,
9,	14,	15,	5,	2,	8,	12,	3,	7,	0,	4,	10,	1,	13,	11,	6,
4,	3,	2,	12,	9,	5,	15,	10,	11,	14,	1,	7,	6,	0,	8,	13

S-Box 7

4,	11,	2,	14,	15,	0,	8,	13,	3,	12,	9,	7,	5,	10,	6,	1,
13,	0,	11,	7,	4,	9,	1,	10,	14,	3,	5,	12,	2,	15,	8,	6,
1,	4,	11,	13,	12,	3,	7,	14,	10,	15,	6,	8,	0,	5,	9,	2,
6,	11,	13,	8,	1,	4,	10,	7,	9,	5,	0,	15,	14,	2,	3,	12

S-Box 8

13,	2,	8,	4,	6,	15,	11,	1,	10,	9,	3,	14,	5,	0,	12,	7,
1,	15,	13,	8,	10,	3,	7,	4,	12,	5,	6,	11,	0,	14,	9,	2,
7,	11,	4,	1,	9,	12,	14,	2,	0,	6,	10,	13,	15,	3,	5,	8,
2,	1,	14,	7,	4,	10,	8,	13,	15,	12,	9,	0,	3,	5,	6,	11

Once we have completed the S-box substitutions, the result is a 32-bit value that we permute using a *P-box*, as shown in Table 15-7. (This table is read like Table 15-1.)

Table 15-7. The P-Box Permutation for Data Blocks in DES

16,	7,	20,	21,	29,	12,	28,	17,	1,	15,	23,	26,	5,	18,	31,	10,
2,	8,	24,	14,	32,	27,	3,	9,	19,	13,	30,	6,	22,	11,	4,	25

At this point, it is convenient to think of the operations in the round as a function, typically denoted as f. If b_j is the jth six-bit block of R_{int}, S_j is the jth S-box, and P is the P-box permutation, this function is defined as:

$$f = P(S_1(b_1), S_2(b_2), \ldots, S_8(b_8))$$

The last operation in each round is to compute the XOR of the 32-bit result of f and the original left block passed into the round, L_{i-1}. Once this is complete, we swap the left and right blocks and begin the next round. In the last round, however, we do not swap the left and right blocks. All together, the computations for L_i and R_i in each round can be concisely expressed as follows:

$$L_i = R_{i-1}$$
$$R_i = L_{i-1} \oplus f(R_{i-1}, K_i)$$

When all 16 rounds have been completed, we concatenate the final right block, R_{16}, with the final left block, L_{16}, to produce the 64-bit block $R_{16}L_{16}$. (Recall that the left and right blocks are not swapped in the final round; thus, we have the last right block on the left and the last left block on the right.) The final step is to permute $R_{16}L_{16}$ as shown in Table 15-8. This permutation is aptly named the *final permutation*. It simply undoes what the initial permutation did earlier. When enciphering data, the result is a 64-bit block of ciphertext; when deciphering data, it is the original 64-bit block of plaintext.

Table 15-8. The Final Permutation for Data Blocks in DES

40,	8,	48,	16,	56,	24,	64,	32,	39,	7,	47,	15,	55,	23,	63,	31,
38,	6,	46,	14,	54,	22,	62,	30,	37,	5,	45,	13,	53,	21,	61,	29,
36,	4,	44,	12,	52,	20,	60,	28,	35,	3,	43,	11,	51,	19,	59,	27,
34,	2,	42,	10,	50,	18,	58,	26,	33,	1,	41,	9,	49,	17,	57,	25

Interface for DES

des_cipher

```
void des_encipher(const unsigned char *plaintext, unsigned char *ciphertext,
    unsigned char *key);
```

Return Value   None.

Description   Uses DES to encipher one 64-bit block of plaintext specified by `plaintext`. Specify the 64-bit key in `key`. (Recall that every eighth bit of this key is ignored, resulting in a 56-bit key.) The 64-bit block of ciphertext is returned in `ciphertext`. It is the responsibility of the caller to manage the storage required in `ciphertext`. To encipher a large buffer of data, call *des_encipher* in accordance with a block cipher mode (see the example later in this chapter). For efficiency, *des_encipher* can reuse the subkeys computed during a previous call. To enable this, set *key* to NULL in subsequent calls.

Complexity $O(1)$

des_decipher

```
void des_decipher(const unsigned char *ciphertext, unsigned char *plaintext,
   unsigned char *key);
```

Return Value   None.

Description   Uses DES to decipher one 64-bit block of ciphertext specified by *ciphertext*. It is assumed that *ciphertext* contains data previously enciphered with *des_encipher*. Specify the 64-bit key in *key*. (Recall that every eighth bit of this key is ignored, resulting in a 56-bit key.) The 64-bit block of plaintext is returned in *plaintext*. It is the responsibility of the caller to manage the storage required in *plaintext*. To decipher a large buffer of data, call *des_decipher* in accordance with the block cipher mode used to encipher the data. For efficiency, *des_decipher* can reuse the subkeys computed during a previous call. To enable this, set *key* to NULL in subsequent calls.

Complexity $O(1)$

Implementation and Analysis of DES

Considering the amount of bit twiddling in DES, it probably comes as no surprise that it is frequently implemented in hardware. Even the figures and terminology associated with DES (diagrams drawn with boxes and lines, and terms such as *S-boxes* and *P-boxes*) tend to suggest a certain affinity toward hardware implementations. Nevertheless, software implementations have their place as well. In software, it is helpful to have several basic operations to assist in carrying out the numerous permutations, transformations, and substitutions that DES requires. For this purpose, the implementation presented here makes use of the bit operations presented in Chapter 14, *Data Compression*. The details of each permutation, transformation, and substitution are defined by the tables at the beginning of Example 15-2. These match the tables presented earlier in the text.

des_encipher

The *des_encipher* operation (see Example 15-2) enciphers a 64-bit block of plaintext using DES. Since one of the nice properties of DES is that the same process can be used both to encipher and decipher data, *des_encipher* simply calls *des_main*, which *des_decipher* calls as well. The *des_main* function uses its

direction argument to determine whether to encipher or decipher the data provided in *source*. The *direction* argument simply alters the order in which subkeys are applied. In the case of *des_encipher*, we set *direction* to *encipher*.

The *des_main* function begins by testing whether **key** is NULL. This allows a caller
of *des_encipher* to reuse subkeys computed during a previous call. To accommodate this, we declare the **subkeys** array as static. If **key** is not NULL, we compute
the subkeys. To do this, we perform the steps presented earlier. The key transformation is performed using the function *permute*, which permutes bits in a buffer
according to a specified table. Assuming that in each position *i* of a table there is
some value *p*, *permute* permutes the buffer passed to it by moving the bit at position *p* to position *i*.

To transform the key, we pass *permute* the table **Des_Transform** (the same table
as in Table 15-1). The necessary rotations are performed by calling the bit operation *bit_rot_left*. This operation rotates a buffer to the left by a specified number of
bits. To rotate the 28-bit subkey blocks the correct amount for each round, we
pass *bit_rot_left* the appropriate element from the table **Des_Rotations** (the same
table as in Table 15-2). We apply the permuted choice to each subkey by calling
permute and passing it the table **Des_Permuted** (the same table as in Table 15-3).

To encipher a data block, we begin by performing the initial permutation. To do
this, we call *permute* and pass it the table **Des_Initial** (the same table as in
Table 15-4). Next, we divide the data into two 32-bit blocks, **lblk** and **rblk**.
Recall that most of the work in enciphering data takes place in a series of operations repeated over 16 rounds. The majority of each round is spent computing the
value of the function *f*, which is stored in **fblk** as we go.

We begin each round by performing an expansion permutation on **rblk**. To do
this, we call *permute* and pass it the table **Des_Expansion** (the same table as in
Table 15-5). Next, we call the bit operation *bit_xor* to compute the XOR of the
expanded right block and the appropriate subkey. The subkey depends on the
round we are executing and whether we are enciphering or deciphering data.
Once the XOR has been computed, we perform a series of S-box substitutions on
the result. **Des_Sbox** defines the eight S-boxes used by DES (the same S-boxes as
in Table 15-6). We look up each substitution exactly as described earlier. That is,
for each six-bit block *j* in the current **fblk**, the first and last bits are joined to
determine the appropriate row in the table defined by **Des_Sbox**, and the middle
four bits are joined to form the column. We complete the computation of *f* by performing the P-box permutation. To do this, we call *permute* and pass it the table
Des_Pbox (the same table as in Table 15-7). We complete each round by computing the XOR of **lblk** and the value of function *f*, and swapping **lblk** and **rblk**.

We repeat this process 16 times, once for each round. After all 16 rounds are complete, we copy **rblk** into the first 32 bits of **target** and **lblk** into the second 32

bits (effectively negating the last swap of the left and right blocks, as is required). At last, we perform the final permutation by calling *permute* and passing it the table `Des_Final` (the same table as in Table 15-8).

The runtime complexity of *des_encipher* is $O(1)$ because all of the steps in enciphering a block of data run in a constant amount of time.

des_decipher

The *des_decipher* operation (see Example 15-2) deciphers a 64-bit block of ciphertext enciphered using DES. Like *des_encipher*, *des_decipher* actually calls *des_main* to decipher the data, but with `direction` set to `decipher`. Thus, *des_decipher* works just like *des_encipher*, except that the subkeys are applied in reverse order. Specifically, in *des_main*, for each round i (starting at 0), we apply the subkey in element $15 - i$ of `subkeys`.

The runtime complexity of *des_decipher* is $O(1)$ because all of the steps in deciphering a block of data run in a constant amount of time.

Example 15-2. Implementation of DES

```
/*****************************************************************************
*                                                                           *
*  -------------------------------- des.c --------------------------------  *
*                                                                           *
*****************************************************************************/

#include <math.h>
#include <stdlib.h>
#include <string.h>

#include "bit.h"
#include "encrypt.h"

/*****************************************************************************
*                                                                           *
*  Define a mapping for the key transformation.                             *
*                                                                           *
*****************************************************************************/

static const int DesTransform[56] = {

   57, 49, 41, 33, 25, 17,  9,  1, 58, 50, 42, 34, 26, 18,
   10,  2, 59, 51, 43, 35, 27, 19, 11,  3, 60, 52, 44, 36,
   63, 55, 47, 39, 31, 23, 15,  7, 62, 54, 46, 38, 30, 22,
   14,  6, 61, 53, 45, 37, 29, 21, 13,  5, 28, 20, 12,  4

};
```

Example 15-2. Implementation of DES (continued)

```c
/****************************************************************************
*                                                                          *
*  Define the number of rotations for computing subkeys.                   *
*                                                                          *
****************************************************************************/

static const int DesRotations[16] = {

   1, 1, 2, 2, 2, 2, 2, 2, 1, 2, 2, 2, 2, 2, 2, 1

};

/****************************************************************************
*                                                                          *
*  Define a mapping for the permuted choice for subkeys.                   *
*                                                                          *
****************************************************************************/

static const int DesPermuted[48] = {

   14, 17, 11, 24,  1,  5,  3, 28, 15,  6, 21, 10,
   23, 19, 12,  4, 26,  8, 16,  7, 27, 20, 13,  2,
   41, 52, 31, 37, 47, 55, 30, 40, 51, 45, 33, 48,
   44, 49, 39, 56, 34, 53, 46, 42, 50, 36, 29, 32

};

/****************************************************************************
*                                                                          *
*  Define a mapping for the initial permutation of data blocks.            *
*                                                                          *
****************************************************************************/

static const int DesInitial[64] = {

   58, 50, 42, 34, 26, 18, 10,  2, 60, 52, 44, 36, 28, 20, 12,  4,
   62, 54, 46, 38, 30, 22, 14,  6, 64, 56, 48, 40, 32, 24, 16,  8,
   57, 49, 41, 33, 25, 17,  9,  1, 59, 51, 43, 35, 27, 19, 11,  3,
   61, 53, 45, 37, 29, 21, 13,  5, 63, 55, 47, 39, 31, 23, 15,  7

};

/****************************************************************************
*                                                                          *
*  Define a mapping for the expansion permutation of data blocks.          *
*                                                                          *
****************************************************************************/

static const int DesExpansion[48] = {

   32,  1,  2,  3,  4,  5,  4,  5,  6,  7,  8,  9,
    8,  9, 10, 11, 12, 13, 12, 13, 14, 15, 16, 17,
```

Example 15-2. Implementation of DES (continued)

```
    16, 17, 18, 19, 20, 21, 20, 21, 22, 23, 24, 25,
    24, 25, 26, 27, 28, 29, 28, 29, 30, 31, 32,  1

};

/****************************************************************************
 *                                                                          *
 *  Define tables for the S-box substitutions performed for data blocks.    *
 *                                                                          *
 ****************************************************************************/

static const int DesSbox[8][4][16] = {

    {
    {14,  4, 13,  1,  2, 15, 11,  8,  3, 10,  6, 12,  5,  9,  0,  7},
    { 0, 15,  7,  4, 14,  2, 13,  1, 10,  6, 12, 11,  9,  5,  3,  8},
    { 4,  1, 14,  8, 13,  6,  2, 11, 15, 12,  9,  7,  3, 10,  5,  0},
    {15, 12,  8,  2,  4,  9,  1,  7,  5, 11,  3, 14, 10,  0,  6, 13},
    },

    {
    {15,  1,  8, 14,  6, 11,  3,  4,  9,  7,  2, 13, 12,  0,  5, 10},
    { 3, 13,  4,  7, 15,  2,  8, 14, 12,  0,  1, 10,  6,  9, 11,  5},
    { 0, 14,  7, 11, 10,  4, 13,  1,  5,  8, 12,  6,  9,  3,  2, 15},
    {13,  8, 10,  1,  3, 15,  4,  2, 11,  6,  7, 12,  0,  5, 14,  9},
    },

    {
    {10,  0,  9, 14,  6,  3, 15,  5,  1, 13, 12,  7, 11,  4,  2,  8},
    {13,  7,  0,  9,  3,  4,  6, 10,  2,  8,  5, 14, 12, 11, 15,  1},
    {13,  6,  4,  9,  8, 15,  3,  0, 11,  1,  2, 12,  5, 10, 14,  7},
    { 1, 10, 13,  0,  6,  9,  8,  7,  4, 15, 14,  3, 11,  5,  2, 12},
    },

    {
    { 7, 13, 14,  3,  0,  6,  9, 10,  1,  2,  8,  5, 11, 12,  4, 15},
    {13,  8, 11,  5,  6, 15,  0,  3,  4,  7,  2, 12,  1, 10, 14,  9},
    {10,  6,  9,  0, 12, 11,  7, 13, 15,  1,  3, 14,  5,  2,  8,  4},
    { 3, 15,  0,  6, 10,  1, 13,  8,  9,  4,  5, 11, 12,  7,  2, 14},
    },

    {
    { 2, 12,  4,  1,  7, 10, 11,  6,  8,  5,  3, 15, 13,  0, 14,  9},
    {14, 11,  2, 12,  4,  7, 13,  1,  5,  0, 15, 10,  3,  9,  8,  6},
    { 4,  2,  1, 11, 10, 13,  7,  8, 15,  9, 12,  5,  6,  3,  0, 14},
    {11,  8, 12,  7,  1, 14,  2, 13,  6, 15,  0,  9, 10,  4,  5,  3},
    },

    {
    {12,  1, 10, 15,  9,  2,  6,  8,  0, 13,  3,  4, 14,  7,  5, 11},
    {10, 15,  4,  2,  7, 12,  9,  5,  6,  1, 13, 14,  0, 11,  3,  8},
    { 9, 14, 15,  5,  2,  8, 12,  3,  7,  0,  4, 10,  1, 13, 11,  6},
    { 4,  3,  2, 12,  9,  5, 15, 10, 11, 14,  1,  7,  6,  0,  8, 13},
    },
```

Example 15-2. Implementation of DES (continued)

```
    {
    { 4, 11,  2, 14, 15,  0,  8, 13,  3, 12,  9,  7,  5, 10,  6,  1},
    {13,  0, 11,  7,  4,  9,  1, 10, 14,  3,  5, 12,  2, 15,  8,  6},
    { 1,  4, 11, 13, 12,  3,  7, 14, 10, 15,  6,  8,  0,  5,  9,  2},
    { 6, 11, 13,  8,  1,  4, 10,  7,  9,  5,  0, 15, 14,  2,  3, 12},
    },

    {
    {13,  2,  8,  4,  6, 15, 11,  1, 10,  9,  3, 14,  5,  0, 12,  7},
    { 1, 15, 13,  8, 10,  3,  7,  4, 12,  5,  6, 11,  0, 14,  9,  2},
    { 7, 11,  4,  1,  9, 12, 14,  2,  0,  6, 10, 13, 15,  3,  5,  8},
    { 2,  1, 14,  7,  4, 10,  8, 13, 15, 12,  9,  0,  3,  5,  6, 11},
    },

};

/*************************************************************************
*                                                                       *
*  Define a mapping for the P-box permutation of data blocks.           *
*                                                                       *
*************************************************************************/

static const int DesPbox[32] = {

    16,  7, 20, 21, 29, 12, 28, 17,  1, 15, 23, 26,  5, 18, 31, 10,
     2,  8, 24, 14, 32, 27,  3,  9, 19, 13, 30,  6, 22, 11,  4, 25

};

/*************************************************************************
*                                                                       *
*  Define a mapping for the final permutation of data blocks.           *
*                                                                       *
*************************************************************************/

static const int DesFinal[64] = {

    40,  8, 48, 16, 56, 24, 64, 32, 39,  7, 47, 15, 55, 23, 63, 31,
    38,  6, 46, 14, 54, 22, 62, 30, 37,  5, 45, 13, 53, 21, 61, 29,
    36,  4, 44, 12, 52, 20, 60, 28, 35,  3, 43, 11, 51, 19, 59, 27,
    34,  2, 42, 10, 50, 18, 58, 26, 33,  1, 41,  9, 49, 17, 57, 25

};

/*************************************************************************
*                                                                       *
*  Define a type for whether to encipher or decipher data.              *
*                                                                       *
*************************************************************************/

typedef enum DesEorD_ {encipher, decipher} DesEorD;
```

Example 15-2. Implementation of DES (continued)

```
/***************************************************************************
 *                                                                         *
 *  ----------------------------- permute -----------------------------    *
 *                                                                         *
 ***************************************************************************/

static void permute(unsigned char *bits, const int *mapping, int n) {

unsigned char       temp[8];

int                 i;

/***************************************************************************
 *                                                                         *
 *  Permute the buffer using an n-entry mapping.                           *
 *                                                                         *
 ***************************************************************************/

memset(temp, 0, (int)ceil(n / 8));

for (i = 0; i < n; i++)
   bit_set(temp, i, bit_get(bits, mapping[i] - 1));

memcpy(bits, temp, (int)ceil(n / 8));

return;

}

/***************************************************************************
 *                                                                         *
 *  ----------------------------- des_main -----------------------------   *
 *                                                                         *
 ***************************************************************************/

static int des_main(const unsigned char *source, unsigned char *target, const
   unsigned char *key, DesEorD direction) {

static unsigned char subkeys[16][7];

unsigned char       temp[8],
                    lkey[4],
                    rkey[4],
                    lblk[6],
                    rblk[6],
                    fblk[6],
                    xblk[6],
                    sblk;

int                 row,
                    col,
                    i,
```

Example 15-2. Implementation of DES (continued)

```
                    j,
                    k,
                    p;

/*************************************************************************
*                                                                       *
*  If key is NULL, use the subkeys as computed in a previous call.      *
*                                                                       *
*************************************************************************/

if (key != NULL) {

   /*************************************************************************
   *                                                                    *
   *  Make a local copy of the key.                                     *
   *                                                                    *
   *************************************************************************/

   memcpy(temp, key, 8);

   /*************************************************************************
   *                                                                    *
   *  Permute and compress the key into 56 bits.                        *
   *                                                                    *
   *************************************************************************/

   permute(temp, DesTransform, 56);

   /*************************************************************************
   *                                                                    *
   *  Split the key into two 28-bit blocks.                             *
   *                                                                    *
   *************************************************************************/

   memset(lkey, 0, 4);
   memset(rkey, 0, 4);

   for (j = 0; j < 28; j++)
      bit_set(lkey, j, bit_get(temp, j));

   for (j = 0; j < 28; j++)
      bit_set(rkey, j, bit_get(temp, j + 28));

   /*************************************************************************
   *                                                                    *
   *  Compute the subkeys for each round.                               *
   *                                                                    *
   *************************************************************************/

   for (i = 0; i < 16; i++) {
```

Example 15-2. Implementation of DES (continued)

```
    /*************************************************************************
    *                                                                       *
    *  Rotate each block according to its round.                            *
    *                                                                       *
    *************************************************************************/

    bit_rot_left(lkey, 28, DesRotations[i]);
    bit_rot_left(rkey, 28, DesRotations[i]);

    /*************************************************************************
    *                                                                       *
    *  Concatenate the blocks into a single subkey.                         *
    *                                                                       *
    *************************************************************************/

    for (j = 0; j < 28; j++)
       bit_set(subkeys[i], j, bit_get(lkey, j));

    for (j = 0; j < 28; j++)
       bit_set(subkeys[i], j + 28, bit_get(rkey, j));

    /*************************************************************************
    *                                                                       *
    *  Do the permuted choice permutation.                                  *
    *                                                                       *
    *************************************************************************/

    permute(subkeys[i], DesPermuted, 48);

  }

}

/*************************************************************************
*                                                                       *
*  Make a local copy of the source text.                                *
*                                                                       *
*************************************************************************/

memcpy(temp, source, 8);

/*************************************************************************
*                                                                       *
*  Do the initial permutation.                                          *
*                                                                       *
*************************************************************************/

permute(temp, DesInitial, 64);

/*************************************************************************
*                                                                       *
*  Split the source text into a left and right block of 32 bits.        *
*                                                                       *
*************************************************************************/
```

Example 15-2. Implementation of DES (continued)

```
memcpy(lblk, &temp[0], 4);
memcpy(rblk, &temp[4], 4);

/*************************************************************************
*                                                                       *
*  Encipher or decipher the source text.                                *
*                                                                       *
*************************************************************************/

for (i = 0; i < 16; i++) {

   /*************************************************************************
   *                                                                       *
   *  Begin the computation of f.                                          *
   *                                                                       *
   *************************************************************************/

   memcpy(fblk, rblk, 4);

   /*************************************************************************
   *                                                                       *
   *  Permute and expand the copy of the right block into 48 bits.         *
   *                                                                       *
   *************************************************************************/

   permute(fblk, DesExpansion, 48);

   /*************************************************************************
   *                                                                       *
   *  Apply the appropriate subkey for the round.                          *
   *                                                                       *
   *************************************************************************/

   if (direction == encipher) {

      /*************************************************************************
      *                                                                       *
      *  For enciphering, subkeys are applied in increasing order.            *
      *                                                                       *
      *************************************************************************/

      bit_xor(fblk, subkeys[i], xblk, 48);
      memcpy(fblk, xblk, 6);

      }

   else {

      /*************************************************************************
      *                                                                       *
      *  For deciphering, subkeys are applied in decreasing order.            *
      *                                                                       *
      *************************************************************************/
```

Example 15-2. Implementation of DES (continued)

```
      bit_xor(fblk, subkeys[15 - i], xblk, 48);
      memcpy(fblk, xblk, 6);

}

/***************************************************************************
*                                                                         *
*  Do the S-box substitutions.                                            *
*                                                                         *
***************************************************************************/

p = 0;

for (j = 0; j < 8; j++) {

   /***********************************************************************
   *                                                                     *
   *   Compute a row and column into the S-box tables.                   *
   *                                                                     *
   ***********************************************************************/

   row = (bit_get(fblk, (j * 6)+0) * 2) + (bit_get(fblk, (j * 6)+5) * 1);
   col = (bit_get(fblk, (j * 6)+1) * 8) + (bit_get(fblk, (j * 6)+2) * 4) +
         (bit_get(fblk, (j * 6)+3) * 2) + (bit_get(fblk, (j * 6)+4) * 1);

   /***********************************************************************
   *                                                                     *
   *  Do the S-box substitution for the current six-bit block.           *
   *                                                                     *
   ***********************************************************************/

   sblk = (unsigned char)DesSbox[j][row][col];

   for (k = 4; k < 8; k++) {

      bit_set(fblk, p, bit_get(&sblk, k));
      p++;

   }

}

/***************************************************************************
*                                                                         *
*  Do the P-box permutation to complete f.                                *
*                                                                         *
***************************************************************************/

permute(fblk, DesPbox, 32);
```

Example 15-2. Implementation of DES (continued)

```
/***************************************************************************
*                                                                          *
*   Compute the XOR of the left block and f.                               *
*                                                                          *
***************************************************************************/

bit_xor(lblk, fblk, xblk, 32);

/***************************************************************************
*                                                                          *
*   Set the left block for the round.                                      *
*                                                                          *
***************************************************************************/

memcpy(lblk, rblk, 4);

/***************************************************************************
*                                                                          *
*   Set the right block for the round.                                     *
*                                                                          *
***************************************************************************/

memcpy(rblk, xblk, 4);

}

/***************************************************************************
*                                                                          *
*   Set the target text to the rejoined final right and left blocks.       *
*                                                                          *
***************************************************************************/

memcpy(&target[0], rblk, 4);
memcpy(&target[4], lblk, 4);

/***************************************************************************
*                                                                          *
*   Do the final permutation.                                              *
*                                                                          *
***************************************************************************/

permute(target, DesFinal, 64);

return 0;

}

/***************************************************************************
*                                                                          *
*   ---------------------------- des_encipher ----------------------------  *
*                                                                          *
***************************************************************************/
```

Example 15-2. Implementation of DES (continued)

```
void des_encipher(const unsigned char *plaintext, unsigned char *ciphertext,
   const unsigned char *key) {

des_main(plaintext, ciphertext, key, encipher);

return;

}

/***************************************************************************
*                                                                         *
*  --------------------------- des_decipher ---------------------------   *
*                                                                         *
***************************************************************************/

void des_decipher(const unsigned char *ciphertext, unsigned char *plaintext,
   const unsigned char *key) {

des_main(ciphertext, plaintext, key, decipher);

return;

}
```

DES Example: Block Cipher Modes

Most block ciphers, such as DES, encipher and decipher data in 64-bit blocks. Since nearly all of the work done with ciphers involves more data than this, we end up invoking the cipher over and over again to process all of the blocks. The specific manner in which a block cipher is invoked repeatedly is called a *block cipher mode*.

The simplest way to process several blocks of data is to append each block of ciphertext we generate to others generated before it. This primitive approach is called *ECB*, or *electronic code book*. Its simplicity makes it very popular, but it is relatively insecure. Its main problem is that for any given key, a specific block of plaintext always enciphers to the same block of ciphertext wherever it appears in the data. This means that if an adversary cracks even a small section of the data, he can begin to develop a code book for cracking other sections as well. A better approach is *CBC*, or *cipher block chaining*.

CBC mode avoids the problems of ECB by augmenting a block cipher with simple operations and *feedback*. Feedback makes each block of ciphertext depend in some way on actions performed earlier. In CBC mode, previous blocks of ciphertext serve as feedback so that even the same block of plaintext is likely to encipher into a different block of ciphertext each time it appears.

For previous blocks of ciphertext to serve as feedback, before we encipher a block of plaintext, we XOR it with the block of ciphertext generated before it. When we decipher the ciphertext, we XOR each deciphered block back with the block of ciphertext it follows. Simply stated:

$$C_i = E_K(P_i \oplus C_{i-1})$$
$$P_i = C_{i-1} \oplus D_K(C_i)$$

where C_i and P_i are the ith blocks of ciphertext and plaintext from buffers C and P, and E_K and D_K are the encipher and decipher operations using key K.

Usually we add one random block of data to the beginning of the plaintext. This is so that even when an adversary has some idea what the first block of plaintext contains, it cannot be used to start replicating the chaining sequence. This block is called the *initialization vector*. We encipher it normally, without any feedback, then use it as the feedback when enciphering and deciphering the first real block of plaintext.

Example 15-3 presents an implementation of two functions, *cbc_encipher* and *cbc_decipher*, that encipher and decipher a buffer of data using DES in CBC mode. The *cbc_encipher* function takes a buffer of plaintext containing `size` bytes and enciphers it using `key` as the key. It assumes that the first block of plaintext is actually the 64-bit initialization vector. The *cbc_decipher* function takes a buffer of ciphertext containing `size` bytes and deciphers it using `key` as the key. For symmetry, the initialization vector is deciphered as well and is returned as the first block of plaintext.

The runtime complexities of *cbc_encipher* and *cbc_decipher* are both $O(n)$, where n is the number of blocks enciphered or deciphered. This is because the two functions simply call the $O(1)$ operations *des_encipher* and *des_decipher*, respectively, once for each block.

Example 15-3. Implementation of Functions for DES in CBC Mode

```
/*****************************************************************************
*                                                                           *
*  -------------------------------- cbc.c --------------------------------   *
*                                                                           *
*****************************************************************************/

#include <stdlib.h>

#include "bit.h"
#include "cbc.h"
#include "encrypt.h"

/*****************************************************************************
*                                                                           *
*  --------------------------- cbc_encipher ---------------------------      *
*                                                                           *
*****************************************************************************/
```

Example 15-3. Implementation of Functions for DES in CBC Mode (continued)

```c
void cbc_encipher(const unsigned char *plaintext, unsigned char *ciphertext,
   const unsigned char *key, int size) {

unsigned char        temp[8];

int                  i;

/***************************************************************************
*                                                                         *
*  Encipher the initialization vector.                                    *
*                                                                         *
***************************************************************************/

des_encipher(&plaintext[0], &ciphertext[0], key);

/***************************************************************************
*                                                                         *
*  Encipher the buffer using DES in CBC mode.                             *
*                                                                         *
***************************************************************************/

i = 8;

while (i < size) {

   bit_xor(&plaintext[i], &ciphertext[i - 8], temp, 64);
   des_encipher(temp, &ciphertext[i], NULL);
   i = i + 8;

}

return;

}

/***************************************************************************
*                                                                         *
*  --------------------------- cbc_decipher ---------------------------   *
*                                                                         *
***************************************************************************/

void cbc_decipher(const unsigned char *ciphertext, unsigned char *plaintext,
   const unsigned char *key, int size) {

unsigned char        temp[8];

int                  i;

/***************************************************************************
*                                                                         *
*  Decipher the initialization vector.                                    *
*                                                                         *
***************************************************************************/
```

Example 15-3. Implementation of Functions for DES in CBC Mode (continued)

```
des_decipher(&ciphertext[0], &plaintext[0], key);

/****************************************************************************
*                                                                          *
*  Decipher the buffer using DES in CBC mode.                              *
*                                                                          *
****************************************************************************/

i = 8;

while (i < size) {

    des_decipher(&ciphertext[i], temp, NULL);
    bit_xor(&ciphertext[i - 8], temp, &plaintext[i], 64);
    i = i + 8;

}

 return;

}
```

Description of RSA

RSA (Rivest-Shamir-Adleman) is one of the most popular asymmetric, or public-key, ciphers. RSA is asymmetric because the key used to encipher data is not the same key used to decipher it. Like DES, RSA is a block cipher, but the block size varies depending on the size of the keys. If the amount of data to be encrypted is not an even multiple of this size, it is padded in some application-specific way.

One important implication of RSA being an asymmetric cipher is that when transmitting data across a network, the key used to encipher the data does not have to be transmitted with the data itself. Thus, there is less chance of having the key compromised. RSA is also useful when parties enciphering data are not allowed to decipher the data of others. Parties who wish to encipher data use one key, which is considered public, while parties allowed to decipher the data use a second key, which they keep private.

RSA is considered very secure, but it runs considerably slower than DES. As with DES, the security of RSA has never been proven, but it is related to the difficult problem of factoring large numbers (numbers containing at least 200 decimal digits). Since no efficient solutions are known for this problem, it is conjectured that there are no efficient ways to crack RSA.

RSA is based on principles that are less obtuse than the numerous permutations and substitutions performed in DES. Fundamentally, enciphering and deciphering data revolves around *modular exponentiation,* an operation in *modular arithmetic.* Modular arithmetic is integer arithmetic as usual except that when we work modulo n, every result x is replaced with a member of $\{0, 1, \ldots, n - 1\}$ so that $x \bmod n$ is the remainder of x/n. For example, 40 mod 11 = 7 because 40/11 = 3 with a remainder of 7. Modular exponentiation is the process of computing $a^b \bmod n$.

Computing Public and Private Keys

In RSA, the public key and private key work together as a pair. The public key is used to encipher a block of data, after which only the corresponding private key can be used to decipher it. When generating keys, we follow a few steps to ensure that this marriage works. These steps also ensure that there is no practical way to determine one key from the other.

To begin, we select two large prime numbers, which are called p and q (see the related topics at the end of the chapter). Considering today's factoring technology, these each should be at least 200 decimal digits to be considered secure in practice. We then compute n, the product of these numbers:

$$n = pq$$

Next, we choose a small odd integer e, which will become part of the public key. The most important consideration in choosing e is that it should have no factors in common with $(p - 1)(q - 1)$. In other words, e is relatively prime with $(p - 1)$ $(q - 1)$. For example, if $p = 11$ and $q = 19$, then $n = (11)(19) = 209$. Here we might choose $e = 17$ because $(p - 1)(q - 1) = (10)(18) = 180$, and 17 and 180 have no common factors. Common choices for e are 3, 17, and 65,537. Using one of these values does not jeopardize the security of RSA because deciphering data is a function of the private key.

Once we have chosen a value for e, we compute a corresponding value d, which will become part of the private key. To do this, we compute the multiplicative inverse of e, modulo $(p - 1)(q - 1)$, as follows:

$$d = e^{-1} \bmod (p-1)(q-1)$$

The way to think of this is: what value of d satisfies $ed \bmod (p - 1)(q - 1) = 1$? For example, in the equation $17d \bmod 180 = 1$, one possible value for d is 53. Other possibilities are 233, 413, 593, and so forth. An extension of Euclid's algorithm is used to compute multiplicative modular inverses in practice (see the related topics at the end of the chapter). In this book, code is provided for using d and e but not for deriving them.

Now that we have values for both e and d, we publish (e, n) as the public key P and keep (d, n) secret as the private key S, as shown:

$$P = (e, n)$$
$$S = (d, n)$$

Parties who encipher data use P. Those who decipher data use S. To ensure that even someone who knows P cannot compute S, the values used for p and q must never be revealed.

The security offered by P and S together comes from the fact that multiplication is a good *one-way function*. One-way functions are fundamental to cryptography. Simply stated, a one-way function is a function that is relatively easy to compute in one direction but impractical to reverse. For example, in RSA, multiplying p and q is a one-way function because although multiplying p and q is easy, factoring n back into p and q is extremely time-consuming, provided the values chosen for p and q are large enough.

The steps performed to compute P and S have their origin in some interesting properties of *Euler's function* (pronounced "oiler"). In particular, these properties allow us to do useful things with modular exponentiation. Euler's function, denoted $\phi(n)$, defines how many numbers less than n are *relatively prime* with n. Two numbers are said to be relatively prime if their only common factor is 1. As an example of Euler's function, $\phi(8) = 4$ because there are four numbers less than 8 that are relatively prime with 8, namely 1, 3, 5, and 7.

Euler's function has two properties that are particularly relevant to RSA. First, when n is prime, $\phi(n) = n - 1$. This is because the only factors of n are 1 and n; thus, n is relatively prime with all of the $n - 1$ numbers before it. Another interesting property is that $\phi(n)$ is the *exponential period* modulo n for numbers relatively prime with n. This means that for any number $a < n$ relatively prime with n, $a^{\phi(n)}$ mod $n = 1$. For example, 1^4 mod $8 = 1$, 3^4 mod $8 = 1$, 5^4 mod $8 = 1$, and 7^4 mod $8 = 1$. Multiplying both sides of this equation by a yields:

$$(a)(a^{\phi(n)} \bmod n) = (1)(a), \text{ or } a^{\phi(n)+1} \bmod n = a$$

Hence, 1^5 mod $8 = 1$, 3^5 mod $8 = 3$, 5^5 mod $8 = 5$, and 7^5 mod $8 = 7$. This algebraic adjustment is powerful because for some equation $c = m^e$ mod n, it lets us find a value d so that c^d mod $n = m$. This is the identity that allows us to encipher data in RSA and then decipher the data back as shown below:

$$c^d \bmod n = (m^e)^d \bmod n = m^{ed} \bmod n = m^{\phi(n)+1} \bmod n = m \bmod n$$

The relationship of Euler's function with exponential periods guarantees that any block of data we encipher will decipher again uniquely. To find d, we solve the equation $d = e^{-1}\phi(n) + 1$. Unfortunately, there is not always an integer solution to $d = e^{-1}\phi(n) + 1$. For example, consider if $e = 5$ and $n = 13$. In this case, $d = (1/5)((13 - 1) + 1) = (1/5)(13)$. To deal with this, we compute d modulo $\phi(n)$. In other words, $d = (e^{-1}\phi(n) + 1) \bmod \phi(n)$, which can be simplified to:

$$d = e^{-1} \bmod \phi(n)$$

We can make this simplification because $(\phi(n) + 1) \bmod \phi(n) = (\phi(n) + 1) - \phi(n) = 1$. We can verify this by inserting any number in place of $\phi(n)$. Notice the similarity between this equation and the one used for d earlier in the steps for computing keys. This provides a way to compute d from e and n. Of course, since e and n are public and potentially known to an adversary, one might ask: doesn't this give an adversary the same opportunity to compute the private key? At this point it is worth examining where RSA's security comes from.

RSA gets its security from the critical fact that Euler's function is *multiplicative*. This means that if p and q are relatively prime (which they are if we choose them both to be prime), then $\phi(pq) = \phi(p)\phi(q)$. Thus, if we have two primes p and q, and $n = pq$, then $\phi(n) = (p-1)(q-1)$, and most importantly:

$$d = e^{-1} \bmod (p-1)(q-1)$$

Therefore, even though an adversary might know both e and n, in order to compute d, she would have to know $\phi(n)$, which can only be determined in a practical manner by knowing both p and q. Since these are not known, the adversary is left to factor n, an extremely time-consuming process, provided the values chosen for p and q are large enough.

Enciphering and Deciphering Data Blocks

To encipher and decipher data with RSA, we first need to choose a block size. This must be less than n. For example, if p and q are primes containing 200 decimal digits, n will be just under 400 decimal digits. Therefore, we should choose a block size small enough to store only those numbers with less than this many decimal digits. In practice, we often choose the block size in bits to be the largest power of 2 less than n. For example, if n were 209, we would choose a block size of 7 bits because $2^7 = 128$ is less than 209, but $2^8 = 256$ is greater.

To encipher a block of plaintext M_i, the ith block of data from a buffer M, we use the public key (e, n) to take the numerical value of M_i, raise it to the power of e, and take the result modulo n. This yields a block of ciphertext C_i. The modulo n operation ensures that C_i will fit into the same size block as the plaintext. Thus, to encipher a block of plaintext:

$$C_i = M_i^e \bmod n$$

It was mentioned earlier that Euler's function is the basis for using modular exponentiation to encipher data using this equation and, in the equation that follows, for being able to get the original plaintext back. To decipher a block of ciphertext C_i, the ith block of ciphertext from a buffer C, we use the private key (d, n) to take the numeric value of C_i, raise it to the power of d, and take the result modulo n. This yields the original block of plaintext M_i. Thus, to decipher a block of ciphertext:

$$M_i = C_i^d \bmod n$$

Interface for RSA

rsa_encipher

void rsa_encipher(Huge *plaintext*, Huge **ciphertext*, RsaPubKey *pubkey*);

Return Value   None.

Description   Uses RSA to encipher one block of plaintext specified by *plaintext*. Specify the public key (e, n) in the *RsaPubKey* structure *pubkey*. A block the same size as *plaintext* is returned in *ciphertext*. It is the responsibility of the caller to manage the storage required in *ciphertext*. To encipher a large buffer of data, call *rsa_encipher* in accordance with a block cipher mode (see the example earlier in this chapter).

Complexity $O(1)$

rsa_decipher

void rsa_decipher(Huge *ciphertext*, Huge **plaintext*, RsaPriKey *prikey*);

Return Value   None.

Description   Uses RSA to decipher one block of ciphertext specified by *ciphertext*. Specify the private key (d, n) in the *RsaPriKey* structure *prikey*. A block the same size as *ciphertext* is returned in *plaintext*. It is the responsibility of the caller to manage the storage required in *plaintext*. To decipher a large buffer of data, call *rsa_decipher* in accordance with the block cipher mode used to decipher the data.

Complexity $O(1)$

Implementation and Analysis of RSA

Because encryption with RSA requires little more than computing $a^b \bmod n$, a basic implementation is relatively simple: all we need is a function to perform modular exponentiation. However, to make RSA secure, recall that we must use large integers. This complicates things. Specifically, all arithmetic must be performed with integers that are twice the size of the keys. (We will see in a moment that this doubling is required for the modular exponentiation process.) Thus, if the keys are 200 decimal digits, we need an abstract datatype that supports integers with at least 400 decimal digits.

Since support for large-integer arithmetic is not provided in this book, the RSA implementation presented here must depend on another library. Several are available. Instead of providing this support, the datatype *Huge* has been defined (see Example 15-1). In a secure implementation we can typedef this to a large-integer abstract datatype of our choice. The only other requirement is that we replace each operator in expressions containing *Huge* integers with operations defined for the type. For purposes of illustration in the implementation presented here, *Huge* is made a typedef to an unsigned long integer, an intrinsic type that usually offers 10 decimal digits. This means that the implementation as it exists in Example 15-4 supports keys up to only 5 decimal digits. Thus, the implementation is functional, but it would not be considered secure without redefining *Huge* to a larger type.

rsa_encipher

The *rsa_encipher* operation (see Example 15-4) enciphers a block of plaintext using RSA. It does this by calling the function *modexp*, which computes a^b mod n, where a is the block of plaintext, and b and n are members e and n of the public key. For efficiency, *modexp* uses a method called *binary square and multiply* to perform modular exponentiation.

The binary square and multiply method avoids the huge intermediate result produced by a^b when a and b are both large. For example, imagine computing a^b mod n when a, b, and n are all integers containing 200 decimal digits. The result is a 40,000-digit integer modulo a 200-digit integer! Since this eventually yields an integer of 200 decimal digits, the goal is to avoid the 40,000-digit intermediate result.

The binary square and multiply method computes a^b mod n primarily as the product of several squares (see Figure 15-4). We start with the binary representation of b and process bits from the right. For each bit in b, we square a, take the result modulo n, and store this value back into a. Each time we encounter a bit in b that is 1, we multiply the current value of a times another register y (initially 1) and store the result back into y. Once we reach the most significant bit in b, y contains the value of a^b mod n. Throughout the process, the largest value ever computed is a^2. Therefore, if a is an integer containing 200 decimal digits, we never have to deal with integers larger than 400 digits, which is a considerable improvement over the 40,000-digit number mentioned a moment ago. The shaded areas of Figure 15-4 illustrate this process for 5^{11} mod 53 = 48,828,125 mod 53 = 20. In this calculation, the largest value we end up handling is $42^2 = 1764$, as opposed to $5^{11} = 48,828,125$.

The runtime complexity of *rsa_encipher* is $O(1)$ because all of the steps in enciphering a block of data run in a constant amount of time. Since the block size is constant, the loop in *modexp* runs in a constant amount of time.

b	y		a	
1011	$a \bmod n$		$a^2 \bmod n$	
	$5 \bmod 53 = 5$		$5^2 \bmod 53 = 25$	
101	$(a \bmod n)\ (a^2 \bmod n)\ \bmod\ n\ =\ a^3 \bmod n$		$(a^2 \bmod n)^2\ \bmod\ n\ =\ a^4 \bmod n$	
	(5)(25) mod 53 = 19		(25)^2 mod 53 = 42	
10			$(a^4 \bmod n)^2\ \bmod\ n\ =\ a^8 \bmod n$	
			(42)^2 mod 53 = 15	
1	$(a^3 \bmod n)(a^8 \bmod n)\ \bmod\ n\ =\ a^{11} \bmod n$			
	(19)(15) mod 53 = 20			

Figure 15-4. Modular exponentiation using the binary square and multiply method

rsa_decipher

The *rsa_decipher* operation (see Example 15-4) deciphers a block of ciphertext enciphered using RSA. It does this by calling the function *modexp*, which computes $a^b \bmod n$, where a is the block of ciphertext, and b and n are members d and n of the private key. This proceeds in the same manner as described for *rsa_encipher*.

The runtime complexity of *rsa_decipher* is $O(1)$ because all of the steps in deciphering a block of data run in a constant amount of time. Since the block size is constant, the loop in *modexp* runs in a constant amount of time.

Example 15-4. Implementation of RSA

```
/*****************************************************************************
*                                                                           *
*  -------------------------------- rsa.c --------------------------------   *
*                                                                           *
*****************************************************************************/

#include "encrypt.h"

/*****************************************************************************
*                                                                           *
*  ------------------------------- modexp --------------------------------   *
*                                                                           *
*****************************************************************************/

static Huge modexp(Huge a, Huge b, Huge n) {

Huge                y;
```

Example 15-4. Implementation of RSA (continued)

```
/***************************************************************************
 *                                                                         *
 *  Compute pow(a, b) % n using the binary square and multiply method.     *
 *                                                                         *
 ***************************************************************************/

y = 1;

while (b != 0) {

   /***************************************************************************
    *                                                                         *
    *  For each 1 in b, accumulate y.                                         *
    *                                                                         *
    ***************************************************************************/

   if (b & 1)
      y = (y * a) % n;

   /***************************************************************************
    *                                                                         *
    *  Square a for each bit in b.                                            *
    *                                                                         *
    ***************************************************************************/

   a = (a * a) % n;

   /***************************************************************************
    *                                                                         *
    *  Prepare for the next bit in b.                                         *
    *                                                                         *
    ***************************************************************************/

   b = b >> 1;

}

return y;

}

/***************************************************************************
 *                                                                         *
 *  --------------------------- rsa_encipher ---------------------------   *
 *                                                                         *
 ***************************************************************************/

void rsa_encipher(Huge plaintext, Huge *ciphertext, RsaPubKey pubkey) {

*ciphertext = modexp(plaintext, pubkey.e, pubkey.n);

return;

}
```

Example 15-4. Implementation of RSA (continued)

```
/*****************************************************************************
*                                                                           *
*  --------------------------- rsa_decipher ---------------------------     *
*                                                                           *
*****************************************************************************/

void rsa_decipher(Huge ciphertext, Huge *plaintext, RsaPriKey prikey) {

*plaintext = modexp(ciphertext, prikey.d, prikey.n);

return;

}
```

Questions and Answers

Q: Suppose we would like to encrypt a file containing flags that enable or disable certain attributes in an application based on the features a customer has paid for. Which method of encryption presented in this chapter would be best suited to this scenario?

A: Since in this scenario only one party, the application itself, needs to read the file, it makes sense to use a symmetric cipher such as DES. Before installing the file, we encipher it with a key that only the application knows about. Whenever the application needs to read the file, it deciphers it using the same key.

Q: Suppose a party A is making sensitive requests for data across the Internet to another party B. B is the only one who should be able to decipher the data enciphered by A, and A is the only one who should be able to decipher data enciphered by B specifically for A. B also receives requests from several other parties, all of whom should not be able to hear what each other is saying. Which method of encryption from this chapter would be best in this scenario?

A: Since all parties must be able to communicate with *B* but without anyone else being able to decipher the communications, we should use a public-key cipher such as RSA. Consider the case of *A* making a request to *B*. *A* makes his request to *B* by enciphering the request with *B*'s public key. When *B* receives the request, *B* deciphers it using her own private key. Once *B* has validated that *A* sent the request (perhaps using a digital signature), she enciphers a reply using *A*'s public key. Once *A* receives the reply from *B*, *A* deciphers the message using his own private key.

Q: With DES, we encipher and decipher data by performing a series of permutations and substitutions. Exactly how these permutations and substitutions affect the data is essentially a function of 16 subkeys, derived from an initial key that we provide. In general, the security of DES is greatest when most of the subkeys differ from one another. Unfortunately, certain initial keys lead to situations in which all subkeys are identical. These initial keys are called weak keys. DES has four weak keys. What are they?

A: To generate subkeys in DES, we first transform the key from 64 bits to 56 bits. Once the key has been transformed, we divide it into two 28-bit blocks and perform a number of other operations that are repeated during each round. If either of the two 28-bit blocks contains bits that are all the same, these operations have no effect. Thus, we end up with subkeys that are identical for every round, and the initial key is considered weak. The four weak keys of DES and what they become are shown in Table 15-9.

Table 15-9. Weak Keys in DES Before and After the Key Transformation

Key	Becomes
0101 0101 0101 0101	0000000 0000000
1F1F 1F1F 1F1F 1F1F	0000000 FFFFFFF
E0E0 E0E0 F1F1 F1F1	FFFFFFF 0000000
FEFE FEFE FEFE FEFE	FFFFFFF FFFFFFF

Q: *Avoiding weak keys is one security issue in DES. Another issue is avoiding semiweak keys. Semiweak keys come in pairs. Two keys form a semiweak key pair if the subkeys they produce are in the opposite order. This means that if we use one key from the pair to re-encipher the ciphertext generated using the other key, we effectively get the same result as deciphering the ciphertext with the original key. DES has six semiweak key pairs. What are they? Why are semiweak keys a problem?*

A: The problem with semiweak key pairs in DES is that by re-enciphering the ciphertext with one key in the pair we essentially end up performing the same operation as deciphering the ciphertext with the other key. Thus, effectively we have two keys that can decipher the data, which makes semiweak keys undesirable. The six semiweak key pairs of DES are shown in Table 15-10.

Table 15-10. Semiweak Key Pairs in DES

Key 1	Key 2
01FE 01FE 01FE 01FE	FE01 FE01 FE01 FE01
1FE0 1FE0 0EF1 0EF1	E01F E01F F10E F10E
01E0 01E0 01F1 01F1	E001 E001 F101 F101
1EFE 1EFE 0EFE 0EFE	FE1F FE1F FE0E FE0E
011F 011F 010E 010E	1F01 1F01 0E01 0E01
E0FE E0FE F1FE F1FE	FEE0 FEE0 FEF1 FEF1

Q: *Some applications of DES use keys that are generated randomly. In applications like this, what precautions might we take against the use of weak and semiweak keys, if any?*

A: Considering the number of keys listed in Tables 15-9 and 15-10 combined, it's evident that out of 2^{56} possible keys in DES, weak and semiweak keys are rare. Nevertheless, applications that use randomly generated keys often check to make sure a candidate key is not weak or semiweak before using it. On the other hand, since checking every key is somewhat wasteful considering how infrequent weak and semiweak keys are, many applications simply don't worry about them.

Q: *RSA is a block cipher, which means that it processes data one block at a time. Whereas DES always uses a block size of 64 bits, the block size of RSA varies depending on the value of* n, *where* n = pq. *What happens if we mistakenly choose the block size so that some blocks of plaintext contain values greater than or equal to* n?

A: The problem with a block of plaintext containing a value greater than or equal to *n* is that when we encipher and decipher blocks, the modular exponentiation operation is modulo *n*. This means that all blocks generated as either ciphertext or plaintext contain values less than *n*. Therefore, if the original block of plaintext contains a value greater than or equal to *n*, after enciphering and deciphering the block, we will not end up with the plaintext we started with.

Q: *This chapter discussed two common block cipher modes, ECB and CBC. What are some of the advantages each offers? What are some of the drawbacks?*

A: ECB and CBC both have advantages and disadvantages. ECB is simple, but its lack of feedback makes it considerably less secure than CBC. However, by not using feedback, ECB has some flexibilities. For example, with ECB, since no block depends on any other block having been processed before it, we can process blocks out of sequence or in parallel. The most significant advantage of CBC is that it conceals patterns in the plaintext well. However, its use of feedback means that we must encipher blocks in order. On the other hand, deciphering data in CBC mode does not have this restriction. To decipher data, we require feedback only from the ciphertext itself, not any of the blocks deciphered previously.

Related Topics

Finding large prime numbers

An essential part of computing secure keys for RSA. One of the best methods for doing this is the Miller-Rabin algorithm, which also makes use of Euclid's algorithm. Miller-Rabin is probabilistic, so on rare occasions it may yield a number that is in fact composite (in fact, this is extremely rare, but nevertheless possible). For this reason, primes generated in this fashion are sometimes called *industrial-grade primes.*

Modular arithmetic

A type of arithmetic particularly useful in encryption as well as other areas of computer science. Modular arithmetic is integer arithmetic as usual except that when we are working modulo n, every result x is replaced with a member of $\{0, 1, \ldots, n-1\}$ so that $x \bmod n$ is the remainder of x/n.

Arithmetic with large integers

An essential part of secure implementations of RSA. In RSA, to be secure considering current factoring technology, we must choose keys that have at least 200 decimal digits. This means that all integer arithmetic must be performed with integers of at least 400 digits.

Euclid's greatest common divisor algorithm

A method of computing greatest common divisors, and one of the oldest known algorithms. The algorithm is particularly relevant to RSA because we can extend it to help compute multiplicative modular inverses.

CFB (cipher feedback) and OFB (output feedback)

Common block cipher modes in addition to the ECB and CBC modes presented in this chapter. CFB uses ciphertext for feedback in such a way that a block cipher appears more like a *stream cipher*. Stream ciphers process data in continuous streams instead of one block at a time. This can be useful in network applications, where data often arrives in bursts that are not aligned with the block size. OFB is another method of running a block cipher as a stream cipher, but the feedback is independent of both the plaintext and ciphertext.

Cryptographic protocols

Step-by-step procedures executed by two or more parties in order to communicate with each other in a secure manner. It is important to realize that many problems in data security require more than just simply enciphering and deciphering data. Often we need to establish secure protocols, of which ciphers are only a part.

16

Graph Algorithms

Graphs are flexible data structures that model problems defined in terms of relationships or connections between objects (see Chapter 11, *Graphs*). This chapter presents algorithms that work with graphs. As we will see, many graph algorithms resemble the fundamental ones for breadth-first and depth-first search introduced in Chapter 11. Breadth-first and depth-first search are important to many other graph algorithms because they offer good ways of exploring the structure of a graph in a systematic manner.

One significant difference between the algorithms of Chapter 11 and the ones in this chapter, however, is that the algorithms here work with *weighted graphs*. In a weighted graph, each edge is assigned a value, or *weight*, which is represented pictorially as a small number beside the edge. Although weights can mean many things, in general they represent a cost associated with traversing an edge. Weighted graphs and their algorithms have an enormous capacity to model real problems. Example 16-1 is a header for the graph algorithms presented in this chapter.

This chapter covers:

Minimum spanning trees
> Trees that serve as abstractions of many connectivity problems. A minimum spanning tree is a tree that connects all vertices in an undirected, weighted graph at a minimum cost.

Shortest paths
> The result of solving various types of shortest-path problems. A shortest path is a path that connects one vertex to another in a directed, weighted graph at a minimum cost.

Traveling-salesman problem

A surprisingly difficult problem in which we look for the shortest tour that visits every vertex in a complete, undirected, weighted graph exactly once before returning to the first vertex.

Some applications of graph algorithms are:

Efficient pipelines

A practical concern in transporting water, oil, and other liquids. If distribution points for the pipeline are represented as vertices in a graph, and candidate connections between the points as edges are weighted by the cost to connect the points, a minimum spanning tree gives us the best way to lay a pipeline that connects all of the distribution points.

Routing tables (illustrated in this chapter)

Tables used by routers to help direct data through an internet. The purpose of a router is to move data closer to its final destination. In one type of routing, routers periodically compute shortest paths to one another so each knows the best next step for sending data to certain destinations.

Delivery services

Services that typically visit numerous locations to pick up and deliver packages. Solving the traveling-salesman problem can indicate the most efficient way for a vehicle operated by a service to visit every location exactly once before returning to its starting point.

Communication networks

Networks containing many different types of equipment including telephone lines, relay stations, and satellite systems, all of which must be located in an optimal manner. An optimal arrangement can be determined by computing a minimum spanning tree for the weighted graph that models the network.

Routing airplanes

An optimization problem particularly important to airlines and air traffic control agencies. Often airplanes cannot fly directly from one point to another. Instead, they weave their way through airway structures, or highways in the sky, considering winds, monetary charges for traversing airspace, and air traffic control restrictions. The best route between two points is the path with the minimum weight defined in terms of factors like these.

Closed transport systems

Systems in which railroad cars or conveyor carts repeatedly tour several points. Systems like these might be used to deliver parts in a factory or to move inventory in and out of a warehouse. Solving the traveling-salesman problem can indicate the best way to construct the system.

Wiring circuit boards

An optimization problem in electronics manufacturing. Often it is necessary to make the pins of several components on a circuit board electrically equivalent by establishing a connection between them. If each pin is represented as a vertex in a graph, and candidate connections as edges weighted by the amount of wire required for the connection, a minimum spanning tree gives us the best way to connect the pins.

Traffic monitoring

The process of watching changes in traffic flow to determine the best route between two points in a city. To avoid excessive traffic delays, we can use a weighted graph to model the flow of traffic along roadways and look for the path from intersection to intersection with the minimum traffic.

Example 16-1. Header for Graph Algorithms

```
/*****************************************************************************
*                                                                           *
*  ----------------------------- graphalg.h -----------------------------   *
*                                                                           *
*****************************************************************************/

#ifndef GRAPHALG_H
#define GRAPHALG_H

#include "graph.h"
#include "list.h"

/*****************************************************************************
*                                                                           *
*  Define a structure for vertices in minimum spanning trees.               *
*                                                                           *
*****************************************************************************/

typedef struct MstVertex_ {

void              *data;
double            weight;

VertexColor       color;
double            key;

struct MstVertex_ *parent;

} MstVertex;

/*****************************************************************************
*                                                                           *
*  Define a structure for vertices in shortest-path problems.               *
*                                                                           *
*****************************************************************************/
```

Example 16-1. Header for Graph Algorithms (continued)

```
typedef struct PathVertex_ {

void            *data;
double          weight;

VertexColor     color;
double          d;

struct PathVertex_ *parent;

} PathVertex;

/*****************************************************************************
*                                                                           *
*  Define a structure for vertices in traveling-salesman problems.          *
*                                                                           *
*****************************************************************************/

typedef struct TspVertex_ {

void            *data;

double          x,
                y;

VertexColor     color;

} TspVertex;

/*****************************************************************************
*                                                                           *
*  -------------------------- Public Interface --------------------------   *
*                                                                           *
*****************************************************************************/

int mst(Graph *graph, const MstVertex *start, List *span, int (*match)(const
   void *key1, const void *key2));

int shortest(Graph *graph, const PathVertex *start, List *paths, int (*match)
   (const void *key1, const void *key2));

int tsp(List *vertices, const TspVertex *start, List *tour, int (*match)
   (const void *key1, const void *key2));

#endif
```

Description of Minimum Spanning Trees

Picture a number of pegs on a board connected by pieces of string. Assuming that
every peg is reachable from any other by traveling along one or more strings,
imagine a game in which the object is to remove some of the strings until all of

the pegs remain connected using the least amount of string. This is the idea behind a *minimum spanning tree*. Formally stated, given an undirected, weighted graph $G = (V, E)$, a minimum spanning tree is the set T of edges in E that connect all vertices in V at a minimum cost. The edges in T form a tree because each vertex ends up with exactly one parent that precedes it in the span, with the exception of the first vertex, which is the root of the tree.

Prim's Algorithm

One approach to computing a minimum spanning tree is *Prim's algorithm*. Prim's algorithm grows a minimum spanning tree by adding edges one at a time based on which looks best at the moment. The fact that Prim's algorithm adds edges using this approach makes it greedy (see Chapter 1, *Introduction*). Although greedy algorithms often yield approximations rather than optimal solutions, Prim's algorithm actually provides an optimal result.

Fundamentally, the algorithm works by repeatedly selecting a vertex and exploring the edges incident on it to determine if there is a more effective way to span the vertices explored thus far. The algorithm resembles breadth-first search because it explores all edges incident on a vertex before moving deeper in the graph. To determine the vertex to select at each stage, we maintain a color and a key value with every vertex.

Initially, we set all colors to white and we set all key values to ∞, which represents an arbitrarily large value greater than the weight of any edge in the graph. We set the key value of the vertex at which to start the span to 0. As the algorithm progresses, we assign to all vertices except the start vertex a parent in the minimum spanning tree. A vertex is part of the minimum spanning tree only after it is colored black. Before this time, its parent can fluctuate.

Prim's algorithm proceeds as follows. First, from among all white vertices in the graph, we select the vertex u with the smallest key value. Initially, this will be the start vertex since its key value is 0. After we select the vertex, we color it black. Next, for each white vertex v adjacent to u, if the weight of the edge (u, v) is less than the key value of v, we set the key value of v to the weight of (u, v) and we set the parent of v to u. We then repeat this process until all vertices have been colored black. As the minimum spanning tree grows, it consists of all edges in the graph that have a black vertex on either end.

Figure 16-1 illustrates the computation of a minimum spanning tree using Prim's algorithm. In the figure, the key value and parent of each vertex are displayed beside the vertex. The key value is to the left of the slash, and the parent is to the right. The edges shaded in light gray are the edges in the minimum spanning tree as it grows. The minimum spanning tree computed in the figure has a total weight of 17.

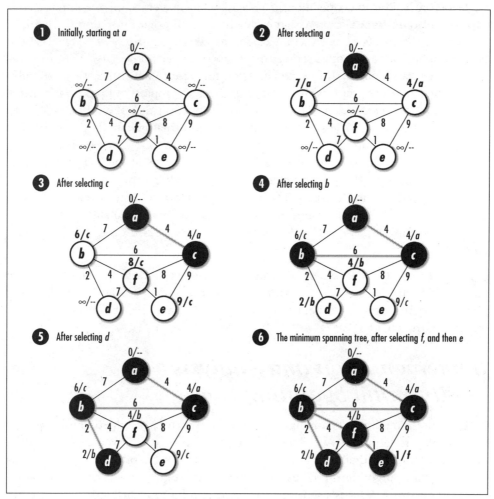

Figure 16-1. Computing a minimum spanning tree using Prim's algorithm

Interface for Minimum Spanning Trees

mst

```
int mst(Graph *graph, const MstVertex *start, List *span, int (*match)
   (const void *key1, const void *key2));
```

Return Value   0 if computing the minimum spanning tree is successful, or −1 otherwise.

Description   Computes a minimum spanning tree for an undirected, weighted graph specified by **graph**. The minimum spanning tree is computed starting from the vertex specified by **start**. The operation modifies **graph**, so a copy should be made before calling the operation, if necessary. Each vertex in *graph* must contain data of type *MstVertex*. Assign a weight to each edge by setting the *weight* member of the *MstVertex* structure passed as *data2* to *graph_ins_edge*. Use the *data* member of each *MstVertex* structure to store data associated with the vertex, such as an identifier. The *match* function for *graph*, which is set by the caller when initializing the graph with *graph_init*, should compare only the *data* members of *MstVertex* structures. This is the same function that should be passed as the *match* argument to *mst*. Once computed, information about the minimum spanning tree is returned in *span*, which is a list of *MstVertex* structures. In *span*, the vertex whose parent is set to NULL is the vertex at the root of the minimum spanning tree. The *parent* member of every other vertex points to the vertex that precedes it in the span. The vertices in *span* point to actual vertices in *graph*, so the caller must ensure that the storage in *graph* remains valid as long as *span* is being accessed. Use *list_destroy* to destroy *span* once it is no longer needed.

Complexity $O(EV^2)$, where V is the number of vertices in the graph and E is the number of edges. However, with a little improvement to the implementation presented here, Prim's algorithm runs in $O(E \lg V)$ time (see the related topics at the end of the chapter).

Implementation and Analysis of Minimum Spanning Trees

To compute a minimum spanning tree for an undirected, weighted graph, we first need a way to represent weighted graphs using the basic abstract datatype for graphs presented in Chapter 11. We also need a way to keep track of the information that Prim's algorithm requires for vertices and edges. This is the point of the *MstVertex* structure; it is used for vertices in graphs for which we plan to compute minimum spanning trees (see Example 16-2). The structure consists of five members: *data* is the data associated with the vertex, *weight* is the weight of the edge incident to the vertex, *color* is the color of the vertex, *key* is the key value of the vertex, and *parent* is the parent of the vertex in the minimum spanning tree.

Building a graph of *MstVertex* structures is nearly the same as building a graph containing other types of data. To insert a vertex into the graph, we call *graph_ins_vertex* and pass an *MstVertex* structure for *data*. Similarly, to insert an edge, we call *graph_ins_edge* and pass *MstVertex* structures for *data1* and *data2*. When we insert a vertex, we set only the *data* member of the *MstVertex* structure. When we insert an edge, we set the *data* member of *data1*, and the *data* and *weight* members of *data2*. In *data2*, the *weight* member is the weight of the edge from the vertex represented by *data1* to the vertex represented by *data2*. In practice, weights are usually computed and stored as floating-point numbers. Since key values are computed from the weights, these are floating-point numbers as well.

The *mst* operation begins by initializing every vertex in the list of adjacency-list structures. We set the initial key value of each vertex to *DBL_MAX*, except the start vertex, whose key value is set to 0.0. Recall that in the graph abstract datatype, a graph was represented as a list of adjacency-list structures, each of which contained one vertex and a set of vertices adjacent to it (see Chapter 11). We use the vertex stored in each adjacency-list structure to maintain the color, key value, and parent of the vertex. The point of maintaining this information in the list of adjacency-list structures, as opposed to vertices in the adjacency lists themselves, is that we can keep it in one place. Whereas a single vertex may appear in numerous adjacency lists, each vertex appears in the list of adjacency-list structures exactly once.

At the center of Prim's algorithm is a single loop that iterates once for each vertex in the graph. We begin each iteration by selecting the vertex that has the smallest key value among the white vertices. We color this vertex black where it resides in the list of adjacency-list structures. Next, we traverse the vertices adjacent to the selected vertex. As we traverse each vertex, we look up its color and key value in the list of adjacency-list structures. Once we have located this information, we compare it with the color and key value of the selected vertex. If the adjacent vertex is white and its key value is less than that of the selected vertex, we set the key value of the adjacent vertex to the weight of the edge between the selected vertex and the adjacent vertex; we also set the parent of the adjacent vertex to the selected vertex. We update this information for the adjacent vertex where it resides in the list of adjacency-list structures. We then repeat this process until all vertices have been colored black.

Once the main loop in Prim's algorithm terminates, we are finished computing the minimum spanning tree. At this point, we insert each black *MstVertex* structure from the list of adjacency-list structures into the linked list *span*. In *span*, the vertex whose parent is set to NULL is the vertex at the root of the minimum spanning tree. The *parent* member of every other vertex points to the vertex that precedes it in the span. The *weight* member of each *MstVertex* structure is not populated because it is needed only for storing weights in adjacency lists. Figure 16-2 shows the list of *MstVertex* structures returned for the minimum spanning tree computed in Figure 16-1.

The runtime complexity of *mst* is $O(EV^2)$, where V is the number of vertices in the graph and E is the number of edges. This comes from the main loop, in which we select vertices and compare weights and key values. For each of the V vertices we select, we first traverse V elements in the list of adjacency-list structures to determine which white vertex has the smallest key value. This part of the main

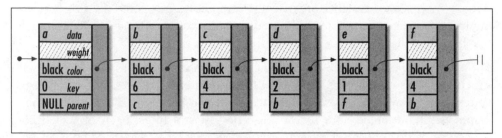

Figure 16-2. The list returned by mst for the minimum spanning tree computed in Figure 16-1

loop is $O(V^2)$ overall. Next, for each vertex adjacent to the vertex we select, we consult the list of adjacency-list structures for information about whether to change its key value and parent. Over all V vertices, the list is consulted E times, once for each of the E edges in all of the adjacency lists together. Each of these consultations requires $O(V)$ time to search the list. Therefore, for all V vertices that we select, an $O(V)$ operation is performed E times. Consequently, this part of the loop is $O(EV^2)$, and the main loop overall is $O(V^2 + EV^2)$, or $O(EV^2)$. Since the loops before and after the main loop are $O(V)$, the runtime complexity of *mst* is $O(EV^2)$. However, recall that with a little improvement (discussed at the end of the chapter), Prim's algorithm runs in $O(E \lg V)$ time.

Example 16-2. Implementation for Computing Minimum Spanning Trees

```
/*****************************************************************************
*                                                                           *
*  -------------------------------- mst.c --------------------------------   *
*                                                                           *
*****************************************************************************/

#include <float.h>
#include <stdlib.h>

#include "graph.h"
#include "graphalg.h"
#include "list.h"

/*****************************************************************************
*                                                                           *
*  --------------------------------- mst ---------------------------------   *
*                                                                           *
*****************************************************************************/

int mst(Graph *graph, const MstVertex *start, List *span, int (*match)(const
   void *key1, const void *key2)) {

AdjList            *adjlist;

MstVertex          *mst_vertex,
                   *adj_vertex;
```

Example 16-2. Implementation for Computing Minimum Spanning Trees (continued)

```
ListElmt            *element,
                    *member;

double              minimum;

int                 found,
                    i;

/***************************************************************************
*                                                                         *
*  Initialize all of the vertices in the graph.                           *
*                                                                         *
***************************************************************************/

found = 0;

for (element = list_head(&graph_adjlists(graph)); element != NULL; element =
   list_next(element)) {

   mst_vertex = ((AdjList *)list_data(element))->vertex;

   if (match(mst_vertex, start)) {

      /*********************************************************************
      *                                                                   *
      *  Initialize the start vertex.                                     *
      *                                                                   *
      *********************************************************************/

      mst_vertex->color = white;
      mst_vertex->key = 0;
      mst_vertex->parent = NULL;
      found = 1;

      }

   else {

      /*********************************************************************
      *                                                                   *
      *  Initialize vertices other than the start vertex.                 *
      *                                                                   *
      *********************************************************************/

      mst_vertex->color = white;
      mst_vertex->key = DBL_MAX;
      mst_vertex->parent = NULL;

      }

   }
```

Example 16-2. Implementation for Computing Minimum Spanning Trees (continued)

```
/***************************************************************************
*                                                                         *
*  Return if the start vertex was not found.                              *
*                                                                         *
***************************************************************************/

if (!found)
   return -1;

/***************************************************************************
*                                                                         *
*  Use Prim's algorithm to compute a minimum spanning tree.               *
*                                                                         *
***************************************************************************/

i = 0;

while (i < graph_vcount(graph)) {

   /***********************************************************************
   *                                                                     *
   *  Select the white vertex with the smallest key value.               *
   *                                                                     *
   ***********************************************************************/

   minimum = DBL_MAX;

   for (element = list_head(&graph_adjlists(graph)); element != NULL; element
      = list_next(element)) {

      mst_vertex = ((AdjList *)list_data(element))->vertex;

      if (mst_vertex->color == white && mst_vertex->key < minimum) {

         minimum = mst_vertex->key;
         adjlist = list_data(element);

      }

   }

   /***********************************************************************
   *                                                                     *
   *  Color the selected vertex black.                                   *
   *                                                                     *
   ***********************************************************************/

   ((MstVertex *)adjlist->vertex)->color = black;

   /***********************************************************************
   *                                                                     *
   *  Traverse each vertex adjacent to the selected vertex.              *
   *                                                                     *
   ***********************************************************************/
```

Example 16-2. Implementation for Computing Minimum Spanning Trees (continued)

```
for (member = list_head(&adjlist->adjacent); member != NULL; member =
   list_next(member)) {

   adj_vertex = list_data(member);

   /********************************************************************
   *                                                                  *
   *  Find the adjacent vertex in the list of adjacency-list structures.  *
   *                                                                  *
   ********************************************************************/

   for (element = list_head(&graph_adjlists(graph)); element != NULL;
      element = list_next(element)) {

      mst_vertex = ((AdjList *)list_data(element))->vertex;

      if (match(mst_vertex, adj_vertex)) {

         /****************************************************************
         *                                                              *
         *  Decide whether to change the key value and parent of the    *
         *  adjacent vertex in the list of adjacency-list structures.   *
         *                                                              *
         ****************************************************************/

         if (mst_vertex->color == white && adj_vertex->weight <
            mst_vertex->key) {

            mst_vertex->key = adj_vertex->weight;
            mst_vertex->parent = adjlist->vertex;

         }

         break;

      }

   }

}

/********************************************************************
*                                                                  *
*  Prepare to select the next vertex.                              *
*                                                                  *
********************************************************************/

i++;

}
```

Example 16-2. Implementation for Computing Minimum Spanning Trees (continued)

```
/***************************************************************************
*                                                                          *
*   Load the minimum spanning tree into a list.                            *
*                                                                          *
***************************************************************************/

list_init(span, NULL);

for (element = list_head(&graph_adjlists(graph)); element != NULL; element =
   list_next(element)) {

   /***************************************************************************
   *                                                                          *
   *   Load each black vertex from the list of adjacency-list structures.     *
   *                                                                          *
   ***************************************************************************/

   mst_vertex = ((AdjList *)list_data(element))->vertex;

   if (mst_vertex->color == black) {

      if (list_ins_next(span, list_tail(span), mst_vertex) != 0) {

         list_destroy(span);
         return -1;

      }

   }

}

return 0;

}
```

Description of Shortest Paths

Finding the *shortest path*, or *minimum-weight path*, from one vertex to another in a graph is an important distillation of many routing problems. Formally stated, given a directed, weighted graph $G = (V, E)$, the shortest path from vertex s to t in V is the set S of edges in E that connect s to t at a minimum cost.

When we find S, we are solving the *single-pair shortest-path problem*. To do this, in actuality we solve the more general *single-source shortest-paths problem*, which solves the single-pair shortest-path problem in the process. In the single-source shortest-paths problem, we compute the shortest paths from a start vertex s to all other vertices reachable from it. We solve this problem because no algorithm is known to solve the single-pair shortest-path problem any faster.

Dijkstra's Algorithm

One approach to solving the single-source shortest-paths problem is *Dijkstra's algorithm* (pronounced "Dikestra"). Dijkstra's algorithm grows a *shortest-paths tree*, whose root is the start vertex *s* and whose branches are the shortest paths from *s* to all other vertices in *G*. The algorithm requires that all weights in the graph be nonnegative. Like Prim's algorithm, Dijkstra's algorithm is another example of a greedy algorithm that happens to produce an optimal result. The algorithm is greedy because it adds edges to the shortest-paths tree based on which looks best at the moment.

Fundamentally, Dijkstra's algorithm works by repeatedly selecting a vertex and exploring the edges incident from it to determine whether the shortest path to each vertex can be improved. The algorithm resembles a breadth-first search because it explores all edges incident from a vertex before moving deeper in the graph. To compute the shortest paths between *s* and all other vertices, Dijkstra's algorithm requires that a color and shortest-path estimate be maintained with every vertex. Typically, shortest-path estimates are represented by the variable *d*.

Initially, we set all colors to white, and we set all shortest-path estimates to ∞, which represents an arbitrarily large value greater than the weight of any edge in the graph. We set the shortest-path estimate of the start vertex to 0. As the algorithm progresses, we assign to all vertices except the start vertex a parent in the shortest-paths tree. The parent of a vertex may change several times before the algorithm terminates.

Dijkstra's algorithm proceeds as follows. First, from among all white vertices in the graph, we select the vertex *u* with the smallest shortest-path estimate. Initially, this will be the start vertex since its shortest-path estimate is 0. After we select the vertex, we color it black. Next, for each white vertex *v* adjacent to *u*, we *relax* the edge (*u*, *v*). When we relax an edge, we determine whether going through *u* improves the shortest path computed thus far to *v*. To make this decision, we add the weight of (*u*, *v*) to the shortest-path estimate for *u*. If this value is less than or equal to the shortest-path estimate for *v*, we assign the value to *v* as its new shortest-path estimate, and we set the parent of *v* to *u*. We then repeat this process until all vertices have been colored black. Once we have computed the shortest-paths tree, the shortest path from *s* to another vertex *t* can be determined by starting at *t* in the tree and following successive parents until we reach *s*. The path in reverse is the shortest path from *s* to *t*.

Figure 16-3 illustrates the computation of the shortest paths between *a* and all other vertices in the graph. The shortest path from *a* to *b*, for example, is ⟨*a*, *c*, *f*, *b*⟩, which has a total weight of 7. The shortest-path estimate and parent of each vertex are displayed beside the vertex. The shortest-path estimate is to the left of the slash, and the parent is to the right. The edges shaded in light gray are the edges in the shortest-paths tree as it changes.

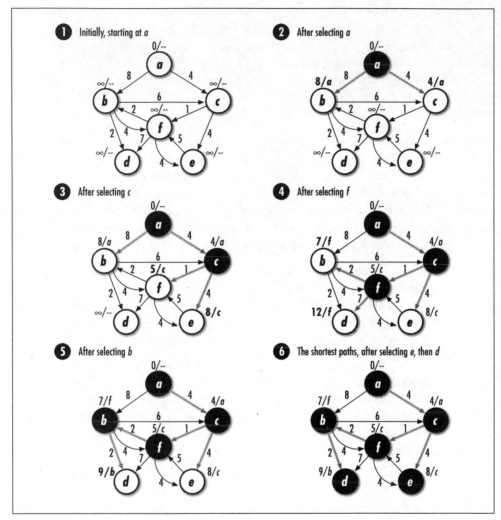

Figure 16-3. Computing shortest paths using Dijkstra's algorithm

Interface for Shortest Paths

shortest

```
int shortest(Graph *graph, const PathVertex *start, List *paths, int (*match)
   (const void *key1, const void *key2));
```

Return Value   0 if computing the shortest paths is successful, or –1 otherwise.

Description   Computes shortest paths between *start* and all other vertices in a directed, weighted graph specified by *graph*. The operation modifies *graph*, so a copy should be made before calling the operation, if necessary. Each vertex in *graph* must contain data of type *PathVertex*. Assign a weight to each edge by setting the *weight* member of the *PathVertex* structure passed as *data2* to *graph_ins_edge*. Use the *data* member of each *PathVertex* structure to store data associated with the vertex, such as an identifier. The *match* function for *graph*, which is set by the caller when initializing the graph with *graph_init*, should compare only the *data* members of *PathVertex* structures. This is the same function that should be passed as the *match* argument to *shortest*. Once computed, information about the shortest paths is returned in *paths*, which is a list of *PathVertex* structures. In *paths*, the parent of the start vertex is set to NULL. The *parent* member of every other vertex points to the vertex that precedes it in the shortest path from the start vertex. The vertices in *paths* point to actual vertices in *graph*, so the caller must ensure that the storage in *graph* remains valid as long as *paths* is being accessed. Use *list_destroy* to destroy *paths* once it is no longer needed.

Complexity $O(EV^2)$, where V is the number of vertices in the graph and E is the number of edges. However, with a little improvement (similar to that discussed for Prim's algorithm at the end of the chapter), Dijkstra's algorithm can run in $O(E \lg V)$ time.

Implementation and Analysis of Shortest Paths

To compute the shortest paths from a vertex to all others reachable from it in a directed, weighted graph, the graph is represented in the same manner as described for minimum spanning trees. However, we use the *PathVertex* structure instead of *MstVertex* for vertices (see Example 16-3). The *PathVertex* structure allows us to represent weighted graphs as well as keep track of the information that Dijkstra's algorithm requires for vertices and edges. The structure consists of five members: *data* is the data associated with the vertex, *weight* is the weight of the edge incident to the vertex, *color* is the color of the vertex, *d* is the shortest-path estimate for the vertex, and *parent* is the parent of the vertex in the shortest-paths tree. We build a graph consisting of *PathVertex* structures in the same manner as described for building graphs with *MstVertex* structures.

The *shortest* operation begins by initializing every vertex in the list of adjacency-list structures. We set the initial shortest-path estimate for each vertex to *DBL_MAX*, except the start vertex, whose estimate is set to 0.0. The vertex stored in each adjacency-list structure is used to maintain the color, shortest-path estimate, and parent of the vertex, for the same reasons as mentioned for computing minimum spanning trees.

At the center of Dijkstra's algorithm is a single loop that iterates once for each vertex in the graph. We begin each iteration by selecting the vertex that has the smallest shortest-path estimate among the white vertices. We color this vertex black where it resides in the list of adjacency-list structures. Next, we traverse the vertices adjacent to the selected vertex. As we traverse each vertex, we look up its color and shortest-path estimate in the list of adjacency-list structures. Once we have located this information, we call *relax* to relax the edge between the selected vertex and the adjacent vertex. If *relax* needs to update the shortest-path estimate and parent of the adjacent vertex, it does so where the adjacent vertex resides in the list of adjacency-list structures. We then repeat this process until all vertices have been colored black.

Once the main loop in Dijkstra's algorithm terminates, we are finished computing the shortest paths from the start vertex to all other vertices reachable from it in the graph. At this point, we insert each black **PathVertex** structure from the list of adjacency-list structures into the linked list **paths**. In **paths**, the parent of the start vertex is set to NULL. The **parent** member of every other vertex points to the vertex that precedes it in the shortest path from the start vertex. The **weight** member of each **PathVertex** structure is not populated because it is needed only for storing weights in adjacency lists. Figure 16-4 shows the list of **PathVertex** structures returned for the shortest paths computed in Figure 16-3.

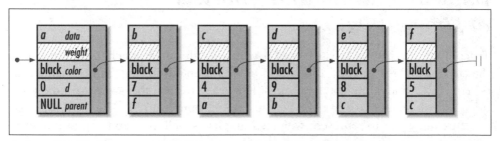

Figure 16-4. The list returned by the operation shortest for the shortest paths computed in Figure 16-3

The runtime complexity of *shortest* is $O(EV^2)$, where V is the number of vertices in the graph and E is the number of edges. This comes from the main loop, in which we select vertices and relax edges. For each of the V vertices we select, we first traverse V elements in the list of adjacency-list structures to determine which white vertex has the smallest shortest-path estimate. This part of the main loop is $O(V^2)$ overall. Next, for each vertex adjacent to the vertex we select, the list of adjacency-list structures is consulted for the information needed to relax the edge between the two vertices. Over all V vertices that we select, the list is consulted E times, once for each of the E edges in all of the adjacency lists together. Each of these consultations requires $O(V)$ time to search the list. Therefore, for all V vertices that we select, an $O(V)$ operation is performed E times. Consequently, this part of the loop is $O(EV^2)$, and the main loop overall is $O(V^2 + EV^2)$, or $O(EV^2)$. Since the loops before and after the main loop are $O(V)$, the runtime complexity of *shortest* is $O(EV^2)$. However, recall that with a little improvement (similar to that discussed for Prim's algorithm at the end of the chapter), Dijkstra's algorithm can run in $O(E \lg V)$ time.

Example 16-3. Implementation for Computing Shortest Paths

```c
/*****************************************************************************
*                                                                           *
*  --------------------------- shortest.c ---------------------------       *
*                                                                           *
*****************************************************************************/

#include <float.h>
#include <stdlib.h>

#include "graph.h"
#include "graphalg.h"
#include "list.h"
#include "set.h"

/*****************************************************************************
*                                                                           *
*  ------------------------------ relax ------------------------------      *
*                                                                           *
*****************************************************************************/

static void relax(PathVertex *u, PathVertex *v, double weight) {

/*****************************************************************************
*                                                                           *
*  Relax an edge between two vertices u and v.                              *
*                                                                           *
*****************************************************************************/

if (v->d > u->d + weight) {

   v->d = u->d + weight;
   v->parent = u;

}

return;

}

/*****************************************************************************
*                                                                           *
*  ----------------------------- shortest ----------------------------     *
*                                                                           *
*****************************************************************************/
```

Example 16-3. Implementation for Computing Shortest Paths (continued)

```
int shortest(Graph *graph, const PathVertex *start, List *paths, int (*match)
   (const void *key1, const void *key2)) {

AdjList          *adjlist;

PathVertex       *pth_vertex,
                 *adj_vertex;

ListElmt         *element,
                 *member;

double           minimum;

int              found,
                 i;

/***************************************************************************
*                                                                         *
*  Initialize all of the vertices in the graph.                           *
*                                                                         *
***************************************************************************/

found = 0;

for (element = list_head(&graph_adjlists(graph)); element != NULL; element =
   list_next(element)) {

   pth_vertex = ((AdjList *)list_data(element))->vertex;

   if (match(pth_vertex, start)) {

      /*********************************************************************
      *                                                                   *
      *  Initialize the start vertex.                                     *
      *                                                                   *
      *********************************************************************/

      pth_vertex->color = white;
      pth_vertex->d = 0;
      pth_vertex->parent = NULL;
      found = 1;

      }

   else {

      /*********************************************************************
      *                                                                   *
      *  Initialize vertices other than the start vertex.                 *
      *                                                                   *
      *********************************************************************/
```

Example 16-3. Implementation for Computing Shortest Paths (continued)

```
      pth_vertex->color = white;
      pth_vertex->d = DBL_MAX;
      pth_vertex->parent = NULL;

   }

}

/*****************************************************************************
 *                                                                           *
 *  Return if the start vertex was not found.                                *
 *                                                                           *
 *****************************************************************************/

if (!found)
   return -1;

/*****************************************************************************
 *                                                                           *
 *  Use Dijkstra's algorithm to compute shortest paths from the start vertex. *
 *                                                                           *
 *****************************************************************************/

i = 0;

while (i < graph_vcount(graph)) {

   /*****************************************************************************
    *                                                                           *
    *  Select the white vertex with the smallest shortest-path estimate.        *
    *                                                                           *
    *****************************************************************************/

   minimum = DBL_MAX;

   for (element = list_head(&graph_adjlists(graph)); element != NULL; element
      = list_next(element)) {

      pth_vertex = ((AdjList *)list_data(element))->vertex;

      if (pth_vertex->color == white && pth_vertex->d < minimum) {

         minimum = pth_vertex->d;
         adjlist = list_data(element);

      }

   }

   /*****************************************************************************
    *                                                                           *
    *  Color the selected vertex black.                                         *
    *                                                                           *
    *****************************************************************************/
```

Example 16-3. Implementation for Computing Shortest Paths (continued)

```c
((PathVertex *)adjlist->vertex)->color = black;

/***********************************************************************
*                                                                     *
*  Traverse each vertex adjacent to the selected vertex.              *
*                                                                     *
***********************************************************************/

for (member = list_head(&adjlist->adjacent); member != NULL; member =
   list_next(member)) {

   adj_vertex = list_data(member);

   /***********************************************************************
   *                                                                     *
   *  Find the adjacent vertex in the list of adjacency-list structures. *
   *                                                                     *
   ***********************************************************************/

   for (element = list_head(&graph_adjlists(graph)); element != NULL;
      element = list_next(element)) {

      pth_vertex = ((AdjList *)list_data(element))->vertex;

      if (match(pth_vertex, adj_vertex)) {

         /******************************************************************
         *                                                                *
         *  Relax the adjacent vertex in the list of adjacency-list       *
         *  structures.                                                   *
         *                                                                *
         ******************************************************************/

         relax(adjlist->vertex, pth_vertex, adj_vertex->weight);

      }

   }

}

/***********************************************************************
*                                                                     *
*  Prepare to select the next vertex.                                 *
*                                                                     *
***********************************************************************/

i++;

}
```

Example 16-3. Implementation for Computing Shortest Paths (continued)

```
/***************************************************************************
 *                                                                         *
 *  Load the vertices with their path information into a list.             *
 *                                                                         *
 ***************************************************************************/

list_init(paths, NULL);

for (element = list_head(&graph_adjlists(graph)); element != NULL; element =
   list_next(element)) {

   /***********************************************************************
    *                                                                     *
    *  Load each black vertex from the list of adjacency-list structures. *
    *                                                                     *
    ***********************************************************************/

   pth_vertex = ((AdjList *)list_data(element))->vertex;

   if (pth_vertex->color == black) {

      if (list_ins_next(paths, list_tail(paths), pth_vertex) != 0) {

         list_destroy(paths);
         return -1;

      }

   }

}

return 0;

}
```

Shortest Paths Example: Routing Tables

One application in which shortest paths play an important role is *routing* data
between networks in an internet. Routing is the process of making informed decisions about how to move data from one point to another. In an internet, this is
accomplished by propagating small sections of the data, or *packets*, along inter-
connected points called *gateways*. As each packet passes through a gateway, a
router looks at where the packet eventually needs to go and decides to which
gateway it should be sent next. The goal of each router is to propagate a packet
closer and closer to its final destination.

In order to propagate a packet closer to its destination, each router maintains
information about the structure, or *topology*, of the internet. It stores this

information in a *routing table*. A routing table contains one entry for each gateway the router knows how to reach. Each entry specifies the next gateway to which packets destined for another gateway should be sent.

So that packets are continually sent along the best route possible, routers periodically update their routing tables to reflect changes in the internet. In one type of routing, called *shortest path first routing*, or *SPF routing*, every router maintains its own map of the internet so that it can update its routing table by computing shortest paths between itself and other destinations. Its map is a directed, weighted graph whose vertices are gateways and whose edges are connections between the gateways. Each edge is weighted by the performance most recently observed for a connection. From time to time, routers exchange information about topology and performance using a protocol designed especially for this purpose.

Example 16-4 is a function, *route,* that computes the information necessary to update one entry in a routing table using SPF routing. The function accepts the list of path information returned in the **paths** argument of *shortest*. It uses this information to determine to which gateway a router should send a packet next to reach its destination most effectively.

To complete an entire table for a specific gateway, we first call *shortest* with the gateway passed as **start**. Next, for each destination to be included in the routing table, we call *route* with the destination passed as **destination**. We pass the same function for **match** as was provided to *graph_init* for the graph from which **paths** was generated. The *route* function follows parent pointers in **paths** from the destination back to the gateway and returns the best choice for moving a packet closer to its destination in **next**. The vertex returned in **next** points to the actual vertex in **paths**, so the storage in **paths** must remain valid as long as **next** is being accessed.

Figure 16-5a illustrates the computation of a routing table for a router at gw_1 in the internet shown (modeled using a graph similar to the one in Figure 16-3). Figure 16-5b illustrates the computation of the routing table for a router at gw_2. Notice how the shortest paths are different depending on where we start in the internet. Also, notice that in Figure 16-5b there is no way to reach gw_1, so there is no entry for it in the table.

The runtime complexity of *route* is $O(n^2)$, where n is the number of gateways in **paths**. This is because we look up in **paths** the parent of each vertex between the destination we are interested in and the starting point in the internet. If the shortest path between us and the destination contains every gateway in **paths**, in the worst case we may have to search the list of gateways n times to find every parent.

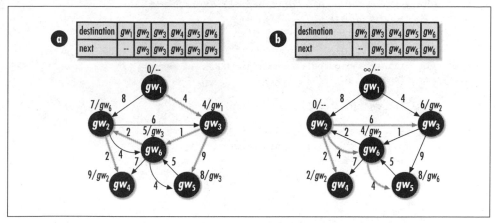

Figure 16-5. Routing tables computed for gateways (a) gw_1 and (b) gw_2, in an internet

Example 16-4. Implementation of a Function for Updating Entries in Routing Tables

```
/*****************************************************************************
*                                                                           *
*  ------------------------------- route.c -------------------------------  *
*                                                                           *
*****************************************************************************/

#include <stdlib.h>

#include "graphalg.h"
#include "list.h"
#include "route.h"

/*****************************************************************************
*                                                                           *
*  -------------------------------- route --------------------------------  *
*                                                                           *
*****************************************************************************/

int route(List *paths, PathVertex *destination, PathVertex **next, int
   (*match)(const void *key1, const void *key2)) {

PathVertex         *temp,
                   *parent;

ListElmt           *element;

int                found;

/*****************************************************************************
*                                                                           *
*  Locate the destination in the list of gateways.                          *
*                                                                           *
*****************************************************************************/
```

*Example 16-4. Implementation of a Function for Updating Entries
in Routing Tables (continued)*

```
found = 0;

for (element = list_head(paths); element != NULL; element =
   list_next(element)) {

   if (match(list_data(element), destination)) {

      temp = list_data(element);
      parent = ((PathVertex *)list_data(element))->parent;
      found = 1;
      break;

   }

}

/****************************************************************************
*                                                                          *
*  Return if the destination is not reachable.                             *
*                                                                          *
****************************************************************************/

if (!found)
   return -1;

/****************************************************************************
*                                                                          *
*  Compute the next gateway in the shortest path to the destination.       *
*                                                                          *
****************************************************************************/

while (parent != NULL) {

   temp = list_data(element);
   found = 0;

   for (element = list_head(paths); element != NULL; element =
      list_next(element)) {

      if (match(list_data(element), parent)) {

         parent = ((PathVertex *)list_data(element))->parent;
         found = 1;
         break;

      }

   }
```

Example 16-4. Implementation of a Function for Updating Entries
in Routing Tables (continued)

```
/***************************************************************************
*                                                                         *
*   Return if the destination is not reachable.                           *
*                                                                         *
***************************************************************************/

if (!found)
   return -1;

}

*next = temp;

return 0;

}
```

Description of the Traveling-Salesman Problem

Imagine a salesman who needs to visit a number of cities as part of the route he works. His goal is to travel the shortest possible distance while visiting every city exactly once before returning to the point at which he starts. This is the idea behind the *traveling-salesman problem.*

In a graph, a tour in which we visit every other vertex exactly once before return-ing to the vertex at which we started is called a *hamiltonian cycle.* To solve the traveling-salesman problem, we use a graph $G = (V, E)$ as a model and look for the hamiltonian cycle with the shortest length. G is a complete, undirected, weighted graph, wherein V is a set of vertices representing the points we wish to visit and E is a set of edges representing connections between the points. Each edge in E is weighted by the distance between the vertices that define it. Since G is complete and undirected, E contains $V(V-1)/2$ edges.

One way to solve the traveling-salesman problem is by exploring all possible per-mutations of the vertices in G. Using this approach, since each permutation repre-sents one possible tour, we simply determine which one results in the tour that is the shortest. Unfortunately, this approach is not at all practical because it does not run in polynomial time. A polynomial-time algorithm is one whose complexity is less than or equal to $O(n^k)$, where k is some constant. This approach does not run in polynomial time because for a set of V vertices, there are $V!$ possible permuta-tions; thus, exploring them all requires $O(V!)$ time, where $V!$ is the factorial of V, which is the product of all numbers from V down to 1.

In general, nonpolynomial-time algorithms are avoided because even for small inputs, problems quickly become intractable. Actually, the traveling-salesman problem is a special type of nonpolynomial-time problem called *NP-complete*. NP-complete problems are those for which no polynomial-time algorithms are known, but for which no proof refutes the possibility either; even so, the likelihood of finding such an algorithm is extremely slim. With this in mind, normally the traveling-salesman problem is solved using an approximation algorithm (see Chapter 1).

Applying the Nearest-Neighbor Heuristic

One way to compute an approximate traveling-salesman tour is to apply the *nearest-neighbor heuristic*. This works as follows. We begin with a tour consisting of only the vertex at the start of the tour. We color this vertex black. All other vertices are white until added to the tour, at which point we color them black as well. Next, for each vertex v not already in the tour, we compute a weight for the edge between the last vertex u added to the tour and v. Recall that the weight of an edge from u to v in the traveling-salesman problem is the distance between u and v. We compute this using the coordinates of the points that each vertex represents. The distance r between two points (x_1, y_1) and (x_2, y_2) is defined by the formula:

$$r = \sqrt{(x_2 - x_1)^2 + (y_2 - y_1)^2}$$

Using this formula, we select the vertex closest to u, color it black, and add it to the tour. We then repeat this process until all vertices have been colored black. At this point, we add the start vertex to the tour again to form a complete cycle.

Figure 16-6 illustrates a solution to the traveling-salesman problem using the nearest-neighbor heuristic. Normally when a graph is drawn for the traveling-salesman problem, the edges connecting every vertex to each other are not explicitly shown since the edges are understood. In the figure, each vertex is displayed along with the coordinates of the point it represents. The dashed lines at each stage show the edges whose distances are being compared. The darkest line is the edge added to the tour. The tour obtained using the nearest-neighbor heuristic has a length of 15.95. The optimal tour has a length of 14.71, which is about 8% shorter.

The nearest-neighbor heuristic has some interesting properties. Like the other algorithms in this chapter, it resembles breadth-first search because it explores all of the vertices adjacent to the last vertex in the tour before exploring deeper in the graph. The heuristic is also greedy because each time it adds a vertex to the tour, it does so based on which looks best at the moment. Unfortunately, the nearest neighbor added at one point may affect the tour in a negative way later. Nevertheless, the heuristic always returns a tour whose length is within a factor of 2 of the

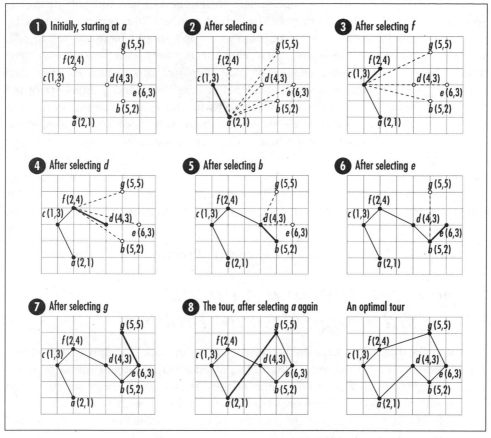

Figure 16-6. Solving the traveling-salesman problem using the nearest-neighbor heuristic

optimal tour length, and in many cases it does better than this. Other techniques exist to improve a tour once we have computed it. One technique is to apply an *exchange heuristic* (see the related topics at the end of the chapter).

Interface for the Traveling-Salesman Problem

tsp

```
int tsp(List *vertices, const TspVertex *start, List *tour, int (*match)
   (const void *key1, const void *key2))
```

Return Value   0 if computing the approximate traveling-salesman tour is successful, or −1 otherwise.

Description   Computes an approximate traveling-salesman tour of the points specified as vertices in *vertices*. The tour begins at the vertex specified by *start*. The operation modifies *vertices*, so a copy should be made before calling the operation, if necessary. Each element in *vertices* must be of type *TspVertex*. Use the *data* member of each *TspVertex* structure to store data associated with the vertex, such as an identifier. Use the *x* and *y* members of the structure to specify the coordinates associated with the vertex. The function specified by *match* determines whether two vertices match. It should only compare the *data* members of *TspVertex* structures. The tour is returned in *tour*, which is a list of *TspVertex* structures. Each vertex appears in *tour* in the order it would be encountered during the tour. The elements in *tour* point to the actual vertices in *vertices*, so the caller must ensure that the storage in *vertices* remains valid as long as *tour* is being accessed. Use *list_destroy* to destroy *tour* once it is no longer needed.

Complexity $O(V^2)$, where V is the number of vertices to visit in the tour.

Implementation and Analysis
of the Traveling-Salesman Problem

To solve the traveling-salesman problem, we begin with a graph that is represented simply as a list of vertices. In this representation, an edge connecting every pair of vertices is implied. Each vertex in the list is a *TspVertex* structure (see Example 16-5). This structure consists of four members: *data* is the data associated with the vertex, *x* and *y* are coordinates for the point the vertex represents, and *color* is the color of the vertex.

The *tsp* operation begins by coloring every vertex white, except the start vertex, which is colored black and added to the tour immediately. The coordinates of the start vertex are also recorded so that we can compute distances between it and every other vertex during the first iteration of the main loop. In the main loop, we add all of the remaining vertices to the tour. During each iteration, we look for the white vertex closest to the last vertex. Each time we add a vertex, we record its coordinates for the next iteration and color the vertex black. After the loop terminates, we add the start vertex again to complete the tour.

The runtime complexity of *tsp* is $O(V^2)$, where V is the number of vertices to visit in the tour. This is because for each of the $V-1$ iterations of the main loop, we search the vertices in the graph to determine which is white and needs a distance computed to it. Notice that $O(V^2)$ is quite an improvement over the runtime complexity for computing an optimal tour, which was $O(V!)$.

Example 16-5. Implementation for Solving the Traveling-Salesman Problem

```
/*****************************************************************************
*                                                                           *
*  ------------------------------- tsp.c ---------------------------------  *
*                                                                           *
*****************************************************************************/

#include <float.h>
#include <math.h>
#include <stdlib.h>

#include "graph.h"
#include "graphalg.h"
#include "list.h"

/*****************************************************************************
*                                                                           *
*  --------------------------------- tsp ---------------------------------  *
*                                                                           *
*****************************************************************************/

int tsp(List *vertices, const TspVertex *start, List *tour, int (*match)
   (const void *key1, const void *key2)) {

TspVertex        *tsp_vertex,
                 *tsp_start,
                 *selection;

ListElmt         *element;

double           minimum,
                 distance,
                 x,
                 y;

int              found,
                 i;

/*****************************************************************************
*                                                                           *
*  Initialize the list for the tour.                                        *
*                                                                           *
*****************************************************************************/

list_init(tour, NULL);

/*****************************************************************************
*                                                                           *
*  Initialize all of the vertices in the graph.                             *
*                                                                           *
*****************************************************************************/

found = 0;
```

Example 16-5. Implementation for Solving the Traveling-Salesman Problem (continued)

```
for (element = list_head(vertices); element != NULL; element =
   list_next(element)) {

   tsp_vertex = list_data(element);

   if (match(tsp_vertex, start)) {

      /*************************************************************************
      *                                                                       *
      *  Start the tour at the start vertex.                                  *
      *                                                                       *
      *************************************************************************/

      if (list_ins_next(tour, list_tail(tour), tsp_vertex) != 0) {

         list_destroy(tour);
         return -1;

      }

      /*************************************************************************
      *                                                                       *
      *  Save the start vertex and its coordinates.                           *
      *                                                                       *
      *************************************************************************/

      tsp_start = tsp_vertex;
      x = tsp_vertex->x;
      y = tsp_vertex->y;

      /*************************************************************************
      *                                                                       *
      *  Color the start vertex black.                                        *
      *                                                                       *
      *************************************************************************/

      tsp_vertex->color = black;
      found = 1;

   }

   else {

      /*************************************************************************
      *                                                                       *
      *  Color all other vertices white.                                      *
      *                                                                       *
      *************************************************************************/

      tsp_vertex->color = white;

   }

}
```

Example 16-5. Implementation for Solving the Traveling-Salesman Problem (continued)

```
/***************************************************************************
*                                                                          *
*  Return if the start vertex was not found.                               *
*                                                                          *
***************************************************************************/

if (!found) {

   list_destroy(tour);
   return -1;

}

/***************************************************************************
*                                                                          *
*  Use the nearest-neighbor heuristic to compute the tour.                 *
*                                                                          *
***************************************************************************/

i = 0;

while (i < list_size(vertices) - 1) {

   /***********************************************************************
   *                                                                      *
   *  Select the white vertex closest to the previous vertex in the tour. *
   *                                                                      *
   ***********************************************************************/

   minimum = DBL_MAX;

   for (element = list_head(vertices); element != NULL; element =
      list_next(element)) {

      tsp_vertex = list_data(element);

      if (tsp_vertex->color == white) {

         distance = sqrt(pow(tsp_vertex->x-x,2.0) + pow(tsp_vertex->y-y,2.0));

         if (distance < minimum) {

            minimum = distance;
            selection = tsp_vertex;

         }

      }

   }
```

Example 16-5. Implementation for Solving the Traveling-Salesman Problem (continued)

```
/***************************************************************************
*                                                                         *
*  Save the coordinates of the selected vertex.                           *
*                                                                         *
***************************************************************************/

x = selection->x;
y = selection->y;

/***************************************************************************
*                                                                         *
*  Color the selected vertex black.                                       *
*                                                                         *
***************************************************************************/

selection->color = black;

/***************************************************************************
*                                                                         *
*  Insert the selected vertex into the tour.                              *
*                                                                         *
***************************************************************************/

if (list_ins_next(tour, list_tail(tour), selection) != 0) {

   list_destroy(tour);
   return -1;

}

/***************************************************************************
*                                                                         *
*  Prepare to select the next vertex.                                     *
*                                                                         *
***************************************************************************/

i++;

}

/***************************************************************************
*                                                                         *
*  Insert the start vertex again to complete the tour.                    *
*                                                                         *
***************************************************************************/

if (list_ins_next(tour, list_tail(tour), tsp_start) != 0) {

   list_destroy(tour);
   return -1;

}
```

Example 16-5. Implementation for Solving the Traveling-Salesman Problem (continued)

```
return 0;

}
```

Questions and Answers

Q: *In the implementations presented for computing minimum spanning trees and shortest paths, weighted graphs are represented by storing the weights of edges in the graphs themselves. What is an alternative to this?*

A: For graphs containing edges weighted by factors that do not change frequently, the approach used in this chapter works well. However, a more general way to think of an edge's weight is as a function $w(u, v)$, where u and v are the vertices that define the edge to which the weight function applies. To determine the weight of an edge, we simply call the function as needed. An advantage to this approach is that it lets us compute weights dynamically in applications where we expect weights to change frequently. On the other hand, a disadvantage is that if the weight function is complicated, it may be inefficient to compute over and over again.

Q: *When solving the traveling-salesman problem, we saw that computing an optimal tour is intractable except when the tour contains very few points. Thus, an approximation algorithm based on the nearest-neighbor heuristic was used. What is another way to approximate a traveling-salesman tour? What is the running time of the approach? How close does the approach come to an optimal tour?*

A: Another approach to solving the traveling-salesman problem using an approximation algorithm is to compute a minimum spanning tree, then traverse the tree using a preorder traversal (see Chapter 9, *Trees*). The running time of this approach is $O(EV^2)$, assuming we use the *mst* operation provided in this chapter. As with the nearest-neighbor heuristic, this approach always produces a tour that has a length within a factor of 2 of the optimal tour length. To verify this, let T_{MST} be the length of the minimum spanning tree, T_{APP} be the length of any approximate tour we compute, and T_{OPT} be the length of the optimal tour. Since both the minimum spanning tree and the optimal tour span all vertices in the tree, and no span is shorter than the minimum spanning tree, $T_{MST} \le T_{OPT}$. Also, $T_{APP} \le 2T_{MST}$ because only in the worst case does an approximate tour trace every edge of the minimum spanning tree twice. Therefore, $T_{APP} \le 2T_{OPT}$. This is summarized as follows:

$$T_{MST} \le T_{OPT}, T_{APP} \le 2T_{MST} \Rightarrow T_{APP} \le 2T_{OPT}$$

Q: *When computing a minimum spanning tree using Prim's algorithm, if we start the algorithm at a different vertex, is it possible to obtain a different tree for the same graph?*

A: Especially in large graphs, as Prim's algorithm runs, it is not uncommon to find several white vertices with the same key value when looking for the one that is the smallest. In this case, we can select any of the choices since all are equally small. Depending on the vertex we select, we end up exploring a different set of edges incident from the vertex. Thus, we can get different edges in the minimum spanning tree. However, although the edges in the minimum spanning tree may vary, the total weight of the tree is always the same, which is the minimum for the graph.

Q: *Recall that when we solve the traveling-salesman problem, we use a graph whose structure is inspected for the hamiltonian cycle with the shortest length. Do all graphs contain hamiltonian cycles?*

A: Not all graphs contain hamiltonian cycles. This is easy to verify in a simple graph that is not connected, or in a directed acyclic graph. However, we never have to worry about this with complete graphs. Complete graphs contain many hamiltonian cycles. Determining whether a graph contains a hamiltonian cycle is another problem that, like the traveling-salesman problem, is NP-complete. In fact, many graph problems fall into this class of difficult problems.

Q: *The implementation of Prim's algorithm presented in this chapter runs in $O(EV^2)$ time. However, a better implementation runs in $O(E \lg V)$. How could we improve the implementation presented here to achieve this?*

A: The implementation of Prim's algorithm in this chapter runs in $O(EV^2)$ time because for each vertex in the graph, we scan the list of vertices to determine which is white and has the minimum key value. We can improve this part of the algorithm dramatically by using a priority queue (see Chapter 10, *Heaps and Priority Queues*). Recall that extracting the minimum value from a priority queue is an $O(1)$ operation, and maintaining the heap property of the priority queue is $O(\lg n)$, where n is the number of elements. This results in a runtime complexity of $O(E \lg V)$ for Prim's algorithm overall. However, the priority queue must support operations for decreasing values already in the queue and for locating a particular value efficiently so that it can be modified. Since the priority queue presented in Chapter 10 does not support these operations, Prim's algorithm was implemented here without this improvement.

Q: *Normally when we compute a minimum spanning tree, we do so for a connected graph. What happens if we try computing a minimum spanning tree for a graph that is not connected?*

A: Recall that a graph is connected if every vertex is reachable from each other by following some path. If we try to compute a minimum spanning tree for a graph that is not connected, we simply get a minimum spanning tree for the connected component in which the start vertex lies.

Related Topics

Bellman-Ford algorithm

Another approach to solving the single-source shortest-paths problem. Unlike Dijkstra's algorithm, the Bellman-Ford algorithm supports graphs whose edges have negative weights. Its runtime complexity is $O(VE)$, where V is the number of vertices in the graph and E is the number of edges.

Kruskal's algorithm

Another approach to computing minimum spanning trees. The algorithm works as follows. To begin, we place every vertex in its own set. Next, we select edges in order of increasing weight. As we select each edge, we determine whether the vertices that define it are in different sets. If this is the case, we insert the edge into a set that is the minimum spanning tree and take the union of the sets containing each vertex; otherwise, we simply move on to the next edge. We repeat this process until all edges have been explored. Kruskal's algorithm has a runtime complexity of $O(E \lg E)$, assuming we use a priority queue to manage the edges, where E is the number of edges in the graph.

All-pairs shortest-paths problem

An additional type of shortest-path problem in which we find the shortest paths between every pair of vertices in a graph. One way to solve this problem is to solve the single-source shortest-paths problem once for each vertex in the graph. However, it can be solved faster using a dedicated approach.

Exchange heuristics

Heuristics designed to help improve approximate traveling-salesman tours that are reasonable to begin with, such as a tour computed using the nearest-neighbor heuristic. Generally, an exchange heuristic works by repeatedly trying to exchange edges already in the tour with others that may be better. As each exchange is made, the length of the tour is recalculated to see if the tour has been improved.

17

Geometric Algorithms

Geometric algorithms solve problems in *computational geometry*. Computational geometry is an area of mathematics in which we perform calculations related to geometric objects, such as points, lines, polygons, and the like. One interesting characteristic of problems in computational geometry is that many have a distinctly visual quality about them. In fact, for many problems we can find solutions simply by looking at visual representations of them. For example, how difficult is it visually to determine whether two line segments intersect? On the other hand, because computing requires more of a computational approach, even coming up with solutions for seemingly simple problems like this can be deceptively challenging. This chapter presents three fundamental geometric algorithms. The first two perform basic operations that are used frequently in solving more complicated problems in computational geometry. The third is a relatively simple example of a three-dimensional geometric algorithm. Example 17-1 is a header for the algorithms presented in this chapter. This chapter covers:

Testing whether line segments intersect

> Using a simple algorithm consisting of two steps: first, we test whether the bounding boxes of the line segments intersect, and then we test whether the line segments straddle each other. If both tests are successful, the two line segments intersect.

Convex hulls

> Minimum-size convex polygons that enclose sets of points. A polygon is convex if any line segment connecting two points inside the polygon lies completely inside the polygon itself.

Arc length on spherical surfaces

> The distance along an arc between two points on the surface of a sphere. Specifically, we calculate the length of the arc that lies in the same plane as

imaginary lines drawn from the center of the sphere to either endpoint of the arc on the sphere's surface.

Some applications of geometric algorithms are:

Farthest-pair problems
Problems in which we determine which two points in a set are located the farthest apart. It can be shown that these points must lie on the convex hull enclosing all of the points. Thus, the number of pairs whose distances are compared can be greatly reduced by first computing a convex hull.

Approximating distances on Earth (illustrated in this chapter)
An interesting application of arc lengths on spherical surfaces. However, since the Earth is not a perfect sphere but an ellipsoid, the distance computed is only an approximation.

Restricted regions
Polygons that enclose areas not to be entered from outside. For example, military organizations define restricted regions in which unauthorized aircraft are not permitted to fly. If the track of an aircraft consists of a series of line segments beginning outside of the region, a simple way to determine whether a proposed route of flight transgresses the region is to test whether any segment on the track intersects with any segment defining the region.

Physical enclosures
Structures that surround a number of objects, such as buildings or natural phenomena. Often one of the requirements in constructing a large enclosure is to build it using the least amount of materials. To do this, we can model the objects as points and compute the convex hull around them.

Robotics
An exciting area of research in which automated, artificially intelligent devices use geometric algorithms for vision and control. For example, a robot with navigational capabilities must be able to move around objects that get in its way and analyze various shapes to recognize where it is.

Cartographic information systems
Database systems containing geographical data generally used for mapping. Often this information is manipulated using geometric algorithms. For example, we might want to compute the distance between two geographical points stored in the system.

Virtual reality systems
Examples are flight simulators, systems for architectural visualization, and systems for molecular modeling. One important aspect of virtual reality systems is their use of computer graphics involving geometric algorithms.

Example 17-1. Header for Geometric Algorithms

```
/***************************************************************************
 *                                                                         *
 * --------------------------- geometry.h ---------------------------       *
 *                                                                         *
 ***************************************************************************/

#ifndef GEOMETRY_H
#define GEOMETRY_H

#include "list.h"

/***************************************************************************
 *                                                                         *
 *  Define an approximation for Pi.                                        *
 *                                                                         *
 ***************************************************************************/

#ifndef PI
#define          PI                    3.14159
#endif


/***************************************************************************
 *                                                                         *
 *  Define macros for comparisons.                                         *
 *                                                                         *
 ***************************************************************************/

#define          MIN(x, y)             (((x) < (y)) ? (x) : (y))
#define          MAX(x, y)             (((x) > (y)) ? (x) : (y))

/***************************************************************************
 *                                                                         *
 *  Define macros for converting between degrees and radians.             *
 *                                                                         *
 ***************************************************************************/

#define          DEGTORAD(deg)         (((deg) * 2.0 * PI) / 360.0)
#define          RADTODEG(rad)         (((rad) * 360.0) / (2.0 * PI))

/***************************************************************************
 *                                                                         *
 *  Define a structure for points in rectilinear coordinates.            *
 *                                                                         *
 ***************************************************************************/

typedef struct Point_ {

double           x,
                 y,
                 z;

} Point;
```

Example 17-1. Header for Geometric Algorithms (continued)

```
/****************************************************************************
*                                                                          *
*   Define a structure for points in spherical coordinates.                *
*                                                                          *
****************************************************************************/

typedef struct SPoint_ {

double            rho,
                  theta,
                  phi;

} SPoint;

/****************************************************************************
*                                                                          *
*   ------------------------- Public Interface -------------------------   *
*                                                                          *
****************************************************************************/

int lint(Point p1, Point p2, Point p3, Point p4);

int cvxhull(const List *P, List *polygon);

void arclen(SPoint p1, SPoint p2, double *length);

#endif
```

Description of Testing Whether Line Segments Intersect

One fundamental problem in computational geometry is determining whether two *line segments* intersect. Line segments are lines that have a beginning and an end. The points that define either end are a line segment's *endpoints*. To determine whether two line segments intersect, we first need to understand a little about lines and line segments in general.

One representation of a line is *point-intercept form*, or $y = mx + b$, where m is the line's slope and b is where the line crosses the y-axis. Using this, for any value of x, we can compute a corresponding value for y (see Figure 17-1a). For a line segment with endpoints $p_1 = (x_1, y_1)$ and $p_2 = (x_2, y_2)$, the slope m and y-intercept b are calculated by applying the following formulas:

$$m = \frac{(y_2 - y_1)}{(x_2 - x_1)}, \; b = y_1 - mx_1$$

Using m and b, the line segment is represented as a line in point-intercept form with endpoints p_1 and p_2 understood (see Figure 17-1b).

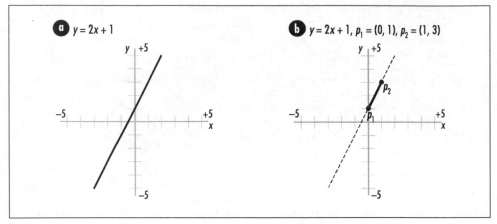

Figure 17-1. (a) A line and (b) a line segment with endpoints p_1 and p_2

Standard Test for Intersecting Line Segments

One way to determine whether two line segments intersect is first to determine the intersection point $p_i = (x_i, y_i)$ of the two lines on which each segment lies, then determine whether p_i is on both segments. If p_i is on both segments, the line segments intersect. We start with the point-intercept representations of the two lines on which the segments lie, which are:

$$y_{line1} = m_{line1}x_{line1} + b_{line1}, \ y_{line2} = m_{line2}x_{line2} + b_{line2}$$

The following formulas are used to compute $p_i = (x_i, y_i)$. Notice that one special case we must avoid when computing x_i is two lines with slopes that are equal. In this case, the denominator in the expression for x_i becomes 0. This occurs when two lines are parallel, in which case the segments will not intersect unless they lie on top of one another to some extent.

$$x_i = \frac{(b_{line2} - b_{line1})}{(m_{line2} - m_{line1})}, \ y_i = m_{line1}x_{line1} + b_{line1}$$

Once we've computed p_i, we perform the following tests to determine whether the point is actually on both line segments. In these tests, $p_1 = (x_1, y_1)$ and $p_2 = (x_2, y_2)$ are the endpoints of one line segment, and $p_3 = (x_3, y_3)$ and $p_4 = (x_4, y_4)$ are the endpoints of the other. If each of the tests is true, the line segments intersect.

$$(x_1 - x_i)(x_i - x_2) \geq 0$$
$$(y_1 - y_i)(y_i - y_2) \geq 0$$
$$(x_3 - x_i)(x_i - x_4) \geq 0$$
$$(y_3 - y_i)(y_i - y_4) \geq 0$$

This approach is common for determining whether line segments intersect. However, because the division required while calculating x_i is prone to round-off error and precision problems, in computing we take a different approach.

Computer Test for Intersecting Line Segments

In computing, to determine whether two lines intersect, a two-step process is used: first, we perform a *quick rejection test*. If this test succeeds, we then perform a *straddle test*. Two line segments intersect only when the quick rejection test and straddle test both succeed.

We begin the quick rejection test by constructing a *bounding box* around each line segment. The bounding box of a line segment is the smallest rectangle that surrounds the segment and has sides that are parallel to the x-axis and y-axis. For a line segment with endpoints $p_1 = (x_1, y_1)$ and $p_2 = (x_2, y_2)$, the bounding box is the rectangle with lower left point $(\min(x_1, x_2), \min(y_1, y_2))$ and upper right point $(\max(x_1, x_2), \max(y_1, y_2))$ (see Figure 17-2). The bounding boxes of two line segments intersect if all of the following tests are true:

$$\max(x_1, x_2) \geq \min(x_3, x_4)$$
$$\max(x_3, x_4) \geq \min(x_1, x_2)$$
$$\max(y_1, y_2) \geq \min(y_3, y_4)$$
$$\max(y_3, y_4) \geq \min(y_1, y_2)$$

If the bounding boxes of the line segments intersect, we proceed with the straddle test. To determine whether one segment with endpoints p_1 and p_2 straddles another with endpoints p_3 and p_4, we compare the *orientation* of p_3 relative to p_2 with that of p_4 relative to p_2 (see Figure 17-2). Each point's orientation conveys whether the point is clockwise or counterclockwise from p_2 with respect to p_1. To determine the orientation of p_3 relative to p_2 with respect to p_1, we look at the sign of:

$$z_1 = (x_3 - x_1)(y_2 - y_1) - (y_3 - y_1)(x_2 - x_1)$$

If z_1 is positive, p_3 is clockwise from p_2. If z_1 is negative, p_3 is counterclockwise from p_2. If it is 0, the points are on the same imaginary line extending from p_1. In this case, the points are said to be *collinear*. To determine the orientation of p_4 relative to p_2 with respect to p_1, we look at the sign of:

$$z_2 = (x_4 - x_1)(y_2 - y_1) - (y_4 - y_1)(x_2 - x_1)$$

If the signs of z_1 and z_2 are different, or if either is 0, the line segments straddle each other. Since if we perform this test, we have already shown that the bounding boxes intersect, the line segments intersect as well.

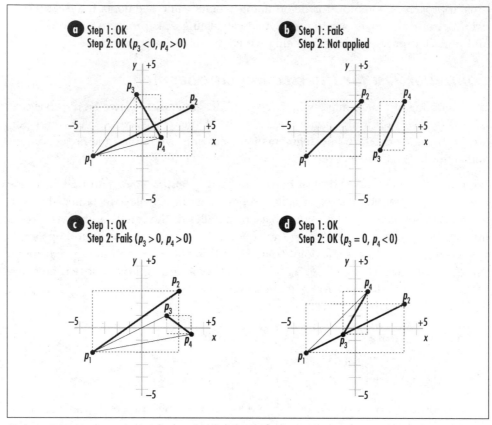

Figure 17-2. Testing whether line segments intersect using the quick rejection test (step 1) and straddle test (step 2)

Figure 17-2 illustrates testing whether various pairs of line segments intersect using the quick rejection and straddle tests. The equations just given come from representing the line segments from p_1 to p_3, p_1 to p_2, and p_1 to p_4 as vectors **U**, **V**, and **W** (see the related topics at the end of the chapter) and using the signs of the z-components of the cross products **U** $\times$ **V** and **W** $\times$ **V** as gauges of orientation.

Interface for Testing Whether Line Segments Intersect

lint

```
int lint(Point p1, Point p2, Point p3, Point p4);
```

Return Value   1 if the two line segments intersect, or 0 otherwise.

Description   Tests whether two line segments intersect. Specify one line segment using its endpoints as *p0* and *p1*. Specify the second line segment using its endpoints as *p3* and *p4*. Each point is a structure of type `Point`. Although `Point` has three members for representing points in three dimensions, we can use it to represent points in two dimensions by setting *z* to 0. Since the *lint* operation works in two dimensions, it ignores the *z*-coordinate of each point.

Complexity $O(1)$

Implementation and Analysis of Testing Whether Line Segments Intersect

To test whether two line segments intersect, we first must have a way to represent each segment. Let *p1* and *p2* define the endpoints of one of the segments and *p3* and *p4* define the endpoints of the other. Each endpoint is a `Point` structure. This structure consists of three members, *x*, *y*, and *z*, that are the coordinates of a point. Recall that we ignore all *z*-coordinates since *lint* works in two dimensions.

The *lint* operation (see Example 17-2) begins by performing the quick rejection test. This test uses two macros, *MIN* and *MAX* (see Example 17-1). These return the minimum and maximum of two values, respectively. The quick rejection test determines whether the bounding boxes of two line segments intersect. If this test succeeds, the algorithm continues with the straddle test; otherwise, it returns immediately that the line segments do not intersect. The straddle test determines the orientation of *p3* relative to *p2* and of *p4* relative to *p2* with respect to *p1*. If the orientations are different, or if either orientation is 0, the straddle test succeeds, and the algorithm returns that the line segments intersect; otherwise, the line segments do not intersect. The quick rejection and straddle tests are performed using the methods described earlier.

The runtime complexity of *lint* is $O(1)$ because all of the steps in testing whether two line segments intersect run in a constant amount of time.

Example 17-2. Implementation for Testing Whether Line Segments Intersect

```
/*****************************************************************************
*                                                                           *
*  ------------------------------- lint.c -------------------------------    *
*                                                                           *
*****************************************************************************/

#include "geometry.h"

/*****************************************************************************
*                                                                           *
*  -------------------------------- lint --------------------------------    *
*                                                                           *
*****************************************************************************/
```

Example 17-2. Implementation for Testing Whether Line Segments Intersect (continued)

```
int lint(Point p1, Point p2, Point p3, Point p4) {

double          z1,
                z2;

int             s1,
                s2;

/***************************************************************************
 *                                                                         *
 *  Perform the quick rejection test.                                      *
 *                                                                         *
 ***************************************************************************/

if (!(MAX(p1.x, p2.x) >= MIN(p3.x, p4.x) && MAX(p3.x, p4.x)
   >= MIN(p1.x, p2.x) && MAX(p1.y, p2.y) >= MIN(p3.y, p4.y)
   && MAX(p3.y, p4.y) >= MIN(p1.y, p2.y))) {

   return 0;

}

/***************************************************************************
 *                                                                         *
 *  Determine whether the line segments straddle each other.               *
 *                                                                         *
 ***************************************************************************/

if ((z1 = ((p3.x - p1.x)*(p2.y - p1.y)) - ((p3.y - p1.y)*(p2.x - p1.x))) < 0)
   s1 = -1;
else if (z1 > 0)
   s1 = 1;
else
   s1 = 0;

if ((z2 = ((p4.x - p1.x)*(p2.y - p1.y)) - ((p4.y - p1.y)*(p2.x - p1.x))) < 0)
   s2 = -1;
else if (z2 > 0)
   s2 = 1;
else
   s2 = 0;

if ((s1 == 0 || s2 == 0) || (s1 != s2))
   return 1;

/***************************************************************************
 *                                                                         *
 *  Return that the line segments do not intersect.                        *
 *                                                                         *
 ***************************************************************************/

return 0;

}
```

Description of Convex Hulls

The convex hull of a set of points is the smallest convex polygon that encloses all points in the set. A polygon is convex if any line segment connecting two points inside the polygon lies completely inside the polygon itself (see Figure 17-3a); otherwise, the polygon is concave (see Figure 17-3b). To picture the convex hull for a set of points, imagine a series of pegs on a board. If we wrap a string tightly around the outermost pegs, the shape of the string is the convex hull.

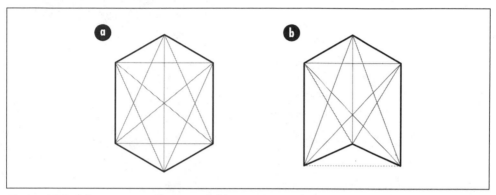

Figure 17-3. (a) A convex polygon and (b) a concave polygon

Jarvis's March

One way to construct the convex hull for a set of points P is to use a method called *Jarvis's march*. Jarvis's march constructs a convex hull in two sections, called the *right chain* and *left chain*. The right chain consists of all points in the convex hull from the lowest point (the one with the smallest y-coordinate) to the highest. If two points are equally low, the lowest point is considered to be the one that is also the furthest to the left (the one with the smallest x-coordinate). The left chain consists of all points from the highest point back to the lowest. If two points are equally high, the highest point is considered to be the one that is also the furthest to the right.

We begin by finding the lowest point in P (as described a moment ago), adding it to the convex hull, and initializing another variable, p_0, to it. Next, we look at each point p_i in P, excluding p_0, and locate the point p_c that is clockwise from all others with respect to p_0. Picture a clock face centered on p_0. In the right chain, we start at the 3 o'clock position and sweep counterclockwise until we encounter a point. In the left chain, we start at 9 o'clock and sweep counterclockwise. Once we find p_c, we add it to the convex hull, we set p_0 to p_c, and repeat the process until p_0 is the point at which we started.

Returning to the peg analogy, in the right chain, selecting each point p_c is similar to tying a string to the current p_0, pulling it taut to the right, and then advancing the string counterclockwise until it touches another point. In the left chain, the process is similar to pulling the string taut to the left before advancing it counterclockwise. Figure 17-4 illustrates this process.

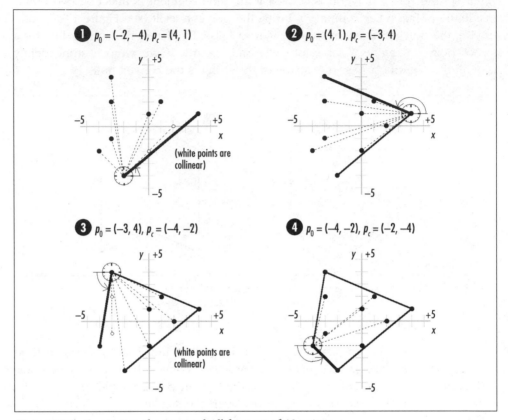

Figure 17-4. Computing the convex hull for a set of 10 points

Computationally, to determine the point clockwise from all other points with respect to p_0, we traverse each point p_i in P, except p_0, and keep track of the best choice for p_c as we go. For each p_i in P, we compare the orientation of p_i relative to the p_c we have found thus far using the expression for z that follows. If z is greater than 0, p_i is clockwise from p_c with respect to p_0, and we reset p_c to the current p_i. One nice thing about this approach is that we do not need to worry about whether we are computing the right or left chain, as the mathematics handles this for us.

$$z = (x_i - x_0)(y_c - y_0) - (y_i - y_0)(x_c - x_0)$$

One special case occurs when z is 0. This means that p_i and p_c are collinear with respect to p_0. In this case, the most clockwise point is considered to be the one furthest from p_0 (in Figure 17-4, see the computation of z where $p_0 = (-2, -4)$,

$p_i = (0, -2)$, and $p_c = (2, 0)$ in step 1, and where $p_0 = (-3, 4)$, $p_i = (-3, 2)$, and $p_c = (-3, -1)$ in step 3). To determine the distance r between $p_0 = (x_0, y_0)$ and a point $p_j = (x_j, y_j)$, where p_j is either p_i or p_c, we use the following equation:

$$r = \sqrt{(x_j - x_0)^2 + (y_j - y_0)^2}$$

Interface for Convex Hulls

cvxhull

```
int cvxhull(const List *P, List *polygon);
```

Return Value   0 if computing the convex hull is successful, or −1 otherwise.

Description   Computes the convex hull for a list of points specified in *P*. Each element in *P* must be of type *Point*. Since the *cvxhull* operation works in two dimensions, like *lint*, it ignores the *z*-coordinate in each *Point* structure. The convex hull is returned in *polygon*, which is a list of *Point* structures. The elements in *polygon* point to the actual points in *P*, so the caller must ensure that the storage in *P* remains valid as long as *polygon* is being accessed. Use *list_destroy* to destroy *polygon* once it is no longer needed.

Complexity $O(nh)$, where n is the total number of points, and h is the number of points in the convex hull.

Implementation and Analysis of Convex Hulls

To compute the convex hull of a set of points, we begin with a list containing each point. Each point in the list is a *Point* structure. This structure consists of three members, *x*, *y*, and *z*, which are the coordinates of a point. Recall that we ignore all *z*-coordinates since the operation works in two dimensions.

The *cvxhull* operation (see Example 17-3) begins by locating the lowest point passed to it in *P*. To determine this, we traverse all points while keeping track of which has the smallest *y*-coordinate. If two points share the smallest *y*-coordinate, we choose the point that has the smallest *x*-coordinate. This results in the lowest and leftmost point. Once we have identified this point, we set *p0* to it.

The actual process of constructing the convex hull takes place within a nested loop. At the start of the outer loop, we insert *p0* into the convex hull. On the first iteration of the loop, *p0* is the lowest point. As the algorithm progresses, each successive iteration of the outer loop yields a new *p0*. Within the inner loop, we traverse each point *pi* in *P* to determine the next *p0*. Specifically, as we traverse each point, *pc* maintains the point determined to be clockwise from all others thus far with respect to the current *p0*. To determine whether a given *pi* is clockwise from the current *pc*, we use the method presented earlier. That is, if *z* is greater than 0, *pi* is clockwise from *pc*, in which case we reset *pc* to *pi*. If *pi* and *pc* are collinear, we set *pc* to *pi* only if *pi* is further from *p0* than *pc*. Thus, once we have traversed all of the points in the list, *pc* is the point that is clockwise to all others with respect to *p0*. At this point, we reset *p0* to *pc* and repeat the process until *p0* is the point at which we started. Once we reach this point, all points in the convex hull have been inserted into *polygon* at the top of the outer loop.

The runtime complexity of *cvxhull* is $O(nh)$, where *n* is the total number of points, and *h* is the number of points in the convex hull. The loop in which the lowest point is determined runs in $O(n)$ time because we must traverse all points to determine which is the lowest. The nested loops together are $O(nh)$ because for each point inserted into the convex hull, we must traverse all other points to determine which is next to insert. Since locating the lowest point and constructing the convex hull are carried out sequentially, the runtime complexity of *cvxhull* is $O(nh)$.

Example 17-3. Implementation for Computing Convex Hulls

```
/*****************************************************************************
*                                                                           *
*  --------------------------------- cvxhull.c ---------------------------   *
*                                                                           *
*****************************************************************************/

#include <math.h>
#include <stdlib.h>

#include "geometry.h"
#include "list.h"

/*****************************************************************************
*                                                                           *
*  ----------------------------------- cvxhull ----------------------------- *
*                                                                           *
*****************************************************************************/

int cvxhull(const List *P, List *polygon) {

ListElmt           *element;

Point              *min,
                   *low,
                   *p0,
                   *pi,
                   *pc;

double             z,
                   length1,
                   length2;

int                count;
```

Example 17-3. Implementation for Computing Convex Hulls (continued)

```
/***************************************************************************
*                                                                         *
*  Find the lowest point in the list of points.                          *
*                                                                         *
***************************************************************************/

min = list_data(list_head(P));

for (element = list_head(P); element != NULL; element = list_next(element)) {

   p0 = list_data(element);

   /***************************************************************************
   *                                                                         *
   *  Keep track of the lowest point thus far.                               *
   *                                                                         *
   ***************************************************************************/

   if (p0->y < min->y) {

      min = p0;
      low = list_data(element);

      }

   else {

      /***************************************************************************
      *                                                                         *
      *  If a tie occurs, use the lowest and leftmost point.                    *
      *                                                                         *
      ***************************************************************************/

      if (p0->y == min->y && p0->x < min->x) {

         min = p0;
         low = list_data(element);

         }

      }

}


/***************************************************************************
*                                                                         *
*  Initialize the list for the convex hull.                               *
*                                                                         *
***************************************************************************/

list_init(polygon, NULL);
```

Example 17-3. Implementation for Computing Convex Hulls (continued)

```
/***************************************************************************
*                                                                         *
*  Perform Jarvis's march to compute the convex hull.                     *
*                                                                         *
***************************************************************************/

p0 = low;

do {

   /***************************************************************************
   *                                                                         *
   *  Insert the new p0 into the convex hull.                                *
   *                                                                         *
   ***************************************************************************/

   if (list_ins_next(polygon, list_tail(polygon), p0) != 0) {

      list_destroy(polygon);
      return -1;

   }

   /***************************************************************************
   *                                                                         *
   *  Find the point pc that is clockwise from all others.                   *
   *                                                                         *
   ***************************************************************************/

   count = 0;

   for (element = list_head(P); element != NULL; element =
      list_next(element)) {

      /***************************************************************************
      *                                                                         *
      *  Skip p0 in the list of points.                                         *
      *                                                                         *
      ***************************************************************************/

      if ((pi = list_data(element)) == p0)
         continue;

      /***************************************************************************
      *                                                                         *
      *  Count how many points have been explored.                              *
      *                                                                         *
      ***************************************************************************/

      count++;
```

Example 17-3. Implementation for Computing Convex Hulls (continued)

```
/************************************************************************
*                                                                      *
*  Assume the first point to explore is clockwise from all others      *
*  until proven otherwise.                                             *
*                                                                      *
************************************************************************/

if (count == 1) {

   pc = list_data(element);
   continue;

}

/************************************************************************
*                                                                      *
*  Determine whether pi is clockwise from pc.                          *
*                                                                      *
************************************************************************/

if ((z = ((pi->x - p0->x) * (pc->y - p0->y)) - ((pi->y - p0->y) * (pc->x
   - p0->x))) > 0) {

   /************************************************************************
   *                                                                      *
   *  The point pi is clockwise from pc.                                  *
   *                                                                      *
   ************************************************************************/

   pc = pi;

   }

else if (z == 0) {

   /************************************************************************
   *                                                                      *
   *  If pi and pc are collinear, select the point furthest from p0.      *
   *                                                                      *
   ************************************************************************/

   length1 = sqrt(pow(pi->x - p0->x, 2.0) + pow(pi->y - p0->y, 2.0));
   length2 = sqrt(pow(pc->x - p0->x, 2.0) + pow(pc->y - p0->y, 2.0));

   if (length1 > length2) {

      /************************************************************************
      *                                                                      *
      *  The point pi is further from p0 than pc.                            *
      *                                                                      *
      ************************************************************************/
```

Example 17-3. Implementation for Computing Convex Hulls (continued)

```
        pc = pi;

    }

  }

}

/*************************************************************************
*                                                                       *
*   Prepare to find the next point for the convex hull.                 *
*                                                                       *
*************************************************************************/

p0 = pc;

/*************************************************************************
*                                                                       *
*   Continue until reaching the lowest point again.                     *
*                                                                       *
*************************************************************************/

} while (p0 != low);

return 0;

}
```

Description of Arc Length on Spherical Surfaces

Many problems require computing the distance between two points. When we are interested in the distance between points along a straight line, we apply the well-known distance formula derived from the Pythagorean theorem. However, if we are interested in the distance between points along a curved surface, the problem becomes more difficult. Fortunately, computing the minimum distance, or *arc length*, between two points on a spherical surface is a special case that is relatively simple. To begin, let's look at two different coordinate systems, *rectilinear coordinates* and *spherical coordinates*.

Rectilinear and Spherical Coordinates

The rectilinear coordinate system is the coordinate system that is most familiar to us. In rectilinear coordinates, a point's location is specified using three values, x, y, z, which are its positions along the x-axis, y-axis, and z-axis. Referring to Figure 17-5, the z-axis is positive going upward. Standing at the arrow looking forward, the x-axis is positive to the right, and the y-axis is positive straight ahead. From this vantage point, the positive directions for x and y look the same as in two dimensions. Thus, to locate (3, 4, 5), for example, we move three units to the right along the *x*-axis, four units ahead parallel to the *y*-axis, and five units up parallel to the *z*-axis (see Figure 17-5).

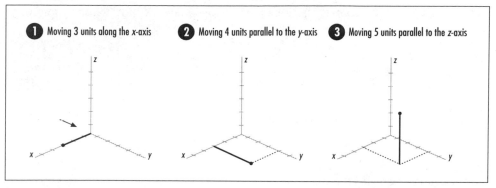

Figure 17-5. Locating the point (3, 4, 5) in a rectilinear coordinate system

In spherical coordinates, a point's location is specified in terms of a distance ρ (rho) and two angles, θ (theta) and ϕ (phi): ρ is the distance along an imaginary line from the origin to the point (a radius), θ is the angle the point forms from the positive *x*-axis toward the positive *y*-axis, and ϕ is the angle the point forms from the positive *z*-axis heading toward the positive *x*-axis. To locate (5, 30, 45), for example, we move five units up the *z*-axis, sweep 45 degrees from the positive *z*-axis toward the positive *x*-axis, and spin 30 degrees from the positive *x*-axis toward the positive *y*-axis (see Figure 17-6). (Notice that it is easier to visualize ϕ before θ even though θ precedes ϕ in the triple.)

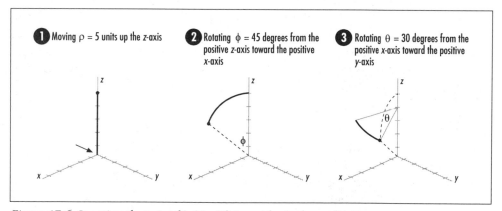

Figure 17-6. Locating the point (5, 30, 45) in a spherical coordinate system

Converting Between Coordinate Systems

When speaking about an arc on a spherical surface, it is often convenient to have its endpoints specified in spherical coordinates. Therefore, the algorithm presented here assumes this representation to begin with. However, to compute an arc's length, we will need its endpoints in rectilinear coordinates. Consequently, the first step is to convert the points $p_1 = (\rho, \theta_1, \phi_1)$ and $p_2 = (\rho, \theta_2, \phi_2)$ to the rectilinear equivalents $p_1 = (x_1, y_1, z_1)$ and $p_2 = (x_2, y_2, z_2)$. To do this, we start with the following equations. Of course, the locations of the points do not change, only their representations.

$$x = \rho \sin\phi \cos\theta$$
$$y = \rho \sin\phi \sin\theta$$
$$z = \rho \cos\phi$$

Another relationship between ρ and the rectilinear coordinates x, y, and z is:

$$\rho = \sqrt{x^2 + y^2 + z^2}$$

This formula calculates the distance from a point to the origin in three dimensions.

Computing the Length of an Arc

Now we are ready to compute the length of the arc between p_1 and p_2 on the sphere. First, we picture two imaginary lines extending from the center of the sphere to each of the points (see Figure 17-7a) and calculate α, the angle between them. To do this, we use the formula:

$$\alpha = \cos^{-1}\left(\frac{x_1 x_2 + y_1 y_2 + z_1 z_2}{\rho^2}\right)$$

where $\cos^{-1}$ is the inverse cosine of the argument in parentheses. Think of an inverse cosine this way: the cosine of what angle gives us the value of the argument in parentheses? The expression in the numerator of the argument comes from treating the imaginary line segments from the center of the sphere to p_1 and p_2 as vectors **U** and **V** (see the related topics at the end of the chapter) and computing the dot product $\mathbf{U} \cdot \mathbf{V}$.

The lines that form α lie in a plane that slices across the sphere. The importance of α is that where the sphere and this plane intersect, a circle is projected onto the plane with the same radius as the sphere (see Figure 17-7b). Since the arc between points p_1 and p_2 lies along a section of this circle, α helps to determine how much of the circle's perimeter the arc covers. This is determined from the percentage $\alpha/2\pi$, since there are 2π radians in a circle. Using this and the circumference of the circle, $2\pi\rho$, we see that the length s of the arc between p_1 and p_2 is $(\alpha/2\pi)(2\pi\rho)$, which simplifies to the equation that follows. This is the equation that is used in the implementation presented later:

$$s = \alpha\rho$$

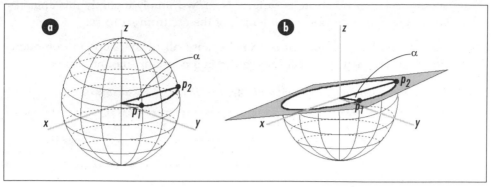

Figure 17-7. The length of an arc as viewed (a) on a sphere and (b) in the plane containing the lines from the center of the sphere to each point

Interface for Arc Length on Spherical Surfaces

arclen

```
void arclen(SPoint p1, SPoint p2, double *length)
```

Return Value   None.

Description   Computes the length of an arc between points *p1* and *p2* on a spherical surface. Each point is a structure of type *Spoint*, a point in spherical coordinates. Specify the radius of the sphere as the `rho` member of each *SPoint* structure. Specify the `theta` and `phi` members of each *SPoint* structure in radians. The length of the arc is returned in `length`.

Complexity   *O*(1)

Implementation and Analysis of Arc Length on Spherical Surfaces

To compute the length of an arc on a spherical surface, we first must have a way to define the arc's endpoints. For this, *arclen* accepts the two points *p1* and *p2*. Each endpoint is an *SPoint* structure. This structure consists of three members, `rho`, `theta`, and `phi`, which are the spherical coordinates for a point expressed in radian measure.

The *arclen* operation (see Example 17-4) begins by converting spherical coordinates into rectilinear coordinates using the equations presented earlier. Recall that this allows us to calculate the angle between the lines extending from the center of the sphere to either point on its surface. Next, we simply multiply this angle by the radius of the sphere to obtain the length of the arc from *p1* to *p2*.

The runtime complexity of *arclen* is $O(1)$ because all of the steps in computing the length of an arc on a spherical surface run in a constant amount of time.

Example 17-4. Implementation for Computing Arc Length on Spherical Surfaces

```
/***************************************************************************
*                                                                         *
*  --------------------------- arclen.c ---------------------------        *
*                                                                         *
***************************************************************************/

#include <math.h>

#include "geometry.h"

/***************************************************************************
*                                                                         *
*  ---------------------------- arclen ----------------------------        *
*                                                                         *
***************************************************************************/

void arclen(SPoint p1, SPoint p2, double *length) {

Point              p1_rct,
                   p2_rct;

double             alpha,
                   dot;

/***************************************************************************
*                                                                         *
*  Convert the spherical coordinates to rectilinear coordinates.          *
*                                                                         *
***************************************************************************/

p1_rct.x = p1.rho * sin(p1.phi) * cos(p1.theta);
p1_rct.y = p1.rho * sin(p1.phi) * sin(p1.theta);
p1_rct.z = p1.rho * cos(p1.phi);

p2_rct.x = p2.rho * sin(p2.phi) * cos(p2.theta);
p2_rct.y = p2.rho * sin(p2.phi) * sin(p2.theta);
p2_rct.z = p2.rho * cos(p2.phi);

/***************************************************************************
*                                                                         *
*  Get the angle between the line segments from the origin to each point. *
*                                                                         *
***************************************************************************/

dot = (p1_rct.x * p2_rct.x) + (p1_rct.y * p2_rct.y) + (p1_rct.z * p2_rct.z);
alpha = acos(dot / pow(p1.rho, 2.0));
```

Example 17-4. Implementation for Computing Arc Length on Spherical Surfaces (continued)

```
/***************************************************************************
*                                                                         *
*  Compute the length of the arc along the spherical surface.             *
*                                                                         *
***************************************************************************/

*length = alpha * p1.rho;

return;

}
```

Arc Length Example: Approximating Distances on Earth

One application of computing arc lengths on spherical surfaces is approximating distances between points on Earth. Sometimes these are called *great-circle distances*. Of course, the earth is not a perfect sphere but an ellipsoid slightly squatter from north to south than east to west. That is, if we were to orbit the earth along the prime meridian, we would find the distance traveled to be less than that of orbiting the earth along the equator. Still, treating the earth as a sphere usually gives reasonable approximations.

To compute the distance between two points on Earth, we first need a way to locate each point. In geography, points are usually located in terms of *latitude* and *longitude*. Latitudes sweep from 0 at the equator to 90 degrees at either pole. For points north of the equator, the letter "N" is appended to the latitude, and for points south, an "S" is appended. Often, degrees north of the equator are thought of as positive and degrees south of the equator as negative. Longitudes sweep from 0 at the prime meridian to 180 degrees in either direction. For points to the west of the prime meridian, the letter "W" is appended to the longitude, and for points to the east, an "E" is appended. Often, degrees west of the prime meridian are thought of as positive and degrees east of the prime meridian as negative. For example, Paris is approximately 49.010 degrees to the north of the equator and 2.548 degrees to the east of the prime meridian. Therefore, its position is 49.010N, 2.548E, or 49.010, −2.548 (see Figure 17-8a).

To approximate the distance between two points on Earth given their latitude and longitude, we first translate each point into spherical coordinates and convert all angles from degrees to radians. Then, we simply compute the length of the arc between the points. Recall that a point in spherical coordinates is given by the triple (r, θ, ϕ). In terms of the earth, r is the distance along an imaginary line from the earth's center to a point on its surface; that is, r is the earth's radius, which is 3440.065 nautical miles. The coordinate θ is the angle the point forms with the prime meridian. Thus, θ corresponds to longitude. However, since positive longitudes are to the west and positive values of θ are the opposite direction, to obtain θ from degrees longitude, we reverse the sign of the longitude. The coordinate ϕ is the angle a point forms with an imaginary line extending vertically from the center of the earth to the north pole. Thus, ϕ corresponds to latitude. However, since latitudes are relative to the equator and not the north pole, to obtain ϕ from degrees latitude, we reverse the sign of the latitude and add 90 degrees.

As an example, to compute the distance between Paris, France (49.010N, 2.548E) and Perth, Australia (31.940S, 115.967E), we begin by converting their latitudes and longitudes to spherical equivalents: (3440.065, 2.548, 40.990) for Paris and (3440.065, 115.967, 121.940) for Perth. Next, we convert the angles in each point to radians. Last, we compute the length of the arc between the points, which is 7706 nautical miles (see Figure 17-8b).

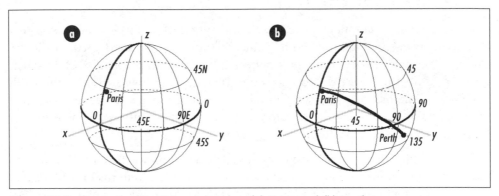

Figure 17-8. Computing the distance between (a) Paris and (b) Perth

This example presents a function, *geodist* (see Examples 17-5 and 17-6), that approximates the distance between two points on Earth using the method just described. The function accepts the latitude and longitude for each point as `lat1` and `lon1`, and `lat2` and `lon2`. It returns the distance between the points in `d`. After performing some initial validation of the latitudes and longitudes, *geodist* converts the latitude and longitude representations into spherical coordinates, stores each representation in `p1` and `p2` with all angles converted to radians, and calls *arclen* to compute the distance.

The runtime complexity of *geodist* is $O(1)$ because all of the steps in computing a great-circle distance run in a constant amount of time.

Example 17-5. Header for a Function for Approximating Distances on Earth

```
/*****************************************************************************
*                                                                           *
*  ------------------------------- geodist.h ------------------------------  *
*                                                                           *
*****************************************************************************/
```

Example 17-5. Header for a Function for Approximating Distances on Earth (continued)

```
#ifndef GEODIST_H
#define GEODIST_H

/**************************************************************************
 *                                                                        *
 *  Define the radius of the earth in nautical miles.                     *
 *                                                                        *
 **************************************************************************/

#define         EARTH_RADIUS        3440.065

/**************************************************************************
 *                                                                        *
 *  ------------------------- Public Interface -------------------------  *
 *                                                                        *
 **************************************************************************/

int geodist(double lat1, double lon1, double lat2, double lon2, double *d);

#endif
```

Example 17-6. Implementation of a Function for Approximating Distances on Earth

```
/**************************************************************************
 *                                                                        *
 *  ---------------------------- geodist.c ----------------------------   *
 *                                                                        *
 **************************************************************************/

#include "geodist.h"
#include "geometry.h"

/**************************************************************************
 *                                                                        *
 *  ----------------------------- geodist -----------------------------   *
 *                                                                        *
 **************************************************************************/

int geodist(double lat1, double lon1, double lat2, double lon2, double *d) {

SPoint          p1,
                p2;

/**************************************************************************
 *                                                                        *
 *  Validate the coordinates.                                             *
 *                                                                        *
 **************************************************************************/

if (lat1 <  -90.0 || lat1 >  90.0 || lat2 <  -90.0 || lat2 >  90.0)
   return -1;

if (lon1 < -180.0 || lon1 > 180.0 || lon2 < -180.0 || lon2 > 180.0)
   return -1;
```

Example 17-6. Implementation of a Function for Approximating Distances on Earth

```
/*****************************************************************************
 *                                                                          *
 *  Convert each latitude and longitude to spherical coordinates in radians *
 *  using the earth's radius for rho.                                       *
 *                                                                          *
 *****************************************************************************/

p1.rho = EARTH_RADIUS;
p1.theta = -1.0 * DEGTORAD(lon1);
p1.phi = (DEGTORAD(-1.0 * lat1)) + DEGTORAD(90.0);

p2.rho = EARTH_RADIUS;
p2.theta = -1.0 * DEGTORAD(lon2);
p2.phi = (DEGTORAD(-1.0 * lat2)) + DEGTORAD(90.0);

/*****************************************************************************
 *                                                                          *
 *  Compute the distance between the points.                                *
 *                                                                          *
 *****************************************************************************/

arclen(p1, p2, d);

return 0;

}
```

Questions and Answers

Q: *One application of geometric algorithms mentioned at the start of this chapter was determining whether the track of an object transgresses a restricted region. If we assume that the track we follow begins outside of the restricted region, a simple approach to this problem is to determine whether any line segment in the track intersects with any line segment defining the restricted region. What is the running time of this approach if we use the* lint *operation presented in this chapter?*

A: The runtime complexity of this approach is $O(nm)$, where n is the number of line segments in the track and m is the number of line segments defining the restricted region. This is because for each of the n line segments in the track, we call *lint* once for each of the m line segments in the restricted region. Since *lint* runs in a constant amount of time, the runtime complexity of the solution overall is $O(nm)$.

Q: *Determining the orientation of two points with respect to a third is an important part of the algorithms presented for determining whether line segments intersect and computing convex hulls. Formally, given points p_1, p_2, and p_3, we determine the orientation of p_3 relative to p_2 with respect to p_1 by treating* *the line segments from* p_1 *to* p_2 *and* p_1 *to* p_3 *as vectors U and V. We then use the sign of the z-component of the cross product U × V as a gauge of orientation. What is the orientation of the points if we compute the cross product V × U? In other words, given a specific orientation of* p_3 *relative to* p_2*, what is the orientation of* p_2 *relative to* p_3*?*

A: The answer to this question is a matter of perspective. Imagine two people facing forward in a room with a door behind them. Unless the two individuals line up perfectly with the door (one in front of the other), person *A* will see person *B* to his left, whereas person *B* will see person *A* to his right, and vice versa. The neat thing about cross products is that they reflect this perspective mathematically. When we compute the orientation of p_3 relative to p_2 with respect to p_1, we get an indication of where p_3 is from the perspective of p_2. For example, p_3 may be clockwise from p_2. When we compute the orientation of p_2 relative to p_3, we get an indication of where p_2 is from the perspective of p_3. These perspectives are always equal but opposite to one another (except in the boundary case when p_2 and p_3 form a straight line with p_1). That is, $U \times V$ is always equal to but of opposite sign as $V \times U$ (if p_2 and p_3 form a straight line with p_1, $U \times V$ and $V \times U$ are both 0, and the line segments from p_1 to p_2 and p_1 to p_3 are collinear). The formula given earlier in the chapter for z_1 when testing for intersecting line segments comes from $U \times V$. To compute $V \times U$, we exchange the positions of x_2 and x_3 and of y_2 and y_3 in the formula. This yields an equivalent result but with the sign reversed. Therefore, if p_3 is clockwise from p_2, for example, this tells us that p_2 is counterclockwise from p_3, as we would expect.

Q: *To test whether two line segments from points* p_1 *to* p_2 *and* p_3 *to* p_4 *intersect, we first examine whether the bounding boxes of the line segments intersect and then compare the orientation of* p_3 *relative to* p_2 *with that of* p_4 *relative to* p_2*. In what situation do the bounding boxes intersect when the orientations of both* p_3 *and* p_4 *are 0? Is it possible to have bounding boxes that do not intersect when the orientations of* p_3 *and* p_4 *are both 0?*

A: Recall that when the orientation of either p_3 or p_4 is 0, it means that the line segment from either p_1 to p_3 or p_1 to p_4 is collinear with the line segment from p_1 to p_2. If the bounding boxes of the two line segments intersect as well, this tells us that at least some parts of the segments overlay each other (see Figure 17-9a). Therefore, the line segments intersect. On the other hand, it is possible to have two line segments that are collinear without intersecting. This occurs when the segments would overlay each other if either were long enough, but neither has the length necessary to do so (see Figure 17-9b).

Q: *In this chapter we learned that the smallest polygon surrounding a set of points is called a·convex hull. This name implies that the polygon is always convex. Why is this?*

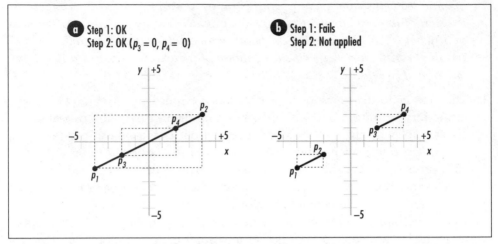

Figure 17-9. Collinear line segments whose bounding boxes (a) intersect and (b) do not intersect

A: Recall that a polygon is convex if any line segment connecting two points inside the polygon lies completely inside the polygon itself; otherwise, the polygon is concave. To understand why a convex hull is always convex, consider a concave polygon that surrounds a set of points. For any sequence of three points p_1, p_2, and p_3 defining a concave region, if we replace the edges from p_1 to p_2 and p_2 to p_3 with a single edge from p_1 to p_3, we can reduce the size of the polygon while keeping p_2 enclosed. We know that the size of the polygon will be reduced because it is always shorter to go from one point to another than through a third point first. We know that p_2 will still be enclosed by the resulting polygon because the angle from p_2 to p_3 is less than the angle from p_1 to p_2. Therefore, since a convex polygon will always be shorter than any concave one that encloses the same points, a convex hull must be convex (see Figure 17-10).

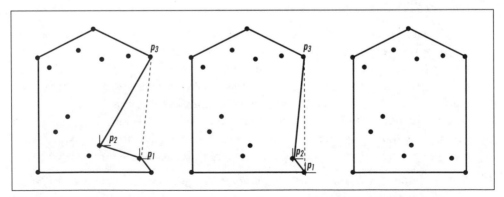

Figure 17-10. Showing that the smallest polygon enclosing a set of points is always convex

Q: *Suppose in the approximation for distances on Earth presented in this chapter we would like to improve the method used in the function* geodist. *Specifically, we would like to do something to take into account the change in the Earth's radius at different latitudes and longitudes. How can we do this?*

A: One way to make this improvement is to use the fact that both points passed into *geodist* have their own value for the spherical coordinate ρ. When we treat the Earth as a perfect sphere, we set the *rho* member of each point to the same value since we are considering the distance from the Earth's center to the surface to be the same everywhere. However, a better approach would be to set *rho* for each point to the actual distance from the center of the Earth to the point and then compute an average of the two *rho* members for the radius of the arc. Although this does not perfect the distance computation, it does generally improve it.

Related Topics

Vectors

Mathematical quantities having both magnitude and direction. A vector consists of several *components*, one for each axis of the coordinate system. If we draw a vector as a line segment starting at the origin, a vector's components are values that describe how far we must move along each axis to reach the point at which the vector ends. Some operations with vectors include addition, subtraction, dot products, cross products, and magnitudes.

Testing whether any two line segments intersect

A generalization of the test provided earlier in this chapter for determining whether two line segments intersect. However, rather than simply applying this test over and over again to test whether any line segments in a set intersect, it is best to use a dedicated approach. Using a dedicated approach, the problem can be solved in $O(n \lg n)$ time, where n is the number of line segments.

Graham's scan

An alternative approach to Jarvis's march for computing convex hulls. Graham's scan works by maintaining a stack of candidate points for the convex hull. Each point is pushed onto the stack once. All points not in the convex hull are eventually popped off the stack so that when the algorithm terminates, the stack contains only the points in the convex hull. Graham's scan has a runtime complexity of $O(n \lg n)$, where n is the number of points in the set to enclose.

Index

About the Author

Kyle Loudon is a software engineer at Jeppesen Dataplan in Los Gatos, California, where he leads the graphical interface development group in developing flight planning software used by commercial airlines, corporate flight departments, and other facets of general aviation. Before Jeppesen, Kyle worked as a system programmer for IBM. Kyle's technical interests include operating systems, networking, and human-computer interaction. Kyle attended Purdue University, where in 1992 he received a B.S. in computer science and a minor in French, and was elected to Phi Beta Kappa. While at Purdue, he coordinated and taught a course for three years in the Department of Computer Science. During this time he also wrote his first book, *Understanding Computers*, a practical and conceptual introduction to computers. Currently he is patiently pursuing an advanced degree while continuing to work in Silicon Valley's software industry.

Aside from computers, Kyle has enjoyed playing and teaching tennis for a number of years. He also enjoys mountain biking, skiing, and on occasion, golf with friends on courses that favor a sometimes overactive slice. In addition, Kyle enjoys various forms of theater, great food, and several styles of music and art; he is a wishful but hopeless pianist and artist himself. Kyle found his present position at Jeppesen after he started flying airplanes in 1992. Currently he is an active pilot holding a commercial pilot certificate with the FAA.

Colophon

Our look is the result of reader comments, our own experimentation, and feedback from distribution channels. Distinctive covers complement our distinctive approach to technical topics, breathing personality and life into potentially dry subjects.

The animals on the cover of *Mastering Algorithms with C* are sea horses. Sea horses are of the family *Syngnathidae*, genus *Hippocampus*. The word "hippocampus" comes from the Greek for "bent horse." The sea horse's unusual-looking body is formed by 50 or so bony plates that encircle the body to create rings of armor. Within their narrow snouts are tubes through which they feed, sucking in plankton and tiny fish larvae. The male sea horse has a pouch in his belly, into which a female lays 100 or more eggs at a time. The male fertilizes the eggs in the pouch and carries them until they hatch, ten days to six weeks later, depending on the sea horse species.

Sea horses are found mostly in shallow tropical and subtropical waters, although there are some ocean-dwelling sea horse species. All sea horses use their pelvic and pectoral fins for steering. They swim slowly, in an upright position, and take frequent breaks. During these breaks they wrap their prehensile tails around a piece of seaweed or coral to anchor themselves. In addition to providing a resting place, the seaweed and coral provide good camouflage for the sea horse.

The largest sea horse species is the Pacific sea horse, measuring approximately 12 inches long. The smallest is the dwarf sea horse, which measures only an inch and a half long.

Jeffrey Liggett was the production editor for *Mastering Algorithms with C*; Cindy Kogut was the copyeditor; Ellie Fountain Maden was the proofreader; Sebastian Banker provided production assistance; Claire Cloutier LeBlanc, Nancy Wolfe Kotary, and Melanie Wang provided quality control. Robert Romano and Rhon Porter created the illustrations using Adobe Photoshop 5 and Macromedia Free-Hand 8. Mike Sierra provided FrameMaker technical support. William Meyers wrote the index with production assistance by Seth Maislin and Brenda Miller.

Hanna Dyer designed the cover of this book based on a series design by Edie Freedman. The illustration is by Lorrie LeJeune. The cover layout was produced by Kathleen Wilson with QuarkXPress 3.32 using the ITC Garamond font. Kathleen Wilson designed the diskette label. Whenever possible, our books use RepKover™, a durable and flexible lay-flat binding. If the page count exceeds RepKover's limit, perfect binding is used.

The inside layout was designed by Alicia Cech based on a series design by Nancy Priest. The inside layout was implemented in FrameMaker 5.5.6 by Mike Sierra. The text and heading fonts are ITC Garamond Light and Garamond Book. This colophon was written by Clairemarie Fisher O'Leary.

More Titles from O'Reilly

C and C++

C++: The Core Language

By Gregory Satir & Doug Brown
1st Edition October 1995
228 pages, ISBN 1-56592-116-X

A first book for C programmers transitioning to C++, an object-oriented enhancement of the C programming language. Designed to get readers up to speed quickly, this book thoroughly explains the important concepts and features and gives brief overviews of the rest of the language. Covers features common to all C++ compilers, including those on UNIX, Windows NT, Windows, DOS, and Macs.

Practical C++ Programming

By Steve Oualline
1st Edition September 1995
584 pages, ISBN 1-56592-139-9

A complete introduction to the C++ language for the beginning programmer and C programmers transitioning to C++. This book emphasizes a practical, real-world approach, including how to debug, how to make your code understandable to others, and how to understand other people's code. Covers good programming style, C++ syntax (what to use and what not to use), C++ class design, debugging and optimization, and common programming mistakes.

Checking C Programs with lint

By Ian F. Darwin
1st Edition October 1988
84 pages, ISBN 0-937175-30-7

The lint program is one of the best tools for finding portability problems and certain types of coding errors in C programs. This handbook introduces you to lint, guides you through running it on your programs, and helps you interpret lint's output.

Practical C Programming, 3rd Edition

By Steve Oualline
3rd Edition August 1997
454 pages, ISBN 1-56592-306-5

Practical C Programming teaches you not only the mechanics of programming, but also how to create programs that are easy to read, maintain, and debug. This third edition introduces popular Integrated Development Environments on Windows systems, as well as UNIX programming utilities, and features a large statistics-generating program to pull together the concepts and features in the language.

High Performance Computing, 2nd Edition

By Kevin Dowd & Charles Severance
2nd Edition July 1998
466 pages, ISBN 1-56592-312-X

This new edition of High Performance Computing gives a thorough overview of the latest workstation and PC architectures and the trends that will influence the next generation. It pays special attention to memory design, tuning code for the best performance, multiprocessors, and benchmarking.

O'REILLY®

TO ORDER: **800-998-9938** • order@oreilly.com • http://www.oreilly.com/
OUR PRODUCTS ARE AVAILABLE AT A BOOKSTORE OR SOFTWARE STORE NEAR YOU.
FOR INFORMATION: **800-998-9938** • **707-829-0515** • info@oreilly.com

UNIX Programming

Programming Python

By Mark Lutz
1st Edition October 1996
906 pages, ISBN 1-56592-197-6

Programming Python describes how to
use Python, an increasingly popular object-
oriented scripting language. This book,
full of running examples, is the most
comprehensive user material available on
Python. It's endorsed by Python creator
Guido van Rossum and complements reference materials that
accompany the software. Includes CD-ROM with Python software
for all major UNIX platforms, as well as Windows, NT, and the Mac.

POSIX Programmer's Guide

By Donald Lewine
1st Edition April 1991
640 pages, ISBN 0-937175-73-0

Most UNIX systems today are POSIX
compliant because the federal government requires it for its purchases.
Given the manufacturer's documentation,
however, it can be difficult to distinguish
system-specific features from those
features defined by POSIX. The *POSIX
Programmer's Guide*, intended as an explanation of the POSIX
standard and as a reference for the POSIX.1 programming
library, helps you write more portable programs.

Programming with curses

By John Strang
1st Edition 1986
78 pages, ISBN 0-937175-02-1

curses is a UNIX library of functions for
controlling a terminal's display screen from
a C program. This handbook helps you make
use of the *curses* library. Describes the original Berkeley version of *curses*.

Power Programming with RPC

By John Bloomer
1st Edition February 1992
522 pages, ISBN 0-937175-77-3

RPC (Remote Procedure Calling) is
the ability to distribute the execution of
functions on remote computers. Written
from a programmer's perspective, this
book shows what you can do with RPCs,
like Sun RPC, the de facto standard on
UNIX systems. It covers related programming topics for Sun
and other UNIX systems and teaches through examples.

POSIX.4

By Bill O. Gallmeister
1st Edition January 1995
568 pages, ISBN 1-56592-074-0

A general introduction to real-time
programming and real-time issues,
this book covers the POSIX.4 standard
and how to use it to solve "real-world"
problems. If you're at all interested in
real-time applications—which include
just about everything from telemetry to
transaction processing—this book is for you. An essential reference.

UNIX Systems Programming for SVR4

By David A. Curry
1st Edition July 1996
620 pages, ISBN 1-56592-163-1

Presents a comprehensive look at the nitty
gritty details on how UNIX interacts with
applications. If you're writing an application
from scratch, or if you're porting an application to any System V.4 platform, you need
this book. It thoroughly explains all UNIX
system calls and library routines related to systems programming,
working with I/O, files and directories, processing multiple input
streams, file and record locking, and memory-mapped files.

UNIX Programming

Pthreads Programming

By Bradford Nichols, Dick Buttlar &
Jacqueline Proulx Farrell
1st Edition September 1996
284 pages, ISBN 1-56592-115-1

POSIX threads, or pthreads, allow multiple
tasks to run concurrently within the same
program. This book discusses when to use
threads and how to make them efficient. It
features realistic examples, a look behind
the scenes at the implementation and performance issues, and
special topics such as DCE and real-time extensions.

Year 2000 in a Nutshell

By Norman Shakespeare
1st Edition September 1998
330 pages, ISBN 1-56592-421-5

This reference guide addresses the awareness,
the managerial aspect, and the technical issues
of the Year 2000 computer dilemma, providing
a compact compendium of solutions and reference information useful for addressing the
problem.

UML in a Nutshell

By Sinan Si Alhir
1st Edition September 1998
290 pages, ISBN 1-56592-448-7

The Unified Modeling Language (UML),
for the first time in the history of systems
engineering, gives practitioners a common
language. This concise quick reference
explains how to use each component of the
language, including its extension mechanisms
and the Object Constraint Language (OCL). A tutorial with realistic
examples brings those new to the UML quickly up to speed.

In a Nutshell Quick References

Java Examples in a Nutshell

By David Flanagan
1st Edition September 1997
414 pages, ISBN 1-56592-371-5

From the author of *Java in a Nutshell*, this
companion book is chock full of practical
real-world programming examples to help
novice Java programmers and experts alike
explore what's possible with Java 1.1. If you
learn best by example, this is the book for you.

Java in a Nutshell, DELUXE EDITION

By David Flanagan, et al.
1st Edition June 1997
628 pages, includes CD-ROM & book
ISBN 1-56592-304-9

Java in a Nutshell, Deluxe Edition, brings
together on CD-ROM five volumes for Java
developers and programmers, linking
related info across books. *Exploring
Java, 2nd Edition*, covers Java basics.
*Java Language Reference, 2nd Edition, Java Fundamental
Classes Reference*, and *Java AWT Reference* provide a definitive set
of documentation on the Java language and the Java 1.1 core API.
Java in a Nutshell, 2nd Edition, our bestselling quick reference,
is included both on the CD-ROM and in a companion desktop
edition. This deluxe library is an indispensable resource for
anyone doing serious programming with Java 1.1.

Java in a Nutshell, Second Edition

By David Flanagan
2nd Edition May 1997
628 pages, ISBN 1-56592-262-X

This second edition of the bestselling Java
book describes all the classes in the Java 1.1
API, with the exception of the still-evolving
Enterprise APIs. And it still has all the great
features that have made this the Java book
most often recommended on the Internet:
practical real-world examples and compact reference information.
It's the only quick reference you'll need.

In a Nutshell Quick References

Java Enterprise in a Nutshell

By David Foanagan, Jim Farley,
William Crawford & Kris Magnusson
1st Edition August 1999 (est.)
600 pages (est.), ISBN 1-56592-483-5

The Java Enterprise APIs are essential building blocks for creating enterprise-wide distributed applications in Java. *Java Enterprise in a Nutshell* covers the RMI, IDL, JDBC, JNDI, and Java servlets APIs, providing a fast-paced tutorial and compact reference material on each of the technologies.

Java Foundation Classes in a Nutshell

By David Flanagan
1st Edition September 1999 (est.)
750 pages (est.), ISBN 1-56592-488-6

Java Foundation Classes in a Nutshell provides an in-depth overview of the important pieces of the Java Foundation Classes (JFC), such as the Swing components and Java 2D. From the author of *Java in a Nutshell*, this book includes compact reference material on all the GUI and graphics related-classes in the numerous java.awt packages.

Java

Java Cryptography

By Jonathan B. Knudsen
1st Edition May 1998
362 pages, ISBN 1-56592-402-9

Java Cryptography teaches you how to write secure programs using Java's cryptographic tools. It includes thorough discussions of the java.security package and the Java Cryptography Extensions (JCE), showing you how to use security providers and even implement your own provider. It discusses authentication, key management, public and private key encryption, and includes a secure talk application that encrypts all data sent over the network. If you work with sensitive data, you'll find this book indispensable.

Java *(continued)*

Java Security

By Scott Oaks
1st Edition May 1998
474 pages, ISBN 1-56592-403-7

This essential Java 1.2 book covers Java's security mechanisms and teaches you how to work with them. It discusses class loaders, security managers, access lists, digital signatures, and authentication and shows how to use these to create and enforce your own security policy.

Java Virtual Machine

By Jon Meyer & Troy Downing
1st Edition March 1997
452 pages, includes diskette
ISBN 1-56592-194-1

This book is a comprehensive programming guide for the Java Virtual Machine (JVM). It gives readers a strong overview and reference of the JVM so that they may create their own implementations of the JVM or write their own compilers that create Java object code. A Java assembler is provided with the book, so the examples can all be compiled and executed.

Java Swing

By Robert Eckstein, Marc Loy &
Dave Wood
1st Edition September 1998
1252 pages, ISBN 1-56592-455-X

The Swing classes eliminate Java's biggest weakness: its relatively primitive user interface toolkit. Java Swing helps you to take full advantage of the Swing classes, providing detailed descriptions of every class and interface in the key Swing packages. It shows you how to use all of the new components, allowing you to build state-of-the-art user interfaces and giving you the context you need to understand what you're doing. It's more than documentation; Java Swing helps you develop code quickly and effectively.

Java

Java Threads, Second Edition

By Scott Oaks and Henry Wong
2nd Edition January 1999
336 pages, ISBN 1-56592-418-5

Revised and expanded to cover Java 2, *Java Threads, 2nd Edition*, shows you how to take full advantage of Java's thread facilities: where to use threads to increase efficiency, how to use them effectively, and how to avoid common mistakes. It thoroughly covers the Thread and ThreadGroup classes, the Runnable interface, and the language's synchronized operator. The book pays special attention to threading issues with Swing, as well as problems like deadlock, race condition, and starvation to help you write code without hidden bugs.

Java Language Reference, Second Edition

By Mark Grand
2nd Edition July 1997
492 pages, ISBN 1-56592-326-X

This book helps you understand the subtle nuances of Java—from the definition of data types to the syntax of expressions and control structures—so you can ensure your programs run exactly as expected. The second edition covers the new language features that have been added in Java 1.1, such as inner classes, class literals, and instance initializers.

Java Fundamental Classes Reference

By Mark Grand & Jonathan Knudsen
1st Edition May 1997
1114 pages, ISBN 1-56592-241-7

The *Java Fundamental Classes Reference* provides complete reference documentation on the core Java 1.1 classes that comprise the *java.lang, java.io, java.net, java.util, java.text, java.math, java.lang.reflect,* and *java.util.zip* packages. Part of O'Reilly's Java documentation series, this edition describes Version 1.1 of the Java Development Kit. It includes easy-to-use reference material and provides lots of sample code to help you learn by example.

Java Servlet Programming

By Jason Hunter with William Crawford
1st Edition November 1998
528 pages, ISBN 1-56592-391-X

Java servlets offer a fast, powerful, portable replacement for CGI scripts. *Java Servlet Programming* covers everything you need to know to write effective servlets. Topics include: serving dynamic Web content, maintaining state information, session tracking, database connectivity using JDBC, and applet-servlet communication.

Java Distributed Computing

By Jim Farley
1st Edition January 1998
384 pages, ISBN 1-56592-206-9

Java Distributed Computing offers a general introduction to distributed computing, meaning programs that run on two or more systems. It focuses primarily on how to structure and write distributed applications and, therefore, discusses issues like designing protocols, security, working with databases, and dealing with low bandwidth situations.

Java Network Programming

By Elliotte Rusty Harold
1st Edition February 1997
442 pages, ISBN 1-56592-227-1

The network is the soul of Java. Most of what is new and exciting about Java centers around the potential for new kinds of dynamic, networked applications. *Java Network Programming* teaches you to work with Sockets, write network clients and servers, and gives you an advanced look at the new areas like multicasting, using the server API, and RMI. Covers Java 1.1.

O'REILLY®

TO ORDER: **800-998-9938** • *order@oreilly.com* • *http://www.oreilly.com/*
OUR PRODUCTS ARE AVAILABLE AT A BOOKSTORE OR SOFTWARE STORE NEAR YOU.
FOR INFORMATION: **800-998-9938** • **707-829-0515** • *info@oreilly.com*

How to stay in touch with O'Reilly

1. Visit Our Award-Winning Web Site

http://www.oreilly.com/

★ "Top 100 Sites on the Web" —*PC Magazine*
★ "Top 5% Web sites" —*Point Communications*
★ "3-Star site" —*The McKinley Group*

Our web site contains a library of comprehensive product information (including book excerpts and tables of contents), downloadable software, background articles, interviews with technology leaders, links to relevant sites, book cover art, and more. File us in your Bookmarks or Hotlist!

2. Join Our Email Mailing Lists

New Product Releases

To receive automatic email with brief descriptions of all new O'Reilly products as they are released, send email to:
listproc@online.oreilly.com
Put the following information in the first line of your message (*not* in the Subject field):
subscribe oreilly-news

O'Reilly Events

If you'd also like us to send information about trade show events, special promotions, and other O'Reilly events, send email to:
listproc@online.oreilly.com
Put the following information in the first line of your message (*not* in the Subject field):
subscribe oreilly-events

3. Get Examples from Our Books via FTP

There are two ways to access an archive of example files from our books:

Regular FTP

- ftp to:
  ftp.oreilly.com
  (login: anonymous
  password: your email address)
- Point your web browser to:
  ftp://ftp.oreilly.com/

FTPMAIL

- Send an email message to:
  ftpmail@online.oreilly.com
  (Write "help" in the message body)

4. Contact Us via Email

order@oreilly.com
To place a book or software order online. Good for North American and international customers.

subscriptions@oreilly.com
To place an order for any of our newsletters or periodicals.

books@oreilly.com
General questions about any of our books.

software@oreilly.com
For general questions and product information about our software. Check out O'Reilly Software Online at **http://software.oreilly.com/** for software and technical support information. Registered O'Reilly software users send your questions to: **website-support@oreilly.com**

cs@oreilly.com
For answers to problems regarding your order or our products.

booktech@oreilly.com
For book content technical questions or corrections.

proposals@oreilly.com
To submit new book or software proposals to our editors and product managers.

international@oreilly.com
For information about our international distributors or translation queries. For a list of our distributors outside of North America check out:
http://www.oreilly.com/www/order/country.html

O'Reilly & Associates, Inc.
101 Morris Street, Sebastopol, CA 95472 USA
TEL   707-829-0515 or 800-998-9938
            (6am to 5pm PST)
FAX   707-829-0104

International Distributors

UK, EUROPE, MIDDLE EAST AND AFRICA (EXCEPT FRANCE, GERMANY, AUSTRIA, SWITZERLAND, LUXEMBOURG, LIECHTENSTEIN, AND EASTERN EUROPE)

INQUIRIES
O'Reilly UK Limited
4 Castle Street
Farnham
Surrey, GU9 7HS
United Kingdom
Telephone: 44-1252-711776
Fax: 44-1252-734211
Email: josette@oreilly.com

ORDERS
Wiley Distribution Services Ltd.
1 Oldlands Way
Bognor Regis
West Sussex PO22 9SA
United Kingdom
Telephone: 44-1243-779777
Fax: 44-1243-820250
Email: cs-books@wiley.co.uk

FRANCE

ORDERS
GEODIF
61, Bd Saint-Germain
75240 Paris Cedex 05, France
Tel: 33-1-44-41-46-16 (French books)
Tel: 33-1-44-41-11-87 (English books)
Fax: 33-1-44-41-11-44
Email: distribution@eyrolles.com

INQUIRIES
Éditions O'Reilly
18 rue Séguier
75006 Paris, France
Tel: 33-1-40-51-52-30
Fax: 33-1-40-51-52-31
Email: france@editions-oreilly.fr

GERMANY, SWITZERLAND, AUSTRIA, EASTERN EUROPE, LUXEMBOURG, AND LIECHTENSTEIN

INQUIRIES & ORDERS
O'Reilly Verlag
Balthasarstr. 81
D-50670 Köln
Germany
Telephone: 49-221-973160-91
Fax: 49-221-973160-8
Email: anfragen@oreilly.de (inquiries)
Email: order@oreilly.de (orders)

CANADA (FRENCH LANGUAGE BOOKS)

Les Éditions Flammarion ltée
375, Avenue Laurier Ouest
Montréal (Québec) H2V 2K3
Tel: 00-1-514-277-8807
Fax: 00-1-514-278-2085
Email: info@flammarion.qc.ca

HONG KONG

City Discount Subscription Service, Ltd.
Unit D, 3rd Floor, Yan's Tower
27 Wong Chuk Hang Road
Aberdeen, Hong Kong
Tel: 852-2580-3539
Fax: 852-2580-6463
Email: citydis@ppn.com.hk

KOREA

Hanbit Media, Inc.
Sonyoung Bldg. 202
Yeksam-dong 736-36
Kangnam-ku
Seoul, Korea
Tel: 822-554-9610
Fax: 822-556-0363
Email: hant93@chollian.dacom.co.kr

PHILIPPINES

Mutual Books, Inc.
429-D Shaw Boulevard
Mandaluyong City, Metro
Manila, Philippines
Tel: 632-725-7538
Fax: 632-721-3056
Email: mbikikog@mnl.sequel.net

TAIWAN

O'Reilly Taiwan
No. 3, Lane 131
Hang-Chow South Road
Section 1, Taipei, Taiwan
Tel: 886-2-23968990
Fax: 886-2-23968916
Email: benh@oreilly.com

CHINA

O'Reilly Beijing
Room 2410
160, FuXingMenNeiDaJie
XiCheng District
Beijing, China PR 100031
Tel: 86-10-86631006
Fax: 86-10-86631007
Email: frederic@oreilly.com

INDIA

Computer Bookshop (India) Pvt. Ltd.
190 Dr. D.N. Road, Fort
Bombay 400 001 India
Tel: 91-22-207-0989
Fax: 91-22-262-3551
Email: cbsbom@giasbm01.vsnl.net.in

JAPAN

O'Reilly Japan, Inc.
Kiyoshige Building 2F
12-Bancho, Sanei-cho
Shinjuku-ku
Tokyo 160-0008 Japan
Tel: 81-3-3356-5227
Fax: 81-3-3356-5261
Email: japan@oreilly.com

ALL OTHER ASIAN COUNTRIES

O'Reilly & Associates, Inc.
101 Morris Street
Sebastopol, CA 95472 USA
Tel: 707-829-0515
Fax: 707-829-0104
Email: order@oreilly.com

AUSTRALIA

WoodsLane Pty., Ltd.
7/5 Vuko Place
Warriewood NSW 2102
Australia
Tel: 61-2-9970-5111
Fax: 61-2-9970-5002
Email: info@woodslane.com.au

NEW ZEALAND

Woodslane New Zealand, Ltd.
21 Cooks Street (P.O. Box 575)
Waganui, New Zealand
Tel: 64-6-347-6543
Fax: 64-6-345-4840
Email: info@woodslane.com.au

LATIN AMERICA

McGraw-Hill Interamericana
Editores, S.A. de C.V.
Cedro No. 512
Col. Atlampa
06450, Mexico, D.F.
Tel: 52-5-547-6777
Fax: 52-5-547-3336
Email: mcgraw-hill@infosel.net.mx

O'REILLY™

O'Reilly & Associates, Inc.
101 Morris Street
Sebastopol, CA 95472-9902
1-800-998-9938

Visit us online at:
http://www.ora.com/
orders@ora.com

O'REILLY WOULD LIKE TO HEAR FROM YOU

Which book did this card come from?

_____

Where did you buy this book?
- ❏ Bookstore   ❏ Computer Store
- ❏ Direct from O'Reilly   ❏ Class/seminar
- ❏ Bundled with hardware/software
- ❏ Other _____

What operating system do you use?
- ❏ UNIX   ❏ Macintosh
- ❏ Windows NT   ❏ PC(Windows/DOS)
- ❏ Other _____

What is your job description?
- ❏ System Administrator   ❏ Programmer
- ❏ Network Administrator   ❏ Educator/Teacher
- ❏ Web Developer
- ❏ Other _____

❏ Please send me O'Reilly's catalog, containing a complete listing of O'Reilly books and software.

Name _____   Company/Organization _____

Address _____

City _____   State _____   Zip/Postal Code _____   Country _____

Telephone _____   Internet or other email address (specify network) _____

Nineteenth century wood engraving
of a bear from the O'Reilly &
Associates Nutshell Handbook®
Using & Managing UUCP.

BUSINESS REPLY MAIL

FIRST CLASS MAIL   PERMIT NO. 80   SEBASTOPOL, CA

Postage will be paid by addressee

O'Reilly & Associates, Inc.
101 Morris Street
Sebastopol, CA 95472-9902